The Editors

ROBERT B. STEPTO is Professor of English, African American Studies, and American Studies at Yale University. He is the author of *A Home Elsewhere: Reading African American Classics in the Age of Obama, Blue as the Lake: A Personal Geography*, and *From Behind the Veil: A Study of Afro-American Narrative*. Among his edited volumes are *Chant of Saints: A Gathering of Literature, Art, and Scholarship, Afro-American Literature: The Reconstruction of Instruction*, and *Harper American Literature*.

JENNIFER RAE GREESON is Assistant Professor of English at the University of Virginia. She is the author of *Our South: Geographic Fantasy and the Rise of National Literature* and of articles related to various aspects of American literature and culture.

W. W. NORTON & COMPANY, INC.
Also Publishes

ENGLISH RENAISSANCE DRAMA
edited by David Bevington et al.

THE NORTON ANTHOLOGY OF AFRICAN AMERICAN LITERATURE
edited by Henry Louis Gates Jr. and Nellie Y. McKay et al.

THE NORTON ANTHOLOGY OF AMERICAN LITERATURE
edited by Nina Baym et al.

THE NORTON ANTHOLOGY OF CHILDREN'S LITERATURE
edited by Jack Zipes et al.

THE NORTON ANTHOLOGY OF CONTEMPORARY FICTION
edited by R. V. Cassill and Joyce Carol Oates

THE NORTON ANTHOLOGY OF DRAMA
edited by J. Ellen Gainor, Stanton B. Garner Jr., and Martin Puchner

THE NORTON ANTHOLOGY OF ENGLISH LITERATURE
edited by M. H. Abrams and Stephen Greenblatt et al.

THE NORTON ANTHOLOGY OF LITERATURE BY WOMEN
edited by Sandra M. Gilbert and Susan Gubar

THE NORTON ANTHOLOGY OF MODERN AND CONTEMPORARY POETRY
edited by Jahan Ramazani, Richard Ellmann, and Robert O'Clair

THE NORTON ANTHOLOGY OF POETRY
edited by Margaret Ferguson, Mary Jo Salter, and Jon Stallworthy

THE NORTON ANTHOLOGY OF SHORT FICTION
edited by R. V. Cassill and Richard Bausch

THE NORTON ANTHOLOGY OF THEORY AND CRITICISM
edited by Vincent B. Leitch et al.

THE NORTON ANTHOLOGY OF WORLD LITERATURE
edited by Sarah Lawall et al.

THE NORTON FACSIMILE OF THE FIRST FOLIO OF SHAKESPEARE
prepared by Charlton Hinman

THE NORTON INTRODUCTION TO LITERATURE
edited by Alison Booth and Kelly J. Mays

THE NORTON READER
edited by Linda H. Peterson and John C. Brereton

THE NORTON SAMPLER
edited by Thomas Cooley

THE NORTON SHAKESPEARE, BASED ON THE OXFORD EDITION
edited by Stephen Greenblatt et al.

For a complete list of Norton Critical Editions, visit
www.wwnorton.com/college/English/nce_home.htm

A NORTON CRITICAL EDITION

Charles W. Chesnutt

THE CONJURE STORIES

AUTHORITATIVE TEXTS

CONTEXTS

CRITICISM

Edited by

ROBERT B. STEPTO
YALE UNIVERSITY

AND

JENNIFER RAE GREESON
UNIVERSITY OF VIRGINIA

W. W. NORTON & COMPANY
New York • London

W. W. Norton & Company has been independent since its founding in 1923, when William Warder Norton and Mary D. Herter Norton first published lectures delivered at the People's Institute, the adult education division of New York City's Cooper Union. The firm soon expanded its program beyond the Institute, publishing books by celebrated academics from America and abroad. By midcentury, the two major pillars of Norton's publishing program—trade books and college texts—were firmly established. In the 1950s, the Norton family transferred control of the company to its employees, and today—with a staff of four hundred and a comparable number of trade, college, and professional titles published each year—W. W. Norton & Company stands as the largest and oldest publishing house owned wholly by its employees.

The text of this book is composed in Fairfield Medium
with the display set in Bernhard Modern.
Book design by Antonina Krass.
Composition by TexTech.
Production managers: Eric Pier-Hocking and Sean Mintus.

Library of Congress Cataloging-in-Publication Data

Chesnutt, Charles W. (Charles Waddell), 1858–1932.
  The conjure stories : authoritative texts, contexts, criticism /
Charles W. Chesnutt ; edited by Robert B. Stepto and Jennifer Rae
Greeson. — 1st ed.
      p. cm. — (Norton critical edition)
  Includes bibliographical references.
  ISBN 978-0-393-92780-1 (pbk.)
  1.   Southern States—Social life and customs—Fiction.   2.   Racially
mixed people—Fiction.   3.   African Americans—Fiction.   4.   Race
relations—Fiction.   5.   Racism—Fiction.   6.   Chesnutt, Charles W.
(Charles Waddell), 1858–1932—Criticism and interpretation.   7.   Chesnutt,
Charles W. (Charles Waddell), 1858–1932—Sources.   I. Stepto, Robert B.
II. Greeson, Jennifer Rae.   III. Title.
  PS1292.C6A6 2011
  813'.4—dc23

                                                                    2011034192

W. W. Norton & Company, Inc., 500 Fifth Avenue
New York, NY 10110-0017
www.wwnorton.com

W. W. Norton & Company Ltd., Castle House
75/76 Wells Street, London W1T 3QT

1 2 3 4 5 6 7 8 9 0

Contents

Criticism 229

Introduction

During the last thirteen years of the nineteenth century, Charles W. Chesnutt wrote numerous stories and sketches in the folk manner, including fourteen Uncle Julius stories, ten of which were conjure tales set in the ante-bellum American South.[1] These stories were well received by the public, so much so that even the slighter tales were rarely rejected by publishers. Five of the stories appeared in major periodicals such as the *Atlantic Monthly* and *Overland Monthly*. Another three saw print in prominent African American journals including the *Southern Workman*. While four stories never came out in magazines, three of these were nonetheless published when Houghton Mifflin brought out a selection of the conjure stories, *The Conjure Woman* (1899). That volume put fully half of the stories before the reading public, and was so immediately successful that Houghton Mifflin agreed to print another collection of Chesnutt's stories, *The Wife of His Youth*, in the following year.

While the stories were thus never lost to the public, most contemporary readers became aware of them when *The Conjure Woman* was reprinted in the 1960s. Moreover, many contemporary readers learned for the first time that there were seven *additional* Uncle Julius stories, including two more conjure stories, when Sylvia Lyons Render collected and edited *The Short Fiction of Charles W. Chesnutt* (1974). In 1993, Richard H. Brodhead edited *The Conjure Woman and Other Conjure Tales*. That volume presents *The Conjure Woman* "in tact," with its selected stories, and additionally offers, in the chronological order of their composition, the seven "Related Tales." This Norton Critical Edition of Chesnutt's conjure tales also prints all fourteen stories, but it does not segregate the stories in *The Conjure Woman* collection from the rest. It presents all fourteen stories in the order in which Chesnutt composed them, mainly so that the reader can discern how Chesnutt experimented with his plots and characters and with the *idea* of the conjure story over time.

---

1. Some ideas and phrasings in part one of this essay first appeared in the opening pages of my 1984 essay, "'The Simple But Intensely Human Inner Life of Slavery': Storytelling and the Revision of History in Charles W. Chesnutt's 'Uncle Julius Stories,'" in Gunter Lenz, ed., *History and Tradition in Afro-American Culture* (Frankfurt: Campus, 1984), pp. 29–55. A selection from that essay is in this volume's Modern Criticism section.

The following chronology is helpful here. In the mid-1880s, Chesnutt visited his father-in-law's garden and listened to "'an old colored man's' tale of 'an old man who anointed his head with scuppernong grape juice, which had the remarkable effect of producing a luxuriant crop of hair.'" This storytelling performance—complete with teller, listener, and tale—prompted the writing of "The Goophered Grapevine" (1887), the first of the Uncle Julius stories, and the first conjure tale featuring Aunt Peggy. During 1887–89, three more stories were written ("Po' Sandy," "The Conjurer's Revenge," "Dave's Neckliss"), and all were quickly printed in either the *Atlantic Monthly* or the *Overland Monthly*. These four stories constitute the first phase of Chesnutt's efforts.

After writing "Dave's Neckliss"—the first tale not involving a conjurer—Chesnutt declared in a letter to Albion Tourgée that he would go no further with Uncle Julius or with efforts to simulate Negro dialect.[2] With that, he went to work on a very different kind of story, "The Sheriff's Children." However, over the next eight years (1889–97), Chesnutt did not exactly drop the Uncle Julius story altogether. Three more were produced ("The Dumb Witness," "A Deep Sleeper," "Lonesome Ben"), all of them fascinating in terms of Chesnutt's ambition to vary his form, to plot without recourse to "conjured" events, and to tell a tale of the folk in "standard" English. These stories form phase two. They bear a special relationship to those in phase one in that all seven stories were written before Walter Hines Page, in his capacity as an editor at Houghton Mifflin, informed Chesnutt that his house would consider publishing a volume of his stories if they could see more conjure stories of a high quality.

Page's letter was dated 30 March 1898. It seems likely that neither he nor Chesnutt would have predicted that *The Conjure Woman* would see print within a year. Matters proceeded expeditiously largely because Chesnutt sat down and wrote six new conjure stories in less than two months. Four of these passed muster at Houghton Mifflin and were immediately placed in *The Conjure Woman* manuscript. One, "Hot-Foot Hannibal," also appeared in the January 1899 issue of the *Atlantic Monthly*.

Over the course of writing these stories, Chesnutt pursued a number of experiments but never altered the tripartite narrative structure of the conventional framed tale. In a typical story, John, the transplanted white northerner who has recently arrived to the very region in North Carolina in which Chesnutt grew up (see this vol-

---

2. Chesnutt's letter to Albion W. Tourgée appears in the Contexts section.

ume's map, "the Terrain of Chesnutt's Conjure Tales"), dominates
the opening unit of the frame.[3] After John has commented variously
on the singularities of black folk stories set in slavery times, Julius
relates one such story to John and his wife, Annie, who are occasionally joined in their act of listenership by Annie's sister, Mabel. Annie
presides over the frame's closure even though in some instances she
must share the actual narration of the unit with John.

The opening unit of the frame (which will be referred to as the prologue) performs several narrative chores. John's monologue invariably
yields to an exchange—either a dialogue with Julius or a three-way
conversation including Annie—that establishes the conditions for a
storytelling performance. Frequently, this exchange is followed by a
second, briefer monologue in which the characteristics and qualities
of Julius's tales are described. From the point of view of narrative
structure, these statements perform the dual function of providing a
bridge between the prologue and the tale while completing the first
phrasing of a typical story's narrative rhythm: framing the exchange
with John's monologues prefigures the tripartite structure of the
story as a whole.

The prologue also has the responsibility of establishing the site of
the storytelling performance as well as the site of the events within
Julius's tale. Most of the tales (nine) are related after all three principal characters are comfortably situated on John and Annie's piazza
(i.e., porch or gallery), a detail that brilliantly keeps before us the
fact that John and Annie are indeed the new northern owners of old
southern plantation spaces, and that Julius is now employed by them
on the site where he had been a slave. In this regard, as Chesnutt
surely had in mind, the piazza is a mischievously complicated revision of the log on which all three first sat democratically while Julius
told his first tale of "The Goophered Grapevine."

The four remaining stories occur while Julius, John, and Annie
are out for business or pleasure in the carriage. In his new life of
wage labor, Julius is John and Annie's coachman; the carriage trips
are one way in which the stories enact the employer-employee relationship that looms in each story as a whole. But more is at work: the
carriage is the piazza-in-motion, and the resulting change in venue
for storytelling performances advances Chesnutt's strategy for the
eventual creation of a semi-fictive community not unlike Faulkner's
Yoknapatawpha or Zora Neale Hurston's Eatonville. (The marvelous
maps created for this volume help make this point.)

3. See the first entry in the Contexts section: Sarah Ingle, "The Terrain of Chesnutt's Con-
    jure Tales."

In these stories, the site of storytelling and that of the tale's episodes are closely allied. Just as most of the stories are told on the piazza of what was once the McAdoo plantation, nearly half of the tales (six) involve black folk who were once McAdoo slaves—like Uncle Julius. The remaining tales of slaves on the neighboring McSwayne, McGee, McLean, and McDonald plantations repeat and yet vary what might be termed the predominating McAdoo tale and geography. Having some of the stories sited on these plantations, in addition to the McAdoo plantation, helps Chesnutt make one of his great points: when you shift about among these plantations, from one slaveholder to another or from the plight of one slave to another, what variations do you actually see? Mightn't McAdoo and McDonald and the rest be slightly different "names" for the same thing?

In thirteen of the fourteen stories, Julius tells the tale within the frame. Even in the one odd case, "The Dumb Witness," he appears as a storyteller, for it is upon his tale of the Murchison family that John constructs the story he himself tells. Ten of the tales involve a conjurer; within these, some variation in plot and narrative structure occurs when the conjure woman is replaced by a conjure man, or when she is a woman other than Aunt Peggy—Tenie in "Po' Sandy" being the most notable example. In a later tale, "The Gray Wolf's Ha'nt," two conjurers appear when Aunt Peggy attempts to aid a McAdoo slave named Dan in escaping the fate a conjure man has prepared for him. However, the doubling of folk magicians and fantastic occurrences does not yield a stronger, more inventive tale. The most memorable of these stories turn on the conjurations of an ingenious conjure woman (Aunt Peggy, Tenie), or, as is the case with "Dave's Neckliss," they verge on the fantastic simply because people can be so cruel to each other, especially when they are caught up in the "system" of slavery.

Annie's domination of the closing unit of the frame—the epilogue—reflects certain familiar theories about how women run things without necessarily having a full voice on every matter. Invariably, it is a remark from her such as "Is that story true?" or "What a system it was . . ." or even "That story doesn't appeal to me . . ." that effects the transition from the tale back to the frame. These remarks usually prompt a conversation about the tale, involving Julius as well as John, which balances the exchange in the prologue. It also usually provides an opportunity for further commentary on the merits of Julius's storytelling. In some instances, the sole substantial comment on Julius's tale appears in this conversation and not in one of John's earlier monologues. When this occurs, Annie, not John, is the critic or authorial voice judging tale and culture alike. Her achievement of this authority through the management of conversation anticipates that which Julius achieves through the manipulation of the entire storytelling event. Indeed, in many stories, there seems to be a direct correlation between Annie's ability to "have the last word" and Julius's success at fulfilling the apparent ulterior motive behind his storytelling. Julius gets what he seems to want usually through Annie's intervention, and Annie's willingness to intervene is often predicated upon the extent to which she has become a full partner in the *event* of the telling of the tale.

Stories from the 1880s

Taking a closer look at what is established or announced in the first four conjure tales, we note that "The Goophered Grapevine" presents a tale of slavery that is more precisely a tragicomic tale of the economy of slavery. All might have been well if Master McAdoo had been content with the profits from his grapes, not to mention the profits from buying and selling his slave Henry every year. But he foolishly allowed a Yankee to meddle with his grapevines, and in the end the vines died, and Henry, whose health was "entwined" with that of the vines, dies, too. In short, tragedy comes to the slaveholder and slave (to white and black) alike, and it is brought on by a greed that is arguably peculiar to what Annie calls the "system" of slavery.

Comedy in this tale, as in many other tales to come, is located in Chesnutt's portrayal of the slaveholder, Master McAdoo.[4] McAdoo fulfills the comic stereotype of the penny-pinching Scot, and as the names of the other slaveholders (McGee, McSwayne, McDonald, etc.) suggest, Chesnutt is relentless in this particular typecasting of the plantation masters in his stories. Also comic—darkly comic—is the suggestion that whatever the Yankee did to McAdoo's grapes by day, in addition to winning huge sums of McAdoo's cash in card games each night, occasioned the Civil War—or instigated McAdoo's going off to the War.

Comedy appears more controversially in Chesnutt's handling of Negro stereotypes. Uncle Julius barely begins his tale before declaring, to white folks no less, that "ef dey's an'thing a nigger lub, nex' ter 'possum, en chick'n, en watermillyums, it's scuppernon's." Clearly, from the beginning of his first tale, Chesnutt is announcing that he is going to confront head on the persistent stereotypes of colored people. His "Negro humor" also has a subtle side. In "The Goophered Grapevine," Henry prospers and his hair grows when McAdoo's grapes grow. When the grapevines are dormant, or worse, when

---

4. Glenda Carpio provides an excellent discussion of humor in Chesnutt's conjure tales in *Laughing Fit To Kill: Black Humor in the Fictions of Slavery* (New York: Oxford UP, 2008), a selection from which appears in the Modern Criticism section of this Norton Critical Edition.

they are dying, Henry also withers and loses his hair. With the folk description of Negro hair as "grapes" in mind, one might say that Chesnutt is pursuing his own line of racial humor (and commentary) in having Henry's "grapes" grow only when his master's grapes grow, too.

"The Goophered Grapevine" establishes the point that whites and blacks both may seek the services of the conjure woman: Master McAdoo wants Aunt Peggy to "goopher" the grapevines so that the slaves will stop eating his grapes; Henry eats some grapes before he learns that they have been "goophered," and he visits Aunt Peggy to see if she can take the "goopher" off him. Each man knows that he must pay Aunt Peggy handsomely: McAdoo gives her ten dollars and Henry brings her a ham. We are thus introduced to the idea that conjuring, like slavery, has its own economy: Aunt Peggy and the conjure men are the only black people in these stories who are consistently paid for their services, and who are free to demand payment. And they seem to be free in another way as well, for they live in the "Free Black Settlement" out the Wilmington Road, which suggests that they are free Negroes (the Guinea conjure man in "The Conjurer's Revenge" is repeatedly described as being free). In this way, Chesnutt addresses the question of how free people of color may survive in the economy of slavery: they have to be talented and ingenious to survive, and they may well survive by sorcery.[5]

"Po' Sandy" sustains the point made in "The Goophered Grapevine" that a slave's travails include being constantly moved about, from one plantation to another, as the schemes and fancies of the master might dictate. McAdoo's Henry is sold and bought back, sold and bought back; McSwayne's Sandy spends a month here, a month there, with his master's various children, so that they all might share Sandy's talents as a "monst'us" good worker. McSwayne is thus characterized by his generosity as much as McAdoo is marked by his zeal for a dollar. This is expressed again when McSwayne greets Sandy with the news that, while Sandy was away, he swapped Sandy's wife for a "noo woman," Tenie. McSwayne makes things right by "generously" giving Sandy a dollar. Clearly, Chesnutt's point is that even a master's generosity can create a slave's affliction.

Sandy takes up with Tenie and soon worries about being sent away from her, as he was so often sent from his wife. Tenie then divulges that she is a conjure woman and that she can change Sandy into something (a dog? a wolf? a mockingbird?) so that he can't be sent off. Tenie turns Sandy into a tree, and in keeping with familiar

---

5. See Charles W. Chesnutt, "The Free Colored People of North Carolina" (1902), which appears in the Contexts section.

folkloric patterns, Sandy endures three tribulations while a tree (before he is milled, which is, of course, the ultimate catastrophe). First, he is pecked by a woodpecker (nature's infliction); then he is chopped in the side by a slave sent out by McSwayne to chop wood for turpentine boxes (the master's infliction); third, he is stripped of Tenie's protection when *she* is sent off to another plantation by McSwayne's wife (the mistress's infliction). It is then that he is felled for milling, notably so that McSwayne can "generously" provide his wife with a new kitchen.

Tenie is easily one of Chesnutt's most interesting fictive inventions, notably because she is both a conjure woman and a slave. At the beginning of the tale, she claims that she had stopped conjuring after she got religion, but we sense that, as a slave, she has actually hidden her talents as opposed to abandoning them. In contrast to Aunt Peggy and the conjure men, Tenie is not paid for her services, nor is she "free" to ask for payment; she is a conjurer but, most likely because she is a slave, she is not in the *business* of conjuring. Much to the point, Tenie can turn Sandy into a tree, but she cannot save him or herself. When she is sent off to another plantation and Sandy is felled and milled, slavery trumps her sorcery. Tenie is the first of the talented slaves in these conjure stories destined for derangement and death. She is also the first to "do time" in the plantation smokehouse, as if such an incarceration will "cure" her.

"Po' Sandy" ends with Annie distraught and angry about slavery ("What a system it was!") and tearful about Tenie's fate ("poor Tenie!"). The next story, "The Conjurer's Revenge," ends with Annie distraught in a quite different way. She exclaims, "That story does not appeal to me, Uncle Julius, and is not up to your usual mark. It isn't pathetic, it has no moral that I can discover, and I can't see why you should tell it. In fact, it seems to me like nonsense." The story isn't as bad as all that, but Annie's right, the story is different. Chesnutt is boldly experimenting with the composition of the conjurer and with the "social realities" of the conjure tale. In the first two tales, the conjurer is a woman, two different women in fact, living under different pressures: Aunt Peggy is a free black woman (living in the Free Black Settlement) and Tenie is indisputably a slave. In our third tale, "The Conjurer's Revenge," the conjurer is a man who is colored, free, and vengeful. This conjure man also lives "down in de free-nigger sett'ement," as Uncle Julius reports, and he was a "Guinea nigger" who claimed that "his daddy wuz a king, er a guv'ner, er some sorter w'at-you-may-call-'em 'way ober yander in Affiky whar the niggers come fum, befo' he was stoled erway en sol' ter de spekilaters." When Master McGee's slave Primus "abducts" the shote belonging to the conjure man and the conjure man plots his revenge and turns Primus into a mule, Chesnutt has clearly decided to make this tale an *intra-racial* drama in which the abuses of slavery are applied by black men upon each other. There is no woman of the order of Tenie (or later, Sis' Becky) whom Annie can relate to and feel for; there is no overtly heinous deed by a slaveholder that can explain the turn of events. Perhaps these are the reasons the tale doesn't appeal to Annie. But this was a tale that Chesnutt felt he needed to attempt, another truth of slavery he had to pursue in fiction.

One thing Chesnutt did not abandon in creating "The Conjurer's Revenge" was his dark sense of humor. When the conjure man turns Primus into a mule, Chesnutt makes sure that we see the dark comedy of Primus sometimes actually being better off as a mule than as a slave. The white folks in the tale provide a kind of grim comedy as well. Master McGee in particular appears comically foolish when he willingly buys Primus the mule from a wily poor white; the joke being that when McGee buys Primus, he buys a "mule" he "owns" already.

In "Dave's Neckliss," we return to the McAdoo plantation, which is now John and Annie's land and vineyard. It is once again a Sunday afternoon, and, as in "The Conjurer's Revenge," the site of story-telling is John and Annie's piazza. Sufficient time has passed for John and Annie and Julius to be more comfortable in each other's company, and even more social as well. For example, John and Annie do an extraordinary thing when they not only invite Julius up on to the piazza but also urge him to partake of their supper. Chesnutt has Julius respond to these courtesies in two most telling ways: Julius eats and relishes his ham supper *after* John and Annie have finished dining (as if to remind them and himself that they all are still in the American South); and he proceeds to tell them what W. E. B. Du Bois would have termed an "unvarnished" tale of slavery, a tale of the destructiveness of slavery that turns not on Negro sorcery but on man's cruelty to man. John and Annie have been more personable with Julius and he in turn is more personal with them: he tells them a tale he knows because he knew Dave, who slaved on the McAdoo plantation by his side.

Dave was abused, humiliated (the "neckliss" he was forced to wear was a chain with a rotting ham attached to it), and destroyed by the machinations of two men: Wiley, who is indeed a wily slave, and Walker, the poor white overseer, who can't stand any more than Wiley can Dave's place of privilege. Walker is incensed that Dave, a black slave, is literate (which the white Walker probably is not), and outraged by the fact that Master McAdoo actually rewards Dave for this affront by allowing him to establish a slave Sabbath meeting. Wiley also resents Dave's status on the plantation, but wants to bring him down less because he is an "uppity Negro" and more because he wants Dave's woman, Dilsey. Wiley plants a stolen ham in Dave's cabin, Dave is accused of the theft, and Dilsey rebukes him. Dilsey's scorn is the last straw: Dave goes mad and "cures" his pain by hanging himself in the plantation smokehouse. Julius, one of the last people to talk with Dave before he took his life, was unable to help his friend.

While "Dave's Neckliss" is a different kind of Uncle Julius story, notably because Dave's fate is "conjured" by someone not known to be a conjure man or woman, it is a story that Chesnutt had been working toward all along. Wiley is a character prefigured by the conjure man in "The Conjurer's Revenge." He is not free like the conjure man, but he is, as the matter was put before, colored and vengeful. Wiley is specifically described as being "sha'p ez a steel trap," "sly ez de fox," and "'ceitful" [deceitful], all characteristics he shares with the conjure man. It is no mere coincidence that each story takes a turn near the end when the conjure man and Wiley both attempt to set matters straight and "free" their victims before they themselves die. But "Dave's Neckliss" is the darker tale: "The Conjurer's Revenge" explains, if you will, why a slave has a club foot and almost makes something comic out of that; "Dave's Neckliss" portrays the step-by-step of a slave's suicide.

Even more interesting is how Dave sustains and develops features of Tenie's character in "Po' Sandy." Both are slaves with a talent, or, more specifically, with a literacy: Tenie is "literate" in conjure; Dave can literally read and perhaps write and becomes a preacher (a man of the Word) with his master's blessing. Both Tenie and Dave die, and we observe how each descends into madness en route to death. Most particularly, we see in each case how madness is heightened, and possibly occasioned in the first place, by the oppression of solitude that afflicts slaves who can no longer partake of the few gestures toward companionship and community that the slave system allows.

Stories, 1893–1897

In his stories written in the mid-1890s—"A Deep Sleeper," "Lonesome Ben," and "The Dumb Witness"—Chesnutt continues his experiments with plantation tales that are not precisely conjure tales, even though strange things occur. He also introduces a new character, Mabel, Annie's younger sister, who is later identified as John's ward. Adding Mabel creates new opportunities for developing the minor but persistent subject of northerners living in the postbellum South, a subject broached up to this point solely through the presence of John and Annie. With Mabel added to Uncle Julius's listenership, there is also the opportunity to create new moments in the event of his storytelling. We see such a moment in "A Deep Sleeper," when it is Mabel, not Annie, who asks the question that prompts Julius's story. But the bold, even radical, experiment in storytelling in these stories appears in "The Dumb Witness," where John tells the tale, albeit after he has assembled shards of the story from Julius. Mabel may have something to do with that as well. The tale in "The Dumb Witness" is about the Murchison family, and John may well have persisted in finding out what he could about that family since, as we discover later on in "Hot-Foot Hannibal" (1898), Mabel is being courted by a Murchison.

In "A Deep Sleeper," the site for storytelling is again John and Annie's piazza, where they and Julius are now joined by Mabel. The story told is one of the many departure-and-return tales offered in the series; by my count there are eight. The story turns on slave Cindy's "departure" to Master Washington McAdoo's plantation (recall here how often a Chesnutt story commences with this particular expression of servitude), which occasions Skundus's deep sadness, which in turn brings on his deep sleep. About a month later, Cindy returns (or rather, is returned) and Skundus, who many thought had run away, returns to a certain wakefulness as well.

The fact that this story involves a sleepy Negro and a succulent watermelon certainly suggests Chesnutt's willingness to entertain or cajole a particular late-nineteenth-century American readership. But, as we see with other stories, this seems to be a strategy by which he can ease into his story some trenchant truths about slavery. For example, this is the tale in which Chesnutt accurately recreates the runaway/reward posters that were circulated after a slave had absconded. Also, before Julius can tell his tale, he has to explain to Mabel how Skundus and all the rest got their extraordinary names. Needless to say, his explanation exposes another degradation:

> 'Dem names wuz gun ter 'em by ole Marse Dugal' McAdoo, wat I use' ter b'long ter, en dey use' ter b'long ter. Marse Dugal' named all de babies w'at wuz bawn on de plantation. Dese young un's mammy wanted ter call 'em sump'n plain en simple, like 'Rastus' er 'Caesar' er 'George Wash'n'ton'; but ole Marse say no, he want all de niggers on his place ter had diffe'nt names, so he can tell them apart. He'd done use' up all de common names, so he had ter take sump'n else. Dem names he gun Skundus en' his brudders is Hebrew names en' wuz tuk out'n de Bible.

When Mabel asks where in the Bible she might find these names, Julius says he doesn't know, adding that it isn't his fault that he can't read. To be sure, a broad, even minstrel-like, humor is present in moments like these, but the moments are not wholly comic. When the laughter subsides, you are left with the hard truth that a slave mother might not even be able to name her child; she certainly could not if she belonged to "Marse" McAdoo.

Like "The Conjurer's Revenge," "Lonesome Ben" is a tale of intra-racial strife amongst plantation folk. Fearing his master's punishments for being drunk, Ben runs away but doesn't get far because, as Chesnutt chooses to portray the situation, Ben knows about the North Star but can't see it. Starving, Ben ends up eating clay, which eventually lightens his skin and makes him unrecognizable even to his wife and son. Late in the story, Ben runs into his master, Mars Marrabo, who does not recognize him either, and worse, calls him a "yaller nigger" and tells him to get off his land. Once he discovers that he is indeed "yaller," Ben comes to a sad understanding of why his son took one look and ran away from him, and of why his wife, Dasdy, called him names. He also now understands why Primus (most likely the same Primus we met in "The Conjurer's Revenge") declared, when they ran into each other, that Ben was "de mos' mis'able lookin' merlatter I eber seed."

Ben ran away to escape punishment but ended up with an affliction far worse than what was likely in store for him: he is, in his own words, a stranger, a man so lonesome that "he didn' eben hab his own se'f ter 'so'ciate wid." Like Tenie and Dave and other slaves who have become "strangers" by the end of one of Julius's tales, Ben goes off by himself and dies. What is particular about Ben's story is that the vocabulary for describing his difference, his strangeness, is racial: he has not been turned into a mule nor has he become so deranged that he thinks he's a ham; he has only become a light-skinned Negro. In the context of slavery, that has certain implications. We note, for example, that when his wife Dasdy sees him on the road, she asks him, quite remarkably, "Er is yer some low-down free nigger dat doan b'long ter nobody an' doan own nobody?" Folktales often form around three trials or crises. In "Lonesome Ben," Ben is rejected three times by black people, including his wife and child.

"The Dumb Witness" is also a tale of a light-skinned slave (a quadroon, in fact), but here the character, a woman named Viney, endures and outlives her tormentor, Malcolm Murchison, and gains revenge upon him. It is not a conjure tale, per se: there is nothing magical or otherworldly about Viney's transformation into a "dumb witness" who can only speak a "discordant jargon"; she is that way (or, appears to be that way) because Murchison, in a rage, mutilated her mouth. Likewise, there is no sorcery involved in Viney's resuming her command of "standard English" decades later; what happened quite simply was Murchison's death. With that, she resumes her coherent speech, and, once she reveals to young Murchison the will she kept hidden from Malcolm Murchison, the old Murchison place, which has been her home all her life, is restored as well.

The long quarrel between Malcolm Murchison and Viney represents what Gordon Thompson has termed a "seminal biracial event."[6]
Thompson especially has in mind events in Stowe's *Uncle Tom's Cabin*
and in Frederick Douglass's narratives when there is special communication between, say, Uncle Tom and Little Eva, or between the
young Douglass and Mrs. Auld, the mistress who teaches him to read.
With Chesnutt, the event, seen large, is profoundly about *mis*communication. Viney's revenge begins precisely when she invents the
"discordant jargon" that will frustrate Murchison the rest of his life.
What Chesnutt also explores is the biracial event in which the characters are related. When Roger Murchison's letter arrives, informing
Malcolm Murchison that he, Roger, is dying and that Viney knows
where his will and papers are, it states this, too, about Viney: "She is
devoted to you and to the family—she ought to be, for she is of our
blood—and she only knows the secret." This takes matters to
another level: the woman Malcolm treated as a slave, and mutilated
because she was his slave, was "family." Viney is the only slave in the
conjure stories who is expressly described as kin of the master.

The fact that this vital information about Viney appears in a letter
may explain why John is the storyteller in "The Dumb Witness." He's
no doubt pursued a conversation, perhaps with the young Murchison who is about to become Mabel's suitor, about the fortunes of the
family. Perhaps John has even read the letter. In either case, these
are not activities to which Uncle Julius would be privy, not to mention the fact that Julius cannot read. It also could be that John tells
the story because all the legal matters involving wills, claims, contes-
tations, and such are more plausibly related by John instead of Julius.
Chesnutt must have delighted in the opportunity to present such a
legal tangle; it represents one of the few moments in his fiction, especially in the conjure tales, when he could draw on his expertise as a
lawyer.

"The Dumb Witness" clearly presents some of Chesnutt's new
ideas for the narration of his stories. But it is also a tale in which
Chesnutt returns to familiar plot strategies and to features of the
slave regime he wishes to expose again and again. "The Dumb Witness" is obviously another tale of revenge; we can well imagine
Viney's glee over outlasting Malcolm Murchison and living to see
the day when the property is turned over to family other than him. It
is also something of a departure-and-return tale. Viney is banished
from the Murchison house after she tells a family secret and thwarts
Malcolm's marriage to a wealthy northerner. But she is returned to

6. Gordon E. Thompson, *Martyrs and Heroes: The Assimilationist Impulse in Representative
African American Narratives* (still in manuscript as of this writing).

the house as soon as Malcolm realizes that she alone knows where the will is. Finally, like "Dave's Neckliss," "The Dumb Witness" turns on the matter of a slave's literacy. Malcolm Murchison is so desperate to get information out of Viney that he hires a free Negro to teach her to write. We are not surprised that Viney just can't get the hang of it. She can invent being dumb in that manner as well. And of course, the free Negro has found one more way to survive in the economy of slavery: teaching "dumb" slaves pays almost as well as conjuring them.

The 1898 Stories and "The Marked Tree"

As mentioned before, upon learning in early 1898 that Houghton Mifflin wanted to see more conjure stories, Chesnutt devoted himself to writing new tales, producing six more in just seven weeks. Four of the six new stories were accepted and published along with Chesnutt's first three conjure stories in *The Conjure Woman* (1899). Those four stories are: "The Gray Wolf's Ha'nt," "Mars Jeems's Nightmare," "Sis' Becky's Pickanniny," and "Hot-Foot Hannibal." The stories rejected for *The Conjure Woman* were "A Victim of Heredity" and "Tobe's Tribulations." I will comment first on these last two stories.

In "A Victim of Heredity," Julius tells the story of "Marse" McDonald, who visits Aunt Peggy in his zeal to figure out how he can feed his slaves less and less. He pays her a dollar (we recall that even Master McAdoo paid her ten dollars), then steals it back. The next day, when he is supposed to pay Aunt Peggy another dollar, he attempts to pass off a bogus, lead coin, but she is on to his tricks. After conjuring the lead dollar into something looking like an authentic twenty-dollar gold piece, she asks McDonald to change it for her. He gives her three fives and five ones; Aunt Peggy has a payday after all.

This portends what she is going to do for McDonald's nephew, Tom, who has been cheated out his lands and inheritance by his treacherous uncle. Because Tom rescued her from drowning in the river, Aunt Peggy is determined to help him out. She fixes it so that the only food that saves McDonald's "weak en feeble" slaves is chicken, and arranges matters so that McDonald spends all his money, and even mortgages his plantation, to buy chickens. Of course, thanks to Aunt Peggy, the man who is making money in this chicken business is none other than nephew Tom. He gets a payday, too.

Race is handled in quite particular ways in this tale. White people, not black people, visit Aunt Peggy, and she uses her powers to reward the young white man who helped her and to punish the master who sought to cut his slaves' rations and to cheat her in the process. Race and class explain why McDonald is the greediest master in the conjure stories: before he was rich he was an "oberseah" and a "nigger-driber"; Julius's contention being that a rich man that bad must have been a "po' white" along the way. Race and class feature in Aunt Peggy's portrayal as well. Other stories hint at her being free, as when we are told that she lives in the Free Black Settlement, but this story explicitly describes her as the "free-nigger cunjuh 'oman."

"A Victim of Heredity" joins other stories such as "The Dumb Witness" in suggesting that brighter days are ahead once the new generation takes over. To be sure, young Tom plans to buy a plantation and lots of slaves, but he also tells Aunt Peggy that, any time she wants to, she can "hab a cabin on his plantation en a stool by his kitchen fiah" and chicken and tobacco, too. Strangely enough, the framing story also offers a tale of a new generation on the land. John has caught a chicken thief and locks him up in the smokehouse—a detail that cannot help but remind readers of the sad and pitiful incarcerations of Tenie (in "Po' Sandy") and Dave (in "Dave's Neckliss"). But John is not a slaveholder, and the War is over; will this story have a different ending? Yes, it will: Annie intervenes, talks with the sheriff while John is away, and sets the thief free. She does so because the colored thief is a "victim of heredity" who can't help craving chicken. That line of thinking at first presents Annie less favorably than we like to see her, but then we realize that it is an "explanation" to the sheriff that prevents any unreasonable punishment, which was a concern of John's from the start.

"Tobe's Tribulations" did not appear in *The Conjure Woman* but was one of the two tales published in 1900 in different numbers of the African American journal *Southern Workman* (the other was "Lonesome Ben"). Perhaps the editors were attracted to the tale because it is so overtly about a slave's yearning for freedom. When Tobe visits Aunt Peggy, his request is nothing less than "I wants you ter tell me de bes' en easies' way fer ter git ter de Norf en be free." Aunt Peggy speaks the truth when she replies, 'I's feared dey ain't no easy way." In the course of events, Aunt Peggy turns Tobe into a bear, a fox, and then finally a frog. As it turns out, because of "mistakes" and certain shortcomings, Tobe remains a frog in the South the rest of his life. As in "Po' Sandy," conjuring can create change but not freedom.

Both the attractions and frustrations for the reader of this tale involve its comic moments, or efforts at comedy. Chesnutt is at the height of his comic powers when he has Julius tell of a McSwayne slave who escapes North and has the audacity to write a "sassy letter" back to his master and mistress, which includes a bill for his twenty years of service to them. That is funny in itself; it is also amusing to listen to the McSwaynes sputter about how ungrateful that Negro is, after everything they did for him. On the other hand, while it is frustrating enough that Tobe cannot get North, even with Aunt Peggy's help, in part because he cannot "keep his eye on the prize," as it were, it is downright disturbing that Chesnutt pursues a low grade of comedy in these developments. When Tobe is turned into a fox, he can't get away and be free because, as we all know, foxes love chicken and can't pass up a full chicken coop. This is more of the colored chicken-craving nonsense that we witnessed in "Dave's Neckliss," where it led to Wiley's demise. Ten years into the conjure tale oeuvre, it is a stale idea.

There is an intriguing new development in the frame of this conjure tale involving John's requisite commentary on the nature and possible origins of Julius's tales. The development presents nothing less than an anthropological or ethnographic speculation regarding how African American tales may have originated in the commingling of storytelling cultures in the slave societies. John remarks:

> [Julius] had seen life from what was to us a new point of view—from the bottom, as it were; and there clung to his mind, like barnacles to the submerged portion of a ship, all sorts of extravagant beliefs. The simplest phenomena of life were to him fraught with hidden meaning,—some prophesy of good, some presage of evil. The source of these notions I never traced, though they doubtlessly could be easily accounted for. Some perhaps were dim reflections of ancestral fetishism; more were the superstitions, filtered through the Negro intellect, of the Scotch settlers who had founded their homes on Cape Fear at a time when a kelpie haunted every Highland glen, and witches, like bats, darkened the air as they flew by in their nocturnal wanderings.

References to the Scottish presence in the antebellum South abound in Chesnutt's tales, but this comment is of a different order. This refers to what may be shared, perhaps inevitably shared, even in a society that is built on difference and where that difference is fiercely monitored.

One notices that the word "Negro" is capitalized in this passage. Might that have been a particular contribution of editors at the *Southern Workmen*? It is not capitalized, for example, in John's opening remarks in "The Goophered Grapevine," in the printing of that tale in *The Conjure Woman*. Even these small matters tell us much about where Chesnutt's stories are situated in American literary history: at the beginning of the twentieth century, editors and publishers were still undecided about capitalizing "Negro," especially in Southern or "plantation" stories.

In "The Gray Wolf's Ha'nt," both a conjure man and a conjure woman, Aunt Peggy, appear. They match powers when a slave named

Dan seeks Aunt Peggy's help in evading the conjure man, who seeks revenge for the death of his son, killed in a fight with Dan over a slave woman named Mahaly. This will be another tale of intra-racial skirmish and destruction (the third, in fact, in the conjure series). As such, it is also a tale that presents free Negroes who use their advantages to their own selfish and vengeful ends, especially when they are conjure men (or the sons of conjure men). So the conflict is not simply black versus black, but free versus slave; and in this context, the only free person to be trusted is a conjure *woman*. Gender thus has its role in this story: will the free black conjure woman save Dan from the free black conjure man?

The answer is "no." Dan is initially protected by a charm from Aunt Peggy, but the conjure man figures that out and, with the help of a jaybird, washes away the charm. When he meets up with Dan, the conjure man charms Dan who agrees to be turned into something—a gray wolf. One moment in the conjure man's pleasantries with Dan is especially revealing. He says, "I lacks you monst'us well. Fac', I feels lack some er dese days I mought buy you fum yo' marster . . . en 'dop' you fer my son." This is a not-so-subtle reminder that Dan is a slave (and like all slaves, an orphan, as Frederick Douglass claimed) who the free conjure man can buy. Amazingly, it persuades Dan to do the conjure man's bidding. In the end, Dan and Mahaly both die, and their ghosts now haunt the land that John is thinking of clearing.

"The Gray Wolf's Ha'nt" is new in that it is both a revenge and a ghost tale. It is also new in that Aunt Peggy ultimately cannot help or save Dan. Though she is no match for the conjure man now, maybe she will be, by and by. Is Chesnutt thus contemplating new ways to tell the tales? Will Aunt Peggy best the conjure man? Will that tale appear?

"Mars Jeems's Nightmare" is another tale of a hard master, James McLean, the Mars Jeems of the title, who worked his slaves from daylight to dark, underfed them, and wouldn't let them sing or dance in the evening, contending that he bought them to work, not play. One particularly stringent policy of his was to not allow any courting or marrying among the slaves. If a couple got sweet on each other, he'd break them up and send one or the other slave away to his plantation in Robeson County. This is the very thing he does to Solomon and his "gal" once he finds out about them, and when she is sent to Robeson, we have another conjure tale that opens with a slave couple broken up by the whimsies of the master. A new touch is that Miss Libbie, the woman "Mars Jeems" has been courting, chooses this moment to break off *their* romance. Solomon and the master are both without their ladies. Solomon goes to see Aunt Peggy about getting his woman back and about making "Mars Jeem" treat his slaves better. Aunt Peggy's caution that she has to be "kinder keerful 'bout cunj'in' w'ite folks" reminds us that most of these tales are indeed about white and black people coming to her to conjure *slaves*. Putting something in "Mars Jeems's" soup, as Aunt Peggy instructs, is new and dangerous work, and it is a bold move on Chesnutt's part, since he is freely admitting, albeit in fiction, that slaves did tamper with the master's food, especially if he was a hard master.

In the end, Solomon gets his woman back, Miss Libbie takes back "Mars Jeems," and the slaves have better working conditions in part because the hard-driving overseer is dismissed. All this seems to have occurred because "Mars Jeems" was conjured into a Negro, whereupon he learned firsthand the conditions on his plantation. A special sweet potato transforms him back to "Mars Jeems" and into the man who makes life easier for the slaves and wins back his lady's love. "Mars Jeems" appears to be both the old and new genera-tion of plantation owner, but we have to be careful with that thought. The tale is occasioned when John and Julius observe Mars Jeems's grandson cruelly beating a horse. That suggests that reforms can indeed be short-lived and undone by the generations to come. Is the grandson now the proprietor of the plantation? One hopes not.

In the frame for "Mars Jeems's Nightmare," we note that John and Annie are not far along in becoming careful and sensitive listeners to Julius. John opens with unfortunate comments about Julius's acute familiarity with the mental processes of dogs and horses, which he attributes to something more than "use." He greets the end of the tale by chiming, "And they all lived happy ever after," adding, "Did you make that up yourself?" Annie's comment, that it is "a very strange story," is more polite than John's, but it hardly engages what the tale might be relating. Chesnutt, in writing this story late in the conjure series, seems to want to limn once again the early stages of John and Annie's growth into listenership. This would explain why this tale was chosen to be the third in *The Conjure Woman*. In 1898, Chesnutt was writing new stories that would add to the por-trayal of every phase of the relationship between Julius, John, and Annie.

"Sis' Becky's Pickaninny" frames its tale with a scene upon John and Annie's piazza, where John has placed a pillowed chair in which Annie can rest and perhaps deal with her melancholy, her sense of "impending misfortune." The couple has now been in North Car-olina for two years, and while Annie's health has been improving (that being one reason why they sought a milder climate than in their native Ohio), she is still contending with maladies that may be psychological as well as physical. Her attending doctor, for example, worries about her moods more than anything else.

When Julius arrives, he tries to give Annie his rabbit's foot, for good luck. Even after John chides him for his "superstitions," with

Annie suggesting that carrying a rabbit's foot is "ridiculous," Julius persists. He succeeds in giving Annie the rabbit's foot and gives her as well the tale of Becky and her son, Mose. The fact that the story so affects Annie suggests that hers is a would-be mother's melancholy. Perhaps she is having trouble conceiving; perhaps she has reason to fear an impending *maternal* misfortune. Whatever her circumstance, the tale moves her. Julius has sensed something and has told a tale that helps Annie at a difficult moment.

Julius's tale begins once again with two slaves torn apart from each other. Becky has been swapped for a horse (named Lightnin' Bug), and her new master refuses to take Mose as well, declaring, "I doan raise niggers; I raise hosses, en I doan wanter be both'rin' wid no nigger babies." Besides reminding us of the other masters who say things like, "I raise cotton, not niggers," this comment recalls all the ways in which slaves were valued or evaluated along with the "other livestock." Becky is told that she is being taken to Robeson County for a few days, where she is to help out Miss Laura, her former master's daughter. But that is a lie: the strange new master is taking her to a strange place, Bladen County, ever farther away from her Mose.

Without his mother, Mose falls ill, and Aunt Nancy visits Aunt Peggy to see what can be done. Ever the businesswoman, Aunt Peggy haggles with Aunt Nancy (the economy of conjuring makes its demands even when the plight of a child is involved), but eventually says that she will "show 'im [Mose] his mammy." Mose visits Becky first as a hummingbird and then as a mockingbird. With this narrative rhythm established, we expect and even yearn for Mose's third transformation, hoping that Becky and Mose will be reunited as mother and child. This occurs, but not before Aunt Peggy conjures Becky ill and then lames the horse Becky's old master had coveted. Becky's new master swaps Becky for his former horse, having persuaded himself that "a lame hoss wuz better'n a dead nigger."

A fascinating feature of this tale is that the happy reunion of mother and child is not the end of it. The tale continues and presents a future in which Mose turns out to be a "sma't man" who learns to be a blacksmith and is allowed to "hire his time . . . En bimeby he bought his mammy en sot her free, en den he bought hisse'f, en tuk keer er Sis' Becky ez long ez dey bofe libbed." Annie needs to hear a story that creates peace and happiness for a woman, now and ever after, and perhaps it helps to dream of a child who is the creator of that kind of lasting happiness. It is something to believe in. So when John thanks Julius for his "very ingenious fairy tale," Annie does not share his view or his tone, as she did in the tale's prologue. She says, "severely" we are told, "Why John! . . . the story bears the stamp of truth, if ever a story did." She hears a truth because she has become a listener, and part of what she has heard is the unspoken "why" of the tale Julius has told, just for her.

"Hot-Foot Hannibal" is hardly the first conjure tale to present intra-racial strife, but it does stand out as the tale in which field slaves are pitted against house slaves. This is not a tale, like others before it, in which the quarrels are between free Negroes and slaves. This is about who will get to work in the big house near a pretty girl with a name like Chloe, who is her mistress's maid, no less. Will it be a "yaller nigger" like Jeff who Chloe adores, or will it be the darker but smarter Hannibal? Who will leave the field and become a "house boy"?

Hannibal gets his chance first and turns out to be "the best house boy ever." But he also gets presumptuous about how being a good "boy" has earned him the right to Chloe, and how they are going be to married in the spring. Chloe tells Jeff to go see Aunt Peggy about this, making certain that he has "a silber dollah en a silk han'-kercher fer ter pay her wid, fer Aun' Peggy neber lack ter wuk fer nobody fer nuffin." When Aunt Peggy gives Jeff a doll, to be buried under the big house, that will make Hannibal light-headed and hot-footed, Hannibal commences to mess up and is sent back to the field. Jeff now gets his chance as "house boy." He succeeds, but he forgets to return the doll to Aunt Peggy and that creates Hannibal's opportunity for revenge.

Losing the prestige of being "house boy" is only the beginning of Hannibal's fury. It also involves Chloe's preference for a light-skinned young man who is named Jeff, not something faintly ridiculous like Caesar or Pompey or Hannibal. Then there is what he was conjured to be: light-headed and hot-footed, just like some "darkey" in a minstrel show. Hannibal's mammoth fury prevents him from seeing that he will never get Chloe. Even Chloe's mistress wants Chloe to marry Jeff: when Master McAdoo proposes that Chloe marry the new house boy, Mistress says, "Chloe ain' dat kin'er gal." She means that Chloe loves Jeff; she may also mean that she is not going to allow Chloe to marry just any Negro, just because he's the house boy.

It makes sense that "Hot-Foot Hannibal" appeared as the last tale in *The Conjure Woman*. Everyone is "on stage": slaves are quarreling with slaves but "Marse" and Mistress McAdoo are also actors in the drama, calling one slave or another up to the big house, selling Jeff downriver, futilely trying to provide for Chloe at the end. And of course, Aunt Peggy, Chesnutt's central conjure character, is present. The frame is crowded as well. Mabel, Annie's sister who was first introduced in the tales of the mid-1890s, here quarrels with and then, at the end, reconciles with young Malcolm Murchison, most likely the young Murchison who is restoring the family home at the end of "The Dumb Witness." Their marriage is a hopeful, new union of North and South. Their housekeeping at the old Murchison place ideally will introduce a new order of working the land and of caring for the people who will be doing the work. Suggestions of such a future provide Chesnutt with a good note on which to end "Hot-Foot Hannibal." Closure to that story brought closure to a project that he had pursued for more than a decade. A new century was months away and Chesnutt was ready to move on.

Well into the new century, Chesnutt found that he had one more conjure tale to tell, "The Marked Tree." Rightly described by Richard Brodhead as "a late reprise of the conjure formula,"[7] "The Marked Tree" was published in the December 1924/January 1925 issue of the *Crisis*, the journal of the NAACP which was then edited by W. E. B. Du Bois. Yolanda Du Bois (Du Bois's daughter) provided illustrations, thus distinguishing this tale as the only one to be illustrated (the illustrations are presented in the Contexts section of this volume).

In the frame, John is off to see the old Spencer place with a view to urging its purchase by an Ohio cousin. We recall that in the very first story *John* is the Ohioan who writes a cousin in North Carolina regarding properties there. While this indicates that John has been in North Carolina for years and is now the cousin "on location," it also suggests that Chesnutt is deliberately bringing this line of narrative full circle and thus to a close. Perhaps he had already decided that this would be the last conjure tale.

John also offers the second of his commentaries comparing Julius's storytelling to folk traditions other than black or "slave" traditions. In "Tobe's Tribulations," John wonders what storytelling cultures came to be shared by whites and blacks, especially Scots and blacks, in North Carolina. In "The Marked Tree," he quite remarkably compares Julius's stories to the "sagas of Iceland" and the "primitive tales of Ancient Greece." And he goes further, speculating that "Had Julius lived in a happier time for men of his complexion, the world might have had a black Aesop or Grimm or Hoffman." John's respect for Julius's stories was not always evident in the earlier tales, but it is fully on view here when he says, "I have saved a few of them." Over the *long durée* of the conjure tale event, John has become a good listener, a reliable listener, which is all a storyteller can hope for.

The amity between black and white that we see in the frame is in no way present in the tale. Twenty years into the twentieth century, Chesnutt was discouraged about race relations, and had little reason to believe a new generation in the South would bring on better

---

7. Richard H. Brodhead, ed., *The Conjure Woman and Other Conjure Tales: Charles W. Chesnutt* (Durham: Duke UP, 1993), p. 23.

times. "Marse" Aleck Spencer (yet another Scot) needs to raise cash for son Johnny's upcoming wedding, and, at his wife's urging, he decides to sell a slave boy named Isham, Phillis's son. This is a particularly cruel turn of events: Isham and Johnny had been boys together, born on the same day. Even Spencer senses that there is something not quite right about this, but Isham is nonetheless sold. On the day of the wedding, Isham arrives at Phillis's door, bloody and wounded after fighting with his new master. When he dies, Phillis gets revenge for her loss upon the entire family.

There is a big oak tree on the Spencer place where family celebrations are traditionally held. Johnny had been christened beneath that tree; on his wedding day, the young couple is toasted under the tree. When Phillis decides to conjure the tree, Spencers, young and old, begin to die off. In all, nine Spencers die in Julius's grim tale before the very tree that Phillis "marked" falls and kills "Marse" Spencer. Phillis's mark is potent: even after the Spencer tree has been chopped into logs, those logs start a fire that burns the family house down to the ground, "wid eve'ybody in it."

Like Tenie in "Po' Sandy," the other conjurer who is a slave woman, Phillis cannot protect her loved one. She can no more save Isham than Tenie can rescue Sandy. On the other hand, Phillis's sorcery destroys a slaveholding family, if not the system of slavery itself. Phillis brings the Spencer house down to the dust. It would seem, then, that in writing "The Marked Tree" Chesnutt sought to revisit his portrait of Tenie, and to create a slave woman conjurer whose powers change the neighborhood, if not the world. Phillis does not gain her freedom nor can she save her son, but she does gain her revenge.

Perhaps Chesnutt was rethinking Tenie's Sandy as well. In "Po' Sandy," the tree (Sandy) is chopped down and milled into boards for the big house's new kitchen. In "The Marked Tree," the tree (marked in memory of Isham) is also chopped down, but the wood does not build some addition to the property, let alone a space in which Phillis, like Tenie before her, can descend into melancholy and grief. The wood burns down property and kills people. That revision, if you will, to one of Chesnutt's very first stories, renders a dark tale even darker. "The Marked Tree" is Chesnutt's last conjure tale and it makes this point: some slaves did fight back and did so in ways that are still unexplainable. Things happened.

ROBERT B. STEPTO

Acknowledgments

We are indebted to Sarah Ingle and to Kelly Johnston, a GIS Specialist at the University of Virginia Libraries, for creating the maps included in this edition; to Beth M. Howse of the Franklin Library at Fisk University for providing us with Chesnutt's typescripts of "The Dumb Witness"; to Maria Carly Thomas and Walt Hunter for research and proofreading assistance; and to the editorial and production staff at Norton, particularly Carol Bemis and Rivka Genesen.

Note on the Texts

This Norton Critical Edition presents Charles Chesnutt's Julius stories in the order in which he wrote them, as nearly as we are able to establish the chronology. The publication history of each story is included as its first footnote.

With the exception of "The Dumb Witness," each of the fourteen Julius stories was published during Chesnutt's lifetime, and we use the original publication of each story as its authoritative text. Six of the stories were published only in periodicals; three of them were published only in *The Conjure Woman* volume (Houghton Mifflin, 1899). Four of the stories were published first in periodicals, and then collected in *The Conjure Woman*; for these stories, we use the collected versions and indicate significant revisions by Chesnutt in the annotations.

We established the text of "The Dumb Witness" from two typescripts, both incomplete and neither a fair copy, held in the archives of Fisk University; more detailed information is included in the annotation of that story. During his lifetime, Chesnutt published a significantly altered version of "The Dumb Witness" as an episode in his last published novel, *The Colonel's Dream*; the relevant excerpt from the novel is included in the Contexts section of this Norton Critical Edition.

* * *

In thinking about how the individual stories have been presented in relation to each other, the following information is also useful.

Seven of these stories were published together in the volume *The Conjure Woman*, in the following configuration:

The Goophered Grapevine
Po' Sandy
Mars Jeems's Nightmare
The Conjurer's Revenge
Sis' Becky's Pickaninny
The Gray Wolf's Ha'nt
Hot-Foot Hannibal

When Chesnutt originally proposed a volume of his short fiction to Houghton Mifflin in October 1897, he included a total of twenty stories. Of these, seven featured Julius as narrator:

Lonesome Ben
The Dumb Witness
The Goophered Grapevine
Dave's Neckliss
Po' Sandy
The Conjurer's Revenge
A Deep Sleeper

When editor Walter Hines Page replied in March 1898 that his press was interested only in a volume of "'conjure' stories," Chesnutt wrote six additional stories, all of which featured Julius as narrator, in seven weeks. He submitted those stories in the following order:

A Victim of Heredity
The Gray Wolf's Ha'nt
Mars Jeems's Nightmare
Sis' Becky's Pickaninny
Tobe's Tribulations
Hot-Foot Hannibal, or the Long Road

The Chesnutt/Page correspondence surrounding the production of *The Conjure Woman*, as collected by Chesnutt's daughter Helen in her critical biography of her father, is included in the Early Criticism section of this Norton Critical Edition.

The Texts of
THE CONJURE STORIES

The Goophered Grapevine[1]

Some years ago my wife was in poor health, and our family doctor, in whose skill and honesty I had implicit confidence, advised a change of climate.[2] I shared, from an unprofessional standpoint, his opinion that the raw winds, the chill rains, and the violent changes of temperature that characterized the winters in the region of the Great Lakes tended to aggravate my wife's difficulty, and would undoubtedly shorten her life if she remained exposed to them. The doctor's advice was that we seek, not a temporary place of sojourn, but a permanent residence, in a warmer and more equable climate. I was engaged at the time in grape-culture in northern Ohio, and, as I liked the business and had given it much study, I decided to look for some other locality suitable for carrying it on. I thought of sunny France, of sleepy Spain, of Southern California, but there were objections to them all. It occurred to me that I might find what I wanted in some one of our own Southern States. It was a sufficient time after the war for conditions in the South to have become somewhat settled; and I was enough of a pioneer to start a new industry, if I could not find a place where grape-culture had been tried. I wrote to a cousin who had gone into the turpentine business in central North Carolina. He assured me, in response to my inquiries, that no better place could be found in the South than the State and neighborhood where he lived; the climate was perfect for health, and, in conjunction with the soil, ideal for grape-culture; labor was cheap, and land could be bought for a mere song. He gave us a cordial invitation to come and visit him while we looked into the matter. We accepted the invitation, and after several days of leisurely travel, the last hundred miles of which were up a river on a sidewheel steamer, we reached our destination, a quaint old town, which I shall call Patesville,[3] because, for one reason, that is not its name. There was a red brick market-house in the public square, with a tall tower, which held a four-faced clock that struck the hours, and from which there pealed out a curfew at nine o'clock.[4] There were two or three hotels, a court-house, a jail, stores, offices, and all the appurtenances of a county seat and a commercial emporium; for while

---

1. Published in the *Atlantic Monthly* in 1887; reprinted, with significant revisions, as the first story of *The Conjure Woman* in 1899.
2. The majority of this long paragraph was added by Chesnutt in the 1899 edition.
3. Fayetteville, N.C. While Chesnutt rather thinly disguises this place-name, he records the actual names of all other places mentioned in the stories.
4. The Fayetteville Market House (see photo, p. 165) was built in 1838 on the site of the old North Carolina State House, which had been destroyed by fire in 1831. While Fayetteville served as the state capital from 1789–93, the legislature had ratified the Constitution of the United States and chartered the University of North Carolina within the walls of the former building. By contrast, the Market House housed a slave market.

3

Patesville numbered only four or five thousand inhabitants, of all shades of complexion, it was one of the principal towns in North Carolina, and had a considerable trade in cotton and naval stores. This business activity was not immediately apparent to my unaccustomed eyes. Indeed, when I first saw the town, there brooded over it a calm that seemed almost sabbatic in its restfulness, though I learned later on that underneath its somnolent exterior the deeper currents of life—love and hatred, joy and despair, ambition and avarice, faith and friendship—flowed not less steadily than in livelier latitudes.[5]

We found the weather delightful at that season, the end of summer, and were hospitably entertained. Our host was a man of means and evidently regarded our visit as a pleasure, and we were therefore correspondingly at our ease, and in a position to act with the coolness of judgment desirable in making so radical a change in our lives. My cousin placed a horse and buggy at our disposal, and himself acted as our guide until I became somewhat familiar with the country.

I found that grape-culture, while it had never been carried on to any great extent, was not entirely unknown in the neighborhood. Several planters thereabouts had attempted it on a commercial scale, in former years, with greater or less success; but like most Southern industries, it had felt the blight of war and had fallen into desuetude.

I went several times to look at a place that I thought might suit me. It was a plantation of considerable extent, that had formerly belonged to a wealthy man by the name of McAdoo. The estate had been for years involved in litigation between disputing heirs, during which period shiftless cultivation had well-nigh exhausted the soil. There had been a vineyard of some extent on the place, but it had not been attended to since the war, and had lapsed into utter neglect. The vines—here partly supported by decayed and broken-down trellises, there twining themselves among the branches of the slender saplings which had sprung up among them—grew in wild and unpruned luxuriance, and the few scattered grapes they bore were the undisputed prey of the first comer. The site was admirably adapted to grape-raising; the soil, with a little attention, could not have been better; and with the native grape, the luscious scuppernong, as my main reliance in the beginning, I felt sure that I could introduce and cultivate successfully a number of other varieties.

---

5. The narrator, identified in "Po' Sandy" as John, draws on contemporary ideas about the influence of climate on human behavior that associate a warm or tropical climate with slowness and laziness.

One day I went over with my wife to show her the place.[6] We drove out of the town over a long wooden bridge that spanned a spreading mill-pond, passed the long whitewashed fence surrounding the county fair-ground, and struck into a road so sandy that the horse's feet sank to the fetlocks. Our route lay partly up hill and partly down, for we were in the sand-hill county[7]; we drove past cultivated farms, and then by abandoned fields grown up in scrub-oak and short-leaved pine, and once or twice through the solemn aisles of the virgin forest, where the tall pines, well-nigh meeting over the narrow road, shut out the sun, and wrapped us in cloistral solitude. Once, at a cross-roads, I was in doubt as to the turn to take, and we sat there waiting ten minutes—we had already caught some of the native infection of restfulness—for some human being to come along, who could direct us on our way. At length a little negro girl appeared, walking straight as an arrow, with a piggin[8] full of water on her head. After a little patient investigation, necessary to overcome the child's shyness, we learned what we wished to know, and at the end of about five miles from the town reached our destination.

We drove between a pair of decayed gateposts—the gate itself had long since disappeared—and up a straight sandy lane, between two lines of rotting rail fence, partly concealed by jimson-weeds and briers, to the open space where a dwelling-house had once stood, evidently a spacious mansion, if we might judge from the ruined chimneys that were still standing, and the brick pillars on which the sills rested. The house itself, we had been informed, had fallen a victim to the fortunes of war.

We alighted from the buggy, walked about the yard for a while, and then wandered off into the adjoining vineyard. Upon Annie's complaining of weariness I led the way back to the yard, where a pine log, lying under a spreading elm, afforded a shady though somewhat hard seat. One end of the log was already occupied by a venerable-looking colored man. He held on his knees a hat full of grapes, over which he was smacking his lips with great gusto, and a pile of grapeskins near him indicated that the performance[9] was no new thing. We approached him at an angle from the rear, and were close to him before he perceived us. He respectfully rose as we drew near, and was moving away, when I begged him to keep his seat.

"Don't let us disturb you," I said. "There is plenty of room for us all."

---

6. Chesnutt added this paragraph in the 1899 edition.
7. A region of North Carolina that separates the Piedmont area to the Northeast, and the Coastal Plain to the Southeast, with a strip of sandy soil and dunes.
8. A wooden pail.
9. By describing Julius's first appearance as a "performance," "monologue," and so on, the narrator raises the issue of Julius's stature as artist, and the question of his control over the development of the story John will narrate.

He resumed his seat with somewhat of embarrassment.[1] While he had been standing, I had observed that he was a tall man, and, though slightly bowed by the weight of years, apparently quite vigorous. He was not entirely black, and this fact, together with the quality of his hair, which was about six inches long and very bushy, except on the top of his head, where he was quite bald, suggested a slight strain of other than negro blood. There was a shrewdness in his eyes, too, which was not altogether African, and which, as we afterwards learned from experience, was indicative of a corresponding shrewdness in his character.[2] He went on eating the grapes, but did not seem to enjoy himself quite so well as he had apparently done before he became aware of our presence.

"Do you live around here?" I asked, anxious to put him at his ease.

"Yas, suh. I lives des ober yander, behine de nex' san'-hill, on de Lumberton plank-road."

"Do you know anything about the time when this vineyard was cultivated?"

"Lawd bless you, suh, I knows all about it. Dey ain' na'er a man in dis settlement w'at won' tell you ole Julius McAdoo 'uz bawn en raise' on dis yer same plantation. Is you de Norv'n gemman w'at's gwine ter buy de ole vimya'd?"

"I am looking at it," I replied; "but I don't know that I shall care to buy unless I can be reasonably sure of making something out of it."

"Well, suh, you is a stranger ter me, en I is a stranger ter you, en we is bofe strangers ter one anudder, but 'f I 'uz in yo' place, I wouldn' buy dis vimya'd."

"Why not?" I asked.

"Well, I dunno whe'r you b'lieves in cunj'in' er not,—some er de w'ite folks don't, er says dey don't,—but de truf er de matter is dat dis yer ole vimya'd is goophered."

"Is what?" I asked, not grasping the meaning of this unfamiliar word.

"Is goophered,—cunju'd, bewitch'."

He imparted this information with such solemn earnestness, and with such an air of confidential mystery, that I felt somewhat interested, while Annie was evidently much impressed, and drew closer to me.

"How do you know it is bewitched?" I asked.

"I wouldn' spec' fer you ter b'lieve me 'less you know all 'bout de fac's. But ef you en young miss dere doan' min' lis'nin' ter a ole nigger run on a minute er two w'ile you er restin', I kin 'splain to you how it all happen'."

---

1. Chesnutt added this paragraph in the 1899 edition.
2. John gives voice to contemporary biological determinism, which sees both physical and mental characteristics as defined by the inherited "blood" of racial origin.

We assured him that we would be glad to hear how it all happened, and he began to tell us. At first the current of his memory—or imagination—seemed somewhat sluggish; but as his embarrassment wore off, his language flowed more freely, and the story acquired perspective and coherence. As he became more and more absorbed in the narrative, his eyes assumed a dreamy expression, and he seemed to lose sight of his auditors, and to be living over again in monologue his life on the old plantation.

"Ole Mars Dugal' McAdoo," he began, "bought dis place long many years befo' de wah, en I'member well w'en he sot out all dis yer part er de plantation in scuppernon's. De vimes growed monst'us fas', en Mars Dugal' made a thousan' gallon er scuppernon' wine eve'y year.

"Now, ef dey's an'thing a nigger lub, nex' ter 'possum, en chick'n, en watermillyums, it's scuppernon's. Dey ain' nuffin dat kin stan' up side'n de scuppernon' fer sweetness; sugar ain't a suckumstance ter scuppernon'. W'en de season is nigh 'bout ober, en de grapes begin ter swivel up des a little wid de wrinkles er ole age,—w'en de skin git sof' en brown,—den de scuppernon' make you smack yo' lip en roll yo' eye en wush fer mo'; so I reckon it ain' very 'stonishin' dat niggers lub scuppernon'.

"Dey wuz a sight er niggers in de naberhood er de vimya'd. Dere wuz ole Mars Henry, Brayboy's niggers, en ole Mars Jeems McLean's niggers, en Mars Dugal's own niggers; den dey wuz a settlement er free niggers en po' buckrahs down by de Wim'l'ton[3] Road, en Mars Dugal' had de only vimya'd in de naberhood. I reckon it ain' so much so nowadays, but befo' de wah, in slab'ry times, a nigger didn' mine goin' fi' er ten mile in a night, w'en dey wuz sump'n good ter eat at de yuther een'.

"So atter a w'ile Mars Dugal' begin ter miss his scuppernon's. Co'se he 'cuse' de niggers er it, but dey all 'nied it ter de las'. Mars Dugal' sot spring guns en steel traps, en he en de oberseah sot up nights once't er twice't, tel one night Mars Dugal'—he 'uz a monst'us keerless man—got his leg shot full er cow-peas.[4] But somehow er nudder dey couldn' nebber ketch none er de niggers. I dunner how it happen, but it happen des like I tell you, en de grapes kep' on a-goin' des de same.

"But bimeby ole Mars Dugal' fix' up a plan ter stop it. Dey wuz a cunjuh 'oman livin' down 'mongs' de free niggers on de Wim'l'ton Road, en all de darkies fum Rockfish ter Beaver Crick wuz feared er her. She could wuk de mos' powerfulles' kin' er goopher,—could make people hab fits, er rheumatiz, er make 'em des dwinel away en

---

3. Wilmington, N.C., the major port town of the state; *buckrahs*: African American term for a white person.
4. Also known as "black-eyed peas," a popular legume consumed in the Southern states; this colloquial usage, though, seems to refer to small shot, analogous to birdshot.

die; en dey say she went out ridin' de niggers at night, fer she wuz a witch 'sides bein' a cunjuh 'oman.[5] Mars Dugal' hearn 'bout Aun' Peggy's doin's, en begun ter 'flect whe'r er no he couldn' git her ter he'p him keep de niggers off'n de grapevimes. One day in de spring er de year, ole miss pack' up a basket er chick'n en poun'-cake, en a bottle er scuppernon' wine, en Mars Dugal' tuk it in his buggy en driv ober ter Aun' Peggy's cabin. He tuk de basket in, en had a long talk wid Aun' Peggy.

"De nex' day Aun' Peggy come up ter de vimya'd. De niggers seed her slippin' 'roun', en dey soon foun' out what she 'uz doin' dere. Mars Dugal' had hi'ed her ter goopher de grapevimes. She sa'ntered 'roun' 'mongs' de vimes, en tuk a leaf fum dis one, en a grape-hull fum dat one, en a grape-seed fum anudder one; en den a little twig fum here, en a little pinch er dirt fum dere,—en put it all in a big black bottle, wid a snake's toof en a speckle' hen's gall en some ha'rs fum a black cat's tail, en den fill' de bottle wid scuppernon' wine. W'en she got de goopher all ready en fix', she tuk 'n went out in de woods en buried it under de root uv a red oak tree, en den come back en tole one er de niggers she done goopher de grapevimes, en a'er a nigger w'at eat dem grapes 'ud be sho ter die inside'n twel' mont's.

"Atter dat de niggers let de scuppernon's 'lone, en Mars Dugal' didn' hab no 'casion ter fine no mo' fault; en de season wuz mos' gone, w'en a strange gemman stop at de plantation one night ter see Mars Dugal' on some business; en his coachman, seein' de scuppernon's growin' so nice en sweet, slip 'roun' behine de smoke-house, en et all de scuppernon's he could hole. Nobody didn' notice it at de time, but dat night, on de way home, de gemman's hoss runned away en kill' de coachman. W'en we hearn de noos, Aun' Lucy, de cook, she up 'n say she seed de strange nigger eat'n' er de scuppernon's behine de smoke-house; en den we knowed de goopher had b'en er wukkin'. Den one er de nigger chilluns runned away fum de quarters one day, en got in de scuppernon's, en died de nex' week. Wite folks say he die' er de fevuh, but de niggers knowed it wuz de goopher. So you k'n be sho de darkies didn' hab much ter do wid dem scuppernon' vimes.

"W'en de scuppernon' season 'uz ober fer dat year, Mars Dugal' foun' he had made fifteen hund'ed gallon er wine; en one er de niggers hearn him laffin' wid de oberseah fit ter kill, en sayin' dem fifteen hund'ed gallon er wine wuz monst'us good intrus' on de ten dollars he laid out on de vimya'd. So I 'low ez he paid Aun' Peggy ten dollars fer to goopher de grapevimes.

"De goopher didn' wuk no mo' tel de nex' summer, w'en 'long to'ds de middle er de season one er de fiel' han's died; en ez dat lef' Mars

5. By identifying Aunt Peggy as both a "witch" and a "conjure woman," Chesnutt stresses the multiple geographic roots—European as well as African—of the folk stories Julius tells.

Dugal' sho't er han's, he went off ter town fer ter buy anudder. He fotch de noo nigger home wid 'im. He wuz er ole nigger, er de color er a gingy-cake, en ball ez a hoss-apple on de top er his head. He wuz a peart ole nigger, do', en could do a big day's wuk.

"Now it happen dat one er de niggers on de nex' plantation, one er ole Mars Henry Brayboy's niggers, had runned away de day befo', en tuk ter de swamp, en ole Mars Dugal' en some er de yuther nabor w'ite folks had gone out wid dere guns en dere dogs fer ter he'p 'em hunt fer de nigger; en de han's on our own plantation wuz all so flusterated dat we fuhgot ter tell de noo han' 'bout de goopher on de scuppernon' vimes. Co'se he smell de grapes en see de vimes, an atter dahk de fus' thing he done wuz ter slip off ter de grapevimes 'dout sayin' nuffin ter nobody. Nex' mawnin' he tole some er de niggers 'bout de fine bait[6] er scuppernon' he et de night befo'.

"W'en dey tole 'im 'bout de goopher on de grapevimes, he 'uz dat tarrified dat he turn pale, en look des like he gwine ter die right in his tracks. De oberseah come up en axed w'at 'uz de matter; en w'en dey tole 'im Henry be'n eatin' er de scuppernon's, en got de goopher on 'im, he gin Henry a big drink er w'iskey, en 'low dat de nex' rainy day he take 'im ober ter Aun' Peggy's, en see ef she wouldn' take de goopher off'n him, seein' ez he didn' know nuffin erbout it tel he done et de grapes.

"Sho nuff, it rain de nex' day, en de oberseah went ober ter Aun' Peggy's wid Henry. En Aun' Peggy say dat bein' ez Henry didn' know 'bout de goopher, en et de grapes in ign'ance er de conseq'ences, she reckon she mought be able fer ter take de goopher off'n him. So she fotch out er bottle wid some cunjuh medicine in it, en po'd some out in a go'd fer Henry ter drink. He manage ter git it down; he say it tas'e like whiskey wid sump'n bitter in it. She 'lowed dat 'ud keep de goopher off'n him tel de spring; but w'en de sap begin ter rise in de grapevimes he ha' ter come en see her ag'in, en she tell him w'at e's ter do.

"Nex' spring, w'en de sap commence' ter rise in de scuppernon' vime, Henry tuk a ham one night. Whar'd he git de ham? *I* doan know; dey wa'n't no hams on de plantation 'cep'n' w'at 'uz in de smoke-house, but *I* never see Henry 'bout de smoke-house. But ez I wuz a-sayin', he tuk de ham ober ter Aun' Peggy's; en Aun' Peggy tole 'im dat w'en Mars Dugal' begin ter prune de grapevimes, he mus' go en take 'n scrape off de sap whar it ooze out'n de cut een's er de vimes, en 'n'int his ball head wid it; en ef he do dat once't a year de goopher wouldn' wuk agin 'im long ez he done it. En bein' ez he fotch her de ham, she fix' it so he kin eat all de scuppernon' he want.

---

6. Refreshment taken between meals.

"So Henry 'n'int his head wid de sap out'n de big grapevime des ha'f way 'twix' de quarters en de big house, en de goopher nebber wuk agin him dat summer. But de beatenes' thing you eber see happen ter Henry. Up ter dat time he wuz ez ball ez a sweeten' 'tater, but des ez soon ez de young leaves begun ter come out on de grapevimes, de ha'r begun ter grow out on Henry's head, en by de middle er de summer he had de bigges' head er ha'r on de plantation. Befo' dat, Henry had tol'able good ha'r 'roun' de aidges, but soon ez de young grapes begun ter come, Henry's ha'r begun to quirl all up in little balls, des like dis yer reg'lar grapy ha'r, en by de time de grapes got ripe his head look des like a bunch er grapes. Combin' it didn' do no good; he wuk at it ha'f de night wid er Jim Crow,[7] en think he git it straighten' out, but in de mawnin' de grapes 'ud be dere des de same. So he gin it up, en tried ter keep de grapes down by havin' his ha'r cut sho't.

"But dat wa'n't de quares' thing 'bout de goopher. When Henry come ter de plantation, he wuz gittin' a little ole an stiff in de j'ints. But dat summer he got des ez spry en libely ez any young nigger on de plantation; fac', he got so biggity dat Mars Jackson, de oberseah, ha' ter th'eaten ter whip 'im, ef he didn' stop cuttin' up his didos[8] en behave hisse'f. But de mos' cur'ouses' thing happen' in de fall, when de sap begin ter go down in de grapevimes. Fus', when de grapes 'uz gethered, de knots begun ter straighten out'n Henry's ha'r; en w'en de leaves begin ter fall, Henry's ha'r 'mence' ter drap out; en when de vimes 'uz bar', Henry's head wuz baller 'n it wuz in de spring, en he begin ter git ole en stiff in de j'ints ag'in, en paid no mo' 'tention ter de gals dyoin' er de whole winter. En nex' spring, w'en he rub de sap on ag'in, he got young ag'in, en so soopl en libely dat none er de young niggers on de plantation couldn' jump, ner dance, ner hoe ez much cotton ez Henry. But in de fall er de year his grapes 'mence' ter straighten out, en his j'ints ter git stiff, en his ha'r drap off, en de rheumatiz begin ter wrastle wid 'im.

"Now, ef you'd 'a' knowed ole Mars Dugal' McAdoo, you'd 'a' knowed dat it ha' ter be a mighty rainy day when he couldn' fine sump'n fer his niggers ter do, en it ha' ter be a mighty little hole he couldn' crawl thoo, en ha' ter be a monst'us cloudy night when a dollar git by him in de dahkness; en w'en he see how Henry git young in de spring en ole in de fall, he 'lowed ter hisse'f ez how he could make mo' money out'n Henry dan by wukkin' him in de cotton-fiel'. 'Long de nex' spring, atter de sap 'mence' ter rise, en Henry 'n'int 'is head en sta'ted fer ter git young en soopl, Mars Dugal' up 'n tuk Henry ter town, en sole 'im fer fifteen hunder' dollars. Co'se de man w'at bought Henry didn' know nuffin 'bout de goopher, en Mars Dugal' didn' see no 'casion fer ter tell 'im. Long to'ds de fall, w'en de sap went down, Henry begin ter git ole ag'in same ez yuzhal, en his noo marster begin ter git skeered les'n he gwine ter lose his fifteen-hunder'-dollar nigger. He sent fer a mighty fine doctor, but de med'cine didn' 'pear ter do no good; de goopher had a good holt. Henry tole de doctor 'bout de goopher, but de doctor des laff at 'im.

"One day in de winter Mars Dugal' went ter town, en wuz san-terin' 'long de Main Street, when who should he meet but Henry's noo marster. Dey said 'Hoddy,' en Mars Dugal' ax 'im ter hab a seegyar; en atter dey run on awhile 'bout de craps en de weather, Mars Dugal' ax 'im, sorter keerless, like ez ef he des thought of it,—

"'How you like de nigger I sole you las' spring?'

"Henry's marster shuck his head en knock de ashes off'n his seegyar.

"'Spec' I made a bad bahgin when I bought dat nigger. Henry done good wuk all de summer, but sence de fall set in he 'pears ter be sorter pinin' away. Dey ain' nuffin pertickler de matter wid 'im— leastways de doctor say so—'cep'n' a tech er de rheumatiz; but his ha'r is all fell out, en ef he don't pick up his strenk mighty soon, I spec' I'm gwine ter lose 'im.'

"Dey smoked on awhile, en bimeby ole mars say, 'Well, a bahgin 's a bahgin, but you en me is good fren's, en I doan wan' ter see you lose all de money you paid fer dat nigger; en ef w'at you say is so, en I ain't 'sputin' it, he ain't wuf much now. I 'spec's you wukked him too ha'd dis summer, er e'se de swamps down here don't agree wid de san'-hill nigger. So you des lemme know, en ef he gits any wusser I 'll be willin' ter gib yer five hund'ed dollars fer 'im, en take my chances on his livin'.'

"Sho 'nuff, when Henry begun ter draw up wid de rheumatiz en it look like he gwine ter die fer sho, his noo marster sen' fer Mars Dugal', en Mars Dugal' gin him what he promus, en brung Henry home ag'in. He tuk good keer uv 'im dyoin' er de winter,—give 'im w'iskey ter rub his rheumatiz, en terbacker ter smoke, en all he want ter eat,—'caze a nigger w'at he could make a thousan' dollars a year off'n didn' grow on eve'y huckleberry bush.

"Nex' spring, w'en de sap ris en Henry's ha'r commence' ter sprout, Mars Dugal' sole 'im ag'in, down in Robeson County dis time; en he kep' dat sellin' business up fer five year er mo'. Henry nebber say nuffin 'bout de goopher ter his noo marsters, 'caze he know he gwine ter be tuk good keer uv de nex' winter, w'en Mars Dugal' buy him back. En Mars Dugal' made 'nuff money off'n Henry ter buy anudder plantation ober on Beaver Crick.

"But 'long 'bout de een' er dat five year dey come a stranger ter stop at de plantation. De fus' day he 'uz dere he went out wid Mars Dugal' en spent all de mawnin' lookin' ober de vimya'd, en atter dinner dey spent all de evenin' playin' kya'ds. De niggers soon 'skiver' dat he

wuz a Yankee, en dat he come down ter Norf C'lina fer ter l'arn de
w'ite folks how to raise grapes en make wine. He promus Mars Dugal'
he c'd make de grapevimes b'ar twice't ez many grapes, en dat de noo
winepress he wuz a-sellin' would make mo' d'n twice't ez many gal-
lons er wine. En ole Mars Dugal' des drunk it all in, des 'peared ter
be bewitch' wid dat Yankee. W'en de darkies see dat Yankee runnin'
'roun' de vimya'd en diggin' under de grapevimes, dey shuk dere heads,
en 'lowed dat dey feared Mars Dugal' losin' his min'. Mars Dugal' had
all de dirt dug away fum under de roots er all de scuppernon' vimes,
an' let 'em stan' dat away fer a week er mo'. Den dat Yankee made de
niggers fix up a mixtry er lime en ashes en manyo,[9] en po' it 'roun' de
roots er de grapevimes. Den he 'vise Mars Dugal' fer ter trim de vimes
close't, en Mars Dugal' tuck 'n done eve'ything de Yankee tole him ter
do. Dyoin' all er dis time, mind yer, dis yer Yankee wuz libbin' off'n
de fat er de lan', at de big house, en playin' kya'ds wid Mars Dugal'
eve'y night; en dey say Mars Dugal' los' mo'n a thousan' dollars dyoin'
er de week dat Yankee wuz a-ruinin' de grapevimes.

"W'en de sap ris nex' spring, ole Henry 'n'inted his head ez yuzhal,
en his ha'r 'mence' ter grow des de same ez it done eve'y year. De
scuppernon' vimes growed monst's fas', en de leaves wuz greener en
thicker dan dey eber be'n dyoin' my remem'ance; en Henry's ha'r
growed out thicker dan eber, en he 'peared ter git younger 'n younger,
en soopler 'n soopler; en seein' ez he wuz sho't er han's dat spring,
havin' tuk in consid'able noo groun', Mars Dugal' 'cluded he wouldn'
sell Henry 'tel he git de crap in en de cotton chop'. So he kep' Henry
on de plantation.

"But 'long 'bout time fer de grapes ter come on de scuppernon'
vimes, dey 'peared ter come a change ober 'em; de leaves withered
en swivel' up, en de young grapes turn' yaller, en bimeby eve'ybody
on de plantation could see dat de whole vimya'd wuz dyin'. Mars
Dugal' tuk 'n water de vimes en done all he could, but 't wa'n' no use:
dat Yankee had done bus' de watermillyum.[1] One time de vimes picked
up a bit, en Mars Dugal' 'lowed dey wuz gwine ter come out ag'in;
but dat Yankee done dug too close under de roots, en prune de
branches too close ter de vime, en all dat lime en ashes done burn'
de life out'n de vimes, en dey des kep' a-with'in' en a-swivelin'.

"All dis time de goopher wuz a-wukkin'. When de vimes sta'ted ter
wither, Henry 'mence' ter complain er his rheumatiz; en when de
leaves begin ter dry up, his ha'r 'mence' ter drap out. When de vimes
fresh' up a bit, Henry'd git peart ag'in, en when de vimes wither'
ag'in, Henry'd git ole ag'in, en des kep' gittin' mo' en mo' fitten fer
nuffin; he des pined away, en pined away, en fine'ly tuk ter his cabin;

9. Manure.
1. Had done irrevocable or irreparable damage.

en when de big vime whar he got de sap ter 'n'int his head withered en turned yaller en died, Henry died too,—des went out sorter like a cannel. Dey did n't 'pear ter be nuffin de matter wid 'im, 'cep'n' de rheumatiz, but his strenk des dwinel' away 'tel he did n' hab ernuff lef' ter draw his bref. De goopher had got de under holt, en th'owed Henry dat time fer good en all.

"Mars Dugal' tuk on might'ly 'bout losin' his vimes en his nigger in de same year; en he swo' dat ef he could git holt er dat Yankee he'd wear 'im ter a frazzle, en den chaw up de frazzle; en he'd done it, too, for Mars Dugal' 'uz a monst'us brash man w'en he once git started. He sot de vimya'd out ober ag'in, but it wuz th'ee er fo' year befo' de vimes got ter b'arin' any scuppernon's.

"W'en de wah broke out, Mars Dugal' raise' a comp'ny, en went off ter fight de Yankees. He say he wuz mighty glad dat wah come, en he des want ter kill a Yankee fer eve'y dollar he los' 'long er dat grape-raisin' Yankee. En I 'spec' he would 'a' done it, too, ef de Yankees had n' s'picioned sump'n, en killed him fus'. Atter de s'render ole miss move' ter town, de niggers all scattered 'way fum de plantation, en de vimya'd ain' be'n cultervated sence."

"Is that story true?" asked Annie doubtfully, but seriously, as the old man concluded his narrative.

"It's des ez true ez I'm a-settin' here, miss. Dey's a easy way ter prove it: I kin lead de way right ter Henry's grave ober yander in de plantation buryin'-groun'. En I tell yer w'at, marster, I wouldn' 'vise you to buy dis yer ole vimya'd, 'caze de goopher's on it yit, en dey ain' no tellin' w'en it 's gwine ter crap out."

"But I thought you said all the old vines died."

"Dey did 'pear ter die, but a few un 'em come out ag'in, en is mixed in 'mongs' de yuthers. I ain' skeered ter eat de grapes, 'caze I knows de old vimes fum de noo ones; but wid strangers dey ain' no tellin' w'at mought happen. I would n' 'vise yer ter buy dis vimya'd."

I bought the vineyard, nevertheless, and it has been for a long time in a thriving condition, and is often referred to by the local press as a striking illustration of the opportunities open to Northern capital in the development of Southern industries. The luscious scuppernong holds first rank among our grapes, though we cultivate a great many other varieties, and our income from grapes packed and shipped to the Northern markets is quite considerable. I have not noticed any developments of the goopher in the vineyard, although I have a mild suspicion that our colored assistants do not suffer from want of grapes during the season.

I found, when I bought the vineyard, that Uncle Julius had occupied a cabin on the place for many years, and derived a respectable revenue from the product of the neglected grapevines. This, doubtless, accounted for his advice to me not to buy the vineyard, though whether it inspired the goopher story I am unable to state. I believe, however, that the wages I paid him for his services as coachman, for I gave him employment in that capacity, were more than an equivalent for anything he lost by the sale of the vineyard.

Po' Sandy[1]

On the northeast corner of my vineyard in central North Carolina, and fronting on the Lumberton plank-road, there stood a small frame house, of the simplest construction. It was built of pine lumber, and contained but one room, to which one window gave light and one door admission. Its weather-beaten sides revealed a virgin innocence of paint. Against one end of the house, and occupying half its width, there stood a huge brick chimney: the crumbling mortar had left large cracks between the bricks; the bricks themselves had begun to scale off in large flakes, leaving the chimney sprinkled with unsightly blotches. These evidences of decay were but partially concealed by a creeping vine, which extended its slender branches hither and thither in an ambitious but futile attempt to cover the whole chimney. The wooden shutter, which had once protected the unglazed window, had fallen from its hinges, and lay rotting in the rank grass and jimson-weeds beneath. This building, I learned when I bought the place, had been used as a schoolhouse for several years prior to the breaking out of the war, since which time it had remained unoccupied, save when some stray cow or vagrant[2] hog had sought shelter within its walls from the chill rains and nipping winds of winter.

One day my wife requested me to build her a new kitchen. The house erected by us, when we first came to live upon the vineyard, contained a very conveniently arranged kitchen; but for some occult reason my wife wanted a kitchen in the back yard, apart from the dwelling-house, after the usual Southern fashion.[3] Of course I had to build it.

To save expense, I decided to tear down the old schoolhouse, and use the lumber, which was in a good state of preservation, in the construction of the new kitchen. Before demolishing the old house, however, I made an estimate of the amount of material contained in it, and found that I would have to buy several hundred feet of lum-

---

1. Published in the *Atlantic Monthly* in 1888; reprinted, without significant revision, as the second story of *The Conjure Woman*.
2. "Vagrant" has a strong connotation in this context, recalling the vagrancy laws passed by many Southern municipalities. These laws criminalized the unemployment of African American men and supported the establishment of the agricultural labor system often termed sharecropping or peonage.
3. When John calls Annie's assimilation to local custom "occult," Chesnutt stresses the connection between cross-cultural exchange and transfigurative magic or conjure.

ber additional, in order to build the new kitchen according to my wife's plan.

One morning old Julius McAdoo, our colored coachman, harnessed the gray mare to the rockaway,[4] and drove my wife and me over to the sawmill from which I meant to order the new lumber. We drove down the long lane which led from our house to the plank-road; following the plank-road for about a mile, we turned into a road running through the forest and across the swamp to the sawmill beyond. Our carriage jolted over the half-rotted corduroy road[5] which traversed the swamp, and then climbed the long hill leading to the sawmill. When we reached the mill, the foreman had gone over to a neighboring farmhouse, probably to smoke or gossip, and we were compelled to await his return before we could transact our business. We remained seated in the carriage, a few rods from the mill, and watched the leisurely movements of the mill-hands. We had not waited long before a huge pine log was placed in position, the machinery of the mill was set in motion, and the circular saw began to eat its way through the log, with a loud whir which resounded throughout the vicinity of the mill. The sound rose and fell in a sort of rhythmic cadence, which, heard from where we sat, was not unpleasing, and not loud enough to prevent conversation. When the saw started on its second journey through the log, Julius observed, in a lugubrious tone, and with a perceptible shudder:—

"Ugh! but dat des do cuddle my blood!"

"What's the matter, Uncle Julius?" inquired my wife, who is of a very sympathetic turn of mind. "Does the noise affect your nerves?"

"No, Mis' Annie," replied the old man, with emotion, "I ain' narvous; but dat saw, a-cuttin' en grindin' thoo dat stick er timber, en moanin', en groanin', en sweekin', kyars my 'memb'ance back ter ole times, en 'min's me er po' Sandy." The pathetic intonation with which he lengthened out the "po' Sandy" touched a responsive chord in our own hearts.

"And who was poor Sandy?" asked my wife, who takes a deep interest in the stories of plantation life which she hears from the lips of the older colored people. Some of these stories are quaintly humorous; others wildly extravagant, revealing the Oriental cast of the negro's imagination; while others, poured freely into the sympathetic ear of a Northern-bred woman, disclose many a tragic incident of the darker side of slavery.[6]

"Sandy," said Julius, in reply to my wife's question, "was a nigger w'at useter b'long ter ole Mars Marrabo McSwayne. Mars Marrabo's

4. A four-wheeled carriage, open at the sides.
5. A road constructed of trunks of trees laid together transversely across a swampy ground.
6. John rehearses the formulaic categories available for "stories of plantation life" in late-nineteenth-century U.S. literature.

place wuz on de yuther side'n de swamp, right nex' ter yo' place. Sandy wuz a monst'us good nigger, en could do so many things erbout a plantation, en alluz 'ten' ter his wuk so well, dat w'en Mars Marrabo's chilluns growed up en married off, dey all un 'em wanted dey daddy fer ter gin 'em Sandy fer a weddin' present. But Mars Marrabo knowed de res' would n' be satisfied ef he gin Sandy ter a'er one un 'em; so w'en dey wuz all done married, he fix it by 'lowin' one er his chilluns ter take Sandy fer a mont' er so, en den ernudder for a mont' er so, en so on dat erway tel dey had all had 'im de same lenk er time; en den dey would all take him roun' ag'in, 'cep'n' oncet in a w'ile w'en Mars Marrabo would len' 'im ter some er his yuther kinfolks 'roun' de country, w'en dey wuz short er han's; tel bimeby it go so Sandy did n' hardly knowed whar he wuz gwine ter stay fum one week's een' ter de yuther.

"One time w'en Sandy wuz lent out ez yushal, a spekilater come erlong wid a lot er niggers, en Mars Marrabo swap' Sandy's wife off fer a noo 'oman. W'en Sandy come back, Mars Marrabo gin 'im a dollar, en 'lowed he wuz monst'us sorry fer ter break up de fambly, but de spekilater had gin 'im big boot,[7] en times wuz hard en money skase, en so he wuz bleedst ter make de trade. Sandy tuk on some 'bout losin' his wife, but he soon seed dey want no use cryin' ober spilt merlasses; en bein' ez he lacked de looks er de noo 'oman, he tuk up wid her atter she'd be'n on de plantation a mont' er so.

"Sandy en his noo wife got on mighty well tergedder, en de niggers all 'mence' ter talk about how lovin' dey wuz. W'en Tenie[8] wuz tuk sick oncet, Sandy useter set up all night wid 'er, en den go ter wuk in de mawnin' des lack he had his reg'lar sleep; en Tenie would 'a' done anythin' in de worl' for her Sandy.

"Sandy en Tenie hadn' be'n libbin' tergedder fer mo' d'n two mont's befo' Mars Marrabo's old uncle, w'at libbed down in Robeson County, sent up ter fin' out ef Mars Marrabo could n' len' 'im er hire 'im a good han' fer a mont' er so. Sandy's marster wuz one er dese yer easy-gwine folks w'at wanter please eve'ybody, en he says yas, he could len' 'im Sandy. En Mars Marrabo tol' Sandy fer ter git ready ter go down ter Robeson nex' day, fer ter stay a mont' er so.

"It wuz monst'us hard on Sandy fer ter take 'im 'way fum Tenie. It wuz so fur down ter Robeson dat he did n' hab no chance er comin' back ter see her tel de time wuz up; he would n' 'a' mine comin' ten er fifteen mile at night ter see Tenie, but Mars Marrabo's uncle's plantation wuz mo' d'n forty mile off. Sandy wuz mighty sad en cas' down atter w'at Mars Marrabo tol' 'im, en he says ter Tenie, sezee:—

---

7. Profit.
8. Tenie's name derives from the Latin verb "to hold," raising associations both with the wedding vows ("to have and to hold"), and with being able to stand fast (as in the English "tenant" or "tenacious").

"'I'm gittin' monst'us ti'ed er dish yer gwine roun' so much. Here I is lent ter Mars Jeems dis mont', en I got ter do so-en-so; en ter Mars Archie de nex' mont', en I got ter do so-en-so; den I got ter go ter Miss Jinnie's: en hit's Sandy dis en Sandy dat, en Sandy yer en Sandy dere, tel it 'pears ter me I ain' got no home, ner no marster, ner no mistiss, ner no nuffin. I can't eben keep a wife: my yuther ole 'oman wuz sol' away widout my gittin' a chance fer ter tell her good-by; en now I got ter go off en leab you, Tenie, en I dunno whe'r I'm eber gwine ter see you ag'in er no. I wisht I wuz a tree, er a stump, er a rock, er sump'n w'at could stay on de plantation fer a w'ile.'

"Atter Sandy got thoo talkin', Tenie did n' say naer word, but des sot dere by de fier, studyin' en studyin'. Bimeby she up'n' says:—

"'Sandy, is I eber tol' you I wuz a cunjuh 'oman?'

"Co'se Sandy hadn' nebber dremp' er nuffin lack dat, en he made a great 'miration w'en he hear w'at Tenie say. Bimeby Tenie went on:—

"'I ain' goophered nobody, ner done no cunjuh wuk, fer fifteen year er mo'; en w'en I got religion I made up my mine I would n' wuk no mo' goopher. But dey is some things I doan b'lieve it 's no sin fer ter do; en ef you doan wanter be sent roun' fum pillar ter pos', en ef you doan wanter go down ter Robeson, I kin fix things so you won't haf ter. Ef you'll des say de word, I kin turn you ter w'ateber you wanter be, en you kin stay right whar you wanter, ez long ez you mineter.'

"Sandy say he doan keer; he's willin' fer ter do anythin' fer ter stay close ter Tenie. Den Tenie ax 'im ef he doan wanter be turnt inter a rabbit.[9]

"Sandy say, 'No, de dogs mought git atter me.'

"'Shill I turn you ter a wolf?' sez Tenie.

"'No, eve'ybody 's skeered er a wolf, en I doan want nobody ter be skeered er me.'

"'Shill I turn you ter a mawkin'-bird?'

"'No, a hawk mought ketch me. I wanter be turnt inter sump'n w'at 'll stay in one place.'

"'I kin turn you ter a tree,' sez Tenie. 'You won't hab no mouf ner years, but I kin turn you back oncet in a w'ile, so you kin git sump'n ter eat, en hear w'at's gwine on.'

"Well, Sandy say dat 'll do. En so Tenie tuk 'im down by de aidge er de swamp, not fur fum de quarters, en turnt 'im inter a big pine-tree, en sot 'im out 'mongs' some yuther trees. En de nex' mawnin', ez some er de fiel' han's wuz gwine long dere, dey seed a tree w'at dey did n' 'member er habbin' seed befo'; it wuz monst'us quare, en dey wuz bleedst ter 'low dat dey had n' 'membered right, er e'se one er de saplin's had be'n growin' monst'us fas'.

---

9. Likely reference to the "Bre'r Rabbit" tales popularized by Joel Chandler Harris in the 1880s.

"W'en Mars Marrabo 'skiver' dat Sandy wuz gone, he 'lowed Sandy had runned away. He got de dogs out, but de las' place dey could track Sandy ter wuz de foot er dat pine-tree. En dere de dogs stood en barked, en bayed, en pawed at de tree, en tried ter climb up on it; en w'en dey wuz tuk roun' thoo de swamp ter look fer de scent, dey broke loose en made fer dat tree ag'in. It wuz de beatenis' thing de w'ite folks eber hearn of, en Mars Marrabo 'lowed dat Sandy must 'a' clim' up on de tree en jump' off on a mule er sump'n, en rid fur ernuff fer ter spile de scent. Mars Marrabo wanted ter 'cuse some er de yuther niggers er heppin' Sandy off, but dey all 'nied it ter de las'; en eve'ybody knowed Tenie sot too much sto' by Sandy fer ter he'p 'im run away whar she could n' nebber see 'im no mo'.

"W'en Sandy had be'n gone long ernuff fer folks ter think he done got clean away, Tenie useter go down ter de woods at night en turn 'im back, en den dey'd slip up ter de cabin en set by de fire en talk. But dey ha' ter be monst'us keerful, er e'se somebody would 'a' seed 'em, en dat would 'a' spile' de whole thing; so Tenie alluz turnt Sandy back in de mawnin' early, befo' anybody wuz a-stirrin'.

"But Sandy didn' git erlong widout his trials en tribberlations. One day a woodpecker come erlong en 'mence' ter peck at de tree; en de nex' time Sandy wuz turnt back he had a little roun' hole in his arm, des lack a sharp stick be'n stuck in it. Atter dat Tenie sot a sparrer-hawk fer ter watch de tree; en w'en de woodpecker come erlong nex' mawnin' fer ter finish his nes', he got gobble' up mos' 'fo' he stuck his bill in de bark.

"Nudder time, Mars Marrabo sent a nigger out in de woods fer ter chop tuppentime boxes. De man chop a box in dish yer tree, en hack' de bark up two er th'ee feet, fer ter let de tuppentime run. De nex' time Sandy wuz turnt back he had a big skyar on his lef' leg, des lack it be'n skunt; en it tuk Tenie nigh 'bout all night fer ter fix a mixtry ter kyo it up. Atter dat, Tenie sot a hawnet fer ter watch de tree; en w'en de nigger come back ag'in fer ter cut ernudder box on de yuther side'n de tree, de hawnet stung 'im so hard dat de ax slip en cut his foot nigh 'bout off.

"W'en Tenie see so many things happenin' ter de tree, she 'cluded she'd ha' ter turn Sandy ter sump'n e'se; en atter studyin' de matter ober, en talkin' wid Sandy one ebenin', she made up her mine fer ter fix up a goopher mixtry w'at would turn herse'f en Sandy ter foxes, er sump'n, so dey could run away en go some'rs whar dey could be free en lib lack w'ite folks.

"But dey ain' no tellin' w'at 's gwine ter happen in dis worl'. Tenie had got de night sot fer her en Sandy ter run away, w'en dat ve'y day one er Mars Marrabo's sons rid up ter de big house in his buggy, en say his wife wuz monst'us sick, en he want his mammy ter len' 'im a 'oman fer ter nuss his wife. Tenie's mistiss say sen' Tenie; she wuz a good nuss. Young mars wuz in a tarrible hurry fer ter git back home. Tenie wuz washin' at de big house dat day, en her mistiss say she should go right 'long wid her young marster. Tenie tried ter make some 'scuse fer ter git away en hide 'tel night, w'en she would have eve'ything fix' up fer her en Sandy; she say she wanter go ter her cabin fer ter git her bonnet. Her mistiss say it doan matter 'bout de bonnet; her head-hankcher wuz good ernuff. Den Tenie say she wanter git her bes' frock; her mistiss say no, she doan need no mo' frock, en w'en dat one got dirty she could git a clean one whar she wuz gwine. So Tenie had ter git in de buggy en go 'long wid young Mars Dunkin ter his plantation, w'ich wuz mo' d'n twenty mile away; en dey wa'n't no chance er her seein' Sandy no mo' 'tel she come back home. De po' gal felt monst'us bad 'bout de way things wuz gwine on, en she knowed Sandy mus' be a wond'rin' why she did n' come en turn 'im back no mo'.

"W'iles Tenie wuz away nussin' young Mars Dunkin's wife, Mars Marrabo tuk a notion fer ter buil' 'im a noo kitchen; en bein' ez he had lots er timber on his place, he begun ter look 'roun' fer a tree ter hab de lumber sawed out'n. En I dunno how it come to be so, but he happen fer ter hit on de ve'y tree w'at Sandy wuz turnt inter. Tenie wuz gone, en dey wa'n't nobody ner nuffin fer ter watch de tree.

"De two men w'at cut de tree down say dey nebber had sech a time wid a tree befo': dey axes would glansh off, en didn' 'pear ter make no progress thoo de wood; en of all de creakin', en shakin', en wobblin' you eber see, dat tree done it w'en it commence' ter fall. It wuz de beatenis' thing!

"W'en dey got de tree all trim' up, dey chain it up ter a timber waggin, en start fer de sawmill. But dey had a hard time gittin' de log dere: fus' dey got stuck in de mud w'en dey wuz gwine crosst de swamp, en it wuz two er th'ee hours befo' dey could git out. W'en dey start' on ag'in, de chain kep' a-comin' loose, en dey had ter keep a-stoppin' en a-stoppin' fer ter hitch de log up ag'in. W'en dey commence' ter climb de hill ter de sawmill, de log broke loose, en roll down de hill en in 'mongs' de trees, en hit tuk nigh 'bout half a day mo' ter git it haul' up ter de sawmill.

"De nex' mawnin' atter de day de tree wuz haul' ter de sawmill, Tenie come home. W'en she got back ter her cabin, de fus' thing she done wuz ter run down ter de woods en see how Sandy wuz gittin' on. W'en she seed de stump standin' dere, wid de sap runnin' out'n it, en de limbs layin' scattered roun', she nigh 'bout went out'n her min'. She run ter her cabin, en got her goopher mixtry, en den follered de track er de timber waggin ter de sawmill. She knowed Sandy could n' lib mo' d'n a minute er so ef she turnt him back, fer he wuz all chop' up so he'd 'a' be'n bleedst ter die. But she wanted ter turn 'im back long ernuff fer ter 'splain ter 'im dat she had n' went off a-purpose, en lef' 'im ter be chop' down en sawed up. She didn' want Sandy ter die wid no hard feelin's to'ds her.

"De han's at de sawmill had des got de big log on de kerridge, en wuz startin' up de saw, w'en dey seed a 'oman runnin' up de hill, all out er bref, cryin' en gwine on des lack she wuz plumb 'stracted. It wuz Tenie; she come right inter de mill, en th'owed herse'f on de log, right in front er de saw, a-hollerin' en cryin' ter her Sandy ter fergib her, en not ter think hard er her, fer it wa'n't no fault er hern. Den Tenie 'membered de tree didn' hab no years, en she wuz gittin' ready fer ter wuk her goopher mixtry so ez ter turn Sandy back, w'en de mill-hands kotch holt er her en tied her arms wid a rope, en fasten' her to one er de posts in de sawmill; en den dey started de saw up ag'in, en cut de log up inter bo'ds en scantlin's right befo' her eyes. But it wuz mighty hard wuk; fer of all de sweekin', en moanin', en groanin', dat log done it w'iles de saw wuz a-cuttin' thoo it. De saw wuz one er dese yer ole-timey, up-en-down saws, en hit tuk longer dem days ter saw a log 'en it do now. Dey greased de saw, but dat didn' stop de fuss; hit kep' right on, tel fin'ly dey got de log all sawed up.

"W'en de oberseah w'at run de sawmill come fum breakfas', de han's up en tell him 'bout de crazy 'oman—ez dey s'posed she wuz— w'at had come runnin' in de sawmill, a-hollerin' en gwine on, en tried ter th'ow herse'f befo' de saw. En de oberseah sent two er th'ee er de han's fer ter take Tenie back ter her marster's plantation.

"Tenie 'peared ter be out'n her min' fer a long time, en her marster ha' ter lock her up in de smoke-'ouse 'tel she got ober her spells.[1] Mars Marrabo wuz monst'us mad, en hit would 'a' made yo' flesh crawl fer ter hear him cuss, 'caze he say de spekilater w'at he got Tenie fum had fooled 'im by wukkin' a crazy 'oman off on him. W'iles Tenie wuz lock up in de smoke-'ouse, Mars Marrabo tuk 'n' haul de lumber fum de sawmill, en put up his noo kitchen.

"W'en Tenie got quiet' down, so she could be 'lowed ter go 'roun' de plantation, she up'n' tole her marster all erbout Sandy en de pine-tree; en w'en Mars Marrabo hearn it, he 'lowed she wuz de wuss 'stracted nigger he eber hearn of. He didn' know w'at ter do wid Tenie: fus' he thought he'd put her in de po'house; but fin'ly, seein' ez she didn' do no harm ter nobody ner nuffin, but des went 'roun' moanin', en groanin', en shakin' her head, he 'cluded ter let her stay on de plantation en nuss de little nigger chilluns w'en dey mammies wuz ter wuk in de cotton-fiel'.

---

1. In "Dave's Neckliss," Chesnutt further develops the irony, introduced here, of imprisoning an ailing human being in a storage building for "curing" meat.

"De noo kitchen Mars Marrabo buil' wuz n' much use, fer it hadn' be'n put up long befo' de niggers 'mence' ter notice quare things erbout it. Dey could hear sump'n moanin' en groanin' 'bout de kitchen in de night-time, en w'en de win' would blow dey could hear sump'n a-hollerin' en sweekin' lack it wuz in great pain en sufferin'. En it got so atter a w'ile dat it wuz all Mars Marrabo's wife could do ter git a 'oman ter stay in de kitchen in de daytime long ernuff ter do de cookin'; en dey wa'n't naer nigger on de plantation w'at would n' rudder take forty dan ter go 'bout dat kitchen atter dark,—dat is, 'cep'n' Tenie; she didn' 'pear ter min' de ha'nts. She useter slip 'roun' at night, en set on de kitchen steps, en lean up agin de do'-jamb, en run on ter herse'f wid some kine er foolishness w'at nobody could n' make out; fer Mars Marrabo had th'eaten' ter sen' her off'n de plantation ef she say anything ter any er de yuther niggers 'bout de pinetree. But somehow er 'nudder de niggers foun' out all erbout it, en dey all knowed de kitchen wuz ha'nted by Sandy's sperrit. En bimeby hit got so Mars Marrabo's wife herse'f wuz skeered ter go out in de yard atter dark.

"W'en it come ter dat, Mars Marrabo tuk en to' de kitchen down, en use' de lumber fer ter buil' dat ole school'ouse w'at you er talkin' 'bout pullin' down. De school'ouse wuz n' use' 'cep'n' in de daytime, en on dark nights folks gwine 'long de road would hear quare soun's en see quare things. Po' ole Tenie useter go down dere at night, en wander 'roun' de school'ouse; en de niggers all 'lowed she went fer ter talk wid Sandy's sperrit. En one winter mawnin', w'en one er de boys went ter school early fer ter start de fire, w'at should he fin' but po' ole Tenie, layin' on de flo', stiff, en col', en dead. Dere didn' 'pear ter be nuffin pertickler de matter wid her,—she had des grieve' herse'f ter def fer her Sandy. Mars Marrabo didn' shed no tears. He thought Tenie wuz crazy, en dey wa'n't no tellin' w'at she mought do nex'; en dey ain' much room in dis worl' fer crazy w'ite folks, let 'lone a crazy nigger.

"Hit wa'n't long atter dat befo' Mars Marrabo sol' a piece er his track er lan' ter Mars Dugal' McAdoo,—my ole marster,—en dat's how de ole school'ouse happen to be on yo' place. W'en de wah broke out, de school stop', en de ole school'ouse be'n stannin' empty ever sence,—dat is, 'cep'n' fer de ha'nts. En folks sez dat de ole school'ouse, er any yuther house w'at got any er dat lumber in it w'at wuz sawed out'n de tree w'at Sandy wuz turnt inter, is gwine ter be ha'nted tel de las' piece er plank is rotted en crumble' inter dus'.'"

Annie had listened to this gruesome narrative with strained attention.

"What a system it was," she exclaimed, when Julius had finished, "under which such things were possible!"

"What things?" I asked, in amazement. "Are you seriously considering the possibility of a man's being turned into a tree?"

"Oh, no," she replied quickly, "not that;" and then she murmured absently, and with a dim look in her fine eyes, "Poor Tenie!"

We ordered the lumber, and returned home. That night, after we had gone to bed, and my wife had to all appearances been sound asleep for half an hour, she startled me out of an incipient doze by exclaiming suddenly,—

"John, I don't believe I want my new kitchen built out of the lumber in that old schoolhouse."

"You wouldn't for a moment allow yourself," I replied, with some asperity, "to be influenced by that absurdly impossible yarn which Julius was spinning to-day?"

"I know the story is absurd," she replied dreamily, "and I am not so silly as to believe it. But I don't think I should ever be able to take any pleasure in that kitchen if it were built out of that lumber. Besides, I think the kitchen would look better and last longer if the lumber were all new."

Of course she had her way. I bought the new lumber, though not without grumbling. A week or two later I was called away from home on business. On my return, after an absence of several days, my wife remarked to me,—

"John, there has been a split in the Sandy Run Colored Baptist Church,[2] on the temperance question. About half the members have come out from the main body, and set up for themselves. Uncle Julius is one of the seceders,[3] and he came to me yesterday and asked if they might not hold their meetings in the old schoolhouse for the present."

"I hope you didn't let the old rascal have it," I returned, with some warmth. I had just received a bill for the new lumber I had bought.

"Well," she replied, "I couldn't refuse him the use of the house for so good a purpose."

"And I'll venture to say," I continued, "that you subscribed something toward the support of the new church?"

She did not attempt to deny it.

"What are they going to do about the ghost?" I asked, somewhat curious to know how Julius would get around this obstacle.

"Oh," replied Annie, "Uncle Julius says that ghosts never disturb religious worship, but that if Sandy's spirit *should* happen to stray into meeting by mistake, no doubt the preaching would do it good."

2. "Sandy Run," the name of Julius's church, both refers to an actual site in Cumberland County, and resonates with the name of the protagonist of Julius's tale. As an imperative phrase, "Sandy, run!" provides a contrast in the present to the sentimental plantation story Julius has just told about the desire of enslaved people to stay in their places.

3. Identifying Julius as "one of the seceders" aligns him with the Confederates of the Civil War. *Uncle Julius*: When Annie uses "Uncle" as the title for Julius, she employs a strategy typical in the era: "Uncle" assigns a courtesy code to a non-related African American man, which is nevertheless deliberately unequal to the title of a white man ("Mister").

The Conjurer's Revenge[1]

Sunday was sometimes a rather dull day at our place.[2] In the morning, when the weather was pleasant, my wife and I would drive to town, a distance of about five miles, to attend the church of our choice. The afternoons we spent at home, for the most part, occupying ourselves with the newspapers and magazines, and the contents of a fairly good library. We had a piano in the house, on which my wife played with skill and feeling. I possessed a passable baritone voice, and could accompany myself indifferently well when my wife was not by to assist me. When these resources failed us, we were apt to find it a little dull.

One Sunday afternoon in early spring,—the balmy spring of North Carolina, when the air is in that ideal balance between heat and cold where one wishes it could always remain,—my wife and I were seated on the front piazza, she wearily but conscientiously ploughing through a missionary report, while I followed the impossible career of the blonde heroine of a rudimentary novel.[3] I had thrown the book aside in disgust, when I saw Julius coming through the yard, under the spreading elms, which were already in full leaf. He wore his Sunday clothes, and advanced with a dignity of movement quite different from his week-day slouch.[4]

"Have a seat, Julius," I said, pointing to an empty rocking-chair.

"No, thanky, boss, I'll des set here on de top step."

"Oh, no, Uncle Julius," exclaimed Annie, "take this chair. You will find it much more comfortable."

The old man grinned in appreciation of her solicitude, and seated himself somewhat awkwardly.

"Julius," I remarked, "I am thinking of setting out scuppernong vines on that sand-hill where the three persimmon-trees are; and while I'm working there, I think I'll plant watermelons between the vines, and get a little something to pay for my first year's work. The new railroad will be finished by the middle of summer, and I can ship the melons North, and get a good price for them."

1. Published in the *Overland Monthly* in 1889; reprinted, with significant revision, as the fourth story of *The Conjure Woman*.
2. A variant introduction in the *Overland Monthly* version establishes a different version of Annie's character. She appears as "quite a zealous missionary" who suffers from unconscious hypocrisy. She "confine[s] her ministrations chiefly to the colored element of the population," presses tracts on Julius even though she knows he can't read, and takes an "unchristian view" of the abased condition of impoverished local whites.
3. Chesnutt rehearses the alternative genres available for polite middle-class consumption; in this context, plantation tales have far superior entertainment value. *piazza*: a covered veranda extending the length of the front of a house.
4. In the *Overland Monthly* version, Annie here presents Julius with a leather-bound hymnal decorated in red; he asks her for another color of book because of the stereotype that "cullud people lubs red so."

"Ef you er gwine ter hab any mo' ploughin' ter do," replied Julius, "I 'spec' you'll ha' ter buy ernudder creetur, 'ca'se hit's much ez dem hosses kin do ter 'ten' ter de wuk dey got now."

"Yes, I had thought of that. I think I'll get a mule; a mule can do more work, and doesn't require as much attention as a horse."

"I wouldn' 'vise you ter buy no mule," remarked Julius, with a shake of his head.

"Why not?"

"Well, you may 'low hit's all foolis'ness, but ef I wuz in yo' place, I wouldn' buy no mule."

"But that isn't a reason; what objection have you to a mule?"

"Fac' is," continued the old man, in a serious tone, "I doan lack ter dribe a mule. I's alluz afeared I mought be imposin' on some human creetur; eve'y time I cuts a mule wid a hick'ry, 'pears ter me mos' lackly I's cuttin' some er my own relations, er somebody e'se w'at can't he'p deyse'ves."[5]

"What put such an absurd idea into your head?" I asked.

My question was followed by a short silence, during which Julius seemed engaged in a mental struggle.

"I dunno ez hit 's wuf w'ile ter tell you dis," he said, at length. "I doan ha'dly 'spec' fer you ter b'lieve it. Does you 'member dat club-footed man w'at hilt de hoss fer you de yuther day w'en you was gittin' out'n de rockaway down ter Mars Archie McMillan's sto'?"

"Yes, I believe I do remember seeing a club-footed man there."

"Did you eber see a club-footed nigger befo' er sence?"

"No, I can't remember that I ever saw a club-footed colored man," I replied, after a moment's reflection.

"You en Mis' Annie wouldn' wanter b'lieve me, ef I wuz ter 'low dat dat man was oncet a mule?"

"No," I replied, "I don't think it very likely that you could make us believe it."

"Why, Uncle Julius!" said Annie severely, "what ridiculous non-sense!"

This reception of the old man's statement reduced him to silence, and it required some diplomacy on my part to induce him to vouch-safe an explanation. The prospect of a long, dull afternoon was not alluring, and I was glad to have the monotony of Sabbath quiet relieved by a plantation legend.

"W'en I wuz a young man," began Julius, when I had finally pre-vailed upon him to tell us the story, "dat club-footed nigger—his name is Primus—use' ter b'long ter ole Mars Jim McGee ober on de

5. As symbols of agricultural life in the South, mules historically have been associated in U.S. culture with enslaved African American laborers, often to racist ends. An inter-species cross between horse and donkey, mules are designed by their breeders to be infertile, tractable, capable of hard labor, and able to withstand abuse.

Lumbe'ton plank-road. I use' ter go ober dere ter see a 'oman w'at libbed on de plantation; dat 's how I come ter know all erbout it. Dis yer Primus wuz de livelies' han' on de place, alluz a-dancin', en drinkin', en runnin' roun', en singin', en pickin' de banjo; 'cep'n' once in a w'ile, w'en he'd 'low he wa'n't treated right 'bout sump'n ernudder, he'd git so sulky en stubborn dat de w'ite folks could n' ha'dly do nuffin wid 'im.

"It wuz 'gin' de rules fer any er de han's ter go 'way fum de plantation at night; but Primus didn' min' de rules, en went w'en he felt lack it; en de w'ite folks purten' lack dey didn' know it, fer Primus was dange'ous w'en he got in dem stubborn spells, en dey'd ruther not fool wid 'im.

"One night in de spring er de year, Primus slip' off fum de plantation, en went down on de Wim'l'ton Road ter a dance gun by some er de free niggers down dere. Dey wuz a fiddle, en a banjo, en a jug gwine roun' on de outside, en Primus sung en dance' 'tel 'long 'bout two o'clock in de mawnin', w'en he start' fer home. Ez he come erlong back, he tuk a nigh-cut 'cross de cotton-fiel's en 'long by de aidge er de Min'al Spring Swamp, so ez ter git shet er de patteroles[6] w'at rid up en down de big road fer ter keep de darkies fum runnin' roun' nights. Primus was sa'nt'rin' 'long, studyin' 'bout de good time he'd had wid de gals, w'en, ez he wuz gwine by a fence co'nder, w'at sh'd he heah but sump'n grunt. He stopped a minute ter listen, en he heared sump'n grunt ag'in. Den he went ober ter de fence whar he heard de fuss, en dere, layin' in de fence co'nder, on a pile er pine straw, he seed a fine, fat shote.

"Primus look' ha'd at de shote, en den sta'ted home. But somehow er 'nudder he couldn' git away fum dat shote; w'en he tuk one step for'ards wid one foot, de yuther foot 'peared ter take two steps back-'ards, en so he kep' nachly gittin' closeter en closeter ter de shote. It was de beatin'es' thing! De shote des 'peared ter cha'm Primus, en fus' thing you know Primus foun' hisse'f 'way up de road wid de shote on his back.

"Ef Primus had 'a' knowed whose shote dat wuz, he'd 'a' manage' ter git pas' it somehow er 'nudder. Ez it happen', de shote b'long ter a cunjuh man w'at libbed down in de free-nigger sett'ement. Co'se de cunjuh man did n' hab ter wuk his roots but a little w'ile 'fo' he foun' out who tuk his shote, en den de trouble begun. One mawnin', a day er so later, en befo' he got de shote eat up, Primus didn' go ter wuk w'en de hawn blow, en w'en de oberseah wen' ter look fer him, dey wa' no trace er Primus ter be 'skivered nowhar. W'en he did n' come back in a day er so mo', eve'ybody on de plantation 'lowed he had

---

6. Patrols, an element of martial law that enforced restrictions on the behavior of enslaved persons.

runned erway. His marster a'vertise' him in de papers, en offered a big reward fer 'im. De nigger-ketchers fotch out dey dogs, en track' 'im down ter de aidge er de swamp, en den de scent gun out; en dat was de las' anybody seed er Primus fer a long, long time.

"Two er th'ee weeks atter Primus disappear', his marster went ter town one Sad'day. Mars Jim was stan'in' in front er Sandy Camp-bell's bar-room, up by de ole wagon-ya'd, w'en a po' w'ite man fum down on de Wim'l'ton Road come up ter 'im en ax' 'im, kinder keerless lack, ef he didn' wanter buy a mule.

"'I dunno,' says Mars Jim; 'it 'pen's on de mule, en on de price. Whar is de mule?'

"'Des 'roun' heah back er ole Tom McAllister's sto',' says de po' w'ite man.

"'I reckon I'll hab a look at de mule,' says Mars Jim, 'en ef he suit me, I dunno but w'at I mought buy 'im.'

"So de po' w'ite man tuk Mars Jim 'roun' back er de sto', en dere stood a monst'us fine mule. W'en de mule see Mars Jim, he gun a whinny, des lack he knowed him befo'. Mars Jim look' at de mule, en de mule 'peared ter be soun' en strong. Mars Jim 'lowed dey 'peared ter be sump'n fermilyus 'bout de mule's face, 'spesh'ly his eyes; but he hadn' los' naer mule, en didn' hab no recommemb'ance er habin' seed de mule befo'. He ax' de po' buckrah whar he got de mule, en de po' buckrah say his brer raise' de mule down on Rockfish Creek. Mars Jim was a little s'picious er seein' a po' w'ite man wid sech a fine creetur, but he fin'lly 'greed ter gib de man fifty dollars fer de mule,—'bout ha'f w'at a good mule was wuf dem days.

"He tied de mule behin' de buggy w'en he went home, en put 'im ter ploughin' cotton de nex' day. De mule done mighty well fer th'ee er fo' days, en den de niggers 'mence' ter notice some quare things erbout him. Dey wuz a medder on de plantation whar dey use' ter put de hosses en mules ter pastur'. Hit was fence' off fum de corn-fiel' on one side, but on de yuther side'n de pastur' was a terbacker-patch w'at wa'n't fence' off, 'ca'se de beastisses doan none un 'em eat terbacker. Dey doan know w'at's good! Terbacker is lack religion, de good Lawd made it fer people, en dey ain' no yuther creetur w'at kin 'preciate it. De darkies notice' dat de fus' thing de new mule done, w'en he was turnt inter de pastur', wuz ter make fer de terbacker-patch. Co'se dey didn' think nuffin un it, but nex' mawnin', w'en dey went ter ketch 'im, dey 'skivered dat he had eat up two whole rows er terbacker plants. Atter dat dey had ter put a halter on 'im, en tie 'im ter a stake, er e'se dey wouldn' 'a' been naer leaf er terbacker lef' in de patch.

"Ernudder day one er de han's, name' 'Dolphus, hitch' de mule up, en dribe up here ter dis yer vimya'd,—dat wuz w'en ole Mars Dugal' own' dis place. Mars Dugal' had kilt a yearlin', en de naber w'ite folks all sont ober fer ter git some fraish beef, en Mars Jim had sont

'Dolphus fer some too. Dey wuz a wine-press in de ya'd whar 'Dolphus lef' de mule a-stan'in', en right in front er de press dey wuz a tub er grape-juice, des pressed out, en a little ter one side a bairl erbout half full er wine w'at had be'n stan'in' two er th'ee days, en had begun ter git sorter sha'p ter de tas'e. Dey wuz a couple er bo'ds on top er dis yer bairl, wid a rock laid on 'em ter hol' 'em down. Ez I wuz a-sayin', 'Dolphus lef' de mule stan'in' in de ya'd, en went inter de smoke-house fer ter git de beef. Bimeby, w'en he come out, he seed de mule a-stagg'rin' 'bout de ya'd; en 'fo' 'Dolphus could git dere ter fin' out w'at wuz de matter, de mule fell right ober on his side, en laid dere des' lack he was dead.

"All de niggers 'bout de house run out dere fer ter see w'at wuz de matter. Some say de mule had de colic; some say one thing en some ernudder; 'tel bimeby one er de han's seed de top wuz off'n de bairl, en run en looked in.

"'Fo' de Lawd!' he say, 'dat mule drunk! he be'n drinkin' de wine.' En sho' 'nuff, de mule had pas' right by de tub er fraish grape-juice en push' de kiver off'n de bairl, en drunk two er th'ee gallon er de wine w'at had been stan'in' long ernough fer ter begin ter git sha'p.

"De darkies all made a great 'miration 'bout de mule gittin' drunk. Dey never had n' seed nuffin lack it in dey bawn days. Dey po'd water ober de mule, en tried ter sober 'im up; but it wa'n't no use, en 'Dolphus had ter take de beef home on his back, en leabe de mule dere, 'tel he slep' off 'is spree.

"I doan 'member whe'r I tol' you er no, but w'en Primus disappear' fum de plantation, he lef' a wife behin' 'im,—a monst'us good-lookin' yaller gal,[7] name' Sally. W'en Primus had be'n gone a mont' er so, Sally 'mence' fer ter git lonesome, en tuk up wid ernudder young man name' Dan, w'at b'long' on de same plantation.[8] One day dis yer Dan tuk de noo mule out in de cotton-fiel' fer ter plough, en w'en dey wuz gwine 'long de tu'n-row, who sh'd he meet but dis yer Sally. Dan look' 'roun' en he did n' see de oberseah nowhar, so he stop' a minute fer ter run on wid Sally.

"'Hoddy, honey,' sezee. 'How you feelin' dis mawnin'?'

"'Fus' rate,' 'spon' Sally.

"Dey wuz lookin' at one ernudder, en dey didn' naer one un 'em pay no 'tention ter de mule, who had turnt 'is head 'roun' en wuz lookin' at Sally ez ha'd ez he could, en stretchin' 'is neck en raisin' 'is years, en whinnyin' kinder sof' ter hisse'f.

"'Yas, honey,' 'lows Dan, 'en you gwine ter feel fus' rate long ez you sticks ter me. Fer I's a better man dan dat low-down runaway nigger Primus dat you be'n wastin' yo' time wid.'

7. Julius refers to Sally as yellow or light-skinned; presumably she is part white.
8. The following paragraphs of sweet-talking and violence were added by Chesnutt for the version of the story included in *The Conjure Woman*.

"Dan had let go de plough-handle, en had put his arm 'roun' Sally, en wuz des gwine ter kiss her, w'en sump'n ketch' 'im by de scruff er de neck en flung 'im 'way ober in de cotton-patch. W'en he pick' 'isse'f up, Sally had gone kitin' down de tu'n-row, en de mule wuz stan'in' dere lookin' ez ca'm en peaceful ez a Sunday mawnin'.

"Fus' Dan had 'lowed it wuz de oberseah w'at had cotch' 'im wastin' 'is time. But dey wa'n't no oberseah in sight, so he 'cluded it must 'a' be'n de mule. So he pitch' inter de mule en lammed 'im ez ha'd ez he could. De mule tuk it all, en 'peared ter be ez 'umble ez a mule could be; but w'en dey wuz makin' de turn at de een' er de row, one er de plough-lines got under de mule's hin' leg. Dan retch' down ter git de line out, sorter keerless like, w'en de mule haul' off en kick him clean ober de fence inter a brier-patch on de yuther side.

"Dan wuz mighty so' fum 'is woun's en scratches, en wuz laid up fer two er th'ee days. One night de noo mule got out'n de pastur', en went down to de quarters. Dan wuz layin' dere on his pallet, w'en he heard sump'n bangin' erway at de side er his cabin. He raise' up on one shoulder en look' roun', w'en w'at should he see but de noo mule's head stickin' in de winder, wid his lips drawed back over his toofs, grinnin' en snappin' at Dan des' lack he wanter eat 'im up. Den de mule went roun' ter de do', en kick' erway lack he wanter break de do' down, 'tel bimeby somebody come 'long en driv him back ter de pastur'. W'en Sally come in a little later fum de big house, whar she'd be'n waitin' on de w'ite folks, she foun' po' Dan nigh 'bout dead, he wuz so skeered. She 'lowed Dan had had de nightmare; but w'en dey look' at de do', dey seed de marks er de mule's huffs, so dey couldn' be no mistake 'bout w'at had happen'.

"Co'se de niggers tol' dey marster 'bout de mule's gwines-on. Fust he didn' pay no 'tention ter it, but atter a w'ile he tol' 'em ef dey didn' stop dey foolis'ness, he gwine tie some un 'em up. So atter dat dey didn' say nuffin mo' ter dey marster, but dey kep' on noticin' de mule's quare ways des de same.

"'Long 'bout de middle er de summer dey wuz a big camp-meetin' broke out down on de Wim'l'ton Road, en nigh 'bout all de po' w'ite folks en free niggers in de settlement got 'ligion, en lo en behol'! 'mongs' 'em wuz de cunjuh man w'at own' de shote w'at cha'med Primus.

"Dis cunjuh man wuz a Guinea nigger,[9] en befo' he wuz sot free had use' ter b'long ter a gent'eman down in Sampson County. De cunjuh man say his daddy wuz a king, er a guv'ner, er some sorter w'at-you-may-call-'em 'way ober yander in Affiky whar de niggers come fum, befo' he was stoled erway en sol' ter de spekilaters. De

---

9. Not African American, but rather a native of Guinea, West Africa, once a prominent slave trading post.

cunjuh man had he'ped his marster out'n some trouble ernudder wid his goopher, en his marster had sot him free, en bought him a trac' er land down on de Wim'l'ton Road. He purten' ter be a cow-doctor, but eve'ybody knowed w'at he r'al'y wuz.

"De cunjuh man hadn' mo' d'n come th'oo good, befo' he wuz tuk sick wid a col' w'at he kotch kneelin' on de groun' so long at de mou'ners' bench. He kep' gittin' wusser en wusser, en bimeby de rheumatiz tuk holt er 'im, en drawed him all up, 'tel one day he sont word up ter Mars Jim McGee's plantation, en ax' Pete, de nigger w'at tuk keer er de mules, fer ter come down dere dat night en fetch dat mule w'at his marster had bought fum de po' w'ite man dyoin' er de summer.

"Pete didn' know w'at de cunjuh man wuz dribin' at, but he didn' daster stay way; en so dat night, w'en he'd done eat his bacon en his hoe-cake, en drunk his 'lasses-en-water, he put a bridle on de mule, en rid 'im down ter de cunjuh man's cabin. W'en he got ter de do', he lit en hitch' de mule, en den knock' at de do'. He felt mighty jubous 'bout gwine in, but he was bleedst ter do it; he knowed he couldn' he'p 'isse'f.

"'Pull de string,' sez a weak voice, en w'en Pete lif' de latch en went in, de cunjuh man was layin' on de bed, lookin' pale en weak, lack he didn' hab much longer fer ter lib.

"'Is you fotch' de mule?' sezee.

"Pete say yas, en de cunjuh man kep' on.

"'Brer Pete,' sezee, 'I's be'n a monst'us sinner man, en I's done a power er wickedness endyoin' er my days; but de good Lawd is wash' my sins erway, en I feels now dat I's boun' fer de kingdom. En I feels, too, dat I ain' gwine ter git up fum dis bed no mo' in dis worl', en I wants ter ondo some er de harm I done. En dat's de reason, Brer Pete, I sont fer you ter fetch dat mule down here. You 'member dat shote I was up ter yo' plantation inquirin' 'bout las' June?'

"'Yas,' says Brer Pete, 'I 'member yo' axin' 'bout a shote you had los'.'

"'I dunno whe'r you eber l'arnt it er no,' says de cunjuh man, 'but I done knowed yo' marster's Primus had tuk de shote, en I wuz boun' ter git eben wid 'im. So one night I cotch' 'im down by de swamp on his way ter a candy-pullin', en I th'owed a goopher mixtry on 'im, en turnt 'im ter a mule, en got a po' w'ite man ter sell de mule, en we 'vided de money. But I doan want ter die 'tel I turn Brer Primus back ag'in.'

"Den de cunjuh man ax' Pete ter take down one er two go'ds off'n a she'f in de corner, en one er two bottles wid some kin' er mixtry in 'em, en set 'em on a stool by de bed; en den he ax' 'im ter fetch de mule in.

"W'en de mule come in de do', he gin a snort, en started fer de bed, des lack he was gwine ter jump on it.

"'Hol' on dere, Brer Primus!' de cunjuh man hollered. 'I 's mon-st'us weak, en ef you 'mence on me, you won't nebber hab no chance fer ter git turn' back no mo'.'

"De mule seed de sense er dat, en stood still. Den de cunjuh man tuk de go'ds en bottles, en 'mence' ter wuk de roots en yarbs, en de mule 'mence' ter turn back ter a man,—fust his years, den de res' er his head, den his shoulders en arms. All de time de cunjuh man kep' on wukkin' his roots; en Pete en Primus could see he wuz gittin' weaker en weaker all de time.

"'Brer Pete,' sezee, bimeby, 'gimme a drink er dem bitters out'n dat green bottle on de she'f yander. I's gwine fas', en it'll gimme strenk fer ter finish dis wuk.'

"Brer Pete look' up on de mantel-piece, en he seed a bottle in de corner. It was so da'k in de cabin he couldn' tell whe'r it wuz a green bottle er no. But he hilt de bottle ter de cunjuh man's mouf, en he tuk a big mouff'l. He hadn' mo' d'n swallowed it befo' he 'mence' ter holler.

"'You gimme de wrong bottle, Brer Pete; dis yer bottle's got pizen in it, en I's done fer dis time, sho'. Hol' me up, fer de Lawd's sake! 'tel I git th'oo turnin' Brer Primus back.'

"So Pete hilt him up, en he kep' on wukkin' de roots, 'tel he got de goopher all tuk off'n Brer Primus 'cep'n' one foot. He had n' got dis foot mo' d'n half turnt back befo' his strenk gun out enti'ely, en he drap' de roots en fell back on de bed.

"'I can't do no mo' fer you, Brer Primus,' sezee, 'but I hopes you will fergib me fer w'at harm I done you. I knows de good Lawd done fergib me, en I hope ter meet you bofe in glory. I sees de good angels waitin' fer me up yander, wid a long w'ite robe en a starry crown, en I'm on my way ter jine 'em.' En so de cunjuh man died, en Pete en Primus went back ter de plantation.

"De darkies all made a great 'miration w'en Primus come back. Mars Jim let on lack he didn' b'lieve de tale de two niggers tol'; he sez Primus had runned erway, en stay' 'tel he got ti'ed er de swamps, en den come back on him ter be fed. He tried ter 'count fer de shape er Primus' foot by sayin' Primus got his foot smash', er snake-bit, er sump'n, w'iles he wuz erway, en den stayed out in de woods whar he couldn' git it kyoed up straight, 'stidder comin' long home whar a doctor could 'a' 'tended ter it. But de niggers all notice' dey marster didn' tie Primus up, ner take on much 'ca'se de mule wuz gone. So dey 'lowed dey marster must 'a' had his s'picions 'bout dat cunjuh man."

My wife had listened to Julius's recital with only a mild interest. When the old man had finished it she remarked:—

"That story does not appeal to me, Uncle Julius, and is not up to your usual mark. It isn't pathetic, it has no moral that I can discover, and I can't see why you should tell it. In fact, it seems to me like nonsense."[1]

The old man looked puzzled as well as pained. He had not pleased the lady, and he did not seem to understand why.

"I'm sorry, ma'm," he said reproachfully, "ef you doan lack dat tale. I can't make out w'at you means by some er dem wo'ds you uses, but I'm tellin' nuffin but de truf. Co'se I didn' see de cunjuh man tu'n 'im back, fer I wuzn' dere; but I be'n hearin' de tale fer twenty-five yeahs, en I ain' got no 'casion fer ter 'spute it.[2] Dey 's so many things a body knows is lies, dat dey ain' no use gwine roun' findin' fault wid tales dat mought des ez well be so ez not. F' instance, dey's a young nigger gwine ter school in town, en he come out heah de yuther day en 'lowed dat de sun stood still en de yeath turnt roun' eve'y day on a kinder axletree. I tol' dat young nigger ef he didn' take hisse'f 'way wid dem lies, I'd take a buggy-trace ter 'im; fer I sees de yeath stan'in' still all de time, en I sees de sun gwine roun' it, en ef a man can't b'lieve w'at 'e sees, I can't see no use in libbin'—mought 's well die en be whar we can't see nuffin. En ernudder thing w'at proves de tale 'bout dis ole Primus is de way he goes on ef anybody ax' him how he come by dat club-foot. I axed 'im one day, mighty perlite en civil, en he call' me a' ole fool, en got so mad he ain' spoke ter me sence. Hit's monst'us quare. But dis is a quare worl', anyway yer kin fix it," concluded the old man, with a weary sigh.

"Ef you makes up yo' min' not ter buy dat mule, suh," he added, as he rose to go, "I knows a man w'at's got a good hoss he wants ter sell,—leas'ways dat's w'at I heared. I'm gwine ter pra'rmeetin' ternight, en I'm gwine right by de man's house, en ef you'd lack ter look at de hoss, I'll ax 'im ter fetch him roun'."

"Oh, yes," I said, "you can ask him to stop in, if he is passing. There will be no harm in looking at the horse, though I rather think I shall buy a mule."

Early next morning the man brought the horse up to the vineyard. At that time I was not a very good judge of horse-flesh. The horse appeared sound and gentle, and, as the owner assured me, had no bad habits. The man wanted a large price for the horse, but finally agreed to accept a much smaller sum, upon payment of which I became possessed of a very fine-looking animal. But alas for the deceitfulness of appearances! I soon ascertained that the horse was blind in one eye, and that the sight of the other was very defective; and not a month elapsed before my purchase developed most of the diseases

1. Annie's response is different in the *Overland Monthly* version, where she is pleased by the story—captivated by "the spell of the storyteller's art"—until Julius finishes the tale. Then she reprimands him not on aesthetic grounds, but rather because "her conscience . . . warned her that she had been encouraging the dissemination of fictitious narrative on the Sabbath."
2. Chesnutt added the subsequent anti-science, anti-education anecdote for the 1899 edition.

that horse-flesh is heir to, and a more worthless, broken-winded, spavined quadruped never disgraced the noble name of horse. After worrying through two or three months of life, he expired one night in a fit of the colic. I replaced him with a mule, and Julius henceforth had to take his chances of driving some metamorphosed[3] unfortunate.

Circumstances that afterwards came to my knowledge created in my mind a strong suspicion that Julius may have played a more than unconscious part in this transaction. Among other significant facts was his appearance, the Sunday following the purchase of the horse, in a new suit of store clothes, which I had seen displayed in the window of Mr. Solomon Cohen's store[4] on my last visit to town, and had remarked on account of their striking originality of cut and pattern. As I had not recently paid Julius any money, and as he had no property to mortgage, I was driven to conjecture to account for his possession of the means to buy the clothes. Of course I would not charge him with duplicity unless I could prove it, at least to a moral certainty, but for a long time afterwards I took his advice only in small doses and with great discrimination.

Dave's Neckliss[1]

"Have some dinner, Uncle Julius?" said my wife.

It was a Sunday afternoon in early autumn. Our two women-servants had gone to a camp-meeting some miles away, and would not return until evening. My wife had served the dinner, and we were just rising from the table, when Julius came up the lane, and, taking off his hat, seated himself on the piazza.

The old man glanced through the open door at the dinner-table, and his eyes rested lovingly upon a large sugar-cured ham, from which several slices had been cut, exposing a rich pink expanse that would have appealed strongly to the appetite of any hungry Christian.[2]

"Thanky, Miss Annie," he said, after a momentary hesitation, "I dunno ez I keers ef I does tas'e a piece er dat ham, ef yer'll cut me off a slice un it."

"No," said Annie, "I won't. Just sit down to the table and help yourself; eat all you want, and don't be bashful."

---

3. John connects Julius's conjure tale with the classical *Metamorphoses* of Ovid.
4. Entrepreneurial immigrants from Eastern Europe often owned dry-goods stores in rural Southern areas that catered to an African American and laboring white clientele; Chesnutt references this stereotype with the naming of the store.
1. Published in the *Atlantic Monthly* in 1889; submitted to Houghton Mifflin by Chesnutt with his proposal for a story collection, but not included in *The Conjure Woman*.
2. John refers to the prohibition against pork in Jewish dietary laws; the phrase also foreshadows the Eucharistic dimensions the ham will assume over the course of the tale.

Julius drew a chair up to the table, while my wife and I went out on the piazza. Julius was in my employment; he took his meals with his own family, but when he happened to be about our house at meal-times, my wife never let him go away hungry.

I threw myself into a hammock, from which I could see Julius through an open window. He ate with evident relish, devoting his attention chiefly to the ham, slice after slice of which disappeared in the spacious cavity of his mouth. At first the old man ate rapidly, but after the edge of his appetite had been taken off he proceeded in a more leisurely manner. When he had cut the sixth slice of ham (I kept count of them from a lazy curiosity to see how much he *could* eat)[3] I saw him lay it on his plate; as he adjusted the knife and fork to cut it into smaller pieces, he paused, as if struck by a sudden thought, and a tear rolled down his rugged cheek and fell upon the slice of ham before him. But the emotion, whatever the thought that caused it, was transitory, and in a moment he continued his dinner. When he was through eating, he came out on the porch, and resumed his seat with the satisfied expression of countenance that usually follows a good dinner.

"Julius," I said, "you seemed to be affected by something, a moment ago. Was the mustard so strong that it moved you to tears?"

"No, suh, it wa'n't de mustard; I wuz studyin' 'bout Dave."

"Who was Dave, and what about him?" I asked.

The conditions were all favorable to story-telling. There was an autumnal languor in the air, and a dreamy haze softened the dark green of the distant pines and the deep blue of the Southern sky. The generous meal he had made had put the old man in a very good humor. He was not always so, for his curiously undeveloped nature was subject to moods which were almost childish in their variableness. It was only now and then that we were able to study, through the medium of his recollection, the simple but intensely human inner life of slavery. His way of looking at the past seemed very strange to us; his view of certain sides of life was essentially different from ours. He never indulged in any regrets for the Arcadian[4] joyousness and irresponsibility which was a somewhat popular conception of slavery; his had not been the lot of the petted house-servant, but that of the toiling field-hand. While he mentioned with a warm appreciation the acts of kindness which those in authority had shown to him and his people, he would speak of a cruel deed, not with the indignation of one accustomed to quick feeling and spontaneous expression, but with a furtive disapproval which suggested to

3. John's interest in watching Julius eat, as well as his emphasis on Julius's huge mouth and prodigious appetite, are cued by Chesnutt to minstrel-show burlesques of black characters voraciously consuming stereotypical foods.
4. Ideally rural or rustic.

us a doubt in his own mind as to whether he had a right to think or to feel, and presented to us the curious psychological spectacle of a mind enslaved long after the shackles had been struck off from the limbs of its possessor. Whether the sacred name of liberty ever set his soul aglow with a generous fire; whether he had more than the most elementary ideas of love, friendship, patriotism, religion,—things which are half, and the better half, of life to us; whether he even realized, except in a vague, uncertain way, his own degradation, I do not know. I fear not; and if not, then centuries of repression had borne their legitimate fruit. But in the simple human feeling, and still more in the undertone of sadness, which pervaded his stories, I thought I could see a spark which, fanned by favoring breezes and fed by the memories of the past, might become in his children's children a glowing flame of sensibility, alive to every thrill of human happiness or human woe.

"Dave use' ter b'long ter my ole marster," said Julius; "he wuz raise' on dis yer plantation, en I kin 'member all erbout 'im, fer I wuz ole 'nuff ter chop cotton w'en it all happen'. Dave wuz a tall man, en monst'us strong: he could do mo' wuk in a day dan any yuther two niggers on de plantation. He wuz one er dese yer solemn kine er men, en nebber run on wid much foolishness, like de yuther darkies. He use' ter go out in de woods en pray; en w'en he hear de han's on de plantation cussin' en gwine on wid dere dancin' en foolishness, he use' ter tell 'em 'bout religion en jedgmen'-day, w'en dey would haf ter gin account fer eve'y idle word en all dey yuther sinful kyarin's-on.

"Dave had l'arn' how ter read de Bible. Dey wuz a free nigger boy in de settlement w'at wuz monst'us smart, en could write en cipher, en wuz alluz readin' books er papers. En Dave had hi'ed dis free boy fer ter l'arn 'im how ter read. Hit wuz 'g'in' de law, but co'se none er de niggers did n' say nuffin ter de w'ite folks 'bout it. Howsomedever, one day Mars Walker—he wuz de oberseah—foun' out Dave could read. Mars Walker wa'n't nuffin but a po' bockrah, en folks said he couldn' read ner write hisse'f, en co'se he didn' lack ter see a nigger w'at knowed mo' d'n he did; so he went en tole Mars Dugal'. Mars Dugal' sont fer Dave, en ax' 'im 'bout it.

"Dave didn't hardly knowed w'at ter do; but he couldn' tell no lie, so he 'fessed he could read de Bible a little by spellin' out de words. Mars Dugal' look' mighty solemn.

"'Dis yer is a se'ious matter,' sezee; 'it's 'g'in' de law ter l'arn niggers how ter read, er 'low 'em ter hab books. But w'at yer l'arn out'n dat Bible, Dave?'

"Dave wa'n't no fool, ef he wuz a nigger, en sezee:—

"'Marster, I l'arns dat it's a sin fer ter steal, er ter lie, er fer ter want w'at doan b'long ter yer; en I l'arns fer ter love de Lawd en ter 'bey my marster.'

"Mars Dugal' sorter smile' en laf' ter hisse'f, like he 'uz might'ly tickle' 'bout sump'n, en sezee:—

"'Doan 'pear ter me lack readin' de Bible done yer much harm, Dave. Dat's w'at I wants all my niggers fer ter know. Yer keep right on readin', en tell de yuther han's w'at yer be'n tellin' me. How would yer lack fer ter preach ter de niggers on Sunday?'

"Dave say he'd be glad fer ter do w'at he could. So Mars Dugal' tole de oberseah fer ter let Dave preach ter de niggers, en tell 'em w'at wuz in de Bible, en it would he'p ter keep 'em fum stealin' er runnin' erway.

"So Dave 'mence' ter preach, en done de han's on de plantation a heap er good, en most un 'em lef' off dey wicked ways, en 'mence' ter love ter hear 'bout God, en religion, en de Bible; en dey done dey wuk better, en didn' gib de oberseah but mighty little trouble fer ter manage 'em.

"Dave wuz one er dese yer men w'at didn' keer much fer de gals,—leastways he didn' 'tel Dilsey come ter de plantation. Dilsey wuz a monst'us peart, good-lookin', gingybread-colored gal,—one er dese yer high-steppin' gals w'at hol's dey heads up, en won' stan' no foolishness fum no man. She had b'long' ter a gemman over on Rockfish, w'at died, en whose 'state ha' ter be sol' fer ter pay his debts. En Mars Dugal' had be'n ter de oction, en w'en he seed dis gal a-cryin' en gwine on 'bout bein' sol' erway fum her ole mammy, Aun' Mahaly, Mars Dugal' bid 'em bofe in, en fotch 'em ober ter our plantation.

"De young nigger men on de plantation wuz des wil' atter Dilsey, but it didn' do no good, en none un 'em couldn' git Dilsey fer dey junesey,[5] 'tel Dave 'mence' fer ter go roun' Aun' Mahaly's cabin. Dey wuz a fine-lookin' couple, Dave en Dilsey wuz, bofe tall, en well-shape', en soopl'. En dey sot a heap by one ernudder. Mars Dugal' seed 'em tergedder one Sunday, en de nex' time he seed Dave atter dat, sezee:—

"'Dave, w'en yer en Dilsey gits ready fer ter git married, I ain' got no rejections. Dey's a poun' er so er chawin'-terbacker up at de house, en I reckon yo' mist'iss kin fine a frock en a ribbin er two fer Dilsey. Youer bofe good niggers, en yer neenter be feared er bein' sol' 'way fum one ernudder long ez I owns dis plantation; en I 'spec's ter own it fer a long time yit.'

"But dere wuz one man on de plantation w'at didn' lack ter see Dave en Dilsey tergedder ez much ez ole marster did. W'en Mars Dugal' went ter de sale whar he got Dilsey en Mahaly, he bought ernudder han', by de name er Wiley. Wiley wuz one er dese yer shiny-eyed, double-headed little niggers, sha'p ez a steel trap, en sly ez de

5. Sweetheart [Chesnutt's note].

fox w'at keep out'n it. Dis yer Wiley had be'n pesterin' Dilsey 'fo' she come ter our plantation, en had nigh 'bout worried de life out'n her. She didn' keer nuffin fer 'im, but he pestered her so she ha' ter th'eaten ter tell her marster fer ter make Wiley let her 'lone. W'en he come ober to our place it wuz des ez bad, 'tel bimeby Wiley seed dat Dilsey had got ter thinkin' a heap 'bout Dave, en den he sorter hilt off aw'ile, en purten' lack he gin Dilsey up. But he wuz one er dese yer 'ceitful niggers, en w'ile he wuz laffin' en jokin' wid de yuther han's 'bout Dave en Dilsey, he wuz settin' a trap fer ter ketch Dave en git Dilsey back fer hisse'f.

"Dave en Dilsey made up dere min's fer ter git married long 'bout Christmas time, w'en dey'd hab mo' time fer a weddin'. But 'long 'bout two weeks befo' dat time ole mars 'mence' ter lose a heap er bacon. Eve'y night er so somebody 'ud steal a side er bacon, er a ham, er a shoulder, er sump'n, fum one er de smoke-'ouses. De smoke-'ouses wuz lock', but somebody had a key, en manage' ter git in some way er 'nudder. Dey 's mo' ways 'n one ter skin a cat, en dey 's mo' d'n one way ter git in a smoke-'ouse,—leastways dat's w'at I hearn say. Folks w'at had bacon fer ter sell didn' hab no trouble 'bout gittin' rid un it. Hit wuz 'g'in' de law fer ter buy things fum slabes; but Lawd! dat law didn' 'mount ter a hill er peas. Eve'y week er so one er dese yer big covered waggins would come 'long de road, ped-dlin' terbacker en w'iskey. Dey wuz a sight er room in one er dem big waggins, en it wuz monst'us easy fer ter swop off bacon fer sump'n ter chaw er ter wa'm yer up in winter-time. I s'pose de peddlers didn' knowed dey wuz breakin' de law, caze de niggers alluz went at night, en stayed on de dark side er de waggin; en it wuz mighty hard fer ter tell *w'at* kine er folks dey wuz.

"Atter two er th'ee hund'ed er meat had be'n stole', Mars Walker call all de niggers up one ebenin', en tol' 'em dat de fus' nigger he cot stealin' bacon on dat plantation would git sump'n fer ter 'member it by long ez he lib'. En he say he'd gin fi' dollars ter de nigger w'at 'skiver' de rogue. Mars Walker say he s'picion' one er two er de nig-gers, but he couldn' tell fer sho, en co'se dey all 'nied it w'en he 'cuse em un it.

"Dey wa'n't no bacon stole' fer a week er so, 'tel one dark night w'en somebody tuk a ham fum one er de smoke-'ouses. Mars Walker des cusst awful w'en he foun' out de ham wuz gone, en say he gwine ter sarch all de niggers' cabins; w'en dis yer Wiley I wuz tellin' yer 'bout up'n say he s'picion' who tuk de ham, fer he seed Dave comin' 'cross de plantation fum to'ds de smoke-'ouse de night befo'. W'en Mars Walker hearn dis fum Wiley, he went en sarch' Dave's cabin, en foun' de ham hid under de flo'.

"Eve'ybody wuz 'stonish'; but dere wuz de ham. Co'se Dave 'nied it ter de las', but dere wuz de ham. Mars Walker say it wuz des ez he 'spected: he did n' b'lieve in dese yer readin' en prayin' niggers; it wuz all 'pocrisy, en sarve' Mars Dugal' right fer 'lowin' Dave ter be readin' books w'en it wuz 'g'in' de law.

"W'en Mars Dugal' hearn 'bout de ham, he say he wuz might'ly 'ceived en disapp'inted in Dave. He say he wouldn' nebber hab no mo' conference in no nigger, en Mars Walker could do des ez he wuz a mineter wid Dave er any er de res' er de niggers. So Mars Walker tuk'n tied Dave up en gin 'im forty; en den he got some er dis yer wire clof w'at dey uses fer ter make sifters out'n, en tuk'n wrap' it roun' de ham en fasten it tergedder at de little een'. Den he tuk Dave down ter de blacksmif-shop, en had Unker Silas, de plantation blacksmif, fasten a chain ter de ham, en den fasten de yuther een' er de chain roun' Dave's neck. En den he says ter Dave, sezee:—

"'Now, suh, yer'll wear dat neckliss fer de nex' six mont's; en I 'spec's yer ner none er de yuther niggers on dis plantation won' steal no mo' bacon dyoin' er dat time.'

"Well, it des 'peared ez if fum dat time Dave didn' hab nuffin but trouble. De niggers all turnt ag'in' 'im, caze he be'n de 'casion er Mars Dugal' turnin' 'em all ober ter Mars Walker. Mars Dugal' wa'n't a bad marster hisse'f, but Mars Walker wuz hard ez a rock. Dave kep' on sayin' he didn' take de ham, but none un 'em did n' b'lieve 'im.

"Dilsey wa'n't on de plantation w'en Dave wuz 'cused er stealin' de bacon. Ole mist'iss had sont her ter town fer a week er so fer ter wait on one er her darters w'at had a young baby, en she didn' fine out nuffin 'bout Dave's trouble 'tel she got back ter de plantation. Dave had patien'ly endyoed de finger er scawn, en all de hard words w'at de niggers pile' on 'im, caze he wuz sho' Dilsey would stan' by 'im, en wouldn' b'lieve he wuz a rogue, ner none er de yuther tales de darkies wuz tellin' 'bout 'im.

"W'en Dilsey come back fum town, en got down fum behine de buggy whar she b'en ridin' wid ole mars, de fus' nigger 'ooman she met says ter her,—

"'Is yer seed Dave, Dilsey?'

"'No, I ain' seed Dave,' says Dilsey.

"'Yer des oughter look at dat nigger; reckon yer wouldn' want 'im fer yo' junesey no mo'. Mars Walker cotch 'im stealin' bacon, en gone en fasten' a ham roun' his neck, so he can't git it off'n hisse'f. He sut'nly do look quare.' En den de 'ooman bus' out laffin' fit ter kill herse'f. W'en she got thoo laffin' she up'n tole Dilsey all 'bout de ham, en all de yuther lies w'at de niggers be'n tellin' on Dave.

"W'en Dilsey started down ter de quarters, who should she meet but Dave, comin' in fum de cotton-fiel'. She turnt her head ter one side, en purten' lack she did n' seed Dave.

"'Dilsey!' sezee.

"Dilsey walk' right on, en didn' notice 'im.

"'*Oh*, Dilsey!'

"Dilsey didn' paid no 'tention ter 'im, en den Dave knowed some er de niggers be'n tellin' her 'bout de ham. He felt monst'us bad, but he 'lowed ef he could des git Dilsey fer ter listen ter 'im fer a minute er so, he could make her b'lieve he didn' stole de bacon. It wuz a week er two befo' he could git a chance ter speak ter her ag'in; but fine'ly he cotch her down by de spring one day, en sezee:—

"'Dilsey, w'at fer yer won' speak ter me, en purten' lack yer doan see me? Dilsey, yer knows me too well fer ter b'lieve I'd steal, er do dis yuther wick'ness de niggers is all layin' ter me,—yer *knows* I would n' do dat, Dilsey. Yer ain' gwine back on yo' Dave, is yer?'

"But w'at Dave say didn' hab no 'fec' on Dilsey. Dem lies folks b'en tellin' her had p'isen' her min' 'g'in' Dave.

"'I doan wanter talk ter no nigger,' says she, 'w'at be'n whip' fer stealin', en w'at gwine roun' wid sich a lookin' thing ez dat hung roun' his neck. I's a 'spectable gal, *I* is. W'at yer call dat, Dave? Is dat a cha'm fer ter keep off witches, er is it a noo kine er neckliss yer got?'

"Po' Dave didn' knowed w'at ter do. De las' one he had 'pended on fer ter stan' by 'im had gone back on 'im, en dey didn' 'pear ter be nuffin mo' wuf libbin' fer. He couldn' hol' no mo' pra'r-meetin's, fer Mars Walker wouldn' 'low 'im ter preach, en de darkies wouldn' 'a' listen' ter 'im ef he had preach'. He didn' eben hab his Bible fer ter comfort hisse'f wid, fer Mars Walker had tuk it erway fum 'im en burnt it up, en say ef he ketch any mo' niggers wid Bibles on de plantation he'd do 'em wuss'n he done Dave.

"En ter make it still harder fer Dave, Dilsey tuk up wid Wiley. Dave could see him gwine up ter Aun' Mahaly's cabin, en settin' out on de bench in de moonlight wid Dilsey, en singin' sinful songs en playin' de banjer. Dave use' ter scrouch down behine de bushes, en wonder w'at de Lawd sen' 'im all dem tribberlations fer.

"But all er Dave's yuther troubles wa'n't nuffin side er dat ham. He had wrap' de chain roun' wid a rag, so it did n' hurt his neck; but w'eneber he went ter wuk, dat ham would be in his way; he had ter do his task, howsomedever, des de same ez ef he didn' hab de ham. W'eneber he went ter lay down, dat ham would be in de way. Ef he turn ober in his sleep, dat ham would be tuggin' at his neck. It wuz de las' thing he seed at night, en de fus' thing he seed in de mawnin'. W'eneber he met a stranger, de ham would be de fus' thing de stranger would see. Most un 'em would 'mence' ter laf, en whareber Dave went he could see folks p'intin' at him, en year 'em sayin':—

"'W'at kine er collar dat nigger got roun' his neck?' er, ef dey knowed 'im, 'Is yer stole any mo' hams lately?' er 'W'at yer take fer yo' neckliss, Dave?' er some joke er 'nuther 'bout dat ham.

"Fus' Dave didn' mine it so much, caze he knowed he hadn' done nuffin. But bimeby he got so he couldn' stan' it no longer, en he'd hide hisse'f in de bushes w'eneber he seed anybody comin', en alluz kep' hisse'f shet up in his cabin atter he come in fum wuk.

"It wuz monst'us hard on Dave, en bimeby, w'at wid dat ham eberlastin' en etarnally draggin' roun' his neck, he 'mence' fer ter do en say quare things, en make de niggers wonder ef he wa'n't gittin' out'n his mine. He got ter gwine roun' talkin' ter hisse'f, en singin' cornshuckin' songs, en laffin' fit ter kill 'bout nuffin. En one day he tole one er de niggers he had 'skivered a noo way fer ter raise hams,— gwine ter pick 'em off'n trees, en save de expense er smoke-'ouses by kyoin' 'em in de sun. En one day he up'n tole Mars Walker he got sump'n pertickler fer ter say ter 'im; en he tuk Mars Walker off ter one side, en tole 'im he wuz gwine ter show 'im a place in de swamp whar dey wuz a whole trac' er lan' covered wid ham-trees.

"Wen Mars Walker hearn Dave talkin' dis kine er fool-talk, en w'en he seed how Dave wuz 'mencin' ter git behine in his wuk, en w'en he ax' de niggers en dey tole 'im how Dave be'n gwine on, he 'lowed he reckon' he 'd punish' Dave ernuff, en it mou't do mo' harm dan good fer ter keep de ham on his neck any longer. So he sont Dave down ter de blacksmif-shop en had de ham tuk off. Dey wa'n't much er de ham lef' by dat time, fer de sun had melt all de fat, en de lean had all swivel' up, so dey wa'n't but th'ee er fo' poun's lef'.

"W'en de ham had be'n tuk off'n Dave, folks kinder stopped talkin' 'bout 'im so much. But de ham had be'n on his neck so long dat Dave had sorter got use' ter it. He look des lack he'd los' sump'n fer a day er so atter de ham wuz tuk off, en didn' 'pear ter know w'at ter do wid hisse'f; en fine'ly he up'n tuk'n tied a lighterd-knot[6] ter a string, en hid it under de flo' er his cabin, en w'en nobody wuzn' lookin' he'd take it out en hang it roun' his neck, en go off in de woods en holler en sing; en he allus tied it roun' his neck w'en he went ter sleep. Fac', it 'peared lack Dave done gone clean out'n his mine. En atter a w'ile he got one er de quarest notions you eber hearn tell un. It wuz 'bout dat time dat I come back ter de plantation fer ter wuk,—I had be'n out ter Mars Dugal's yuther place on Beaver Crick for a mont' er so. I had hearn 'bout Dave en de bacon, en 'bout w'at wuz gwine on on de plantation; but I didn' b'lieve w'at dey all say 'bout Dave, fer I knowed Dave wa'n't dat kine er man. One day atter I come back, me'n Dave wuz choppin' cotton tergedder, w'en Dave lean' on his hoe, en motion' fer me ter come ober close ter 'im; en den he retch' ober en w'ispered ter me.

"'Julius', sezee, 'did yer knowed yer wuz wukkin' long yer wid a ham?'

"I couldn' 'magine w'at he meant. 'G'way fum yer, Dave,' says I. 'Yer ain' wearin' no ham no mo'; try en fergit 'bout dat; 't ain' gwine ter do yer no good fer ter 'member it.'

---

6. A pine wood knot or root, rich with resin, so called for its ability to light fires easily.

"'Look a-yer, Julius,' sezee, 'kin yer keep a secret?'

"'Co'se I kin, Dave,' says I. 'I doan go roun' tellin' people w'at yuther folks says ter me.'

"'Kin I trus' yer, Julius? Will yer cross yo' heart?'

"'I cross' my heart. 'Wush I may die ef I tells a soul,' says I.

"Dave look' at me des lack he wuz lookin' thoo me en 'way on de yuther side er me, en sezee:—

"'Did yer knowed I wuz turnin' ter a ham, Julius?'

"I tried ter 'suade Dave dat dat wuz all foolishness, en dat he oughtn't ter be talkin' dat-a-way,—hit wa'n't right. En I tole 'im ef he'd des be patien', de time would sho'ly come w'en eve'ything would be straighten' out, en folks would fine out who de rale rogue wuz w'at stole de bacon. Dave 'peared ter listen ter w'at I say, en promise' ter do better, en stop gwine on dat-a-way; en it seem lack he pick' up a bit w'en he seed dey wuz one pusson didn' b'lieve dem tales 'bout 'im.

"Hit wa'n't long atter dat befo' Mars Archie McIntyre, ober on de Wimbleton road, 'mence' ter complain 'bout somebody stealin' chickens fum his hen-'ouse. De chickens kep' on gwine, en at las' Mars Archie tole de han's on his plantation dat he gwine ter shoot de fus' man he ketch in his hen-'ouse. In less'n a week atter he gin dis warnin', he cotch a nigger in de hen-'ouse, en fill' 'im full er squir'l-shot. W'en he got a light, he 'skivered it wuz a strange nigger; en w'en he call' one er his own sarven's, de nigger tole 'im it wuz our Wiley. W'en Mars Archie foun' dat out, he sont ober ter our planta-tion fer ter tell Mars Dugal' he had shot one er his niggers, en dat he could sen' ober dere en git w'at wuz lef un 'im.

"Mars Dugal' wuz mad at fus'; but w'en he got ober dere en hearn how it all happen', he didn' hab much ter say. Wiley wuz shot so bad he wuz sho' he wuz gwine ter die, so he up'n says ter ole marster:—

"'Mars Dugal',' sezee, 'I knows I's be'n a monst'us bad nigger, but befo' I go I wanter git sump'n off'n my mine. Dave didn' steal dat bacon w'at wuz tuk out'n de smoke-'ouse. I stole it all, en I hid de ham under Dave's cabin fer ter th'ow de blame on him—en may de good Lawd fergib me fer it.'

"Mars Dugal' had Wiley tuk back ter de plantation, en sont fer a doctor fer ter pick de shot out'n 'im. En de ve'y nex' mawnin' Mars Dugal' sont fer Dave ter come up ter de big house; he felt kinder sorry fer de way Dave had be'n treated. Co'se it wa'n't no fault er Mars Dugal's, but he wuz gwine ter do w'at he could fer ter make up fer it. So he sont word down ter de quarters fer Dave en all de yuther han's ter 'semble up in de yard befo' de big house at sun-up nex' mawnin'.

"Yearly in de mawnin' de niggers all swarm' up in de yard. Mars Dugal' wuz feelin' so kine dat he had brung up a bairl er cider, en tole de niggers all fer ter he'p deyselves.

"All de han's on de plantation come but Dave; en bimeby, w'en it seem lack he wa'n't comin', Mars Dugal' sont a nigger down ter de quarters ter look fer 'im. De sun wuz gittin' up, en dey wuz a heap er wuk ter be done, en Mars Dugal' sorter got ti'ed waitin'; so he up'n says:—

"'Well, boys en gals, I sont fer yer all up yer fer ter tell yer dat all dat 'bout Dave's stealin' er de bacon wuz a mistake, ez I s'pose yer all done hearn befo' now, en I's mighty sorry it happen'. I wants ter treat all my niggers right, en I wants yer all ter know dat I sets a heap by all er my han's w'at is hones' en smart. En I want yer all ter treat Dave des lack yer did befo' dis thing happen', en mine w'at he preach ter yer; fer Dave is a good nigger, en has had a hard row ter hoe. En de fus' one I ketch sayin' anythin' 'g'in' Dave, I'll tell Mister Walker ter gin 'im forty. Now take ernudder drink er cider all roun', en den git at dat cotton, fer I wanter git dat Persimmon Hill trac' all pick' ober ter-day.'

"W'en de niggers wuz gwine 'way, Mars Dugal' tole me fer ter go en hunt up Dave, en bring 'im up ter de house. I went down ter Dave's cabin, but couldn' fine 'im dere. Den I look' roun' de plantation, en in de aidge er de woods, en 'long de road; but I couldn' fine no sign er Dave. I wuz 'bout ter gin up de sarch, w'en I happen' fer ter run 'cross a foot-track w'at look' lack Dave's. I had wukked 'long wid Dave so much dat I knowed his tracks: he had a monst'us long foot, wid a holler instep, w'ich wuz sump'n skase 'mongs' black folks. So I follered dat track 'cross de fiel' fum de quarters 'tel I got ter de smoke-'ouse. De fus' thing I notice' wuz smoke comin' out'n de cracks; it wuz cu'ous, caze dey hadn' be'n no hogs kill' on de plantation fer six mont' er so, en all de bacon in de smoke-'ouse wuz done kyoed. I couldn' 'magine fer ter sabe my life w'at Dave wuz doin' in dat smoke-'ouse. I went up ter de do' en hollered:—

"'Dave!'

"Dey didn' nobody answer. I didn' wanter open de do', fer w'ite folks is monst'us perickler 'bout dey smoke-'ouses; en ef de oberseah had a-come up en cotch me in dere, he mou't not wanter b'lieve I wuz des lookin' fer Dave. So I sorter knock at de do' en call' out ag'in:—

"'O Dave, hit's me—Julius! Doan be skeered. Mars Dugal' wants yer ter come up ter de big house,—he done 'skivered who stole de ham.'

"But Dave didn' answer. En w'en I look' roun' ag'in en didn' seed none er his tracks gwine way fum de smoke-'ouse, I knowed he wuz in dere yit, en I wuz 'termine' fer ter fetch 'im out; so I push de do' open en look in.

"Dey wuz a pile er bark burnin' in de middle er de flo', en right ober de fier, hangin' fum one er de rafters, wuz Dave; dey wuz a rope roun' his neck, en I didn' haf ter look at his face mo' d'n once fer ter see he wuz dead.[7]

---

7. Julius describes the scene of Dave's suicide as the scene of a lynching—the contemporary mob execution of an African American, usually by hanging and often by burning the body, carried out as an act of white supremacist terrorism.

"Den I knowed how it all happen'. Dave had kep' on gittin' wusser en wusser in his mine, 'tel he des got ter b'lievin' he wuz all done turnt ter a ham; en den he had gone en built a fier, en tied a rope roun' his neck, des lack de hams wuz tied, en had hung hisse'f up in de smoke-'ouse fer ter kyo.

"Dave wuz buried down by de swamp, in de plantation buryin'-groun'. Wiley didn' died fum de woun' he got in Mars McIntyre's hen-'ouse; he got well atter a w'ile, but Dilsey wouldn' hab nuffin mo' ter do wid 'im, en 't wa'n't long 'fo' Mars Dugal' sol' 'im ter a spekilater on his way souf,—he say he didn' want no sich a nigger on de planta-tion, ner in de county, ef he could he'p it. En w'en de een' er de year come, Mars Dugal' turnt Mars Walker off, en run de plantation hisse'f atter dat.

"Eber sence den," said Julius in conclusion, "w'eneber I eats ham, it min's me er Dave.[8] I lacks ham, but I nebber kin eat mo' d'n two er th'ee poun's befo' I gits ter studyin' 'bout Dave, en den I has ter stop en leab de res' fer ernudder time."

There was a short silence after the old man had finished his story, and then my wife began to talk to him about the weather, on which subject he was an authority. I went into the house.[9] When I came out, half an hour later, I saw Julius disappearing down the lane, with a basket on his arm.

At breakfast, next morning, it occurred to me that I should like a slice of ham. I said as much to my wife.

"Oh, no, John," she responded, "you shouldn't eat anything so heavy for breakfast."

I insisted.

"The fact is," she said, pensively, "I couldn't have eaten any more of that ham, and so I gave it to Julius."

A Deep Sleeper[1]

It was four o'clock on Sunday afternoon, in the month of July. The air had been hot and sultry, but a light, cool breeze had sprung up, and occasional cirrus clouds overspread the sun, and for a while sub-dued his fierceness. We were all out on the piazza—as the coolest place we could find—my wife, my sister-in-law and I. The only sounds that broke the Sabbath stillness were the hum of an occasional

---

8. In Julius's conclusion, Chesnutt creates a grotesque echo of Christ's call to the Lord's Supper: "Take, eat; this is my body which is given for you. This do in remembrance of Me" (Matthew 26:26, Luke 22:19 [New Revised Standard Version]).
9. This tale provokes a singular non-response from John and Annie.
1. Published in a short-lived Boston periodical titled *Two Tales* in 1893; submitted to Houghton Mifflin by Chesnutt with his proposal for a story collection, but not included in *The Conjure Woman*.

vagrant bumble-bee, or the fragmentary song of a mocking-bird in a neighboring elm, who lazily trolled a stave of melody, now and then, as a sample of what he could do in the cool of the morning, or after a light shower, when the conditions would be favorable to exertion.

"Annie," said I, "suppose, to relieve the deadly dulness of the afternoon, that we go out and pull the big watermelon, and send for Colonel Pemberton's folks to come over and help us eat it."

"Is it ripe, yet?" she inquired sleepily, brushing away a troublesome fly that had impudently settled on her hair.

"Yes, I think so. I was out yesterday with Julius, and we thumped it, and concluded it would be fully ripe by to-morrow or next day. But I think it is perfectly safe to pull it to-day."

"Well, if you are sure, dear, we'll go. But how can we get it up to the house? It's too big to tote."

"I'll step round to Julius's cabin and ask him to go down with the wheelbarrow and bring it up," I replied.

Julius was an elderly colored man who worked on the plantation and lived in a small house on the place, a few rods from my own residence. His daughter was our cook, and other members of his family served us in different capacities.

As I turned the corner of the house I saw Julius coming up the lane. He had on his Sunday clothes, and was probably returning from the afternoon meeting at the Sandy Run Baptist Church, of which he was a leading member and deacon.

"Julius," I said, "we are going out to pull the big watermelon, and we want you to take the wheelbarrow and go with us, and bring it up to the house."

"Does yer reckon dat watermillun's ripe yit, sah?" said Julius. "Didn' 'pear ter me it went quite plunk enuff yistiddy fer ter be pull' befo' termorrer."

"I think it is ripe enough, Julius."

"Mawnin' 'ud be a better time fer ter pull it, sah, w'en de night air an' de jew's done cool' it off nice."

"Probably that's true enough, but we'll put it on ice, and that will cool it; and I'm afraid if we leave it too long, some one will steal it."

"I 'spec's dat so," said the old man, with a confirmatory shake of the head. "Yer takes chances w'en yer pulls it, en' yer takes chances w'en yer don't. Dey's a lot er po' w'ite trash roun' heah w'at ain' none too good fer ter steal it. I seed some un' 'em loafin' long de big road on mer way home fum chu'ch jes' now. I has ter watch mer own chicken-coop ter keep chick'ns 'nuff fer Sunday eatin'. I'll go en' git de w'eelborrow."

Julius had a profound contempt for poor whites, and never let slip an opportunity for expressing it. He assumed that we shared this sentiment, while in fact our feeling toward this listless race was something entirely different. They were, like Julius himself, the product of a system which they had not created and which they did not know enough to resist.

As the old man turned to go away he began to limp, and put his hand to his knee with an exclamation of pain.

"What's the matter, Julius?" asked my wife.

"Yes, Uncle Julius, what ails you?" echoed her sweet young sister. "Did you stump your toe?"

"No, miss, it's dat mis'able rheumatiz. It ketches me now an' den in de lef' knee, so I can't hardly draw my bref. O Lawdy!" he added between his clenched teeth, "but dat do hurt. Ouch! It's a little better now," he said, after a moment, "but I doan' b'lieve I kin roll dat w'eelborrow out ter de watermillun-patch en' back. Ef it's all de same ter yo', sah, I'll go roun' ter my house en' sen' Tom ter take my place, w'iles I rubs some linimum on my laig."

"That'll be all right, Julius," I said, and the old man, hobbling, disappeared round the corner of the house. Tom was a lubberly, sleepy-looking negro boy of about fifteen, related to Julius's wife in some degree, and living with them.

The old man came back in about five minutes. He walked slowly, and seemed very careful about bearing his weight on the afflicted member.

"I sont 'Liza Jane fer ter wake Tom up," he said. "He's down in de orchard asleep under a tree somewhar. 'Liza Jane knows whar he is. It takes a minute er so fer ter wake 'im up. 'Liza Jane knows how ter do it. She tickles 'im in de nose er de yeah wid a broomstraw; hollerin' doan' do no good. Dat boy is one er de Seben Sleepers. He's wuss'n his gran'daddy used ter be."

"Was his grandfather a deep sleeper, Uncle Julius?" asked my wife's sister.

"Oh, yas, Miss Mabel," said Julius, gravely. "He wuz a monst'us pow'ful sleeper. He slep' fer a mont' once."

"Dear me, Uncle Julius, you must be joking," said my sister-in-law incredulously. I thought she put it mildly.

"Oh, no, ma'm, I ain't jokin'. I never jokes on ser'ous subjec's. I wuz dere w'en it all happen'. Hit wuz a monst'us quare thing."

"Sit down, Uncle Julius, and tell us about it," said Mabel; for she dearly loved a story, and spent much of her time "drawing out" the colored people in the neighborhood.

The old man took off his hat and seated himself on the top step of the piazza. His movements were somewhat stiff and he was very careful to get his left leg in a comfortable position.

"Tom's gran'daddy wuz name' Skundus,"[2] he began. "He had a brudder name' Tushus en' ernudder name' Cottus en' ernudder name'

---

2. A corruption of the Latin name "Secundus," or "the Second."

Squinchus." The old man paused a moment and gave his leg another hitch.

My sister-in-law was shaking with laughter. "What remarkable names!" she exclaimed. "Where in the world did they get them?"

"Dem names wuz gun ter 'em by ole Marse Dugal' McAdoo, wat I use' ter b'long ter, en' dey use' ter b'long ter. Marse Dugal' named all de babies w'at wuz bawn on de plantation. Dese young un's mammy wanted ter call 'em sump'n plain en' simple, like 'Rastus' er 'Cæsar' er 'George Wash'n'ton;' but ole Marse say no, he want all de niggers on his place ter hab diffe'nt names, so he kin tell 'em apart. He'd done use' up all de common names, so he had ter take sump'n else. Dem names he gun Skundus en' his brudders is Hebrew names en' wuz tuk out'n de Bible."

"Can you give me chapter and verse?" asked Mabel.

"No, Miss Mabel, I doan know 'em. Hit ain' my fault dat I ain't able ter read de Bible. But ez I wuz a-sayin', dis yer Skundus growed up ter be a peart, lively kind er boy, en' wuz very well liked on de plantation. He never quo'lled wid de res' er de han's en' alluz behaved 'isse'f en' tended ter his wuk. De only fault he had wuz his sleep'ness. He'd haf ter be woke up ev'y mawnin' ter go ter his wuk, en' w'enever he got a chance he'd fall ersleep. He wuz might'ly nigh gittin' inter trouble mod'n once fer gwine ter sleep in de fiel'. I never seed his beat fer sleepin'. He could sleep in de sun er sleep in de shade. He could lean upon his hoe en' sleep. He went ter sleep walk'n' 'long de road oncet, en' mighty nigh bus't his head open 'gin' a tree he run inter. I did heah he oncet went ter sleep while he wuz in swimmin'. He wuz floatin' at de time, en' come mighty nigh gittin' drownded befo' he woke up. Ole Marse heared 'bout it en' ferbid his gwine in swimmin' enny mo', fer he said he couldn't 'ford ter lose 'im.

"When Skundus wuz growed up he got ter lookin' roun' at de gals, en' one er de likeliest un 'em tuk his eye. It was a gal name' Cindy, w'at libbed wid 'er mammy in a cabin by deyse'ves. Cindy tuk ter Skundus ez much ez Skundus tuk ter Cindy, en' bimeby Skundus axed his marster ef he could marry Cindy. Marse Dugal' b'long' ter de P'isbytay'n Chu'ch en' never 'lowed his niggers ter jump de broomstick, but alluz had a preacher fer ter marry 'em. So he tole Skundus ef him en' Cindy would 'ten' ter dey wuk good dat summer till de crap was laid by, he'd let 'em git married en' hab a weddin' down ter de quarters.

"So Skundus en' Cindy wukked hahd as dey could till 'bout a mont' er so befo' layin' by, w'en Marse Dugal's brudder, Kunnel Wash'n'ton McAdoo, w'at libbed down in Sampson County, 'bout a hunderd mile erway, come fer ter visit Marse Dugal'. Dey wuz five er six folks in de visitin' party, en' our w'ite folks needed a new gal fer ter he'p wait on 'em. Dey picked out de likeliest gal dey could fine 'mongs' de fiel-han's, en' 'cose dat wuz Cindy. Cindy wuz might'ly tickled fer ter be tuk in de house-sarvice, fer it meant better vittles en' better clo's en' easy wuk. She didn' seed Skundus quite as much, but she seed 'im w'eneber she could. Prospe'ity didn' spile Cindy; she didn' git stuck up en' 'bove 'sociatin' wid fiel'-han's, lack some gals in her place 'ud a done.

"Cindy wuz sech a handy gal 'roun' de house, en' her marster's relations lacked her so much, dat w'en dey visit wuz ober, dey wanted ter take Cindy 'way wid 'em. Cindy didn' want ter go en' said so. Her marster wuz a good-natured kind er man, en' would 'a' kep' her on de plantation. But his wife say no, it 'ud nebber do ter be lett'n' de sarvants hab dey own way, er dey soon wouldn' be no doin' nuthin' wid 'em. Ole marster tole 'er he done promus ter let Cindy marry Skundus.

"'O, well,' sez ole Miss, 'dat doan' cut no figger. Dey's too much er dis foolishness 'bout husban's en' wibes 'mongs' de niggers now-a-days. One nigger man is de same as ernudder, en' dey'll be plenty un 'em down ter Wash'n'ton's plantation.' Ole Miss wuz a mighty smart woman, but she didn' know ev'ything.

"'Well,' says ole Marse, 'de craps 'll be laid by in a mont' now, 'en den dey won't be much ter do fer ernudder mont' er six weeks. So we'll let her go down dere an' stay till cotton-pickin' time; I'll jes' len' 'er ter 'em till den. Ef dey wants ter keep 'er en' we finds we doan need 'er, den we'll talk furder 'bout sellin' 'er. We'll tell her dat we jes' gwine let her go down dere wid de chil'en a week er so en' den come back, en' den we won't hab no fuss 'bout it.'

"So dey fixed it dat erway, en' Cindy went off wid 'em, she 'spectin' ter be back in a week er so, en' de w'ite folks not hahdly 'lowin' she'd come back at all. Skundus didn' lack ter hab Cindy go, but he couldn' do nuthin'. He wuz wukkin' off in ernudder part er de plantation w'en she went erway, en' had ter tell her good-by de night befo'.

"Bimeby, w'en Cindy didn' come back in two or th'ee weeks, Skundus 'mence ter git res'less. En' Skundus wuz diff'ent f'um udder folks. Mos' folks w'en dey gits res'less can't sleep good, but de mo' res'lesser Skundus got, de mo' sleepier he 'peared ter git. W'eneber he wuz'n wukkin' er eatin', he'd be sleepin'. Wen de yuther niggers 'ud be skylarkin' 'roun' nights en' Sundays, Skundus 'ud be soun' asleep in his cabin. Things kep' on dis way fer 'bout a mont' atter Cindy went away, w'en one mawnin' Skundus didn't come ter wuk. Dey look' fer 'im 'roun' de plantation, but dey couldn' fin' 'im, en' befo' de day wuz gone, ev'ybody wuz sho' dat Skundus had runned erway.

"Cose dey wuz a great howdydo 'bout it. Nobody hadn' nebber runned erway fum Marse Dugal' befo', an' dey hadn' b'en a runaway nigger in de neighbo'hood fer th'ee er fo' years. De w'ite folks wuz all wukked up, en' dey wuz mo' ridin' er hosses en' mo' hitchin up er buggies d'n a little. Ole Marse Dugal' had a lot er papers printed en' stuck up on trees 'long de roads, en' dey wuz sump'n put in de noospapers—a free nigger f'um down on de Wim'l'ton Road read de paper ter some er our han's—tellin' all 'bout how high Skundus wuz, en' w'at kine er teef he had, en' 'bout a skyah he had on his lef' cheek, en' how sleepy he wuz, en' off'rin' a reward er one hunder' dollars fer whoeber 'ud ketch 'im. But none of 'em eber cotch 'im.

"W'en Cindy fus' went away she wuz kinder down in de mouf fer a day er so. But she went to a fine new house, de folks treated her well en' dere wuz sich good comp'ny 'mongs' her own people, dat she made up 'er min' she might's well hab a good time fer de week er two she wuz gwine ter stay down dere. But w'en de time roll' on en' she didn' heared nothin' 'bout gwine back, she 'mence' ter git kinder skeered she wuz'n nebber gwine ter see her mammy ner Skundus no mo'. She wuz monst'us cut up 'bout it, an' los' 'er appetite en' got so po' en' skinny, her mist'ess sont 'er down ter de swamp fer ter git some roots fer ter make some tea fer 'er health. Her mist'ess sont her 'way 'bout th'ee o'clock en' Cindy didn' come back till atter sundown; en' she say she b'en lookin' fer de roots, dat dey didn' 'pear ter be none er dem kin' er roots fer a mile er so 'long de aidge er de swamp.

"Cindy 'mence' ter git better jes' ez soon as she begun ter drink de root-tea. It wuz a monst'us good med'cine, leas'ways in her case. It done Cindy so much good dat her mist'ess 'cluded she'd take it herse'f en' gib it ter de chil'en. De fus' day Cindy went atter de roots dey wuz some lef' ober, en' her mist'ess tol' 'er fer ter use dat fer de nex' day. Cindy done so, but she tol' 'er mist'ess hit didn' hab no strenk en' didn' do 'er no good. So ev'y day atter dat Marse Wash'n'-ton's wife 'ud sen' Cindy down by de aidge er de swamp fer ter git fresh roots.

"'Cindy,' said one er de fiel'-han's one day, 'yer better keep 'way fum dat swamp. Dey's a ha'nt walkin' down dere.'

"'Go way fum yere wid yo' foolishness,' said Cindy. 'Dey ain' no ha'nts. W'ite folks doan' b'lieve in sich things, fer I heared 'em say so; but yer can't 'spec' nothin' better fum fiel'-han's.'

"Dey wuz one man on de plantation, one er dese yer dandy niggers w'at 'uz alluz runnin' atter de wimmen folks, dat got ter pest'rin' Cindy. Cindy didn' paid no 'tention ter 'im, but he kep' on tryin' fer ter co't her w'en he could git a chance. Fin'ly Cindy tole 'im fer ter let her 'lone, er e'se sump'n' might happen ter 'im. But he didn' min' Cindy, en' one ebenin' he followed her down ter de swamp. He los' track un er, en' ez he wuz a-startin' back out'n de swamp, a great big black ha'nt 'bout ten feet high, en' wid a fence-rail in its han's jump out'n de bushes en' chase 'im cl'ar up in de co'n fiel'. Leas'ways he said it did; en' atter dat none er de niggers wouldn't go nigh de swamp, 'cep'n Cindy, who said it wuz all foolishness—it wuz dis nigger's guilty conscience dat skeered 'im—she hadn' seed no ha'nt en' wuz'n skeered er nuffin' she didn't see.

"Bimeby, w'en Cindy had be'n gone fum home 'bout two mont's, harves'-time come on, en' Marse Dugal' foun' hisse'f short er han's. One er de men wuz down wid de rheumatiz, Skundus wuz gone, en' Cindy wuz gone, en' Marse Dugal tole ole Miss dey wuz no use talkin', he couldn' 'ford ter buy no new han's, en' he'd ha' ter sen' fer Cindy, 'en put her in de fiel'; fer de cotton-crap wuz a monst'us big 'un dat year, en' Cindy wuz one er de bes' cotton-pickers on de plantation. So dey wrote a letter to Marse Wash'n'ton dat day fer Cindy, en' wanted Cindy by de 'een er de mont', en' Marse Wash'n'ton sont her home. Cindy didn't 'pear ter wanter come much. She said she'd got kinder use' ter her noo home; but she didn' hab no mo' ter say 'bout comin' dan she did 'bout goin'. Howsomedever, she went down ter de swamp fer ter git roots fer her mist'ess up ter de las' day she wuz dere.

"W'en Cindy got back home, she wuz might'ly put out 'ca'se Skundus wuz gone, en' hit didn' 'pear ez ef anythin' anybody said ter 'er 'ud comfort 'er. But one mawnin' she said she'd dreamp' dat night dat Skundus wuz gwine ter come back; en' sho' 'nuff, de ve'y nex' mawnin' who sh'd come walkin' out in de fiel' wid his hoe on his shoulder but Skundus, rubbin' his eyes ez ef he hadn' got waked up good yit.

"Dey wuz a great 'miration mongs' de niggers, en' somebody run off ter de big house fer ter tell Marse Dugal'. Bimeby here come Marse Dugal' hisse'f, mad as a hawnit, a-cussin' en' gwine on like he gwine ter hurt somebody; but anybody w'at look close could' 'a' seed he wuz 'mos' tickled ter def fer ter git Skundus back ergin.

"'Whar yer be'n run erway ter, yer good-fer-nuthin', lazy, black nigger?' sez 'e. 'I'm gwine ter gib yer fo' hunderd lashes. I'm gwine ter hang yer up by yer thumbs en' take ev'y bit er yer black hide off'n yer, en' den I'm gwine ter sell yer ter de fus' speci'later w'at comes' long buyin' niggers fer ter take down ter Alabam'. W'at yer mean by runnin' er way fum yer good, kin' marster, yer good-fer-nuthin', wool-headed, black scoun'el?'

"Skundus looked at 'im ez ef he didn' understan'. 'Lawd, Marse Dugal',' sez 'e, 'I doan' know w'at youer talkin' 'bout. I ain' runned erway; I ain' be'n nowhar.'

"'Whar yer be'n fer de las' mon'?' said Marse Dugal'. 'Tell me de truf, er I'll hab yer tongue pulled out by de roots. I'll tar yer all ober yer en' set yer on fiah. I'll—I'll'—Marse Dugal' went on at a tarrable rate, but eve'ybody knowed Marse Dugal' bark uz wuss'n his bite.

"Skundus look lack 'e wuz skeered mos' ter def fer ter heah Marse Dugal' gwine on dat erway, en' he couldn' 'pear to un'erstan' w'at Marse Dugal' was talkin' erbout.

"'I didn' mean no harm by sleep'n in de barn las' night, Marse Dugal',' sez 'e, 'en' ef yer'll let me off dis time, I won' nebber do so no mo'.'

"Well, ter make a long story sho't, Skundus said he had gone ter de barn dat Sunday atternoon befo' de Monday w'en he could't be foun', fer ter hunt aigs, en' wiles he wuz up dere de hay had 'peared so sof' en' nice dat he had laid down fer take a little nap; dat it wuz mawnin' w'en he woke en' foun' hisse'f all covered up whar de hay had fell over on 'im. A hen had built a nes' right on top un 'im, en' it had half-a-dozen aigs in it. He said he hadn't stop fer ter git no brekfus', but had jes' suck' one or two er de aigs en' hurried right straight out in de fiel', fer he seed it wuz late en' all de res' er de han's wuz gone ter wuk.

"'Youer a liar,' said Marse Dugal', 'en' de truf ain't in yer. Yer b'en run erway en' hid in de swamp somewhar ernudder.' But Skundus swo' up en' down dat he hadn' b'en out'n dat barn, en' fin'lly Marse Dugal' went up ter de house en' Skundus went on wid his wuk.

"Well, yer mought know dey wuz a great 'miration in de neighbo'hood. Marse Dugal' sont fer Skundus ter cum up ter de big house nex' day, en' Skundus went up 'spect'n' fer ter ketch forty. But w'en he got dere, Marse Dugal' had fetched up ole Doctor Leach fum down on Rockfish, 'en another young doctor fum town, en' dey looked at Skundus's eyes en' felt of his wris' en' pulled out his tongue, en' hit 'im in de chis', en' put dey yeahs ter his side fer ter heah 'is heart beat; en' den dey up'n made Skundus tell how he felt w'en 'e went ter sleep en' how he felt w'en 'e woke up. Dey stayed ter dinner, en' w'en dey got thoo' talkin' en' eatin' en' drinkin', dey tole Marse Dugal' Skundus had had a catacornered fit,[3] en' had be'n in a trance fer fo' weeks. En' w'en dey l'arned about Cindy, en' how dis yer fit had come on gradg'ly atter Cindy went away, dey 'lowed Marse Dugal' 'd better let Skundus en' Cindy git married, er he'd be liable ter hab some mo' er dem fits. Fer Marse Dugal' didn' want no fittified niggers ef 'e could he'p it.

"Atter dat, Marse Dugal' had Skundus up ter de house lots er times fer ter show 'im off ter folks w'at come ter visit. En' bein' as Cindy wuz back home, en' she en' Skundus wukked hahd, en' he couldn' 'ford fer ter take no chances on dem long trances, he 'lowed em ter got married soon ez cotton-pickin' wuz ober, en' gib 'em a cabin er dey own ter lib in down in de quarters. En' sho' 'nuff, dey didn' had no trouble keep'n' Skundus wak f'm dat time fo'th, fer Cindy

---

3. With the neologism "catacornered fit," Julius conflates the sense of a *cataleptic* fit with that of an oblique or slanted (*catacornered*) act. The malapropism suggests that "deep sleeping" could be a cover for other activity (living in the swamp by Cindy's new plantation, in the case of Skundus, or stealing the watermelon, in the case of Tom) as well as a biological condition.

turned out ter hab a temper of her own, en' made Skundus walk a chalk-line.[4]

"Dis yer boy, Tom," said the old man, straightening out his leg carefully, preparatory to getting up, "is jes' like his gran'daddy. I b'lieve ef somebody didn' wake 'im up he'd sleep till jedgmen' day. Heah 'e comes now. Come on heah wid dat w'eelborrow, yer lazy, good-fer-nuthin' rascal."

Tom came slowly round the house with the wheelbarrow, and stood blinking and rolling his eyes as if he had just emerged from a sound sleep and was not yet half awake.

We took our way around the house, the ladies and I in front, Julius next and Tom bringing up the rear with the wheelbarrow. We went by the well-kept grape-vines, heavy with the promise of an abundant harvest, through a narrow field of yellowing corn, and then picked our way through the watermelon-vines to the spot where the monarch of the patch had lain the day before, in all the glory of its coat of variegated green. There was a shallow concavity in the sand where it had rested, but the melon itself was gone.

Lonesome Ben[1]

There had been some talk among local capitalists about building a cotton mill on Beaver Creek, a few miles from my place on the sand hills in North Carolina, and I had been approached as likely to take an interest in such an enterprise. While I had the matter under advisement it was suggested, as an inducement to my co-operation, that I might have the brick for the mill made on my place—there being clay there suitable for the purpose—and thus reduce the amount of my actual cash investment. Most of my land was sandy, though I had observed several outcroppings of clay along the little creek or branch forming one of my boundaries.

One afternoon in summer, when the sun was low and the heat less oppressive than it had been earlier in the day, I ordered Julius, our old colored coachman, to harness the mare to the rockaway and drive me to look at the clay-banks. When we were ready, my wife, who wished to go with me for the sake of the drive, came out and took her seat by my side.

We reached our first point of destination by a road running across the plantation, between a field of dark-green maize on the one hand and a broad expanse of scuppernong vines on the other. The road led

---

4. Behave with propriety.
1. Rejected by the *Atlantic Monthly* in 1897; submitted to Houghton Mifflin by Chesnutt with his proposal for a story collection, but not included in *The Conjure Woman*; published in the *Southern Workman* in 1900.

us past a cabin occupied by one of my farm-hands. As the carriage
went by at a walk, the woman of the house came to the door and
curtsied. My wife made some inquiry about her health, and she
replied that it was poor. I noticed that her complexion, which naturally was of a ruddy brown, was of a rather sickly hue. Indeed, I had
observed a greater sallowness among both the colored people and
the poor whites thereabouts than the hygienic conditions of the
neighborhood seemed to justify.

After leaving this house our road lay through a cotton field for a
short distance, and then we entered a strip of woods, through which
ran the little stream beside which I had observed the clay. We
stopped at the creek, the road by which we had come crossing it and
continuing over the land of my neighbor, Colonel Pemberton. By the
roadside, on my own land, a bank of clay rose in almost a sheer per-
pendicular for about ten feet, evidently extending back some distance into the low, pine-clad hill behind it, and having also frontage
upon the creek. There were marks of bare feet on the ground along
the base of the bank, and the face of it seemed freshly disturbed and
scored with finger marks, as though children had been playing there.

"Do you think that clay would make good brick, Julius?" I asked
the old man, who had been unusually quiet during the drive. He
generally played with the whip, making little feints at the mare, or
slapping her lightly with the reins, or admonishing her in a familiar
way; but on this occasion the heat or some other cause had rendered
him less demonstrative than usual.

"Yas, suh, I knows it would," he answered.

"How do you know? Has it ever been used for that purpose?"

"No, suh; but I got my reasons fer sayin' so. Ole Mars Dugal
useter hab a brickya'd fu'ther up de branch—I dunno as yer noticed
it, fer it's all growed ober wid weeds an' grass. Mars Dugal said dis
yer clay wouldn' make good brick, but I knowed better."

I judged from the appearance of the clay that it was probably deficient in iron. It was of a yellowish-white tint and had a sort of greasy
look.[2]

"Well," I said, "we'll drive up to the other place and get a sample of
that clay, and then we'll come back this way."

"Hold on a minute, dear," said my wife, looking at her watch,
"Mabel has been over to Colonel Pemberton's all the afternoon. She
said she'd be back at five. If we wait here a little while she'll be along
and we can take her with us."

"All right," I said, "we'll wait for her. Drive up a little farther,
Julius, by that jessamine vine."

2. John's description of the clay resonates with contemporary descriptions of impoverished
   white people in the southern states—precisely those malnourished people who, in a
   grotesque version of "you are what you eat," are shown to be consuming the clay in the
   frame narrative of this tale.

While we were waiting, a white woman wearing a homespun dress and slat-bonnet, came down the road from the other side of the creek, and lifting her skirts slightly, waded with bare feet across the shallow stream. Reaching the clay-bank she stooped and gathered from it, with the aid of a convenient stick, a quantity of the clay which she pressed together in the form of a ball. She had not seen us at first, the bushes partially screening us; but when, having secured the clay, she turned her face in our direction and caught sight of us watching her, she hid the lump of clay in her pocket with a shame-faced look, and hurried away by the road she had come.

"What is she going to do with that, Uncle Julius?" asked my wife. We were Northern settlers, and still new to some of the customs of the locality, concerning which we often looked to Julius for information. He had lived on the place many years and knew the neighborhood thoroughly.

"She's gwineter eat it, Miss Annie," he replied, "w'en she gits outer sight."

"Ugh!" said my wife with a grimace, "you don't mean she's going to eat that great lump of clay?"

"Yas'm I does; dat's jes' w'at I means—gwineter eat eve'y bit un it, an' den come back bimeby fer mo'."

"I should think it would make them sick," she said.

"Dey gits use' ter it," said Julius. "Howsomeber, ef dey eats too much it does make 'em sick; an' I knows w'at I'm er-talkin' erbout. I doan min' w'at dem kinder folks does," he added, looking contemptuously after the retreating figure of the poor-white woman, "but w'eneber I sees black folks eat'n' clay of'n dat partic'lar clay-bank, it alluz sets me ter studyin' 'bout po' lonesome Ben."

"What was the matter with Ben?" asked my wife. "You can tell us while we're waiting for Mabel."

Old Julius often beguiled our leisure with stories of plantation life, some of them folk-lore stories, which we found to be in general circulation among the colored people; some of them tales of real life as Julius had seen it in the old slave days; but the most striking were, we suspected, purely imaginary, or so colored by old Julius's fancy as to make us speculate at times upon how many original minds, which might have added to the world's wealth of literature and art, had been buried in the ocean of slavery.[3]

"W'en ole Mars Marrabo McSwayne owned dat place ober de branch dere, w'at Kunnel Pembe'ton owns now," the old man began, "he useter hab a nigger man name' Ben. Ben wuz one er dese yer big black niggers—he was mo'd'n six foot high an' black ez coal. He wuz

---

3. John provides a list of the various ways that Julius's tales might be categorized: as folklore, as history, or as art.

a fiel'-han' an' a good wukker, but he had one little failin'—he would take a drap er so oncet in a w'ile. Co'se eve'ybody laks a drap now an' den, but it 'peared ter 'fec' Ben mo'd'n it did yuther folks. He didn' hab much chance dat-a-way, but eve'y now an' den he'd git holt er sump'n' somewahr, an' sho's he did, he'd git out'n de narrer road. Mars Marrabo kep' on wa'nin' 'm 'bout it, an' fin'lly he tol' 'im ef he eber ketch 'im in dat shape ag'in he 'uz gwineter gib 'im fo'ty. Ben knowed ole Mars Marrabo had a good 'memb'ance an' alluz done w'at he said, so he wuz monst'us keerful not ter gib 'm no 'casion fer ter use his 'memb'ance on him. An' so fer mos' a whole yeah Ben 'nied hisse'f an' nebber teched a drap er nuffin'.

"But it's ha'd wuk ter larn a ole dog new tricks, er ter make him fergit de ole uns, an' po' Ben's time come bimeby, jes' lak ev'ybody e'se's does. Mars Marrabo sent 'im ober ter dis yer plantation one day wid a bundle er cotton-sacks fer Mars Dugal', an' wiles he wuz ober yere, de ole Debbil sent a' 'oman w'at had cas' her eyes on 'im an' knowed his weakness, fer ter temp' po' Ben wid some licker. Mars Whiskey wuz right dere an' Mars Marrabo wuz a mile erway, an' so Ben minded Mars Whiskey an' fergot 'bout Mars Marrabo. W'en he got back home he couldn' skasely tell Mars Marrabo de message w'at Mars Dugal' had sent back ter 'im.

"Mars Marrabo listen' at 'im 'temp' ter tell it; and den he says, kinder col' and cuttin'-like—he didn' 'pear ter get mad ner nuffin'.

"'Youer drunk, Ben.'

"De way his marster spoke sorter sobered Ben, an' he 'nied it of co'se.

"'Who? Me, Mars Marrabo? *I* ain' drunk; no, marster, *I* ain' drunk. I ain' teched a drap er nuffin' sence las' Chris'mas, suh'.

"'Youer drunk, Ben, an' don't you dare ter 'spute my wo'd, er I'll kill you in yo' tracks! I'll talk ter you Sad'day night, suh, w'en you'll be sober, an' w'en you'll hab Sunday ter 'flect over ou' conve'sation, an' 'nuss yo' woun's.'

"W'en Mars Marrabo got th'oo talkin' Ben wuz mo' sober dan he wuz befo' he got drunk. It wuz Wednesday w'en Ben's marster tol' 'im dis, an' 'twix' den and Friday night Ben done a heap er studyin'. An' de mo' he studied de mo' he didn' lak de way Mars Marrabo talked. He hadn' much trouble wid Mars Marrabo befo', but he knowed his ways, an' he knowed dat de longer Mars Marrabo waited to do a thing de wusser he got 'stid er gittin' better lak mos' folks. An' Ben fin'lly made up his min' he wa'n't gwineter take dat cowhidin'. He 'lowed dat ef he wuz little, like some er de dahkies on de plantation, he wouldn' min' it so much; but he wuz so big dey'd be mo' groun' fer Mars Marrabo ter cover, an' it would hurt dat much mo'. So Ben 'cided ter run erway.

"He had a wife an' two chil'en, an' dey had a little cabin ter dey-se'ves down in de quahters. His wife Dasdy wuz a good-lookin', good-natu'd 'oman, an' 'peared ter set a heap er sto' by Ben. De little boy wuz name' Pete; he wuz 'bout eight er nine years ole, an' had already 'menced ter go out in de fiel' an' he'p his mammy pick cotton, fer Mars Marrabo wuz one er dese yer folks w'at wants ter make eve'y aidge cut.[4] Dis yer little Pete wuz a mighty souple dancer, an' w'en his daddy would set out in de yahd an' pick de banjo fer 'im, Pete could teach de ole folks noo steps—dancin' jes seemed to come nachul ter 'im. Dey wuz a little gal too; Ben didn' pay much 'tention ter de gal, but he wuz monst' us fond er Dasdy an' de boy. He wuz sorry ter leab 'em, an' he didn' tell 'em nuffin' 'bout it fer fear dey'd make a fuss. But on Friday night Ben tuk all de bread an' meat dey wuz in de cabin an' made fer de woods.

"W'en Sad'day come an' Ben didn' 'pear, an' nobody didn' know nuffin' 'bout 'im, Mars Marrabo 'lowed of co'se dat Ben had runned erway. He got up a pahty an' tuk de dawgs out an' follered de scen' down ter de crick an' los' it. Fer Ben had tuk a go'd-full er tar 'long wid' 'im, an' w'en he got ter de crick he had 'n'inted his feet wid tar, an' dat th'owed de houns' off'n de scent. Dey sarched de woods an' follered de roads an' kep' watchin' fer a week, but dey couldn' fin' no sign er Ben. An' den Mars Marrabo got mo' stric', an' wuked his niggers hahder'n eber, ez ef he wanted ter try ter make up fer his loss.

"W'en Ben stahted out he wanted ter go ter de No'th. He didn' know how fur' it wuz, bet he 'lowed he retch dar in fo' er five days. He knowed de No'th Stah, an' de fus night he kep' gwine right straight to'ds it. But de nex' night it was rainin', an' fer two er th'ee nights it stayed cloudy, an' Ben couldn' see de No'th Stah. Howsomeber, he knowed he had got stahted right' an' he kep' gwine right straight on de same way fer a week er mo' 'spectin' ter git ter de No'th eve'y day, w'en one mawin' early, atter he had b'en walkin' all night, he come right smack out on de crick jes whar he had stahted f'om.

"Co'se Ben wuz monst'us disapp'inted. He had been wond'rin' w'y he hadn' got ter de No'th befo', an' behol', heah he wuz back on de ole plantation. He couldn' un'erstan' it at fus', but he wuz so hongry he didn' hab time ter study 'bout nuffin' fer a little w'ile but jes' ter git sump'n' ter eat; fer he had done eat up de bread an' meat he tuk away wid 'im, an' had been libbin' on roas'n-ears an' sweet'n taters he'd slip out'n de woods an' fin' in co'n fiel's 'an 'tater-patches. He look 'cross de crick, an' seed dis yer clay-bank, an' he waded ober an' got all he could eat, an' den tuk a lump wid 'im, an' hid in de woods ag'in 'til he could study de matter ober some.

"Fus' he 'lowed dat he better gib hiss'ef up an' take his lammin'. But jes' den he 'membered de way Mars Marrabo looked at 'im an'

---

4. "To make every edge cut" means to seek maximum return on one's investments.

w'at he said 'bout Sad'day night; an' den he 'lowed dat ef Mars
Marrabo ketch 'im now, he'd wear 'im ter a frazzle an' chaw up de
frazzle, so de wouldn' be nuffin' lef' un 'im at all, an' dat Mars
Marrabo would make a' example an' a warnin' of 'im fer all de niggers
in de naberhood. Fac' is Mars Marrabo prob'ly wouldn' a' done much
ter 'im fer it 'ud be monst'us po' 'couragement fer runaway niggers
ter come back, ef dey gwineter git killed w'en dey come. An' so Ben
waited 'til night, an' den he went back an' got some mo' clay an' eat it
an' hid hisse'f in de woods ag'in.

"Well, hit wuz quare 'bout Ben, but he stayed roun' heah fer a
mont', hidin' in de woods in de daytime, an' slippin'out nights an' gittin' clay ter eat an' water 'fom de crick yanker ter drink. De water in
dat crick wuz cl'ar in dem days, stidder bein' yallar lak it is now."

We had observed that the water, like that of most streams that
take their rise in swamps, had an amber tint to which the sand
and clay background of the bed of the stream imparted an even yel-
lower hue.

"What did he do then, Julius?" asked my wife, who liked to hear
the end of a story.

"Well, Miss, he made up his min' den dat he wuz gwineter staht
fer de No'th ag'in. But wiles he b'en layin' roun' in de woods he had
'mence ter feel monst'us lonesome, an' it 'peared ter him dat he jes'
couldn' go widout seein' Dasdy an' little Pete. Fus' he 'lowed he'd go
up ter de cabin, but he thought 'bout de dogs 'roun' de yahd, an' dat
de yuther dahkies mought see 'im, and so he 'cided he'd better watch
fer 'em 'til dey come long de road—it wuz dis yer same road—w'en
he could come out'n de woods an' talk ter 'em. An' he eben 'lowed he
mought 'suade 'em ter run erway wid 'im an' dey could all get ter de
No'th, fer de nights wuz cl'ar now, an' he couldn' lose de No'th Stah.

"So he waited two er th'ee days, an' sho' nuff long come Dasdy one
mornin', comin' over to Mars Dugal's fer ter fetch some things fer
her missis. She wuz lookin' kinder down in de mouf, fer she thought
a heap er Ben, an' wuz monst'us sorry ter lose 'im, w'iles at de same
time she wuz glad he wuz free, fer she 'lowed he'd done got ter de
Norf long befo'. An' she wuz studyin' 'bout Ben, w'at a fine-lookin'
man he wuz, an' wond'rin' ef she'd eber see 'im any mo'.

"W'en Ben seed her comin' he waited 'til she got close by, an' den
he stepped out 'n de woods an' come face ter face wid her. She didn'
'pear to know who he wuz, an' seem kinder skeered.

"'Hoddy, Dasdy honey,' he said.

"'Huh!' she said, 'pears ter me you'er mighty fermilyer on sho't
acquaintance.'

"'Sho't acquaintance.' Why, doan' yer know me, Dasdy?'

"'No. I doan' know yer f'om a skeercrow. I never seed yer befo' in
my life, an' nebber wants ter see yer ag'in. Whar did yer com f'om

anyhow? Whose nigger is yer? Er is yer some low-down free nigger dat doan b'long ter nobody an' doan own nobody?'

"'W'at fer you talk ter me like dat, honey? I's Ben, yo' Ben. Why doan you know yo' own man?'

"He put out his ahms fer ter draw her ter 'im, but she jes' gib one yell, an' stahted ter run. Ben wuz so 'stonish' he didn' know w'at ter do, an' he stood dere in de road 'til he heared somebody e'se comin', w'en he dahted in de woods ag'in.

"Po' Ben wuz so 'sturbed in his min' dat he couldn' hahdly eat any clay dat day. He couldn' make out w'at wuz de matter wid Dasdy but he 'lowed maybe she'd heared he wuz dead er sump'n', an' thought he wuz a ha'nt, an' dat wuz w'y she had run away. So he watch' by de side er de road, an' nex' mornin' who should come erlong but little Pete, wid a reed over his shoulder, an' a go'd-full er bait, gwine fishin' in de crick.

"Ben called 'im; 'Pete, O Pete! *Little* Pete.'

"Little Pete cocked up his ears an' listened. 'Peared lak he'd heared dat voice befo'. He stahted fer de woods fer ter see who it wuz callin' 'im, but befo' he got dere Ben stepped out an' retched fer 'im.

"'Come heah, honey, an' see yo' daddy, who ain' seenyer fer so long.'

"But little Pete tuk one look at 'im, an' den 'menceter holler an squeal an' kick an' bite an' scratch. Ben wuz so 'stonish' dat he couldn' hol' de boy, who slipped out'n his han's an run to'ds de house ez fas' ez his legs would tote 'im.

"Po' Ben kep' gittin' wus an' wus mixed up. He couldn' make out fer de life er 'im w'at could be de matter. Nobody didn' 'pear ter wanter own 'im. He felt so cas' down dat he didn' notice a nigger man comin' long de road 'til he got right close up on 'im, an' didn' heah dis man w'en he said 'Hoddy' ter 'im.

"'W'at's de matter wid yer?' said de yuther man w'en Ben didn' 'spon'. 'W'at jedge er member er de legislater er hotel-keeper does you b'long ter dat you can't speak ter a man w'en he says hoddy ter yer?'

"Ben kinder come ter hisse'f an' seed it wuz Primus, who b'long ter his marster an' knowed 'im as well as anybody. But befo' he could git de words out'n his mouf Primus went on talkin'.

"'Youer de mos' mis'able lookin' merlatter[5] I eber seed. Dem rags look lak dey be'n run th'oo a sawmill. My marster doan 'low no strange niggers roun' dis yer plantation, an' yo' better take yo' yaller hide 'way f'um yer as fas' as yo' kin.'

"Jes den somebody hollered on de yuther side er de crick, an' Primus stahted off on a run, so Ben didn' hab no chance ter say no mo' ter 'im.

5. Mulatto, a once widely used term for a person of mixed black and white parentage.

"Ben almos' 'lowed he wuz gwine out'n' his min', he wuz so 'ston-ished an' mazed at none er dese yer folks reco'nizir' 'im. He went back in de woods ag'in an' stayed dere all day, wond'rin' w'at he wuz gwineter do. Oncet er twicet he seed folks comin' 'long de road, an' stahted out ter speak ter 'em, but changed his min' an'slip' back ag'in.

"Co'se ef Mars Marrabo had been huntin' Ben he would 'a' foun' 'im. But he had long sence los' all hope er seein' im ag'in, an' so nobody didn' 'sturb Ben in de woods. He stayed hid a day er two mo' an' den he got so lonesome an' homesick fer Dasdy an' little Pete an' de yuther dahkies,—somebody ter talk ter—dat he jes' made up his min' ter go right up ter de house an' gib hisse'f up an' take his med'cine. Mars Marrabo couldn' do nuffin' mo' d'n kill 'im an' he mought's well be dead as hidin' in de woods wid nobody ter talk ter er look at ner nuffin'. He had jes' come out 'n de woods an' stahted up dis ve'y road, w'en who sh'd come 'long in a hoss 'n buggy but ole Mars Marrabo, drivin' ober ter dat yuther brickyahd youer gwinter see now. Ben run out 'n de woods, and fell down on his knees in de road right in front er Mars Marrabo. Mars Marrabo had to pull on de lines an' hol' de hoss up ter keep 'im f'um runnin' ober Ben.

"'Git out'n de road, you fool nigger,' says Mars Marrabo, 'does yer wanter git run ober? Who's nigger is you, anyhow?'

"'I's yo' nigger, Mars Marrabo; doan yer know Ben, w'at runned erway?'

"'Yas, I knows my Ben w'at runned erway. Does you know whar he is?'

"'Why, I's yo' Ben, Mars Marrabo. Doan yer know me, marster?"

"'No, I doan know yer, yer yaller rascal! W'at de debbil yer mean by tellin' me sich a lie? Ben wuz black ez a coal an' straight ez an' arrer. Youer yaller ez dat clay-bank, an' crooked ez a bair'l-hoop. I reckon youer some 'stracted nigger, tun't out by some marster w'at doan wanter take keer er yer. You git off'n my plantation, an' doan show yo' clay-cullud hide aroun' yer no more, er I'll hab yer sent ter jail an' whip.'

"Mars Marrabo drove erway an' lef' po' Ben mo' dead 'n alive. He crep' back in de bushes an' laid down an' wep' lak a baby. He didn' hab no wife, no chile, no frien's, no marster—he'd be'n willin ernuff to git 'long widout a marster, w'en he had one, but it 'peared lak a sin fer his own marster ter 'ny 'im an' cas' 'im off dat-a-way. It 'peared ter 'im he mought jes' ez well be dead ez livin', fer he wuz all alone in de worl', wid nowhar ter go, an' nobody didn' hab nuffin' ter say ter 'im but ter 'buse 'im an' drive 'im erway.

"Atter he got ober his grievin' spell he 'mence ter wonder w'at Mars Marrabo meant by callin' 'im yaller, an' ez long ez nobody didn' seem ter keer whuther dey seed 'im er not, he went down by de crick in broad daylight, an' kneel down by de water an' looked at his face.

Fus' he didn' reco'nize hisse'f an' glanshed back ter see ef dey wa'n't
somebody lookin' ober his shoulder—but dey wa'n't. An' w'en he
looked back in de water he seed de same thing—he wa'n't black no
mo', but had turnt ter a light yaller.'

"Ben didn' knowed w'at ter make er it fer a minute er so. Fus' he
'lowed he must hab de yaller fever, er de yaller janders,[6] er sump'n
lak dat'! But he had knowed rale dark folks ter hab janders befo', and
it hadn't nebber 'fected 'em dat-a-way. But bimeby he got up o'ff'n 'is
han's an' knees an' wuz stan'in' lookin' ober de crick at de clay-bank,
an' wond'rin' ef de clay he'd b'en eat'n' hadn' turnt 'im yaller w'en he
heared sump'n say jes' ez plain ez wo'ds.

"'Turnt ter clay! turnt ter clay! turnt ter clay!'

"He looked all roun', but he couldn' see nobody but a big bullfrog
settin' on a log on de yuther side er de crick. An' w'en he turnt roun'
an' sta'ted back in de woods, he heared de same thing behin' 'im.

"'Turnt ter clay! turnt ter clay! turnt ter clay!'

"Dem wo'ds kep' ringin' in 'is yeahs 'til he fin'lly 'lowed dey wuz
boun' ter be so, er e'se dey wouldn' a b'en tol' ter 'im, an' dat he had
libbed on clay so long an' had eat so much, dat he must 'a' jes nach'ly
turnt ter clay!"

"Imperious Caesar, turned to clay,
Might stop a hole to keep the wind away,"[7]
I murmured parenthentically.

"Yas, suh," said the old man, "turnt ter clay. But you's mistook in
de name, suh; hit wuz Ben, you 'member, not Caesar. Ole Mars
Marrabo did hab a nigger name Caesar, but dat wuz anudder one."

"Don't interrupt him, John," said my wife impatiently. "What happened then, Julius?"

"Well, po' Ben didn' know w'at ter do. He had be'n lonesome
ernuff befo', but now he didn' eben hab his own se'f ter 'so'ciate wid,
fer he felt mo' lak a stranger 'n he did lak Ben. In a day er so mo' he
'mence ter wonder whuther he wuz libbin' er not. He had hearn
'bout folks turnin' ter clay w'en dey wuz dead, an' he 'lowed maybe he
wuz dead an' didn' knowed it, an' dat wuz de reason w'y eve'body run
erway f'm 'im an' wouldn' hab nuffin' ter do wid 'im. An' ennyhow, he
'lowed ef he wa'n't dead, he mought's well be.[8] He wande'ed roun' a
day 'er so mo', an' fin'lly de lonesomeness, an' de sleepin' out in de
woods, 'mongs' de snakes an' sco'pions, an' not habbin' nuffin' fit ter
eat, 'mence ter tell on him, mo' an' mo', an' he kep' gittin' weakah an'
weakah 'til one day, w'en he went down by de crick fer ter git a drink
er water, he foun' his limbs gittin' so stiff hit 'uz all he could do ter
crawl up on de bank an' lay down in de sun. He laid dere 'til he died,

6. Jaundice.
7. John slightly misquotes *Hamlet* 5.1: "Imperious Caesar, *dead and* turn'd to clay/Might
   stop a hole to keep the wind away."
8. Julius gives a description of the condition described by sociologists as "social death."

an' de sun beat down on 'im, an' beat down on 'im, an' beat down on 'im, fer th'ee er fo' days, 'til it baked 'im as ha'd as a brick. An' den a big win' come erlong an' blowed a tree down, an' it fell on 'im an' smashed 'im all ter pieces, an' groun' 'im ter powder. An' den a big rain come erlong, an' washed 'im in de crick, 'an eber sence den de water in dat crick's b'en jes' as yer sees it now. An dat wuz de een' er po' lonesome Ben, an' dat's de reason w'y I knows dat clay'll make brick an' w'y I doan nebber lak ter see no black folks eat'n it."

My wife came of a family of reformers, who could never contemplate an evil without seeking an immediate remedy. When I decided that the bank of edible clay was not fit for brickmaking, she asked me if I would not have it carted away, suggesting at the same time that it could be used to fill a low place in another part of the plantation.

"It would be too expensive," I said.

"Oh, no," she replied, "I don't think so. I have been talking with Uncle Julius about it, and he says he has a nephew who is out of employment, and who will take the contract for ten dollars, if you will furnish the mule and cart, and board him while the job lasts."

As I had no desire to add another permanent member to my household, I told her it would be useless; that if the people did not get clay there they would find it elsewhere, and perhaps an inferior quality which might do greater harm, and that the best way to stop them from eating it was to teach them self-respect, when she had opportunity, and those habits of industry and thrift whereby they could get their living from the soil in a manner less direct but more commendable.

The Dumb Witness[1]

The old Murchison[2] place was situated on the Lumberton plank road, about two miles from my vineyard on the North Carolina sandhills. Old Julius, our colored coachman, had driven me over one Spring morning to see young Murchison, the responsible manager of the property, about some walnut timber I wished to purchase from him for shipment. I had noticed many resources of the country that

---

1. Tentatively accepted by the *Atlantic Monthly* in 1897, but never published; submitted to Houghton Mifflin by Chesnutt with his proposal for a story collection, but not included in *The Conjure Woman*. Reworked by Chesnutt into an episode in the novel *The Colonel's Dream* (1905), but not published as a stand-alone story in his lifetime. This text is established from two partial typescripts, both marked with Chesnutt's manuscript revisions and corrections, held in the archives of Fisk University. The earlier typescript is complete except for a missing second page; of the second typescript, which incorporates the revisions indicated on the first, only seven of twenty-three numbered pages survive. Where the second (revised) typescript is available, we use its wording over that of the first—with the significant exception of the last paragraphs of the story, noted below.
2. The college Chesnutt directed in Fayetteville, the State Colored Normal School (now Fayetteville State University), is located on Murchison Road. The largest and most important African American neighborhood in Fayetteville in the nineteenth century was called Murchison Heights.

the easy-going Southerners had not thought of developing; and I took advantage of them when I found it convenient and profitable to do so.

We entered the lane leading to the house by passing between two decaying gateposts. This entrance had evidently once possessed some pretensions to elegance, for the massive posts had been faced with dressed lumber and finished with ornamental tops, some fragments of which still remained; and the one massive hinge, hanging by a slender rust-eaten nail, had been wrought into a fantastic shape. As we drove through the gateway, a green lizard scampered down from the top of one of the posts, where he had been sunning himself, and a rattlesnake lying in the path lazily uncoiled his mottled brown length and, sounding his rattle the meanwhile, wriggled slowly off into the rank grass and weeds.

The house stood well back from the road, on the crest of one of the regular undulations of the sandhill country. It was partly concealed, when approached from the road, by intervening trees and shrubbery, which had once formed a well ordered pleasaunce,[3] but now grew in wild and tangled profusion, so that it was difficult to distinguish one bush or tree from another. The lane itself was partially overgrown, and the mare's fetlocks swept the dew from the grass, where it had not yet been dried by the morning sun.

As we drew nearer, the house stood clearly revealed. It was apparently of more ancient date than any I had seen in the neighborhood. It was a large two-story frame house, built in the colonial style, with a low-pitched roof, and a broad piazza along the front, running the full length of both stories and supported by huge round columns, and suggesting distantly, in its general effect, the portico of a Greek temple. The roof had sunk on one side, and the shingles were old and cracked and moss-grown; while several of the windows in the upper part of the house were boarded up, and others filled with sash from which the glass had apparently long since been broken.

For a space of several rods on each side of the house the ground was bare of grass and shrubbery, and scarcely less forbidding than the road we had traveled. It was rough and uneven, lying in little hillocks and hollows, as though it had been dug over at hazard, or explored by some rampant drove of hogs. At one side, beyond this barren area, lay an enclosed kitchen garden, in which a few collards and okra-plants and tomato-vines struggled desperately against neglect and drought and poverty of soil.

A casual glance might have led one not informed to the contrary to believe the place untenanted, so lonely and desolate did it seem. But as we approached we became aware of two figures on the long piazza. At one end of it, in a massive armchair of carved oak, a man

3. Pleasure-garden.

was seated—apparently a very old man, for he was bent and wrinkled. His thin white hair hung down upon his shoulders. His face was of a high-bred and strongly marked type, with something of the hawk-like contour usually associated with extreme acquisitiveness. His eyes were turned toward the opposite end of the piazza, where a woman was also seated. She seemed but little younger than the man, and her face was enough like his, in a feminine way, to suggest that they might be related in some degree, unless this inference were negatived by the woman's complexion, which disclosed a strong infusion of darker blood. She wore a homespun frock and a muslin cap and sat bolt upright, with her hands folded on her lap, looking toward her *vis-à-vis* at the other end of the piazza.

As we drew up a short distance from the door, the old man rose, as we supposed, to come forward and greet us. But, instead of stopping at the steps and facing outward, he continued his course to the other end of the piazza, and halted before the woman.

"Viney," he said, in a sharply imperative voice, "my uncle says you will tell me where he put the papers. I am tired of this nonsense. I insist upon knowing immediately."

The woman made no reply, but her faded eyes seemed to glow for a moment, like the ashes of a dying fire fanned by some random breath of air.

"Why do you not answer me?" he continued, with increasing vehemence. "I tell you I insist upon knowing. It is imperative that I should know, and know at once. My interests are suffering for every day's delay. The papers—where are the papers?"

Still the woman sat silent, though her figure seemed to stiffen as she leaned slightly toward him. He grew visibly more impatient at her silence, and began to threaten her.

"Tell me immediately, you hussy, or you will have reason to regret it. You take liberties that cannot be permitted. I will not put up with it," he said, shaking his fist as he spoke. "I shall have to have you whipped."

The slumberous fire in the woman's eyes flamed up for a moment. She rose from her seat, and drawing herself up to her full height— she was a tall woman, though bowed somewhat with years—began to speak, I thought at first in some foreign tongue. But after a moment I knew that no language or dialect, at least none of European origin, could consist of such a discordant jargon, such a meaningless cacophony as that which fell from the woman's lips. And as she went on, pouring out a flood of sounds that were not words, and which yet seemed now and then vaguely to suggest words, as clouds suggest the shapes of mountains and trees and strange beasts, the old man seemed to bend like a reed before a storm, and began to expostulate, accompanying his words with deprecatory gestures.

"Yes, Viney, good Viney," he said in soothing tones—"I know it was wrong, and I've always regretted it—always, from the very day [ ].[4] But you shouldn't bear malice, Viney, it isn't Christian. The Bible says you should bless them that curse you, and do good to them that despitefully use you.[5] But I was good to you before, Viney, and I was good to you afterwards, and I know you have forgiven me—good Viney, noble-hearted Viney!—and you are going to tell me. Now, *do* tell me where the papers are," he added, pleadingly, offering to take her hand, which lay on the arm of the chair.

She drew her hand away, as she muttered something in the same weird tones she had employed before. The old man bent toward her, in trembling eagerness, but seemed disappointed.

"Try again, Viney," he said, "that's a good girl. Your old master thinks a great deal of you, Viney. He is your best friend."

Again she made an inarticulate response. He seemed to comprehend, and turning from her, came down the steps, muttering to himself, took up a spade that stood at one end of the steps, passed by us without seeming conscious of our presence, and hastening with tottering footsteps to one side of the yard began digging furiously.

I had been so much interested in this curious drama that I had forgotten for the time being the business that brought me there. The old woman, however, when the man had gone, rose from her seat and went into the house, without giving us more than a look.

"What's the matter with them, Julius?" I said, returning with a start to the world of reality.

The old man pointed to his head.

"Dey's bofe 'stracted, suh," he said, "out'n dey min'. Dey's be'en dat-a-way fer yeahs an' yeahs."

At that moment the young man of the house came out to the door, and greeted us pleasantly. He asked me to alight from the carriage, and led me to the chair the old man had occupied. It was a massive oak affair, with carved arms and back and a wooden seat, and looked as though it might be of ancient make, perhaps an heirloom. I found young Murchison was a frank and manly young fellow, and quite capable of looking out for his own interests. I struck a bargain with him, on terms that were fair to both. When I had concluded my business and invited him to call and see me sometime, I got into the carriage, and Julius drove down the lane and out into the road again. In going out, we passed near the old man, who was still muttering to himself and digging rapidly, but with signs of weariness.

---

4. An illegible word or words, lost in the decomposition of the edge of the typescript page, should complete this sentence.
5. Luke 6:28: "Bless them that curse you, and pray for them which despitefully use you" (King James Version); "bless those who curse you, pray for those who abuse you" (New Revised Standard Version).

He did not look up as we went by, but seemed entirely absorbed in his strange pursuit.

In the evening, after supper, Julius came up to the house. We sat out on the porch, my wife and her sister and Julius and I. We cut a large watermelon, and when Julius had eaten the half we gave to him, he told us the story of old man Murchison's undoing. The air was cool, the sky was clear, the stars shone with a brightness unknown in higher latitudes. The voices of the night came faintly from the distant woods, and there could have been no more romantic setting for the story of jealousy, revenge and disappointment which the old white-haired negro told us, in his own quaint dialect—a story of things possible only in an era which, happily, has passed from our history, as, in God's own time—and may it be soon!—it will from all the earth. Some of the facts in this strange story, circumstances of which Julius was ignorant, though he had the main facts correct—I learned afterwards from other sources, but I have woven them all together here in orderly sequence.

The Murchison family had occupied their ancestral seat on the sandhills for a hundred years or more. There were not many rich families in that part of North Carolina, and this one, by reason of its wealth and other things was easily the most conspicuous in several counties. The first great man of the family, General Arthur Murchison, had won distinction in the war of independence, and during all the Revolutionary period had been one of the most ardent of the Carolina patriots. After peace was established he had taken high place in the councils of the State. Elected a delegate to the Constitutional Convention at Philadelphia in 1787, it was largely due to his efforts that North Carolina adopted the Federal Constitution the following year. His son became a distinguished jurist, whose name is still a synonym for legal learning and juridical wisdom in North Carolina. Roger Murchison, the son of Judge Murchison—the generations had followed one another rapidly in a country of warm skies and early marriages—was the immediate predecessor of Malcolm Murchison, the demented old man who was nominal owner of the estate at the time of my visit to the house.

In Roger Murchison the family may be said to have begun to decline from the eminence it had attained in the career of Judge Murchison. In the first place, Roger Murchison did not marry, thus seemingly indicating a lack of the family pride which would have made him wish to continue the name in the direct line. Again, though his career in college had been brilliant; though the wealth and standing of the family gave him social and political prestige; and though he had held high office under the State and National governments, he had never while in public life especially distinguished himself for eloquence or statesmanship, but had, on the contrary, enjoyed a life of ease and pleasure and had wasted what his friends thought rare gifts. He was fond of cards, of fast horses, of rare wines, and of gay society. It is not surprising, therefore, that he spent very little time on his property, preferring the life of cities to the comparative dullness of plantation life with such colorless distractions as a neighboring small town could offer.

He had inherited a large estate, including several plantations, and numerous slaves. During his frequent absences from home, in the last fifteen years of his life, he left his property under the management of a nephew, Malcolm Murchison, the orphan son of a younger brother, and his own prospective heir. Young Malcolm was a youth of unusual strength of character and administrative capacity, and even before he had attained his majority showed himself a better manager than his uncle had ever been. So well, indeed, did he manage the estate that his uncle left it for ten years practically in his hands, looking to him only for the means he required to lead his own life in other places. It is true he appeared periodically and assumed the role of proprietor, but Malcolm was the man to whom the community and the slaves looked as both the present and the future master.

Young Murchison kept bachelor's hall in the great house. The only women about the establishment were an old black cook, and the housekeeper, a tall, comely young quadroon—she had too a dash of Indian blood, which perhaps gave her straighter and blacker hair than she would otherwise have had, and also perhaps endowed her with some other qualities which found their natural expression in the course of subsequent events—if indeed her actions needed anything more than common human nature to account for them.[6] The duties of young Murchison's housekeeper were not onerous; compared with the toiling field-hand she led a life of ease and luxury.

The one conspicuous vice of Malcolm Murchison was avarice. If he had other failings, they were the heritage of the period, and he shared them with his contemporaries of the same caste. Perhaps it was his avarice that kept him from marrying; it was cheaper to have his clothing and his table looked after by a slave than by a woman who would not have been content with her food and clothing. At any rate, for ten or fifteen years he remained single, and ladies never set foot in the Murchison house. Men sometimes came and smoked and drank, played cards, bought and sold produce or slaves, but the foot of a white woman had not touched the floor for

6. In the revised typescript of the story, Chesnutt here cancels the following sentence: "We like to speak of Negro cunning, of Indian revengefulness, of the low morality of inferior races, when, alas! Our own race excels in all these things, when it wishes, because it lends to evil purposes a higher intelligence and a wider experience than inferior races can command."

fifteen years, when Mrs. Martha Todd[7] came from Pennsylvania to the neighboring town of Patesville to visit a cousin living there, who had married a resident of the town.

Malcolm Murchison met Mrs. Todd while she was driving on the road one day. He knew her companion, in response to whose somewhat distant bow he lifted his hat. Attracted by the stranger's appearance, he made inquiries about her in the town, and learned that she was a widow and rich in her own right. He sought opportunities to meet her, courted her, and after a decent interval of hesitation on her part—she had only just put off mourning for her first husband—received her promise to be his wife.

He broke the news to his housekeeper by telling her to make the house ready for a mistress. The housekeeper had been in power too long to yield gracefully, or perhaps she foresaw and dreaded the future. Some passionate strain of the mixed blood in her veins—a very human blood—broke out in a scene of hysterical violence. She pleaded, remonstrated, raged. He listened calmly through it all—he had anticipated some such scene—and at the end said to her:

"You had better be quiet and obedient. I have heard what you have to say—this once—and it will be useless for you to repeat it, for I shall not listen again. If you are reasonable, I will send you to the other plantation. If not, I will leave you here, with your new mistress."

She was silent for the time being, but raged inwardly. The next day she stole away from home, went to the town, sought out the new object of Murchison's devotion, and told her something—just what she told no one but herself and the lady ever knew.

When Murchison called in the evening, Mrs. Todd sent down word that she was not at home. With the message came a note:

"I have had my wedded happiness spoiled once. A burnt child dreads the fire—I do not care to go twice through the same experience. I have learned some things about you that will render it impossible for me ever to marry you. It is needless to seek an explanation."

He went away puzzled and angry. His housekeeper wore an anxious look, which became less anxious as she observed his frame of mind. He had been wondering where Mrs. Todd had got the information—he could not doubt what it was—that had turned her from him. Suddenly a suspicion flashed into his mind. He went away early the next morning and made investigations. In the afternoon he came home with all the worst passions of weak humanity, clad with irresponsible power, flaming in his eyes.

---

7. As Candace Waid points out in her essay in this Norton Critical Edition, Chesnutt names Murchison's love interest after the most famous widow of the postwar era, Mary Todd Lincoln.

"I will teach you," he said to his housekeeper, who quailed before him—"to tell tales about your master. I will put it out of your power to dip your tongue in where you are not concerned."

There was no one to say him nay. The law made her his. It was a lonely house, and no angel of mercy stayed his hand.[8]

About a week later he received a letter—a bulky envelope. On breaking the seal, he found the contents to consist of two papers, one of which was a letter from a friend and political associate of his uncle. It was dated at Washington, and announced the death of his uncle Roger as the result of an accident. A team of spirited horses had run away with him and thrown him out of the carriage, inflicting a fatal injury. The letter stated that his uncle had lingered for a day, during which he had dictated a letter to his nephew; that his body had been embalmed and placed in a vault, to await the disposition of his relatives or representatives. His uncle's letter was enclosed with the one above, and ran as follows:

"My dear Malcolm:—This is the last communication I shall ever make to you, I am sorry to say—though I don't know that I ought to complain, for I have always been a philosopher, and have had a good time to boot. There must be an end to all things, and I cannot escape the common fate.

"You have been a good nephew and a careful manager, and I have not forgotten the fact. I have left a will in which you are named as my sole heir, barring some small provision for my sister Mary. With the will you will find several notes, and mortgages securing them, on plantations in the neighborhood—I do not need to specify, as they explain themselves; also some bonds and other securities of value and your grandmother's diamond necklace. I do not say here where they are, lest this letter might fall into the wrong hands; but your housekeeper Viney knows their hiding place. She is devoted to you and to the family—she ought to be, for she is of our blood—and she only knows the secret. I would not have told her, of course, had I not thought of just some such chance as this which has befallen me. She does not know the value of the papers, but simply that they are important.

"And now Malcolm, my boy, goodbye. I am crossing the river and I reach back to clasp your hand once more—just once.

"Your dying Uncle,
"Roger Murchison."

Malcolm Murchison took this letter to Viney. She had been banished from the house to a cabin in the yard, where she was waited on by the old black cook. He felt a little remorseful as he looked at her;

---

8. A manuscript marking here indicates that Chesnutt intended that another passage be inserted at the end of this sentence. The passage does not survive with the extant typescript.

for, after all, she was a woman, and there had been excuses for what she had done; and he had begun to feel, in some measure, that there was not sufficient excuse for what he had done.

She looked at him with an inscrutable face as he came in, and he felt very uncomfortable under the look.

"Viney," he said, not unkindly, "I'm sorry I went so far, and I'm glad you're getting better."

Her expression softened, a tear rolled down her cheek, and he felt correspondingly relieved. It is so easy to forgive our own sins against others.

"Your old Master Roger is dead. I have just received a letter telling me how it happened. He was thrown from a buggy in a runaway and injured so badly that he died the same day.[9] He had time to write me a letter, in which he says you can tell me where he put certain papers that you know about. Can you tell"—he remembered her condition[1]— "can you show me where they are?"

A closer observer than Malcolm Murchison might have detected at this moment another change in the woman's expression. Perhaps it was in her eyes more than elsewhere; for into their black depths there sprang a sudden fire. Beyond this, however, and a slight quickening of her pulse, of which there was no visible manifestation, she gave no sign of special feeling; and even if these had been noticed they might have been attributed to the natural interest felt at hearing of her old master's death.

The only answer Viney made was to lift her hand and point it to her mouth.

"Yes, I know," he said hastily, "you can't tell me—not now at least—but you can surely point out the place to me."

She shook her head and pointed again to her mouth.

"Is it hidden in some place that you can't lead me to, when you are able to get up?"

She nodded her head.

"Will it require words to describe it so that I can find it?"

Again she nodded affirmatively.

He reflected a moment. "Is it in the house?" he asked.

She shook her head.

"In the yard?"

Again she made a negative sign.

"In the barn?"

No.

"In the fields?"

No.

9. Again, a manuscript marking indicates that Chesnutt intended that another passage be inserted here. The passage does not survive with the extant manuscript.
1. With editorial markings, Chesnutt rewords the typed phrase "he thought of her mutilation."

He tried for an hour, naming every spot he could think of as a possible hiding-place for the papers, but with no avail. Every question was answered in the negative.

When he had exhausted his ingenuity in framing questions he went away very much disappointed. He had been patiently waiting for his reward for many years, and now when it should be his, it seemed to elude his grasp.

"Never mind," he said, "we will wait until you are better, and then perhaps you may be able to speak intelligibly. In the meantime you shall not want for anything."

He had her removed to the house, and saw that she received every attention. She was fed with dainty food, and such care as was possible was given to her wound. In due time it healed. But she did not even then seem able to articulate, even in whispers, and all his attempts to learn of her the whereabouts of the missing papers were met by the same failure. She seemed willing enough, but unable to tell what he wished to know. There was apparently some mystery which only words could unravel.

It occurred to him more than once how simple it would be for her to write down the few words necessary to his happiness. But, alas! she might as well have been without hands, for any use she could make of them in that respect. Slaves were not taught to write, for too much learning would have made them mad. But Malcolm Murchison was a man of resources—he would have her taught to write. So he employed a teacher—a free colored man who had picked up some fragments of learning, and who could be trusted to hold his tongue, to teach Viney to read and write. But somehow she made poor progress.[2] She was handicapped of course by her loss of speech. It was unfamiliar work too for the teacher, who would not have been expert with a pupil equipped with all the normal faculties. Perhaps she had begun too old, or her mind was too busily occupied with other thoughts to fix it on the tedious and painful steps by which the art of expression in writing is acquired. Whatever the reason, she manifested a remarkable stupidity while seemingly anxious to learn; and in the end Malcolm was compelled to abandon the attempt to teach her.

Several years passed in vain efforts to extract from Viney in some way the wished-for information. Meantime Murchison's affairs did not prosper. Several other relatives claimed a share in his uncle's estate, on the ground that he had died intestate. In the absence of the will, their claims could not be successfully disputed. Every legal means of delay was resorted to, and the authorities were disposed, in

2. Here Chesnutt cancels the following phrase: "Ignorant people learn with their voices as well as with their minds."

view of the remarkable circumstances of the case, to grant every possible favor. But the law fixed certain limits to delay in the settlement of an estate, and in the end he was obliged either to compromise the adverse claims or allow them to be fixed by legal process. And while certain of what his own rights were, he was compelled to see a large part of what was rightfully his go into hands where it would be difficult to trace or recover it if the will were found. Some of the estates against which he suspected the hidden notes and mortgages were held were sold and otherwise disposed of. His worry interfered with proper attention to his farming operations, and one crop was almost a failure. The factor to whom he shipped his cotton went bankrupt owing him a large balance, and he fell into debt, and worried himself into a fever. The woman Viney nursed him through it, and was always present at his side, a mute reproach for his cruelty, a constant reminder of his troubles. Her presence was the worst of things for him, and yet he could not bear to have her out of his sight; for in her lay the secret he longed for and which he hoped at some time in some miraculous way to extract from her.

When he rose from his sick-bed after an illness of three months, he was but the wreck of the strong man he had once been. His affairs had fallen into hopeless disorder. His slaves, except Viney, were sold to pay his debts, and there remained to him of the almost princely inheritance he had expected only the old place on the sand-hills and his slave Viney, who still kept house for him. His mind was vacant and wandering, except on the one subject of the hidden will, and he spent most of the time in trying to extract from Viney the secret of its hiding-place. A young nephew came and lived with him and did what was necessary to hold the remnant of the estate together.

When the war came Viney was freed, with the rest of her brethren in bondage. But she did not leave the old place. There was some gruesome attraction in the scene of her suffering; or perhaps it was the home instinct. The society of humankind did not possess the same attraction for her as if she had not been deprived of the power of speech. She stayed on and on, doing the simple housework for the demented old man and his nephew, until the superstitious negroes and poor-whites of the neighborhood said that she too shared the old man's affliction. Day after day they sat on the porch, when her indoor work was done, the old man resting in the carved oaken arm-chair, and she in her splint-bottom chair; or the old man commanding, threatening, expostulating, entreating her to try, just once more, to tell him his uncle's message—she replying in the meaningless inarticulate mutterings that we had heard; or the old man digging, digging furiously, and she watching him from the porch, with the same inscrutable eyes, though dulled somewhat by age, that had flashed upon him for a moment in the dimly-lighted cabin where she lay on her bed of pain.

The summer following the visit I made to the old Murchison place I accompanied my wife North on a trip to our former home. On my return several weeks later I had occasion again to visit young Murchison, and drove over one morning to the house. As we drove up the lane I noticed a surprising change in the surroundings. A new gate had been hung, upon a pair of ugly cast-iron hinges. The grass in the path had been mowed, and the weeds and shrubs bordering it had been cut down. The neglected pleasure-garden had been reduced to some degree of order, and the ground around the house had been plowed and harrowed, and the young blades of grass were shooting up and covering the surface with a greenish down. The house itself had shared in the general improvement. The roof had been repaired and the broken windows mended, and from certain indications in the way of ladders and pails in the yard, I inferred that it was intended to paint the house. This however was merely a supposition, for house-painting is an art that languishes in the rural districts of the South.

Julius had been noticing my interest in these signs of prosperity, with a pleased expression that boded further surprises.

"What's been going on here, Julius?" I asked.

"Ole Mars Murchison done dead, suh—died las' mont', an' eve'ything goes ter young Mistah Roger. He's done 'mence' ter fix de ole place up. He be'n ober ter yo' place lookin' 'roun', an' say he's gwineter hab his'n lookin' lak yo'n befo' de yeah's ober."[3]

We stopped the rockaway in front of the house. As we drew up an old woman came out in whom I recognized one of the strange couple I had seen on the porch on my former visit. She seemed intelligent enough, to judge by her appearance, and I ventured to address her.

"Is Mr. Murchison at home?"

"Yes, sir," she answered, "I'll call him."

Her articulation was not distinct, but her words were intelligible. I was never more surprised in my life.

"What does this mean, Julius?" I inquired, turning to the old man, who was grinning and chuckling to himself in great glee at my manifest astonishment. "Has she recovered her speech?"

---

3. Both early and revised typescript versions of the end of the story survive, and the only differences between the two are in Chesnutt's renderings of Viney's and Julius's speech. From this point forward in the revised typescript, however, Chesnutt clearly cancelled the final paragraphs. Because we have no later revision with which to replace the cancelled paragraphs, we revert here to the earlier typescript's version. The most significant change is that Viney, who delivers her single line in dialect in the revised typescript, here speaks Standard English.

"She had nebber lost it, suh. Ole Viney could 'a' talked all de time, ef she had had a min' ter. W'en Ole Mars Malcolm wuz dead she tuck 'n showed young Mistah Roger whar de will an' de papahs wuz hid. An' whar you reckon dey wuz, suh?"

"I give it up, Julius. Enlighten me."

"Dey wa'n't in de house, ner de yahd, ner de bahn, ner de field'. Dey wuz hid in de seat er dat ole oak ahm-cheer on de piazza yander, w'at Ole Mars Ma'colm be'n settin' in all dese years."

A Victim of Heredity;
or Why the Darkey Loves Chicken[1]

I went to North Carolina a few years after the war with some hopeful views in regard to the colored people. It was my idea that with the larger opportunities of freedom they would improve gradually and learn in due time to appreciate the responsibilities of citizenship. This opinion, based on simple faith in human nature, which is much the same the world over, I never saw any good reason to change.

There were a few of my dusky neighbors, however, who did not shake off readily the habits formed under the old system, and I suffered more or less, from time to time, from petty thievery. So long as it was confined to grapes on the vine, or roasting-ears, or hanging fruit, or an occasional watermelon, I did not complain so much; but one summer, after several raids upon my hen-house, I determined to protect my property. I therefore kept close watch one night, and caught a chicken-thief in the very act. I locked him up in a strongly-built smokehouse, where I thought he would be safe until morning.[2]

I made up my mind, before I went to sleep, that an example must be made of this miscreant. Knowing that the law in North Carolina, as elsewhere, was somewhat elastic, and the degree of punishment for crime largely dependent upon the vigor of the prosecution, I decided that five years in the penitentiary would be about right for this midnight marauder. It would give him time to break off the habit of stealing, and would strike terror to the hearts of other evil-doers.

In the morning I went down to the smokehouse to inspect my captive. He was an insignificant looking fellow, and seemed very much frightened. I sent him down something to eat, and told him I was going to have him taken to jail.

1. Written by Chesnutt in 1898 specifically for *The Conjure Woman*; rejected for the volume; published in *Self-Culture Magazine* (Cleveland), 1900.
2. This opening episode resonates worryingly with the earlier stories featuring smokehouses, "Po' Sandy" and "Dave's Neckliss." John puts himself in the place of the slaveholders from both earlier stories, by using his smokehouse to confine a person (as is done to Tenie in the former story), and by thwarting a chicken-stealer by lying in wait for him (as is done to Wiley in the latter story).

During breakfast I turned the matter over in my mind, and concluded that five years' imprisonment would be a punishment rather disproportioned to the offence, and that perhaps two years in the penitentiary would be an equally effective warning.

One of my servants was going to town toward noon, with a load of grapes for shipment to the nearest market, and I wrote a note to the sheriff, Mr. Weems, requesting him to send a constable out to take charge of the thief. The ink was scarcely dry before it occurred to me that over-severity in the punishment of crime was often productive of harm, and had seldom resulted in any good, and that in all probability, taking everything into consideration, a year in jail in the neighborhood would be ample punishment, and a more impressive object-lesson than a longer term in the more distant penitentiary.[3]

During the afternoon I learned, upon inquiry, that my captive had a large family and a sick wife; that because of a trifling disposition he was without steady employment, and therefore dependent upon odd jobs for a livelihood. But while these personal matters might be proper subjects of consideration for the humanitarian, I realized that any false sentiment on my part would be dangerous to social order; and that property must be protected, or soon there would be no incentive to industry and thrift. I determined that the thief should have at least six months in jail, if I had to support his family during his incarceration.

I was sitting on the front piazza, indulging in a quiet smoke during the hot part of the afternoon, just after having arrived at this final conclusion, when old Julius came around the house, and, touching his hat, asked at what time my wife wished the rockaway brought round for our afternoon drive.

"I hardly think we shall go to-day," I replied, "until the constable has come and taken that thief to jail. By the way, Julius," I added with some severity, "why is it that your people can't let chickens alone?"

The old man shook his head sadly.

"It's a myst'ry, suh," he answered with a sigh, "dat ev'ybody doan understan'. Ef dey did, some un 'em mought make mo' 'lowance."

My wife came out of the house and took a seat in an armchair near me, behind the honeysuckle vine.

"I am asking Julius to explain," I said, "why his people are so partial to chickens."

"I think it unkind, John," returned my wife, "to charge upon a whole race the sins of one worthless individual. There are thieves wherever there is portable property, and I don't imagine colored people like chicken better than other people."

---

3. Although they are often used interchangeably, the term "jail" refers to a temporary local facility where individuals may be detained for minor offenses, or while they await trial. A "penitentiary," by contrast, refers to a long-term detention facility reserved for those convicted of major crimes.

Old Julius shook his head dissentingly. "I is bleedzd ter differ fum you dere, ma'm," he said, with as much positiveness as he was capable of in conversation with white people; "cullud folks is mo' fonder er chick'n 'n w'ite folks. Dey can't he'p but be."

"Why so?" I asked. "Is it in the blood?"

"You's hit it, suh, de fus' sta't-off. Yas, suh, dat is de fac', tooby sho', en no mistake erbout it."

"Why, Uncle Julius!" exclaimed my wife with some show of indignation. "You ought to be ashamed to slander your race in that way."

"I begs yo' pardon, ma'm, ef it hu'ts yo' feelin's, but I ain' findin' no fault wid *dem. Dey* ain' 'sponsible fer dey tas'e fer chick'n-meat. A w'ite man's ter blame fer dat."

"Well," I said, "that statement is interesting. Sit down and tell us all about it."

Julius took a seat on the top step, and laying his ragged straw hat beside him, began:

"Long yeahs befo' de wah dey wuz a monst'us rich w'ite gent'e-man, name' Mars Donal' McDonal', w'at useter lib down on de yuther side er de Wim'l'ton Road. He had n' alluz be'n rich, fer w'en he fus' come ter dis county he wuz po', en he wukked fer a yeah er so as oberseah fer anudder w'ite man, 'tel he had save' money 'nuff ter buy one er two niggers, en den he rented a place on sheers, en bimeby he had bought a plantation en bought some mo' niggers en raise' some, 'tel he 'mence' ter be so well-off dat folks mos' fergot he had eber be'n a nigger-driber. He kep' on gittin' richer en richer, 'tel fin'lly he wuz one er de riches' men in de county.

"But he wa'n't sat'sfied. He had a neffy, name' Tom, en Mars Donal' had be'n lef' gyardeen fer, dis yer neffy er his'n, en he had manage' so dat w'en young Mars Tom growed up dey wa'n't nuffin at all lef' er de fine proputty w'at young Mars Tom's daddy had own' w'en he died.

"Folks said Mars Donal' had rob' his neffy, but dey wa'n't no way ter prove it. En mo'd'n dat, Mars Donal' didn' 'pear ter lak Mars Tom a-tall atter he growed up, en turnt 'im out in de worl' ter shif' fer hisse'f widout no money ner nuffin.

"Mars Tom had be'n co'tin' fer lo! dese many yeahs his secon' cousin, young Miss 'Liza M'Guire, who useter lib on de yuther side er de ribber, en young Mars Tom wanter ter marry Miss 'Liza monst'us bad. But w'en Mars Tom come er age, en Mars Donal' say all his proputty done use' up on his edication, Miss 'Liza's daddy say he wouldn' 'low her ter marry Mars Tom 'tel he make some money, er show her daddy how he wuz gwine ter suppo't Miss 'Liza ef he married her.[4]

---

4. Tom and Eliza are central characters in Harriet Beecher Stowe's *Uncle Tom's Cabin* (1852), and one of the most famous scenes from that novel involves Eliza's flight across the Ohio River to freedom.

"De young folks wa'n't 'lowed ter see one ernudder ve'y often, but Mars Tom had a batteau down on de ribber en he useter paddle ober sometimes ter meet Miss 'Liza whuther er no.

"One eb'nin' Mars Tom went down ter de ribber en ontied his batteau en wuz startin' ter cross w'en he heared somebody holler. He looked roun' en he see hit wuz a' ole nigger 'oman had fell in de ribber. She had sunk once, en wuz gwine down ag'in, w'en Mars Tom cotch 'er en pull't' er out, en gin er a drink er sump'n he had in a flas', en den tied his boat en he'ped 'er up de bank ter de top, whar she could git 'long by herse'f.

"Now, dis yer 'oman w'at Mars Tom pull't out'n de ribber des happen' ter be ole Aun' Peggy, de free-nigger cunjuh 'oman w'at libbed down by de Wim'l'ton Road. She had be'n diggin' roots fer her cunj'in', en had got too close ter de ribber, en had fell in whar de water wuz deep en strong, en had come monst'us close ter bein' drownded. Aun' Peggy knowed all 'bout Mars Tom en his uncle ole Mars Donal', en his junesey Miss 'Liza, en she made up her min' dat she wuz gwine ter do sump'n fer young Mars Tom de fus' chanst she got. She wuz wond'rin' wot kinder goopher she could wuk fer Mars Tom, w'en who should come ter see her one day but ole Mars Donal' hisse'f.

"Now, w'y Mars Donal' come ter go ter see ole Aun' Peggy wuz dis erway. Mars Donal' had be'n gittin' richer en richer, en closeter en closeter, 'tel he'd got so he'd mos' skin a flea fer his hide en taller. But he wa'n't sat'sfied, en he kep' on projickin' wid one thing en fig'rin' on ernudder, fer ter see how he could git mo' en mo'. He wuz a'ready wukkin' his niggers ez ha'd ez dey could stan', but he got his 'count-book out one day en 'mence' ter cackilate w'at it cos' 'im ter feed his niggers, en it 'peared ter be a monst'us sum. En he 'lowed ter hisse'f dat ef he could feed his niggers fer 'bout half er w'at it had be'n costin' 'im, he'd save a heap er money ev'y yeah.

"Co'se ev'ybody knowed, en Mars Donal' knowed, dat a fiel'-han' had ter hab so much bacon en so much meal and so much merlasses a week ter make 'im fittin' ter do his wuk. But Mars Donal' 'lowed dey mought be some way ter fool de niggers, er sump'n; so he tuk a silber dollar en went down ter see ole Aun' Peggy.

"Aun' Peggy laid de silber dollar on de mantelpiece en heared w'at he had to say, en den she 'lowed she'd wuk her roots, en he'd hafter come back nex' day en fetch her ernudder silber dollar, en she'd tell 'im w'at he sh'd do.

"Mars Donal' sta'ted out, en bein' ez Aun' Peggy's back wuz tu'nt, he 'lowed he'd take dat silber dollar 'long wid 'im, bein' ez she hadn' tole 'im nuffin, en he'd gin it ter her nex' day. But w'en he pick' up de silber dollar, it wuz so hot it bu'nt 'is han', he laid it down rale quick en went off rubbin' his han' en cussin' kinder sof' ter hisse'f.

"De nex' day he went back, en Aun' Peggy gun 'im a goopher mixtry in a bottle.

"'You take dis yer mixtry,' sez she, 'en put it on yo' niggers' rashuns de nex' time you gibs 'em out, en den stidder 'lowin' yo' han's a poun' er bacon en a peck er meal en a qua't er merlasses, you gin 'em half a poun' er bacon en half a peck er meal en a pint er merlasses, en dey won' know de diffe'nce. Fac', dis yer goopher mixtry'll make de half look des lak de whole, en atter de niggers has once eat some er dat conju'd meat en meal en merlasses, it's gwine ter take dey ap'tites erway so dey'll be des ez well sat'sfied ez ef dey had a side a bacon en a bairl er flour.'

"W'en Mars Donal' sta'ted erway Aun' Peggy sez, sez she:

"'You done fergot dat yuther dollar, ain' you, Mars Donal'?'

"'Oh, yes, Peggy', sezee, 'but heah it is.' En Mars Donal' retch' down in his pocket en pull't out a han'ful er gol' en silber, en picked out a lead dollar en handed it ter Aun' Peggy. Aun' Peggy seed de dollar wuz bad, but she tuk it en didn' let on. But ez Mars Donal' wuz turnin' ter go 'way, Aun' Peggy sprinkle' sump'n on dat lead dollar, en sez she:

"'O Mars Donal' kin I get you ter change a twenty-dollar gol' piece fer me?'

"'Yas, I reckon,' sezee.

"Aun' Peggy handed him de lead dollar, en he looked at it en bit it en sounded it on de table, en it 'peared ter be a bran'-noo gol' piece; so he tuk'n pull't out his pu'se en gun Aun' Peggy th'ee five-dollar gol' pieces en five good silber dollars, en den he tuk his goopher mixtry en went 'long home wid it.

"W'en Mars Donal' had gone, Aun' Peggy sont a mawkin'-bird fer ter tell young Mars Tom ter came en see her.

"Mars Tom wuz gwine 'long de road one eb'nin' w'en he heared a mawkin'-bird singin' right close ter 'im, en de mawkin'-bird seem' ter be a-sayin':

> "'Go see ole Aun' Peggy,
>   She wants ter see you bad,
>   She'll show you how ter git back
>   De lan' yo' daddy had.'

"Mars Tom wuz studyin' 'bout sump'n e'se, en he didn' pay no 'tention ter w'at de mawkin'-bird say. So pretty soon he heahs de mawkin'-bird ag'in:

> "'Go en see Aun' Peggy,
>   She wants ter see you bad,
>   She's gwine ter he'p you git back
>   The gol' yo' daddy had.'

"But Mars Tom had sump'n e'se on his min', en he wuz gwine on down de road right pas' whar Aun' Peggy lib' w'en de mawkin'-bird

come up en mos' pe'ched on his shoulders, en sez, des ez plain ez ef
he wuz talkin':

> "'Go see ole Aun' Peggy,
> 　Er e'se you'll wush you had;
> She'll show you how ter marry
> De gal you wants so bad.'

"Dat happen' ter be des w'at Mars Tom wuz studyin' erbout, en he
'mence' ter 'low dey mought be sump'n in w'at dis yer mawkin'-bird
say, so he up'n' goes ter see Aun' Peggy.

"Aun' Peggy say how glad she wuz ter see 'im, en tol' 'im how she'd
be'n wantin' ter do sump'n fer 'im. En den she 'splained 'bout Mars
Donal', en tole Mars Tom sum-p'n w'at he mus' go en do.

"'But I ain' got no money, Aun' Peggy,' sezee.

"'Nemmine', sez Aun' Peggy, 'You borry all de money you kin rake
en scrape, en you git all de credit you kin; en I ain' be'n cunj'in' all
dese yeahs fer nuffin, en I'll len' you some money. But you do des ez I
tell you, en doan git skeert, en ev'y-thing'll tu'n out des exac'ly ez I say.'

"Ole Mars Donal' sprinkle' de goopher mixtry on his niggers'
rashons, nex' Sun-day mawnin', en den sarved out half rashuns, des
ez Aun' Peggy say, en sho' 'nuff, de niggers didn' 'pear ter notice no
diffe'nce, des ez Aun' Peggy say. En all de week none er de han's
didn' say nuffin 'bout not habbin' 'nuff ter eat, en dey 'peared ter be
des ez well sat'sfied ez ef dey 'd got dey reg'lar rashuns.

"Mars Donal' figgered up his books at de een' er a week er so en
foun' he had sabe' so much money dat he 'mence' ter wonder ef he
couldn' sabe some mo'. En bein' ez de niggers wuz all gittin' 'long so
nice, en de cotton had be'n laid by, en de fiel'-han's wouldn' hab ter
wuk so tarrable ha'd fer a mont' er so, Mars Donal' 'lowed he'd use
Aun' Peggy's goopher some mo', en so he tuk'n sprinkle' some mo' er
de mixtry on de nex' week's rashuns en den cut de rashuns in two
once mo'; stidder givin' de han's a half a peck er meal en a pint er
merlasses en half a poun' er bacon, he gun 'em a qua'ter er a peck er
meal en half a pint er merlasses en fo' ounces er meat fer a week's
rashuns. De goopher wukked des de same ez it had befo', en de niggers didn' 'pear ter notice no diffe'nce. Mars Donal' wuz tickle' mos'
ter def, en kep' dis up right along fer th'ee er fo' weeks.

"But Mars Donal' had be'n so busy fig'rin' up his profits en
countin' his money, dat he hadn' be'n payin' ez close 'tention ter his
niggers ez yushal, en fus' thing he knowed, w'en de ha'd wuk begun
ag'in, he 'skivered dat mos' er his niggers wuz so weak en feeble dat
dey couldn' ha'dly git 'roun' de plantation; 'peared ez ef dey had des
use' up all de strenk dey had, en den des all gun out at once.

"Co'se Mars Donal' got skeert, en 'mence' ter gib' em dey reg'lar
rashuns. But somehow er nuther dey didn' 'pear ter hab no ap'tite, en

dey would n' come fer dey rashuns w'en dey week wuz up, but 'lowed dey had 'nuff ter las' 'em fer a mont'. En meanw'iles dey kep' on gittin po'er an po'er, en weaker en weaker, 'tel Mars Donal' got so skeert he hasten' back ter see ole Aun' Peggy en ax' her ter take dat goopher off'n his niggers.

"Aun' Peggy knowed w'at Mars Donal' had done 'bout cuttin' down de rashuns, but she wa'n't ready to finish up wid Mars Donal' yit; so she didn' let on, but des gun 'im ernudder mixtry, en tol' 'im fer to sprinkle dat on de niggers' nex' rashuns.

"Mars Donal' sprinkle' it on, 'but it did n' do no good, en nex' week he come back ag'in.

"'Dis yer mixtry ain' got no power, Peggy,' sezee. 'It ain' 'sturb' de yuther goopher a-tall.'

"'I doan unnerstan' dis,' sez Aun' Peggy; 'how did you use dat fus' mixtry I gun you?'

"Well, den Mars Donal' 'lowed how he had sprinkle' it on de fus' time, en how it wukked so good dat he had sprinkle' it on de nex' time en cut de rashuns in two ag'in.

"'Uh huh, uh huh!' 'spon' Aun' Peggy, 'look w'at you gone en done! You wa'n't sat'sfied wid w'at I tol' you, en now you gone en got ev'y-thing all mess' up. I knows how to take dat fus' goopher off, but now you gone en double de strenk, en I doan know whuther I kin fin' out how to take it off er no. Anyhow, I got ter wuk my roots fer a week er so befo' I kin tell. En w'ile's I is wukkin', you mought gib yo' niggers sump'n a little better ter eat, en day mought pick up a little. S'posen you tries roas' po'k?'

"So Mars Donal' killt all 'is hawgs en fed his niggers on roas' po'k fer a week; but it didn' do 'em no good, en at de een' er de week he went back ter Aun' Peggy ag'in.

"'I's monst'us sorry,' she sez, 'but it ain' my fault. I's wukkin' my roots ez ha'd ez I kin, but I ain' foun' out how ter take de goopher off yit. S'pos'n you feed yo' han's on roas' beef fer a week er so?'

"So Mars Donal' killt all 'is cows en fed de niggers on roas' beef fer a week, but dey didn' pick up. En all dis time dey wa'n' wukkin', en Mars Donal's craps wuz gittin 'way behin', en he wuz gwine mos' 'tracted fer fear he wuz bleedzd ter lose dem five hund'ed nig-gers w'at he sot so much sto' by. So he goes back ter ole Aun' Peggy ag'in.

"'Peggy,' sezee, 'you is got ter do sump'n fer me, er e'se I'll be in de po'-house fus' thing I know.'

"'Well, suh,' sez Aun' Peggy, 'I's be'n doin' all I knows how, but dey's a root I's bleedzd ter hab, en it doan grow nowhar but down in Robeson County. En I got ter go down dere en gether it on a Friday night in de full er de moon. En I won't be back yer fer a week or ten days.'

"Mars Donal' wuz mos' out'n his min' wid waitin' en losin' money. 'But s'posen dem niggers dies on my han's w'iles you er gone,' sezee, 'w'at is I gwine ter do?'

"Aun' Peggy studied en studied, en den she up en sez, sez she:

"'Well, ef dey dies I reckon you'll hatter bury 'em. Dey is one thing you mought try, en I s'pec's its 'bout de only thing w'at'll keep yo' niggers alibe 'tel I gits back. You mought see ef dey won' eat chick'n.'

"Well, Mars Donal' wanted ter sabe his niggers. Dey wuz all so po' en so skinny en so feeble dat he couldn' sell 'em ter nobody, en dey wouldn' eat muffin' e'se, so he des had ter feed 'em on chick'n. W'en he had use' up all de chick'ns on his place, he went roun' ter his nabers ter buy chick'ns, en dey say dey wuz sorry, but dey'd sol' all dey chick'ns ter a man in town. Mars Donal' went ter dis yer man, en he say dem chick'ns doan b'long ter him but ter ernudder man w'at wuz geth'in' chick'ns fer ter ship ter Wim'l'ton, er de No'f, er some'ers. Mars Donal' say he des bleedzd ter hab chick'ns, en fer dat man to see de yuther gent'eman en ax 'im w'at he'd take fer dem chick'ns. De nex' day de man say Mars Donal' could hab de chick'ns fer so much, w'ich wuz 'bout twicet ez much ez chick'ns had be'n fetchin' in de market befo'. It mos' broke Mars Donal's hea't, but he 'lowed dem chick'ns would las' 'tel Aun' Peggy come back en tuk de goopher off'n de niggers.

"But w'en de een' er de week wuz retch', ole Aun' Peggy hadn' come back, en Mars Donal' had ter hab mo' chick'ns, fer chick'n-meat des barely 'peared ter keep de niggers alibe; en so he went out in de country for ter hunt fer chick'ns. En ev'ywhar he'd go, dis yuther man had be'n befo' 'im en had bought up all de chick'ns, er contracted fer 'em all, en Mars Donal' had ter go back ter dis man in town en pay two prices ter git chick'ns ter feed his niggers.

"De nex' week it wuz de same way, en Mars Donal' 'mence' ter git desp'rit. He sont way off in two er th'ee counties, fer ter hunt chick'ns, but high er low, no matter whar, dis yuther man had be'n befo', 'tel it 'peared lak he had bought up all de chick'ns in No'f Ca'lina.

"But w'at wuz dribin' Mars Donal' mos' crazy wuz de money he had ter spen' fer dese chick'ns. It has mos' broke his hea't fer ter kill all his hawgs, en he had felt wuss w'en he hatter kill all his cows. But w'en dis yer chick'n business begun, it come mighty nigh ruinin' 'im. Fus', he spen' all de money he had saved feedin' de niggers. Den he spent all de money he had in de bank, er sto'ed away. Den he bor-ried all de money he could on his notes, en he des 'bout retch' de pint whar he'd hatter mawgidge his plantation fer ter raise mo' money ter buy chick'ns fer his niggers, w'en one day Aun' Peggy come back fum Robeson County en tol' Mars Donal' she had foun' de root she 'uz lookin' fer, en gun 'im a mixtry fer ter take de goopher off 'n de niggers.

"'Dis yer mixtry'; sez she, "'ll fetch yo' niggers ap'tites back en make 'em eat dey rashuns en git dey strenk ag'in. But you is use' dat yuther mixtry so strong, en put dat goopher on so ha'd, dat I 'magine its got in dey blood, en I's feared dey ain' nobody ner nuffin kin eber take it all off 'n 'em.[5] So I 'spec's you'll hatter gib yo' niggers chick'n at leas' oncet a week ez long ez dey libs, ef you wanter git de wuk out 'n 'em dat you oughter.

"Dey wuz so many niggers on ole Mars Donal's plantation," continued Julius, "en dey got scattered roun' so befo' de wah en sence, dat dey ain' ha'dly no cullu'd folks in No'f Ca'lina but w'at's got some er de blood er dem goophered niggers in dey vames. En so eber sence den, all de niggers in No'f Ca'lina has ter hab chick'n at leas' oncet er week fer ter keep dey healt' en strenk. En dat's w'y cullu' folks laks chick'n mo'd'n w'ite folks."

"What became of Tom and his sweet-heart?" asked my wife.

"Yas'm," said Julius, "I wuz a-comin' ter dat. De nex' week atter de goopher wuz tuk off 'n de niggers, Mars Tom come down ter Aun' Peggy en paid her back de money he borried. En he tol' Aun' Peggy he had made mo' money buyin' chick'ns en sellin' 'em ter his Uncle Donal' dan his daddy had lef' 'im w'en he died, en he say he wuz gwine ter marry Miss 'Liza en buy a big plantation en a lot er niggers en hol' up his head 'mongs' de big w'ite folks des lak he oughter. En he tol' Aun' Peggy he wuz much bleedzd ter her, en ef she got ti'ed cunj'in' en wanter res' en lib easy, she could hab a cabin on his plantation en a stool by his kitchen fiah, en all de chick'n en wheat-bread she wanter eat, en all de terbacker she wanter smoke ez long ez she mought stay in dis worl' er sin en sorrer."

I had occasion to visit the other end of the vineyard shortly after Julius had gone shambling down the yard toward the barn. I left word that the constable should be asked to wait until my return. I was detained longer than I expected, and when I came back I asked if the officer had arrived.

"Yes," my wife replied, "he came."

"Where is he?" I asked.

"Why, he's gone."

"Did he take the chicken-thief?"

"I'll tell you, John," said my wife, with a fine thoughtful look, "I've been thinking more or less about the influence of heredity and environment, and the degree of our responsibility for the things we do, and while I have not been able to get everything reasoned out, I think

5. Julius's tale creates a fabulous mirror on the way that contemporary debates about (as Annie puts it) "the influence of heredity and environment" often devolved into pronouncements about racial predispositions—characteristics that were "in the blood."

I can trust my intuitions. The constable came awhile after you left, but I told him that you had changed your mind, and that he might send in his bill for the time lost and you would pay for it."

"And what am I going to do with Sam Jones?" I asked.

"Oh," she replied, "I told Julius he might unlock the smokehouse and let him go."

The Gray Wolf's Ha'nt[1]

It was a rainy day at the vineyard. The morning had dawned bright and clear. But the sky had soon clouded, and by nine o'clock there was a light shower, followed by others at brief intervals. By noon the rain had settled into a dull, steady downpour. The clouds hung low, and seemed to grow denser instead of lighter as they discharged their watery burden, and there was now and then a muttering of distant thunder. Outdoor work was suspended, and I spent most of the day at the house, looking over my accounts and bringing up some arrears of correspondence.

Towards four o'clock I went out on the piazza, which was broad and dry, and less gloomy than the interior of the house, and composed myself for a quiet smoke. I had lit my cigar and opened the volume I was reading at that time, when my wife, whom I had left dozing on a lounge, came out and took a rocking-chair near me.

"I wish you would talk to me, or read to me—or something," she exclaimed petulantly. "It's awfully dull here to-day."

"I'll read to you with pleasure," I replied, and began at the point where I had found my bookmark:—

"'The difficulty of dealing with transformations so many-sided as those which all existences have undergone, or are undergoing, is such as to make a complete and deductive interpretation almost hopeless. So to grasp the total process of redistribution of matter and motion as to see simultaneously its several necessary results in their actual interdependence is scarcely possible. There is, however, a mode of rendering the process as a whole tolerably comprehensible. Though the genesis of the rearrangement of every evolving aggregate is in itself one, it presents to our intelligence'"—[2]

"John," interrupted my wife, "I wish you would stop reading that nonsense and see who that is coming up the lane."

---

1. Written by Chesnutt in 1898 specifically for *The Conjure Woman*; included as the sixth story of the volume.
2. This passage is drawn from Herbert Spencer's influential *System of Synthetic Philosophy* (1862–1897). John quotes "with pleasure" from Spencer's remarks on "The Interpretation of Evolution" and "The Instability of the Homogenous."

I closed my book with a sigh. I had never been able to interest my wife in the study of philosophy, even when presented in the simplest and most lucid form.

Some one was coming up the lane; at least, a huge faded cotton umbrella was making progress toward the house, and beneath it a pair of nether extremities in trousers was discernible. Any doubt in my mind as to whose they were was soon resolved when Julius reached the steps and, putting the umbrella down, got a good dash of the rain as he stepped up on the porch.

"Why in the world, Julius," I asked, "didn't you keep the umbrella up until you got under cover?"

"It's bad luck, suh, ter raise a' umbrella in de house, en w'iles I dunno whuther it 's bad luck ter kyar one inter de piazzer er no, I 'lows it's alluz bes' ter be on de safe side. I didn' s'pose you en young missis 'u'd be gwine on yo' dribe ter-day, but bein' ez it's my pa't ter take you ef you does, I 'lowed I'd repo't fer dooty, en let you say whuther er no you wants ter go."

"I'm glad you came, Julius," I responded. "We don't want to go driving, of course, in the rain, but I should like to consult you about another matter. I'm thinking of taking in a piece of new ground. What do you imagine it would cost to have that neck of woods down by the swamp cleared up?"

The old man's countenance assumed an expression of unwonted seriousness, and he shook his head doubtfully.

"I dunno 'bout dat, suh. It mought cos' mo', en it mought cos' less, ez fuh ez money is consarned. I ain' denyin' you could cl'ar up dat trac' er lan' fer a hund'ed er a couple er hund'ed dollahs,—ef you wants ter cl'ar it up. But ef dat 'uz my trac' er lan', I wouldn' 'sturb it, no, suh, I wouldn'; sho's you bawn, I wouldn'."

"But why not?" I asked.

"It ain' fittin' fer grapes, fer noo groun' nebber is."

"I know it, but—"

"It ain' no yeathly good fer cotton, 'ca'se it 's too low."

"Perhaps so; but it will raise splendid corn."

"I dunno," rejoined Julius deprecatorily. "It's so nigh de swamp dat de 'coons'll eat up all de cawn."

"I think I'll risk it," I answered.

"Well, suh," said Julius, "I wushes you much joy er yo' job. Ef you has bad luck er sickness er trouble er any kin', doan blame *me*. You can't say ole Julius didn' wa'n you."

"Warn him of what, Uncle Julius?" asked my wife.

"Er de bad luck w'at follers folks w'at 'sturbs dat trac' er lan'. Dey is snakes en sco'pions in dem woods. En ef you manages ter 'scape de p'isen animals, you is des boun' ter hab a ha'nt ter settle wid,—ef you doan hab two."

"Whose haunt?" my wife demanded, with growing interest.

"De gray wolf's ha'nt, some folks calls it,—but I knows better."

"Tell us about it, Uncle Julius," said my wife. "A story will be a godsend to-day."

It was not difficult to induce the old man to tell a story, if he were in a reminiscent mood. Of tales of the old slavery days he seemed indeed to possess an exhaustless store,—some weirdly grotesque, some broadly humorous; some bearing the stamp of truth, faint, perhaps, but still discernible; others palpable inventions, whether his own or not we never knew, though his fancy doubtless embellished them. But even the wildest was not without an element of pathos,— the tragedy, it might be, of the story itself; the shadow, never absent, of slavery and of ignorance; the sadness, always, of life as seen by the fading light of an old man's memory.

"Way back yander befo' de wah," began Julius, "ole Mars Dugal' McAdoo useter own a nigger name' Dan. Dan wuz big en strong en hearty en peaceable en good-nachu'd most er de time, but dange'ous ter aggervate. He alluz done his task, en nebber had no trouble wid de w'ite folks, but woe be unter de nigger w'at 'lowed he c'd fool wid Dan, fer he wuz mos' sho' ter git a good lammin'. Soon ez eve'ybody foun' Dan out, dey didn' many un 'em 'temp' ter 'sturb 'im. De one dat did would 'a' wush' he hadn', ef he could 'a' libbed long ernuff ter do any wushin'.

"It all happen' dis erway. Dey wuz a cunjuh man w'at libbed ober t' other side er de Lumbe'ton Road. He had be'n de only cunjuh doctor in de naber-hood fer lo! dese many yeahs, 'tel ole Aun' Peggy sot up in de bizness down by de Wim'l'ton Road. Dis cunjuh man had a son w'at libbed wid 'im, en it wuz dis yer son w'at got mix' up wid Dan,— en all 'bout a 'oman.

"Dey wuz a gal on de plantation name' Mahaly. She wuz a monst'us lackly gal,—tall en soopl', wid big eyes, en a small foot, en a lively tongue, en w'en Dan tuk ter gwine wid 'er eve'y-body 'lowed dey wuz well match', en none er de yuther nigger men on de plantation das' ter go nigh her, fer dey wuz all feared er Dan.

"Now, it happen' dat dis yer cunjuh man's son wuz gwine 'long de road one day, w'en who sh'd come pas' but Mahaly. En de minute dis man sot eyes on Mahaly, he 'lowed he wuz gwine ter hab her fer hisse'f. He come up side er her en 'mence' ter talk ter her; but she didn' paid no 'tention ter 'im, fer she wuz studyin' 'bout Dan, en she didn' lack dis nigger's looks nohow. So w'en she got ter whar she wuz gwine, dis yer man wa'n't no fu'ther 'long dan he wuz w'en he sta'ted.

"Co'se, atter he had made up his min' fer ter git Mahaly, he 'mence' ter 'quire 'roun', en soon foun' out all 'bout Dan, en w'at a dange'ous nigger he wuz. But dis man 'lowed his daddy wuz a cunjuh man, en so he'd come out all right in de een'; en he kep' right on atter Mahaly.

Meanw'iles Dan's marster had said dey could git married ef dey wanter, en so Dan en Mahaly had tuk up wid one ernudder, en wuz libbin' in a cabin by dey-se'ves, en wuz des wrop' up in one ernudder.

"But dis yer cunjuh man's son didn' 'pear ter min' Dan's takin' up wid Mahaly, en he kep' on hangin' 'roun' des de same, 'tel fin'lly one day Mahaly sez ter Dan, sez she:—

"'I wush you'd do sump'n ter stop dat free nigger man fum follerin' me 'roun'. I doan lack him nohow, en I ain' got no time fer ter was'e wid no man but you.'

"Co'se Dan got mad w'en he heared 'bout dis man pest'rin' Mahaly, en de nex' night, w'en he seed dis nigger comin' 'long de road, he up en ax' 'im w'at he mean by hangin' 'roun' his 'oman. De man didn' 'spon' ter suit Dan, en one wo'd led ter ernudder, 'tel bimeby dis cunjuh man's son pull' out a knife en sta'ted ter stick it in Dan; but befo' he could git it drawed good, Dan haul' off en hit 'im in de head so ha'd dat he nebber got up. Dan 'lowed he'd come to atter a w'ile en go 'long 'bout his bizness, so he went off en lef 'im layin' dere on de groun'.

"De nex' mawnin' de man wuz foun' dead. Dey wuz a great 'miration made 'bout it, but Dan didn' say nuffin, en none er de yuther niggers hadn' seed de fight, so dey wa'n't no way ter tell who done de killin'. En bein' ez it wuz a free nigger, en dey wa'n't no w'ite folks 'speshly int'rusted, dey wa'n't nuffin done 'bout it, en de cunjuh man come en tuk his son en kyared 'im 'way en buried 'im.

"Now, Dan hadn' meant ter kill dis nigger, en w'iles he knowed de man hadn' got no mo' d'n he desarved, Dan 'mence' ter worry mo' er less. Fer he knowed dis man's daddy would wuk his roots en prob'ly fin' out who had killt 'is son, en make all de trouble fer 'im he could. En Dan kep' on studyin' 'bout dis 'tel he got so he didn' ha'dly das' ter eat er drink fer fear dis cunjuh man had p'isen' de vittles er de water. Fin'lly he 'lowed he'd go ter see Aun' Peggy, de noo cunjuh 'oman w'at had moved down by de Wim'l'ton Road, en ax her fer ter do sump'n ter pertec' 'im fum dis cunjuh man. So he tuk a peck er 'taters en went down ter her cabin one night.

"Aun' Peggy heared his tale, en den sez she:—

"'Dat cunjuh man is mo' d'n twice't ez ole ez I is, en he kin make monst'us powe'ful goopher. W'at you needs is a life-cha'm, en I'll make you one ter-morrer; it's de on'y thing w'at'll do you any good. You leabe me a couple er ha'rs fum yo' head, en fetch me a pig ter-morrer night fer ter roas', en w'en you come I'll hab de cha'm all ready fer you.'

"So Dan went down ter Aun' Peggy de nex' night,—wid a young shote,—en Aun' Peggy gun 'im de cha'm. She had tuk de ha'rs Dan had lef' wid 'er, en a piece er red flannin, en some roots en yarbs, en had put 'em in a little bag made out'n 'coon-skin.

"'You take dis cha'm,' sez she, 'en put it in a bottle er a tin box, en bury it deep unner de root er a live-oak tree, en ez long ez it stays dere safe en soun', dey ain' no p'isen kin p'isen you, dey ain' no rattlesnake kin bite you, dey ain' no sco'pion kin sting you. Dis yere cunjuh man mought do one thing er 'nudder ter you, but he can't kill you. So you neenter be at all skeered, but go 'long 'bout yo' bizness en doan bother yo' min'.'

"So Dan went down by de ribber, en 'way up on de bank he buried de cha'm deep unner de root er a live-oak tree, en kivered it up en stomp' de dirt down en scattered leaves ober de spot, en den went home wid his min' easy.

"Sho' 'nuff, dis yer cunjuh man wukked his roots, des ez Dan had 'spected he would, en soon l'arn' who killt his son. En co'se he made up his min' fer ter git eben wid Dan. So he sont a rattlesnake fer ter sting 'im, but de rattlesnake say de nigger's heel wuz so ha'd he couldn' git his sting in. Den he sont his jay-bird fer ter put p'isen in Dan's vittles, but de p'isen did n' wuk. Den de cunjuh man 'low' he'd double Dan all up wid de rheumatiz, so he couldn' git 'is han' ter his mouf ter eat, en would hafter sta've ter def; but Dan went ter Aun' Peggy, en she gun 'im a' 'intment ter kyo de rheumatiz. Den de cunjuh man 'lowed he'd bu'n Dan up wid a fever, but Aun' Peggy tol' 'im how ter make some yarb tea fer dat. Nuffin dis man tried would kill Dan, so fin'lly de cunjuh man 'lowed Dan mus' hab a life-cha'm.

"Now, dis yer jay-bird de cunjuh man had wuz a monst'us sma't creeter,—fac', de niggers 'lowed he wuz de ole Debbil hisse'f, des settin' roun' waitin' ter kyar dis ole man erway w'en he 'd retch' de een' er his rope. De cunjuh man sont dis jay-bird fer ter watch Dan en fin' out whar he kep' his cha'm. De jay-bird hung roun' Dan fer a week er so, en one day he seed Dan go down by de ribber en look at a live-oak tree; en den de jay-bird went back ter his marster, en tol' 'im he 'spec' de nigger kep' his life-cha'm under dat tree.

"De cunjuh man lafft en lafft, en he put on his bigges' pot, en fill' it wid his stronges' roots, en b'iled it en b'iled it, 'tel bimeby de win' blowed en blowed, 'tel it blowed down de live-oak tree. Den he stirred some more roots in de pot, en it rained en rained 'tel de water run down de ribber bank en wash' Dan's life-cha'm inter de ribber, en de bottle went bobbin' down de current des ez onconsarned ez ef it wa'n't takin' po' Dan's chances all 'long wid it. En den de cunjuh man lafft some mo', en 'lowed ter hisse'f dat he wuz gwine ter fix Dan now, sho' 'nuff; he wa'n't gwine ter kill 'im des yet, fer he could do sump'n ter 'im w'at would hu't wusser 'n killin'.

"So dis cunjuh man 'mence' by gwine up ter Dan's cabin eve'y night, en takin' Dan out in his sleep en ridin' 'im roun' de roads en fiel's ober de rough groun'. In de mawnin' Dan would be ez ti'ed ez ef he hadn' be'n ter sleep. Dis kin' er thing kep' up fer a week er so, en

Dan had des 'bout made up his min' fer ter go en see Aun' Peggy
ag'in, w'en who sh'd he come across, gwine 'long de road one day,
to'ds sundown, but dis yer cunjuh man. Dan felt kinder skeered at
fus'; but den he 'membered 'bout his life-cha'm, w'ich he hadn' be'n
ter see fer a week er so, en 'lowed wuz safe en soun' unner de live-
oak tree, en so he hilt up 'is head en walk' 'long, des lack he didn'
keer nuffin 'bout dis man no mo' d'n any yuther nigger. W'en he got
close ter de cunjuh man, dis cunjuh man sez, sezee:—

"'Hoddy, Brer Dan? I hopes you er well?'

"W'en Dan seed de cunjuh man wuz in a good humor en didn'
'pear ter bear no malice, Dan 'lowed mebbe de cunjuh man hadn'
foun' out who killt his son, en so he 'termine' fer ter let on lack he
didn' know nuffin, en so sezee:—

"'Hoddy, Unk' Jube?'—dis ole cunjuh man's name wuz Jube. 'I's
p'utty well, I thank you. How is you feelin' dis mawnin'?'

"'I's feelin' ez well ez a' ole nigger could feel w'at had los' his only
son, en his main 'pen'ence in 'is ole age.

"'But den my son wuz a bad boy,' sezee, 'en I couldn' 'spec' nuffin
e'se. I tried ter l'arn him de arrer er his ways en make him go ter
chu'ch en pra'r-meetin'; but it wa'n't no use. I dunno who killt 'im, en
I doan wanter know, fer I'd be mos' sho' ter fin' out dat my boy had
sta'ted de fuss. Ef I'd 'a' had a son lack you, Brer Dan, I'd 'a' be'n a
proud nigger; oh, yas, I would, sho 's you bawn. But you ain' lookin' ez
well ez you oughter, Brer Dan. Dey's sump'n de matter wid you, en
w'at's mo', I 'spec' you dunno w'at it is.'

"Now, dis yer kin' er talk nach'ly th'owed Dan off'n his gya'd, en
fus' thing he knowed he wuz talkin' ter dis ole cunjuh man des lack
he wuz one er his bes' frien's. He tol' 'im all 'bout not feelin' well in
de mawnin', en ax' 'im ef he could tell w'at wuz de matter wid 'im.

"'Yas,' sez de cunjuh man. 'Dey is a witch be'n ridin' you right
'long. I kin see de marks er de bridle on yo' mouf. En I'll des bet yo'
back is raw whar she's be'n beatin' you.'

"'Yas,' 'spon' Dan, 'so it is.' He hadn' notice it befo', but now he felt
des lack de hide had be'n tuk off'n 'im.

"'En yo' thighs is des raw whar de spurrers has be'n driv' in you,'
sez de cunjuh man. 'You can't see de raw spots, but you kin feel 'em.'

"'Oh, yas,' 'lows Dan, 'dey does hu't pow'ful bad.'

"'En w'at's mo',' sez de cunjuh man, comin' up close ter Dan en
whusp'in' in his yeah, 'I knows who it is be'n ridin' you.'

"'Who is it?' ax' Dan. 'Tell me who it is.'

"'It's a' ole nigger 'oman down by Rockfish Crick. She had a pet
rabbit, en you cotch' 'im one day, en she's been squarin' up wid you
eber sence. But you better stop her, er e'se you'll be rid ter def in a
mont' er so.'

"'No,' sez Dan, 'she can't kill me, sho'.'

"'I dunno how dat is,' said de cunjuh man, 'but she kin make yo' life mighty mis'able. Ef I wuz in yo' place, I'd stop her right off.'

"'But how is I gwine ter stop her?' ax' Dan. 'I dunno nuffin 'bout stoppin' witches.'

"'Look a heah, Dan,' sez de yuther; 'you is a good young man. I lacks you monst'us well. Fac', I feels lack some er dese days I mought buy you fum yo' marster, ef I could eber make money ernuff at my biz-ness dese hard times, en 'dop' you fer my son. I lacks you so well dat I'm gwine ter he'p you git rid er dis yer witch fer good en all; fer des ez long ez she libs, you is sho' ter hab trouble, en trouble, en mo' trouble.'

"'You is de bes' frien' I got, Unk' Jube,' sez Dan, 'en I'll 'member yo' kin'ness ter my dyin' day. Tell me how I kin git rid er dis yer ole witch w'at's be'n ridin' me so ha'd.'

"'In de fus' place,' sez de cunjuh man, 'dis ole witch nebber comes in her own shape, but eve'y night, at ten o'clock, she tu'ns herse'f inter a black cat, en runs down ter yo' cabin en bridles you, en mounts you, en dribes you out th'oo de chimbly, en rides you ober de roughes' places she kin fin'. All you got ter do is ter set fer her in de bushes 'side er yo' cabin, en hit her in de head wid a rock er a lighterd-knot w'en she goes pas'.'

"'But,' sez Dan, 'how kin I see her in de da'k? En s'posen I hits at her en misses her? Er s'posen I des woun's her, en she gits erway,— w'at she gwine do ter me den?'

"'I is done studied 'bout all dem things,' sez de cunjuh man, 'en it 'pears ter me de bes' plan fer you ter foller is ter lemme tu'n you ter some creetur w'at kin see in de da'k, en w'at kin run des ez fas' ez a cat, en w'at kin bite, en bite fer ter kill; en den you won't hafter hab no trouble atter de job is done. I dunno whuther you'd lack dat er no, but dat is de sho'es' way.'

"'I doan keer,' 'spon' Dan. 'I'd des ez lief be anything fer a' hour er so, ef I kin kill dat ole witch. You kin do des w'at you er mineter.'

"'All right, den,' sez de cunjuh man, 'you come down ter my cabin at half-past nine o'clock ter-night, en I'll fix you up.'

"Now, dis cunjuh man, w'en he had got th'oo talkin' wid Dan, kep' on down de road 'long de side er de plantation, 'tel he met Mahaly comin' home fum wuk des atter sundown.

"'Hoddy do, ma'm,' sezee; 'is yo' name Sis' Mahaly, w'at b'longs ter Mars Dugal' McAdoo?'

"'Yas,' 'spon' Mahaly, 'dat's my name, en I b'longs ter Mars Dugal'.'

"'Well,' sezee, 'yo' husban' Dan wuz down by my cabin dis ebenin', en he got bit by a spider er sump'n, en his foot is swoll' up so he can't walk. En he ax' me fer ter fin' you en fetch you down dere ter he'p 'im home.'

"Co'se Mahaly wanter see w'at had happen' ter Dan, en so she sta'ted down de road wid de cunjuh man. Ez soon ez he got her inter his cabin, he shet de do', en sprinkle' some goopher mixtry on her, en tu'nt her ter a black cat. Den he tuk 'n put her in a bairl, en put a bo'd on de bairl, en a rock on de bo'd, en lef' her dere 'tel he got good en ready fer ter use her.

"'Long 'bout half-pas' nine o'clock Dan come down ter de cunjuh man's cabin. It wuz a wa'm night, en de do' wuz stan'in' open. De cunjuh man 'vited Dan ter come in, en pass' de time er day wid 'im. Ez soon ez Dan 'mence' talkin', he heared a cat miauin' en scratchin' en gwine on at a tarrable rate.

"'Wat's all dat fuss 'bout?' ax' Dan.

"'Oh, dat ain' nuffin but my ole gray tomcat,' sez de cunjuh man. 'I has ter shet 'im up sometimes fer ter keep 'im in nights, en co'se he doan lack it.

"'Now,' 'lows de cunjuh man, 'lemme tell you des w'at you is got ter do. W'en you ketches dis witch, you mus' take her right by de th'oat en bite her right th'oo de neck. Be sho' yo' teef goes th'oo at de fus' bite, en den you won't nebber be bothe'd no mo' by dat witch. En w'en you git done, come back heah en I'll tu'n you ter yo'se'f ag'in, so you kin go home en git yo' night's res'.'

"Den de cunjuh man gun Dan sump'n nice en sweet ter drink out'n a new go'd, en in 'bout a minute Dan foun' hisse'f tu'nt ter a gray wolf; en soon ez he felt all fo' er his noo feet on de groun', he sta'ted off fas' ez he could fer his own cabin, so he could be sho' en be dere time ernuff ter ketch de witch, en put a' een' ter her kyarin's-on.

"Ez soon ez Dan wuz gone good, de cunjuh man tuk de rock off'n de bo'd, en de bo'd off'n de bairl, en out le'p' Mahaly en sta'ted fer ter go home, des lack a cat er a 'oman er anybody e'se would w'at wuz in trouble; en it wa'n't many minutes befo' she wuz gwine up de path ter her own do'.

"Meanw'iles, w'en Dan had retch' de cabin, he had hid hisse'f in a bunch er jimson weeds in de ya'd. He hadn' wait' long befo' he seed a black cat run up de path to'ds de do'. Des ez soon ez she got close ter 'im, he le'p' out en ketch' her by de th'oat, en got a grip on her, des lack de cunjuh man had tol' 'im ter do. En lo en behol'! no sooner had de blood 'mence' ter flow dan de black cat tu'nt back ter Mahaly, en Dan seed dat he had killt his own wife. En w'iles her bref wuz gwine she call' out:

"'O Dan! O my husban'! come en he'p me! come en sabe me fum dis wolf w'at's killin' me!'

"W'en po' Dan sta'ted to'ds her, ez any man nach'ly would, it des made her holler wuss en wuss; fer she didn' knowed dis yer wolf wuz her Dan. En Dan des had ter hide in de weeds, en grit his teef en hol' hisse'f in, 'tel she passed out'n her mis'ry, callin' fer Dan ter de las', en wond'rin' w'y he did n' come en he'p her. En Dan 'lowed ter hisse'f he'd ruther 'a' be'n killt a dozen times 'n ter 'a' done w'at he had ter Mahaly.

"Dan wuz mighty nigh 'stracted, but w'en Mahaly wuz dead en he got his min' straighten' out a little, it didn' take 'im mo' d'n a minute er so fer ter see th'oo all de cunjuh man's lies, en how de cunjuh man had fooled 'im en made 'im kill Mahaly, fer ter git eben wid 'im fer killin' er his son. He kep' gittin' madder en madder, en Mahaly hadn' much mo' d'n drawed her' las bref befo' he sta'ted back ter de cunjuh man's cabin ha'd ez he could run.

"W'en he got dere, de do' wuz stan'in' open; a lighterd-knot wuz flick'rin' on de h'a'th, en de ole cunjuh man wuz settin' dere noddin' in de corner. Dan le'p' in de do' en jump' fer dis man's th'oat, en got de same grip on 'im w'at de cunjuh man had tol' 'im 'bout half a' hour befo'. It wuz ha'd wuk dis time, fer de ole man's neck wuz monst'us tough en stringy, but Dan hilt on long ernuff ter be sho' his job wuz done right. En eben den he didn' hol' on long ernuff; fer w'en he tu'nt de cunjuh man loose en he fell ober on de flo', de cunjuh man rollt his eyes at Dan, en sezee:—

"'I's eben wid you, Brer Dan, en you er eben wid me; you killt my son en I killt yo' 'oman. En ez I doan want no mo' d'n w'at 's fair 'bout dis thing, ef you'll retch up wid yo' paw en take down dat go'd hangin' on dat peg ober de chimbly, en take a sip er dat mixtry, it'll tu'n you back ter a nigger ag'in, en I kin die mo' sad'sfied 'n ef I lef' you lack you is.'

"Dan nebber 'lowed fer a minute dat a man would lie wid his las' bref, en co'se he seed de sense er gittin' tu'nt back befo' de cunjuh man died; so he clumb on a chair en retch' fer de go'd, en tuk a sip er de mixtry. En ez soon ez he 'd done dat de cunjuh man lafft his las' laf, en gapsed out wid 'is las' gaps:—

"'Uh huh! I reckon I's square wid you now fer killin' me, too; fer dat goopher on you is done fix' en sot now fer good, en all de cunj'in' in de worl' won't nebber take it off.

'Wolf you is en wolf you stays,
All de rest er yo' bawn days.'

"Co'se Brer Dan couldn' do nuffin. He knowed it wa'n't no use, but he clumb up on de chimbly en got down de go'ds en bottles en yuther cunjuh fixin's, en tried 'em all on hisse'f, but dey didn' do no good. Den he run down ter ole Aun' Peggy, but she didn' know de wolf langwidge, en couldn't 'a' tuk off dis yuther goopher nohow, eben ef she'd 'a' unnerstood w'at Dan wuz sayin'. So po' Dan wuz bleedgd ter be a wolf all de rest er his bawn days.

"Dey foun' Mahaly down by her own cabin nex' mawnin', en eve'y-body made a great 'miration 'bout how she'd be'n killt. De niggers 'lowed a wolf had bit her. De w'ite folks say no, dey ain' be'n no wolves 'roun' dere fer ten yeahs er mo'; en dey didn' know w'at ter make out'n it. En w'en dey couldn' fin' Dan nowhar, dey 'lowed he'd

quo'lled wid Mahaly en killt her, en run erway; en dey didn' know
w'at ter make er dat, fer Dan en Mahaly wuz de mos' lovin' couple on
de plantation. Dey put de dawgs on Dan's scent, en track' 'im down
ter ole Unk' Jube's cabin, en foun' de ole man dead, en dey didn'
know w'at ter make er dat; en den Dan's scent gun out, en dey didn'
know w'at ter make er dat. Mars Dugal' tuk on a heap 'bout losin' two
er his bes' han's in one day, en ole missis 'lowed it wuz a jedgment on
'im fer sump'n he 'd done. But dat fall de craps wuz monst'us big, so
Mars Dugal' say de Lawd had temper' de win' ter de sho'n ram, en
make up ter 'im fer w'at he had los'.

"Dey buried Mahaly down in dat piece er low groun' you er talkin'
'bout cl'arin' up. Ez fer po' Dan, he didn' hab nowhar e'se ter go, so
he des stayed 'roun' Mahaly's grabe, w'en he wa'n't out in de yuther
woods gittin' sump'n ter eat. En sometimes, w'en night would come,
de niggers useter heah him howlin' en howlin' down dere, des fittin'
ter break his hea't. En den some mo' un 'em said dey seed Mahaly's
ha'nt dere 'bun'ance er times, colloguin'[3] wid dis gray wolf. En eben
now, fifty yeahs sence, long atter ole Dan has died en dried up in de
woods, his ha'nt en Mahaly's hangs 'roun' dat piece er low groun', en
eve'body w'at goes 'bout dere has some bad luck er 'nuther; fer ha'nts
doan lack ter be 'sturb' on dey own stompin'-groun'."

The air had darkened while the old man related this harrowing
tale. The rising wind whistled around the eaves, slammed the loose
window-shutters, and, still increasing, drove the rain in fiercer gusts
into the piazza. As Julius finished his story and we rose to seek shelter within doors, the blast caught the angle of some chimney or
gable in the rear of the house, and bore to our ears a long, wailing
note, an epitome, as it were, of remorse and hopelessness.

"Dat's des lack po' ole Dan useter howl," observed Julius, as he
reached for his umbrella, "en w'at I be'n tellin' you is de reason I
doan lack ter see dat neck er woods cl'ared up. Co'se it b'longs ter
you, en a man kin do ez he choose' wid 'is own. But ef you gits
rheumatiz er fever en agur, er ef you er snake-bit er p'isen' wid some
yarb er 'nuther, er ef a tree falls on you, er a ha'nt runs you en makes
you git 'stracted in yo' min', lack some folks I knows w'at went foolin'
'roun' dat piece er lan', you can't say I neber wa'ned you, suh, en tol'
you w'at you mought look fer en be sho' ter fin'."

When I cleared up the land in question, which was not until the following year, I recalled the story Julius had told us, and looked in vain
for a sunken grave or perhaps a few weather-bleached bones of some
denizen of the forest. I cannot say, of course, that some one had not
been buried there; but if so, the hand of time had long since removed

3. Julius creates a verb form of the noun "colloquy."

any evidence of the fact. If some lone wolf, the last of his pack, had once made his den there, his bones had long since crumbled into dust and gone to fertilize the rank vegetation that formed the under-growth of this wild spot. I did find, however, a bee-tree in the woods, with an ample cavity in its trunk, and an opening through which convenient access could be had to the stores of honey within. I have reason to believe that ever since I had bought the place, and for many years before, Julius had been getting honey from this tree. The gray wolf's haunt had doubtless proved useful in keeping off too inquisitive people, who might have interfered with his monopoly.

Mars Jeems's Nightmare[1]

We found old Julius very useful when we moved to our new residence. He had a thorough knowledge of the neighborhood, was familiar with the roads and the watercourses, knew the qualities of the various soils and what they would produce, and where the best hunting and fishing were to be had. He was a marvelous hand in the management of horses and dogs, with whose mental processes he manifested a greater familiarity than mere use would seem to account for, though it was doubtless due to the simplicity of a life that had kept him close to nature. Toward my tract of land and the things that were on it—the creeks, the swamps, the hills, the meadows, the stones, the trees—he maintained a peculiar personal attitude, that might be called predial rather than proprietary.[2] He had been accustomed, until long after middle life, to look upon himself as the property of another. When this relation was no longer possible, owing to the war, and to his master's death and the dispersion of the family, he had been unable to break off entirely the mental habits of a lifetime, but had attached himself to the old plantation, of which he seemed to consider himself an appurtenance. We found him useful in many ways and entertaining in others, and my wife and I took quite a fancy to him.

Shortly after we became established in our home on the sand-hills, Julius brought up to the house one day a colored boy of about seventeen, whom he introduced as his grandson, and for whom he solicited employment. I was not favorably impressed by the youth's appearance,—quite the contrary, in fact; but mainly to please the old man I hired Tom—his name was Tom[3]—to help about the stables,

---

1. Written by Chesnutt in 1898 for *The Conjure Woman*; included as the third story of the volume.
2. John characterizes Julius's attitude toward the land as more closely connected with serf-dom on it ("predial"), than with ownership of it ("proprietary").
3. With John's repetition, Chesnutt stresses the overdetermination—post–*Uncle Tom's Cabin*—of "Tom" as a name for an African American man.

weed the garden, cut wood and bring water, and in general to make himself useful about the outdoor work of the household.

My first impression of Tom proved to be correct. He turned out to be very trifling, and I was much annoyed by his laziness, his carelessness, and his apparent lack of any sense of responsibility. I kept him longer than I should, on Julius's account, hoping that he might improve; but he seemed to grow worse instead of better, and when I finally reached the limit of my patience, I discharged him.

"I am sorry, Julius," I said to the old man; "I should have liked to oblige you by keeping him; but I can't stand Tom any longer. He is absolutely untrustworthy."

"Yas, suh," replied Julius, with a deep sigh and a long shake of the head, "I knows he ain' much account, en dey ain' much 'pen'ence ter be put on 'im. But I wuz hopin' dat you mought make some 'lowance fuh a' ign'ant young nigger, suh, en gib 'im one mo' chance."

But I had hardened my heart. I had always been too easily imposed upon, and had suffered too much from this weakness. I determined to be firm as a rock in this instance.

"No, Julius," I rejoined decidedly, "it is impossible. I gave him more than a fair trial, and he simply won't do."

When my wife and I set out for our drive in the cool of the evening,—afternoon is "evening" in Southern parlance,—one of the servants put into the rockaway two large earthenware jugs. Our drive was to be down through the swamp to the mineral spring at the foot of the sand-hills beyond. The water of this spring was strongly impregnated with sulphur and iron, and, while not particularly agreeable of smell or taste, was used by us, in moderation, for sanitary reasons.

When we reached the spring, we found a man engaged in cleaning it out. In answer to an inquiry he said that if we would wait five or ten minutes, his task would be finished and the spring in such condition that we could fill our jugs. We might have driven on, and come back by way of the spring, but there was a bad stretch of road beyond, and we concluded to remain where we were until the spring should be ready. We were in a cool and shady place. It was often necessary to wait awhile in North Carolina; and our Northern energy had not been entirely proof against the influences of climate and local custom.

While we sat there, a man came suddenly around a turn of the road ahead of us. I recognized in him a neighbor with whom I had exchanged formal calls. He was driving a horse, apparently a high-spirited creature, possessing, so far as I could see at a glance, the marks of good temper and good breeding; the gentleman, I had heard it suggested, was slightly deficient in both. The horse was rearing and plunging, and the man was beating him furiously with a buggy-whip.

When he saw us, he flushed a fiery red, and, as he passed, held the
reins with one hand, at some risk to his safety, lifted his hat, and
bowed somewhat constrainedly as the horse darted by us, still pant-
ing and snorting with fear.

"He looks as though he were ashamed of himself," I observed.

"I'm sure he ought to be," exclaimed my wife indignantly. "I think
there is no worse sin and no more disgraceful thing than cruelty."

"I quite agree with you," I assented.

"A man w'at 'buses his hoss is gwine ter be ha'd on de folks w'at
wuks fer 'im," remarked Julius. "Ef young Mistah McLean doan
min', he'll hab a bad dream one er dese days, des lack 'is grandaddy
had way back yander, long yeahs befo' de wah."

"What was it about Mr. McLean's dream, Julius?" I asked. The
man had not yet finished cleaning the spring, and we might as well
put in time listening to Julius as in any other way. We had found
some of his plantation tales quite interesting.

"Mars Jeems[4] McLean," said Julius, "wuz de grandaddy er dis yer
gent'eman w'at is des gone by us beatin' his hoss. He had a big plantation en a heap er niggers. Mars Jeems wuz a ha'd man, en monst'us
stric' wid his han's. Eber sence he growed up he nebber 'peared ter
hab no feelin' fer nobody. W'en his daddy, ole Mars John McLean,
died, de plantation en all de niggers fell ter young Mars Jeems. He
had be'n bad 'nuff befo', but it wa'n't long atterwa'ds 'tel he got so
dey wuz no use in libbin' at all ef you ha' ter lib roun' Mars Jeems.
His niggers wuz bleedzd ter slabe fum daylight ter da'k, w'iles yuther
folks's didn' hafter wuk 'cep'n' fum sun ter sun;[5] en dey didn' git no
mo' ter eat dan dey oughter, en dat de coa'ses' kin'! Dey wa'n't 'lowed
ter sing, ner dance, ner play de banjo w'en Mars Jeems wuz roun' de
place; fer Mars Jeems say he wouldn' hab no sech gwines-on,—said
he bought his han's ter wuk, en not ter play, en w'en night come dey
mus' sleep en res', so dey'd be ready ter git up soon in de mawnin' en
go ter dey wuk fresh en strong.

"Mars Jeems didn' 'low no co'tin' er juneseyin' roun' his plantation,—said he wanted his niggers ter put dey min's on dey wuk, en
not be wastin' dey time wid no sech foolis'ness. En he wouldn' let his
han's git married,—said he wuzn' raisin' niggers, but wuz raisin' cotton. En w'eneber any er de boys en gals 'ud 'mence ter git sweet on
one ernudder, he'd sell one er de yuther un 'em, er sen' 'em way
down in Robeson County ter his yuther plantation, whar dey could
n' nebber see one ernudder.

---

4. James.
5. Julius draws a distinction between being required to work all day long (from sun to sun),
   and the more draconian system of being required to work as well during the dawn and
   twilight hours (from daylight to dark).

"Ef any er de niggers eber complained, dey got fo'ty; so co'se dey didn' many un 'em complain. But dey didn' lack it, des de same, en nobody couldn' blame 'em, fer dey had a ha'd time. Mars Jeems didn' make no 'lowance fer nachul bawn laz'ness, ner sickness, ner trouble in de min', ner nuffin; he wuz des gwine ter git so much wuk outer eve'y han', er know de reason w'y.

"Dey wuz one time de niggers 'lowed, fer a spell, dat Mars Jeems mought git bettah. He tuk a lackin' ter Mars Marrabo McSwayne's oldes' gal, Miss Libbie, en useter go ober dere eve'y day er eve'y ebenin', en folks said dey wuz gwine ter git married sho'. But it 'pears dat Miss Libbie heared 'bout de gwines-on on Mars Jeems's plantation, en she des 'lowed she couldn' trus' herse'f wid no sech a man; dat he mought git so useter 'busin' his niggers dat he'd 'mence ter 'buse his wife atter he got useter habbin' her roun' de house. So she 'clared she wuzn' gwine ter hab nuffin mo' ter do wid young Mars Jeems.

"De niggers wuz all monst'us sorry w'en de match wuz bust' up, fer now Mars Jeems got wusser 'n he wuz befo' he sta'ted sweethea'tin'. De time he useter spen' co'tin' Miss Libbie he put in findin' fault wid de niggers, en all his bad feelin's 'ca'se Miss Libbie th'owed 'im ober he 'peared ter try ter wuk off on de po' niggers.

"W'iles Mars Jeems wuz co'tin' Miss Libbie, two er de han's on de plantation had got ter settin' a heap er sto' by one ernudder. One un 'em wuz name' Solomon, en de yuther wuz a 'oman w'at wukked in de fiel' 'long er 'im—I fe'git dat 'oman's name, but it doan 'mount ter much in de tale nohow. Now, whuther 'ca'se Mars Jeems wuz so tuk up wid his own junesey dat he didn' paid no 'tention fer a w'ile ter w'at wuz gwine on 'twix' Solomon en his junesey, er whuther his own co'tin' made 'im kin' er easy on de co'tin' in de qua'ters, dey ain' no tellin'. But dey's one thing sho', dat w'en Miss Libbie th'owed 'im ober, he foun' out 'bout Solomon en de gal monst'us quick, en gun Solomon fo'ty, en sont de gal down ter de Robeson County planta-tion, en tol' all de niggers ef he ketch 'em at any mo' sech foolish-ness, he wuz gwine ter skin 'em alibe en tan dey hides befo' dey ve'y eyes. Co'se he wouldn' 'a' done it, but he mought 'a' made things wusser 'n dey wuz. So you kin 'magine dey wa'n't much lub-makin' in de qua'ters fer a long time.

"Mars Jeems useter go down ter de yuther plantation sometimes fer a week er mo', en so he had ter hab a oberseah ter look atter his wuk w'iles he 'uz gone. Mars Jeems's oberseah wuz a po' w'ite man name' Nick Johnson,—de niggers called 'im Mars Johnson ter his face, but behin' his back dey useter call 'im Ole Nick, en de name suited 'im ter a T. He wuz wusser 'n Mars Jeems ever da'ed to be. Co'se de darkies didn' lack de way Mars Jeems used 'em, but he wuz de marster, en had a right ter do ez he please'; but dis yer Ole Nick wa'n't nuffin but a po' buckrah, en all de niggers 'spised 'im ez much

ez dey hated 'im, fer he did n' own nobody, en wa'n't no bettah 'n a
nigger, fer in dem days any 'spectable pusson would ruther be a nigger dan a po' w'ite man.

"Now, atter Solomon's gal had be'n sont away, he kep' feelin' mo'
en mo' bad erbout it, 'tel fin'lly he 'lowed he wuz gwine ter see ef dey
couldn' be sump'n done fer ter git 'er back, en ter make Mars Jeems
treat de darkies bettah. So he tuk a peck er co'n out'n de ba'n one
night, en went ober ter see ole Aun' Peggy, de free-nigger cunjuh
'oman down by de Wim'l'ton Road.

"Aun' Peggy listen' ter 'is tale, en ax' him some queshtuns, en den
tol' 'im she 'd wuk her roots, en see w'at dey'd say 'bout it, en ter-
morrer night he sh'd come back ag'in en fetch ernudder peck er co'n,
en den she'd hab sump'n fer ter tell 'im.

"So Solomon went back de nex' night, en sho' 'nuff, Aun' Peggy tol'
'im w'at ter do. She gun 'im some stuff w'at look' lack it be'n made by
poundin' up some roots en yarbs wid a pestle in a mo'tar.

"'Dis yer stuff,' sez she, 'is monst'us pow'ful kin' er goopher. You
take dis home, en gin it ter de cook, ef you kin trus' her, en tell her
fer ter put it in yo' marster's soup de fus' cloudy day he hab okra soup
fer dinnah. Min' you follers de d'rections.'

"'It ain' gwineter p'isen 'im, is it?' ax' Solomon, gittin' kin' er
skeered; fer Solomon wuz a good man, en didn' want ter do nobody
no rale ha'm.

"'Oh, no,' sez ole Aun' Peggy, 'it's gwine ter do 'im good, but he'll
hab a monst'us bad dream fus'. A mont' fum now you come down
heah en lemme know how de goopher is wukkin'. Fer I ain' done
much er dis kin' er cunj'in' er late yeahs, en I has ter kinder keep
track un it ter see dat it doan 'complish no mo' d'n I 'lows fer it ter
do. En I has ter be kinder keerful 'bout cunj'in' w'ite folks; so be
sho' en lemme know, w'ateber you do, des w'at is gwine on roun' de
plantation.'

"So Solomon say all right, en tuk de goopher mixtry up ter de big
house en gun it ter de cook, en tol' her fer ter put it in Mars Jeems's
soup de fus' cloudy day she hab okra soup fer dinnah. It happen' dat
de ve'y nex' day wuz a cloudy day, en so de cook made okra soup fer
Mars Jeems's dinnah, en put de powder Solomon gun her inter de
soup, en made de soup rale good, so Mars Jeems eat a whole lot of it
en 'peared ter enjoy it.

"De nex' mawnin' Mars Jeems tol' de oberseah he wuz gwine 'way on
some bizness, en den he wuz gwine ter his yuther plantation, down in
Robeson County, en he didn' 'spec' he 'd be back fer a mont' er so.

"'But,' sezee, 'I wants you ter run dis yer plantation for all it 's
wuth. Dese yer niggers is gittin' monst'us triflin' en lazy en keerless,
en dey ain' no 'pen'ence ter be put in 'em. I wants dat stop', en w'iles
I 'm gone erway I wants de 'spenses cut 'way down en a heap mo' wuk

done. Fac', I wants dis yer plantation ter make a reco'd dat'll show w'at kinder oberseah you is.'

"Ole Nick didn' said nuffin but 'Yas, suh,' but de way he kinder grin' ter hisse'f en show' his big yaller teef, en snap' de rawhide he useter kyar roun' wid 'im, made col' chills run up and down de backbone er dem niggers w'at heared Mars Jeems a-talkin'. En dat night dey wuz mo'nin' en groanin' down in de qua'ters, fer de niggers all knowed w'at wuz comin'.

"So, sho' 'nuff, Mars Jeems went erway nex' mawnin', en de trouble begun. Mars Johnson sta'ted off de ve'y fus' day fer ter see w'at he could hab ter show Mars Jeems w'en he come back. He made de tasks bigger en de rashuns littler, en w'en de niggers had wukked all day, he'd fin' sump'n fer 'em ter do roun' de ba'n er som'ers atter da'k, fer ter keep 'em busy a' hour er so befo' dey went ter sleep.

"About th'ee er fo' days atter Mars Jeems went erway, young Mars Dunkin McSwayne rode up ter de big house one day wid a nigger settin' behin' 'im in de buggy, tied ter de seat, en ax' ef Mars Jeems wuz home. Mars Johnson wuz at de house, and he say no.

"'Well,' sez Mars Dunkin, sezee, 'I fotch dis nigger ober ter Mistah McLean fer ter pay a bet I made wid 'im las' week w'en we wuz playin' kya'ds te'gedder. I bet 'im a nigger man, en heah's one I reckon'll fill de bill. He wuz tuk up de yuther day fer a stray nigger, en he couldn' gib no 'count er hisse'f, en so he wuz sol' at oction, en I bought 'im. He's kinder brash, but I knows yo' powers, Mistah Johnson, en I reckon ef anybody kin make 'im toe de ma'k, you is de man.'

"Mars Johnson grin' one er dem grins w'at show' all his snaggle teef, en make de niggers 'low he look lack de ole debbil, en sezee ter Mars Dunkin:—

"'I reckon you kin trus' me, Mistah Dunkin, fer ter tame any nigger wuz eber bawn. De nigger doan lib w'at I can't take down in 'bout fo' days.'

"Well, Ole Nick had 'is han's full long er dat noo nigger; en w'iles de res' er de darkies wuz sorry fer de po' man, dey 'lowed he kep' Mars Johnson so busy dat dey got along better 'n dey'd 'a' done ef de noo nigger had nebber come.

"De fus' thing dat happen', Mars Johnson sez ter dis yer noo man:—

"'W'at 's yo' name, Sambo?'[6]

"'My name ain' Sambo,' 'spon' de noo nigger.

"'Did I ax you w'at yo' name wa'n't?' sez Mars Johnson. 'You wants ter be pa'tic'lar how you talks ter me. Now, w'at is yo' name, en whar did you come fum?'

"'I dunno my name,' sez de nigger, 'en I doan 'member whar I come fum. My head is all kin' er mix' up.'

6. Like "Tom," another stereotypical name for an African American man.

"'Yas,' sez Mars Johnson, 'I reckon I'll ha' ter gib you sump'n fer ter cl'ar yo' head. At de same time, it'll l'arn you some manners, en atter dis mebbe you'll say "suh" w'en you speaks ter me.'

"Well, Mars Johnson haul' off wid his rawhide en hit de noo nigger once. De noo man look' at Mars Johnson fer a minute ez ef he didn' know w'at ter make er dis yer kin' er l'arnin'. But w'en de oberseah raise' his w'ip ter hit him ag'in, de noo nigger des haul' off en made fer Mars Johnson, en ef some er de yuther niggers hadn' stop' 'im, it 'peared ez ef he mought 'a' made it wa'm fer Ole Nick dere fer a w'ile. But de oberseah made de yuther niggers he'p tie de noo nigger up, en den gun 'im fo'ty, wid a dozen er so th'owed in fer good measure, fer Ole Nick wuz nebber stingy wid dem kin' er rashuns. De nigger went on at a tarrable rate, des lack a wil' man, but co'se he wuz bleedzd ter take his med'cine, fer he wuz tied up en could n' he'p hisse'f.

"Mars Johnson lock' de noo nigger up in de ba'n, en didn' gib 'im nuffin ter eat fer a day er so, 'tel he got 'im kin'er quiet' down, en den he tu'nt 'im loose en put 'im ter wuk. De nigger 'lowed he wa'n't useter wukkin', en wouldn' wuk, en Mars Johnson gun 'im anudder fo'ty fer laziness en impidence, en let 'im fas' a day er so mo', en den put 'im ter wuk ag'in. De nigger went ter wuk, but did n' 'pear ter know how ter han'le a hoe. It tuk des 'bout half de oberseah's time lookin' atter 'im, en dat po' nigger got mo' lashin's en cussin's en cuffin's dan any fo' yuthers on de plantation. He didn' mix' wid ner talk much ter de res' er de niggers, en couldn' 'pear ter git it th'oo his min' dat he wuz a slabe en had ter wuk en min' de w'ite folks, spite er de fac' dat Ole Nick gun 'im a lesson eve'y day. En fin'lly Mars Johnson 'lowed dat he couldn' do nuffin wid 'im; dat ef he wuz his nigger, he'd break his sperrit er break 'is neck, one er de yuther. But co'se he wuz only sont ober on trial, en ez he didn' gib sat'sfaction, en he hadn' heared fum Mars Jeems 'bout w'en he wuz comin' back; en ez he wuz feared he'd git mad some time er 'nuther en kill de nigger befo' he knowed it, he 'lowed he'd better sen' 'im back whar he come fum. So he tied 'im up en sont 'im back ter Mars Dunkin.

"Now, Mars Dunkin McSwayne wuz one er dese yer easy-gwine gent'emen w'at didn' lack ter hab no trouble wid niggers er nobody e'se, en he knowed ef Mars Ole Nick couldn' git 'long wid dis nigger, nobody could. So he tuk de nigger ter town dat same day, en sol' 'im ter a trader w'at wuz gittin' up a gang er lackly niggers fer ter ship off on de steamboat ter go down de ribber ter Wim'l'ton en fum dere ter Noo Orleens.

"De nex' day atter de noo man had be'n sont away, Solomon wuz wukkin' in de cotton-fiel', en w'en he got ter de fence nex' ter de woods, at de een' er de row, who sh'd he see on de yuther side but ole Aun' Peggy. She beckon' ter 'im,—de oberseah wuz down on de yuther side er de fiel',—en sez she:—

"'W'y ain' you done come en 'po'ted ter me lack I tol' you?'

"'W'y, law! Aun' Peggy,' sez Solomon, 'dey ain' nuffin ter 'po't. Mars Jeems went away de day atter we gun 'im de goopher mixtry, en we ain' seed hide ner hair un 'im sence, en co'se we doan know nuffin 'bout w'at 'fec' it had on 'im.'

"'I doan keer nuffin 'bout yo' Mars Jeems now; w'at I wants ter know is w'at is be'n gwine on 'mongs' de niggers. Has you be'n gittin' 'long any better on de plantation?'

"'No, Aun' Peggy, we be'n gittin' 'long wusser. Mars Johnson is stric'er 'n he eber wuz befo', en de po' niggers doan ha'dly git time ter draw dey bref, en dey 'lows dey mought des ez well be dead ez alibe.'

"'Uh huh!' sez Aun' Peggy, sez she, 'I tol' you dat 'uz monst'us pow'-ful goopher, en its wuk doan 'pear all at once.'

"'Long ez we had dat noo nigger heah,' Solomon went on, 'he kep' Mars Johnson busy pa't er de time; but now he 's gone erway, I s'pose de res' un us'll ketch it wusser 'n eber.'

"'W'at's gone wid de noo nigger?' sez Aun' Peggy, rale quick, battin' her eyes en straight'nin' up.

"'Ole Nick done sont 'im back ter Mars Dunkin, who had fotch 'im heah fer ter pay a gamblin' debt ter Mars Jeems,' sez Solomon, 'en I heahs Mars Dunkin has sol' 'im ter a nigger-trader up in Patesville, w'at 's gwine ter ship 'im off wid a gang ter-morrer.'

"Ole Aun' Peggy 'peared ter git rale stirred up w'en Solomon tol' 'er dat, en sez she, shakin' her stick at 'im:—

"'W'y didn' you come en tell me 'bout dis noo nigger bein' sol' erway? Didn' you promus me, ef I 'd gib you dat goopher, you 'd come en 'po't ter me 'bout all w'at wuz gwine on on dis plantation? Co'se I could 'a' foun' out fer myse'f, but I 'pended on yo' tellin' me, en now by not doin' it I's feared you gwine spile my cunj'in'. You come down ter my house ter-night en do w'at I tells you, er I'll put a spell on you dat'll make yo' ha'r fall out so you'll be bal', en yo' eyes drap out so you can't see, en yo' teef fall out so you can't eat, en yo' years grow up so you can't heah. W'en you is foolin' wid a cunjuh 'oman lack me, you got ter min' yo' P's en Q's er dey'll be trouble sho' 'nuff.'

"So co'se Solomon went down ter Aun' Peggy's dat night, en she gun 'im a roasted sweet'n' 'tater.

"'You take dis yer sweet'n' 'tater,' sez she,—'I done goophered it 'speshly fer dat noo nigger, so you better not eat it yo'se'f er you'll wush you hadn',—en slip off ter town, en fin' dat strange man, en gib 'im dis yer sweet'n' 'tater. He mus' eat it befo' mawnin', sho', ef he doan wanter be sol' erway ter Noo Orleens.'

"'But s'posen de patteroles ketch me, Aun' Peggy, w'at I gwine ter do?' sez Solomon.

"'De patteroles ain' gwine tech you, but ef you doan fin' dat nigger, *I'm* gwine git you, en you'll fin' me wusser 'n de patteroles. Des hol' on a minute, en I'll sprinkle you wid some er dis mixtry out'n dis yer bottle, so de patteroles can't see you, en you kin rub yo' feet wid some er dis yer grease out'n dis go'd, so you kin run fas', en rub some un it on yo' eyes so you kin see in de da'k; en den you mus' fin' dat noo nigger en gib 'im dis yer 'tater, er you gwine ter hab mo' trouble on yo' han's 'n you eber had befo' in yo' life er eber will hab sence.'

"So Solomon tuk de sweet'n' 'tater en sta'ted up de road fas' ez he could go, en befo' long he retch' town. He went right 'long by de patteroles, en dey didn' 'pear ter notice 'im, en bimeby he foun' whar de strange nigger was kep', en he walked right pas' de gyard at de do' en foun' 'im. De nigger couldn' see 'im, ob co'se, en he couldn' 'a' seed de nigger in de da'k, ef it hadn' be'n fer de stuff Aun' Peggy gun 'im ter rub on 'is eyes. De nigger wuz layin' in a co'nder, 'sleep, en Solomon des slip' up ter 'im, en hilt dat sweet'n' 'tater 'fo' de nigger's nose, en he des nach'ly retch' up wid his han', en tuk de 'tater en eat it in his sleep, widout knowin' it. W'en Solomon seed he'd done eat de 'tater, he went back en tol' Aun' Peggy, en den went home ter his cabin ter sleep, 'way 'long 'bout two o'clock in de mawnin'.

"De nex' day wuz Sunday, en so de niggers had a little time ter deyse'ves. Solomon wuz kinder 'sturb' in his min' thinkin' 'bout his junesey w'at 'uz gone away, en wond'rin' w'at Aun' Peggy had ter do wid dat noo nigger; en he had sa'ntered up in de woods so's ter be by hisse'f a little, en at de same time ter look atter a rabbit-trap he'd sot down in de aidge er de swamp, w'en who sh'd he see stan'in' unner a tree but a w'ite man.

"Solomon didn' knowed de w'ite man at fus', 'tel de w'ite man spoke up ter 'im.

"'Is dat you, Solomon?' sezee.

"Den Solomon reco'nized de voice.

"'Fer de Lawd's sake, Mars Jeems! is dat you?'

"'Yas, Solomon,' sez his marster, 'dis is me, er w'at's lef er me.'

"It wa'n't no wonder Solomon hadn' knowed Mars Jeems at fus', fer he wuz dress' lack a po' w'ite man, en wuz barefooted, en look' monst'us pale en peaked, ez ef he'd des come th'oo a ha'd spell er sickness.

"'You er lookin' kinder po'ly, Mars Jeems,' sez Solomon. 'Is you be'n sick, suh?'

"'No, Solomon,' sez Mars Jeems, shakin' his head, en speakin' sorter slow en sad, 'I ain' be'n sick, but I's had a monst'us bad dream,—fac', a reg'lar, nach'ul nightmare. But tell me how things has be'n gwine on up ter de plantation sence I be'n gone, Solomon.'

"So Solomon up en tol' 'im 'bout de craps, en 'bout de hosses en de mules, en 'bout de cows en de hawgs. En w'en he 'mence' ter tell 'bout de noo nigger, Mars Jeems prick' up 'is yeahs en listen', en eve'y now en den he'd say, 'Uh huh! uh huh!' en nod 'is head. En bimeby, w'en he'd ax' Solomon some mo' queshtuns, he sez, sezee:—

"'Now, Solomon, I doan want you ter say a wo'd ter nobody 'bout meetin' me heah, but I wants you ter slip up ter de house, en fetch me some clo's en some shoes,—I fergot ter tell you dat a man rob' me back yander on de road en swap' clo's wid me widout axin' me whuther er no,—but you neenter say nuffin 'bout dat, nuther. You go en fetch me some clo's heah, so nobody won't see you, en keep yo' mouf shet, en I'll gib you a dollah.'

"Solomon wuz so 'stonish' he lack ter fell ober in his tracks, w'en Mars Jeems promus' ter gib 'im a dollah. Dey su't'nly wuz a change come ober Mars Jeems, w'en he offer' one er his niggers dat much money. Solomon 'mence' ter 'spec' dat Aun' Peggy's cunj'ation had be'n wukkin' monst'us strong.

"Solomon fotch Mars Jeems some clo's en shoes, en dat same eb'nin' Mars Jeems 'peared at de house, en let on lack he des dat minute got home fum Robeson County. Mars Johnson was all ready ter talk ter 'im, but Mars Jeems sont 'im wo'd he wa'n't feelin' ve'y well dat night, en he'd see 'im ter-morrer.

"So nex' mawnin' atter breakfus' Mars Jeems sont fer de oberseah, en ax' 'im fer ter gib 'count er his styoa'd-ship. Ole Nick tol' Mars Jeems how much wuk be'n done, en got de books en showed 'im how much money be'n save'. Den Mars Jeems ax' 'im how de darkies be'n behabin', en Mars Johnson say dey be'n behabin' good, most un 'em, en dem w'at didn' behabe good at fus' change dey conduc' atter he got holt un 'em a time er two.

"'All,' sezee, ''cep'n' de noo nigger Mistah Dunkin fotch ober heah en lef' on trial, w'iles you wuz gone.'

"'Oh, yas,' 'lows Mars Jeems, 'tell me all 'bout dat noo nigger. I heared a little 'bout dat quare noo nigger las' night, en it wuz des too redik'lus. Tell me all 'bout dat noo nigger.'

"So seein' Mars Jeems so good-nachu'd 'bout it, Mars Johnson up en tol' 'im how he tied up de noo han' de fus' day en gun 'im fo'ty 'ca'se he wouldn' tell 'im 'is name.

"'Ha, ha, ha!' sez Mars Jeems, laffin' fit ter kill, 'but dat is too funny fer any use. Tell me some mo' 'bout dat noo nigger.'

"So Mars Johnson went on en tol' 'im how he had ter starbe de noo nigger 'fo' he could make 'im take holt er a hoe.

"'Dat wuz de beatinis' notion fer a nigger,' sez Mars Jeems, 'puttin' on airs, des lack he wuz a w'ite man! En I reckon you didn' do nuffin ter 'im?'

"'Oh, no, suh,' sez de oberseah, grinnin' lack a chessy-cat, 'I didn' do nuffin but take de hide off'n 'im.'

"Mars Jeems lafft en lafft, 'tel it 'peared lack he wuz des gwine ter bu'st. 'Tell me some mo' 'bout dat noo nigger, oh, tell me some mo'. Dat noo nigger int'rusts me, he do, en dat is a fac'.'

"Mars Johnson didn' quite un'erstan' w'y Mars Jeems sh'd make sich a great 'miration 'bout de noo nigger, but co'se he want' ter please de gent'eman w'at hi'ed 'im, en so he 'splain' all 'bout how many times he had ter cowhide de noo nigger, en how he made 'im do tasks twicet ez big ez some er de yuther han's, en how he 'd chain 'im up in de ba'n at night en feed 'im on co'n-bread en water.

"'Oh! but you is a monst'us good oberseah; you is de bes' oberseah in dis county, Mistah Johnson,' sez Mars Jeems, w'en de oberseah got th'oo wid his tale; 'en dey ain' nebber be'n no nigger-breaker lack you roun' heah befo'. En you desarbes great credit fer sendin' dat nigger 'way befo' you sp'ilt 'im fer de market. Fac', you is sech a monst'us good oberseah, en you is got dis yer plantation in sech fine shape, dat I reckon I doan need you no mo'. You is got dese yer darkies so well train' dat I 'spec' I kin run 'em myse'f fum dis time on. But I does wush you had 'a' hilt on ter dat noo nigger 'tel I got home, fer I'd 'a' lack ter 'a' seed 'im, I su't'nly should.'

"De oberseah wuz so 'stonish' he didn' ha'dly know w'at ter say, but fin'lly he ax' Mars Jeems ef he wouldn' gib 'im a riccommen' fer ter git ernudder place.

"'No, suh,' sez Mars Jeems, 'somehow er 'nuther I doan lack yo' looks sence I come back dis time, en I 'd much ruther you wouldn' stay roun' heah. Fac', I's feared ef I'd meet you alone in de woods some time, I mought wanter ha'm you. But layin' dat aside, I be'n lookin' ober dese yer books er yo'n w'at you kep' w'iles I wuz 'way, en fer a yeah er so back, en dere's some figgers w'at ain' des cl'ar ter me. I ain' got no time fer ter talk 'bout 'em now, but I 'spec' befo' I settles wid you fer dis las' mont', you better come up heah ter-morrer, atter I's look' de books en 'counts ober some mo', en den we'll straighten ou' business all up.'

"Mars Jeems 'lowed atterwa'ds dat he wuz des shootin' in de da'k w'en he said dat 'bout de books, but howsomeber, Mars Nick Johnson lef' dat naberhood 'twix' de nex' two suns, en nobody roun' dere nebber seed hide ner hair un 'im sence. En all de darkies t'ank de Lawd, en 'lowed it wuz a good riddance er bad rubbage.

"But all dem things I done tol' you ain' nuffin 'side'n de change w'at come ober Mars Jeems fum dat time on. Aun' Peggy's goopher had made a noo man un 'im enti'ely. De nex' day atter he come back, he tol' de han's dey neenter wuk on'y fum sun ter sun, en he cut dey tasks down so dey didn' nobody hab ter stan' ober 'em wid a rawhide er a hick'ry. En he 'lowed ef de niggers want ter hab a dance in de big ba'n any Sad'day night, dey mought hab it. En bimeby, w'en Solomon seed how good Mars Jeems wuz, he ax' 'im ef he wouldn' please sen' down ter de yuther plantation fer his junesey. Mars Jeems say su't'nly, en gun Solomon a pass en a note ter de oberseah on de yuther plantation, en sont Solomon down ter Robeson County wid a hoss en buggy fer ter fetch his junesey back. W'en de niggers see how fine Mars Jeems gwine treat 'em, dey all tuk ter sweethea'tin' en juneseyin' en singin' en dancin', en eight er ten couples got married, en bimeby eve'ybody 'mence' ter say Mars Jeems McLean got a finer plantation, en slicker-lookin' niggers, en dat he 'uz makin' mo' cotton en co'n, dan any yuther gent'eman in de county. En Mars Jeems's own junesey, Miss Libbie, heared 'bout de noo gwines-on on Mars Jeems's plantation, en she change' her min' 'bout Mars Jeems en tuk 'im back ag'in, en 'fo' long dey had a fine weddin', en all de darkies had a big feas', en dey wuz fiddlin' en dancin' en funnin' en frolic'in' fum sundown 'tel mawnin'."

"And they all lived happy ever after," I said, as the old man reached a full stop.

"Yas, suh," he said, interpreting my remarks as a question, "dey did. Solomon useter say," he added, "dat Aun' Peggy's goopher had turnt Mars Jeems ter a nigger, en dat dat noo han' wuz Mars Jeems hisse'f. But co'se Solomon didn' das' ter let on 'bout w'at he 'spicioned, en ole Aun' Peggy would 'a' 'nied ef she had be'n ax', fer she'd 'a' got in trouble sho', ef it 'uz knowed she 'd be'n cunj'in' de w'ite folks.

"Dis yer tale goes ter show," concluded Julius sententiously, as the man came up and announced that the spring was ready for us to get water, "dat w'ite folks w'at is so ha'd en stric', en doan make no 'lowance fer po' ign'ant niggers w'at ain' had no chanst ter l'arn, is li'ble ter hab bad dreams, ter say de leas', en dat dem w'at is kin' en good ter po' people is sho' ter prosper en git 'long in de worl'."

"That is a very strange story, Uncle Julius," observed my wife, smiling, "and Solomon's explanation is quite improbable."

"Yes, Julius," said I, "that was powerful goopher. I am glad, too, that you told us the moral of the story; it might have escaped us otherwise. By the way, did you make that up all by yourself?"

The old man's face assumed an injured look, expressive more of sorrow than of anger, and shaking his head he replied:—

"No, suh, I heared dat tale befo' you er Mis' Annie dere wuz bawn, suh. My mammy tol' me dat tale w'en I wa'n't mo' d'n knee-high ter a hopper-grass."

I drove to town next morning, on some business, and did not return until noon; and after dinner I had to visit a neighbor, and did not get back until supper-time. I was smoking a cigar on the back piazza in the early evening, when I saw a familiar figure carrying a bucket of water to the barn. I called my wife.

"My dear," I said severely, "what is that rascal doing here? I thought I discharged him yesterday for good and all."

"Oh, yes," she answered, "I forgot to tell you. He was hanging round the place all the morning, and looking so down in the mouth, that I told him that if he would try to do better, we would give him one more chance. He seems so grateful, and so really in earnest in his promises of amendment, that I'm sure you'll not regret taking him back."

I was seriously enough annoyed to let my cigar go out. I did not share my wife's rose-colored hopes in regard to Tom; but as I did not wish the servants to think there was any conflict of authority in the household, I let the boy stay.

Sis' Becky's Pickaninny[1]

We had not lived in North Carolina very long before I was able to note a marked improvement in my wife's health. The ozone-laden air of the surrounding piney woods, the mild and equable climate, the peaceful leisure of country life, had brought about in hopeful measure the cure we had anticipated. Toward the end of our second year, however, her ailment took an unexpected turn for the worse. She became the victim of a settled melancholy, attended with vague forebodings of impending misfortune.[2]

"You must keep up her spirits," said our physician, the best in the neighboring town. "This melancholy lowers her tone too much, tends to lessen her strength, and, if it continue too long, may be fraught with grave consequences."

I tried various expedients to cheer her up. I read novels to her. I had the hands on the place come up in the evening and serenade her with plantation songs. Friends came in sometimes and talked, and frequent letters from the North kept her in touch with her former home. But nothing seemed to rouse her from the depression into which she had fallen.

One pleasant afternoon in spring, I placed an armchair in a shaded portion of the front piazza, and filling it with pillows led my wife out of the house and seated her where she would have the pleasantest view of a somewhat monotonous scenery. She was scarcely placed when old Julius came through the yard, and, taking off his tattered straw hat, inquired, somewhat anxiously:—

"How is you feelin' dis afternoon, ma'm?"

"She is not very cheerful, Julius," I said. My wife was apparently without energy enough to speak for herself.

---

1. Written by Chesnutt in 1898 specifically for *The Conjure Woman*; included as the fifth story of the volume.
2. Annie's "ailment," as John describes it, seems related to neurasthenia, a condition thought by turn-of-the-century physicians to afflict elite American women disproportionately. Since the couple is childless, too, the nature of the story Julius concocts in response to her "ailment" suggests that Annie may have suffered a miscarriage or other problems related to childbearing.

The old man did not seem inclined to go away, so I asked him to sit down. I had noticed, as he came up, that he held some small object in his hand. When he had taken his seat on the top step, he kept fingering this object,—what it was I could not quite make out.

"What is that you have there, Julius?" I asked, with mild curiosity.

"Dis is my rabbit foot, suh."

This was at a time before this curious superstition had attained its present jocular popularity among white people, and while I had heard of it before, it had not yet outgrown the charm of novelty.

"What do you do with it?"

"I kyars it wid me fer luck, suh."

"Julius," I observed, half to him and half to my wife, "your people will never rise in the world until they throw off these childish superstitions and learn to live by the light of reason and common sense. How absurd to imagine that the fore-foot of a poor dead rabbit, with which he timorously felt his way along through a life surrounded by snares and pitfalls, beset by enemies on every hand, can promote happiness or success, or ward off failure or misfortune!"

"It is ridiculous," assented my wife, with faint interest.

"Dat's w'at I tells dese niggers roun' heah," said Julius. "De fo'-foot ain' got no power. It has ter be de hin'-foot, suh,—de lef' hin'-foot er a grabe-ya'd rabbit, killt by a cross-eyed nigger on a da'k night in de full er de moon."

"They must be very rare and valuable," I said.

"Dey is kinder ska'ce, suh, en dey ain' no 'mount er money could buy mine, suh. I mought len' it ter anybody I sot sto' by, but I wouldn' sell it, no indeed, suh, I wouldn'."

"How do you know it brings good luck?" I asked.

"'Ca'se I ain' had no bad luck sence I had it, suh, en I's had dis rabbit foot fer fo'ty yeahs. I had a good marster befo' de wah, en I wa'n't sol' erway, en I wuz sot free; en dat 'uz all good luck."

"But that doesn't prove anything," I rejoined. "Many other people have gone through a similar experience, and probably more than one of them had no rabbit's foot."

"Law, suh! you doan hafter prove 'bout de rabbit foot! Eve'ybody knows dat; leas'ways eve'ybody roun' heah knows it. But ef it has ter be prove' ter folks w'at wa'n't bawn en raise' in dis naberhood, dey is a' easy way ter prove it. Is I eber tol' you de tale er Sis' Becky en her pickaninny?"[3]

"No," I said, "let us hear it." I thought perhaps the story might interest my wife as much or more than the novel I had meant to read from.

"Dis yer Becky," Julius began, "useter b'long ter ole Kunnel Pen'leton, who owned a plantation down on de Wim'l'ton Road, 'bout

3. A once popular, now highly derogatory term for a black child.

ten miles fum heah, des befo' you gits ter Black Swamp. Dis yer
Becky wuz a fiel'-han', en a monst'us good 'un. She had a husban'
oncet, a nigger w'at b'longed on de nex' plantation, but de man w'at
owned her husban' died, en his lan' en his niggers had ter be sol' fer
ter pay his debts. Kunnel Pen'leton 'lowed he'd 'a' bought dis nigger,
but he had be'n bettin' on hoss races, en didn' hab no money, en so
Becky's husban' wuz sol' erway ter Fuhginny.

"Co'se Becky went on some 'bout losin' her man, but she couldn'
he'p herse'f; en 'sides dat, she had her pickaninny fer ter comfo't her.
Dis yer little Mose wuz de cutes', blackes', shiny-eyedes' little nigger
you eber laid eyes on, en he wuz ez fon' er his mammy ez his mammy
wuz er him. Co'se Becky had ter wuk en didn' hab much time ter
was'e wid her baby. Ole Aun' Nancy, de plantation nuss down at de
qua'ters, useter take keer er little Mose in de daytime, en atter de
niggers come in fum de cotton-fiel' Becky 'ud git her chile en kiss 'im
en nuss 'im, en keep 'im 'tel mawnin'; en on Sundays she'd hab 'im in
her cabin wid her all day long.

"Sis' Becky had got sorter useter gittin' 'long widout her husban',
w'en one day Kunnel Pen'leton went ter de races. Co'se w'en he
went ter de races, he tuk his hosses, en co'se he bet on 'is own
hosses, en co'se he los' his money; fer Kunnel Pen'leton didn' nebber
hab no luck wid his hosses, ef he did keep hisse'f po' projeckin' wid
'em. But dis time dey wuz a hoss name' Lightnin' Bug, w'at b'longed ter
ernudder man, en dis hoss won de sweep-stakes; en Kunnel Pen'leton tuk a lackin' ter dat hoss, en ax' his owner w'at he wuz willin' ter
take fer 'im.

"'I'll take a thousan' dollahs fer dat hoss,' sez dis yer man, who had
a big plantation down to'ds Wim'l'ton, whar he raise' hosses fer ter
race en ter sell.

"Well, Kunnel Pen'leton scratch' 'is head, en wonder whar he wuz
gwine ter raise a thousan' dollahs; en he didn' see des how he could
do it, fer he owed ez much ez he could borry a'ready on de skyo'ity he
could gib. But he wuz des boun' ter hab dat hoss, so sezee:—

"'I'll gib you my note fer 'leven hund'ed dollahs fer dat hoss.'

"De yuther man shuck 'is head, en sezee:—

"'Yo' note, suh, is better 'n gol', I doan doubt; but I is made it a rule
in my bizness not ter take no notes fum nobody. Howsomeber, suh,
ef you is kinder sho't er fun's, mos' lackly we kin make some kin' er
bahg'in. En w'iles we is talkin', I mought 's well say dat I needs
ernudder good nigger down on my place. Ef you is got a good one ter
spar', I mought trade wid you.'

"Now, Kunnel Pen'leton didn' r'ally hab no niggers fer ter spar',
but he 'lowed ter hisse'f he wuz des bleedzd ter hab dat hoss, en so he
sez, sezee:—

"'Well, I doan lack ter, but I reckon I'll haf ter. You come out ter my plantation ter-morrer en look ober my niggers, en pick out de one you wants.'

"So sho' 'nuff nex' day dis yer man come out ter Kunnel Pen'leton's place en rid roun' de plantation en glanshed at de niggers, en who sh'd he pick out fum 'em all but Sis' Becky.

"'I needs a noo nigger 'oman down ter my place,' sezee, 'fer ter cook en wash, en so on; en dat young 'oman'll des fill de bill. You gimme her, en you kin hab Lightnin' Bug.'"

"Now, Kunnel Pen'leton didn' lack ter trade Sis' Becky, 'ca'se she wuz nigh 'bout de bes' fiel'-han' he had; en 'sides, Mars Dugal' didn' keer ter take de mammies 'way fum dey chillun w'iles de chillun wuz little. But dis man say he want Becky, er e'se Kunnel Pen'leton couldn' hab de race hoss.

"'Well,' sez de kunnel, 'you kin hab de 'oman. But I doan lack ter sen' her 'way fum her baby. W'at'll you gimme fer dat nigger baby?'

"'I doan want de baby,' sez de yuther man. 'I ain' got no use fer de baby.'

"'I tell yer w'at I'll do,' 'lows Kunnel Pen'leton, 'I'll th'ow dat pickaninny in fer good measure.'

"But de yuther man shuck his head. 'No,' sezee, 'I's much erbleedzd, but I doan raise niggers; I raises hosses, en I doan wanter be both'rin' wid no nigger babies. Nemmine de baby. I'll keep dat 'oman so busy she 'll fergit de baby; fer niggers is made ter wuk, en dey ain' got no time fer no sich foolis'ness ez babies.'

"Kunnel Pen'leton didn' wanter hu't Becky's feelin's,—fer Kunnel Pen'leton wuz a kin'-hea'ted man, en nebber lack' ter make no trouble fer nobody,—en so he tol' Becky he wuz gwine sen' her down ter Robeson County fer a day er so, ter he'p out his son-in-law in his wuk; en bein' ez dis yuther man wuz gwine dat way, he had ax' 'im ter take her 'long in his buggy.

"'Kin I kyar little Mose wid me, marster?' ax' Sis' Becky.

"'N-o,' sez de kunnel, ez ef he wuz studyin' whuther ter let her take 'im er no; 'I reckon you better let Aun' Nancy look atter yo' baby fer de day er two you 'll be gone, en she'll see dat he gits ernuff ter eat 'tel you gits back.'

"So Sis' Becky hug' en kiss' little Mose, en tol' 'im ter be a good little pickaninny, en take keer er hisse'f, en not fergit his mammy w'iles she wuz gone. En little Mose put his arms roun' his mammy en lafft en crowed des lack it wuz monst'us fine fun fer his mammy ter go 'way en leabe 'im.

"Well, dis yer hoss trader sta'ted out wid Becky, en bimeby, atter dey'd gone down de Lumbe'ton Road fer a few miles er so, dis man tu'nt roun' in a diffe'nt d'rection, en kep' goin' dat erway, 'tel bimeby

Sis' Becky up 'n ax' 'im ef he wuz gwine' ter Robeson County by a noo road.

"'No, nigger,' sezee, 'I ain' gwine ter Robeson County at all. I's gwine ter Bladen County, whar my plantation is, en whar I raises all my hosses.'

"'But how is I gwine ter git ter Mis' Laura's plantation down in Robeson County?' sez Becky, wid her hea't in her mouf, fer she 'mence' ter git skeered all er a sudden.

"'You ain' gwine ter git dere at all,' sez de man. 'You b'longs ter me now, fer I done traded my bes' race hoss fer you, wid yo' ole marster. Ef you is a good gal, I'll treat you right, en ef you doan behabe yo'se'f,—w'y, w'at e'se happens 'll be yo' own fault.'

"Co'se Sis' Becky cried en went on 'bout her pickaninny, but co'se it did n' do no good, en bimeby dey got down ter dis yer man's place, en he put Sis' Becky ter wuk, en fergot all 'bout her habin' a pickaninny.

"Meanw'iles, w'en ebenin' come, de day Sis' Becky wuz tuk 'way, little Mose 'mence' ter git res'less, en bimeby, w'en his mammy didn' come, he sta'ted ter cry fer 'er. Aun' Nancy fed 'im en rocked 'im en rocked 'im; en fin'lly he des cried en cried 'tel he cried hisse'f ter sleep.

"De nex' day he didn' 'pear ter be as peart ez yushal, en w'en night come he fretted en went on wuss 'n he did de night befo'. De nex' day his little eyes 'mence' ter lose dey shine, en he wouldn' eat nuffin, en he 'mence' ter look so peaked dat Aun' Nancy tuk 'n kyared 'im up ter de big house, en showed 'im ter her ole missis, en her ole missis gun her some med'cine fer 'im, en 'lowed ef he didn' git no better she sh'd fetch 'im up ter de big house ag'in, en dey 'd hab a doctor, en nuss little Mose up dere. Fer Aun' Nancy's ole missis 'lowed he wuz a lackly little nigger en wu'th raisin'.

"But Aun' Nancy had l'arn' ter lack little Mose, en she didn' wanter hab 'im tuk up ter de big house. En so w'en he didn' git no better, she gethered a mess er green peas, and tuk de peas en de baby, en went ter see ole Aun' Peggy, de cunjuh 'oman down by de Wim'l'ton Road. She gun Aun' Peggy de mess er peas, en tol' her all 'bout Sis' Becky en little Mose.

"'Dat is a monst'us small mess er peas you is fotch' me,' sez Aun' Peggy, sez she.

"'Yas, I knows,' 'lowed Aun' Nancy, 'but dis yere is a monst'us small pickaninny.'

"'You 'll hafter fetch me sump'n mo',' sez Aun' Peggy, 'fer you can't 'spec' me ter was'e my time diggin' roots en wukkin' cunj'ation fer nuffin.'

"'All right,' sez Aun' Nancy, 'I'll fetch you sump'n mo' nex' time.'

"'You bettah,' sez Aun' Peggy, 'er e'se dey'll be trouble. W'at dis yer little pickaninny needs is ter see his mammy. You leabe 'im heah 'tel ebenin' en I'll show 'im his mammy.'

"So w'en Aun' Nancy had gone 'way, Aun' Peggy tuk 'n wukked her roots, en tu'nt little Mose ter a hummin'-bird, en sont 'im off fer ter fin' his mammy.

"So little Mose flewed, en flewed, en flewed away, 'tel bimeby he got ter de place whar Sis' Becky b'longed. He seed his mammy wukkin' roun' de ya'd, en he could tell fum lookin' at her dat she wuz trouble' in her min' 'bout sump'n, en feelin' kin' er po'ly. Sis' Becky heared sump'n hummin' roun' en roun' her, sweet en low. Fus' she 'lowed it wuz a hummin'-bird; den she thought it sounded lack her little Mose croonin' on her breas' way back yander on de ole planta-tion. En she des 'magine' it wuz her little Mose, en it made her feel bettah, en she went on 'bout her wuk pearter 'n she'd done sence she'd be'n down dere. Little Mose stayed roun' 'tel late in de ebenin', en den flewed back ez hard ez he could ter Aun' Peggy. Ez fer Sis' Becky, she dremp all dat night dat she wuz holdin' her pickaninny in her arms, en kissin' him, en nussin' him, des lack she useter do back on de ole plantation whar he wuz bawn. En fer th'ee er fo' days Sis' Becky went 'bout her wuk wid mo' sperrit dan she'd showed sence she'd be'n down dere ter dis man's plantation.

"De nex' day atter he come back, little Mose wuz mo' pearter en better 'n he had be'n fer a long time. But to'ds de een' er de week he 'mence' ter git res'less ag'in, en stop' eatin', en Aun' Nancy kyared 'im down ter Aun' Peggy once mo', en she tu'nt 'im ter a mawkin'-bird dis time, en sont 'im off ter see his mammy ag'in.

"It didn' take him long fer ter git dere, en w'en he did, he seed his mammy standin' in de kitchen, lookin' back in de d'rection little Mose wuz comin' fum. En dey wuz tears in her eyes, en she look' mo' po'ly en peaked 'n she had w'en he wuz down dere befo'. So little Mose sot on a tree in de ya'd en sung, en sung, en sung, des fittin' ter split his th'oat. Fus' Sis' Becky didn' notice 'im much, but dis mawkin'-bird kep' stayin' roun' de house all day, en bimeby Sis' Becky des 'magine' dat mawkin'-bird wuz her little Mose crowin' en crowin', des lack he useter do w'en his mammy would come home at night fum de cotton-fiel'. De mawkin'-bird stayed roun' dere 'mos' all day, en w'en Sis' Becky went out in de ya'd one time, dis yer mawkin'-bird lit on her shoulder en peck' at de piece er bread she wuz eatin', en fluttered his wings so dey rub' up agin de side er her head. En w'en he flewed away 'long late in de ebenin', des 'fo' sundown, Sis' Becky felt mo' better 'n she had sence she had heared dat hummin'-bird a week er so pas'. En dat night she dremp 'bout ole times ag'in, des lack she did befo'.

"But dis yer totin' little Mose down ter ole Aun' Peggy, en dis yer gittin' things fer ter pay de cunjuh 'oman, use' up a lot er Aun' Nancy's time, en she begun ter git kinder ti'ed. 'Sides dat, w'en Sis' Becky had be'n on de plantation, she had useter he'p Aun' Nancy wid de young uns ebenin's en Sundays; en Aun' Nancy 'mence' ter miss 'er monst'us, 'speshly sence she got a tech er de rheumatiz herse'f, en so she 'lows ter ole Aun' Peggy one day:—

"'Aun' Peggy, ain' dey no way you kin fetch Sis' Becky back home?'

"'Huh!' sez Aun' Peggy, 'I dunno 'bout dat. I'll hafter wuk my roots en fin' out whuther I kin er no. But it'll take a monst'us heap er wuk, en I can't was'e my time fer nuffin. Ef you'll fetch me sump'n ter pay me fer my trouble, I reckon we kin fix it.'

"So nex' day Aun' Nancy went down ter see Aun' Peggy ag'in.

"'Aun' Peggy,' sez she, 'I is fotch' you my bes' Sunday head-hankercher. Will dat do?'

"Aun' Peggy look' at de head-hankercher, en run her han' ober it, en sez she:—

"'Yas, dat'll do fus'-rate. I's be'n wukkin' my roots sence you be'n gone, en I 'lows mos' lackly I kin git Sis' Becky back, but it's gwine take fig'rin' en studyin' ez well ez cunj'in'. De fus' thing ter do'll be ter stop fetchin' dat pickaninny down heah, en not sen' 'im ter see his mammy no mo'. Ef he gits too po'ly, you lemme know, en I'll gib you some kin' er mixtry fer ter make 'im fergit Sis' Becky fer a week er so. So 'less'n you comes fer dat, you neenter come back ter see me no mo' 'tel I sen's fer you.'

"So Aun' Peggy sont Aun' Nancy erway, en de fus' thing she done wuz ter call a hawnet fum a nes' unner her eaves.

"'You go up ter Kunnel Pen'leton's stable, hawnet,' sez she, 'en sting de knees er de race hoss name' Lightnin' Bug. Be sho' en git de right one.'

"So de hawnet flewed up ter Kunnel Pen'leton's stable en stung Lightnin' Bug roun' de laigs, en de nex' mawnin' Lightnin' Bug's knees wuz all swoll' up, twice't ez big ez dey oughter be. W'en Kunnel Pen'leton went out ter de stable en see de hoss's laigs, hit would 'a' des made you trimble lack a leaf fer ter heah him cuss dat hoss trader. Howsomeber, he cool' off bimeby en tol' de stable boy fer ter rub Lightnin' Bug's laigs wid some linimum. De boy done ez his marster tol' 'im, en by de nex' day de swellin' had gone down consid'able. Aun' Peggy had sont a sparrer, w'at had a nes' in one er de trees close ter her cabin, fer ter watch w'at wuz gwine on 'roun' de big house, en w'en dis yer sparrer tol' 'er de hoss wuz gittin' ober de swellin', she sont de hawnet back fer ter sting 'is knees some mo', en de nex' mawnin' Lightnin' Bug's laigs wuz swoll' up wuss 'n befo'.

"Well, dis time Kunnel Pen'leton wuz mad th'oo en th'oo, en all de way 'roun', en he cusst dat hoss trader up en down, fum A ter Izzard. He cusst so ha'd dat de stable boy got mos' skeered ter def, en went off en hid hisse'f in de hay.

"Ez fer Kunnel Pen'leton, he went right up ter de house en got out his pen en ink, en tuk off his coat en roll' up his sleeves, en writ a letter ter dis yer hoss trader, en sezee:—

"'You is sol' me a hoss w'at is got a ringbone er a spavin[4] er sump'n, en w'at I paid you fer wuz a soun' hoss. I wants you ter sen' my nigger 'oman back en take yo' ole hoss, er e'se I'll sue you, sho 's you bawn.'

"But dis yer man wa'n't skeered a bit, en he writ back ter Kunnel Pen'leton dat a bahg'in wuz a bahg'in; dat Lightnin' Bug wuz soun' w'en he sol' 'im, en ef Kunnel Pen'leton didn' knowed ernuff 'bout hosses ter take keer er a fine racer, dat wuz his own fune'al. En he say Kunnel Pen'leton kin sue en be cusst for all he keer, but he ain' gwine ter gib up de nigger he bought en paid fer.

"W'en Kunnel Pen'leton got dis letter he wuz madder 'n he wuz befo', 'speshly 'ca'se dis man 'lowed he didn' know how ter take keer er fine hosses. But he couldn' do nuffin but fetch a lawsuit, en he knowed, by his own 'spe'ience, dat lawsuits wuz slow ez de seben-yeah eetch and cos' mo' d'n dey come ter, en he 'lowed he better go slow en wait awhile.

"Aun' Peggy knowed w'at wuz gwine on all dis time, en she fix' up a little bag wid some roots en one thing en ernudder in it, en gun it ter dis sparrer er her'n, en tol' 'im ter take it 'way down yander whar Sis' Becky wuz, en drap it right befo' de do' er her cabin, so she'd be sho' en fin' it de fus' time she come out'n de do'.

"One night Sis' Becky dremp' her pickaninny wuz dead, en de nex' day she wuz mo'nin' en groanin' all day. She dremp' de same dream th'ee nights runnin', en den, de nex' mawnin' atter de las' night, she foun' dis yer little bag de sparrer had drap' in front her do'; en she 'lowed she 'd be'n cunju'd, en wuz gwine ter die, en ez long ez her pickaninny wuz dead dey wa'n't no use tryin' ter do nuffin nohow. En so she tuk 'n went ter bed, en tol' her marster she'd be'n cunju'd en wuz gwine ter die.

"Her marster lafft at her, en argyed wid her, en tried ter 'suade her out'n dis yer fool notion, ez he called it,—fer he wuz one er dese yer w'ite folks w'at purten' dey doan b'liebe in cunj'in',—but hit wa'n't no use. Sis' Becky kep' gittin' wusser en wusser, 'tel fin'lly dis yer man 'lowed Sis' Becky wuz gwine ter die, sho' 'nuff. En ez he knowed dey hadn' be'n nuffin de matter wid Lightnin' Bug w'en he traded 'im, he 'lowed mebbe he could kyo' 'im en fetch 'im roun' all right, leas'ways good 'nuff ter sell ag'in. En anyhow, a lame hoss wuz better 'n a dead nigger. So he sot down en writ Kunnel Pen'leton a letter.

"'My conscience,' sezee, 'has be'n troublin' me 'bout dat ringbone' hoss I sol' you. Some folks 'lows a hoss trader ain' got no conscience, but dey doan know me, fer dat is my weak spot, en de reason I ain' made no mo' money hoss tradin'. Fac' is,' sezee, 'I is got so I can't sleep nights fum studyin' 'bout dat spavin' hoss; en I is made up my min' dat, w'iles a bahg'in is a bahg'in, en you seed Lightnin' Bug befo' you traded fer 'im, principle is wuth mo' d'n money er hosses er niggers. So ef

---

4. *ringbone, spavin*: inflammatory disorders of the leg of a horse, causing lameness.

you'll sen' Lightnin' Bug down heah, I'll sen' yo' nigger 'oman back, en we'll call de trade off, en be ez good frien's ez we eber wuz, en no ha'd feelin's.'

"So sho' 'nuff, Kunnel Pen'leton sont de hoss back. En w'en de man w'at come ter bring Lightnin' Bug tol' Sis' Becky her pickaninny wa'n't dead, Sis' Becky wuz so glad dat she 'lowed she wuz gwine ter try ter lib 'tel she got back whar she could see little Mose once mo'. En w'en she retch' de ole plantation en seed her baby kickin' en crowin' en holdin' out his little arms to'ds her, she wush' she wuzn' cunju'd en didn' hafter die. En w'en Aun' Nancy tol' 'er all 'bout Aun' Peggy, Sis' Becky went down ter see de cunjuh 'oman, en Aun' Peggy tol' her she had cunju'd her. En den Aun' Peggy tuk de goopher off'n her, en she got well, en stayed on de plantation, en raise' her pickaninny. En w'en little Mose growed up, he could sing en whistle des lack a mawkin'-bird, so dat de w'ite folks useter hab 'im come up ter de big house at night, en whistle en sing fer 'em, en dey useter gib 'im money en vittles en one thing er ernudder, w'ich he alluz tuk home ter his mammy; fer he knowed all 'bout w'at she had gone th'oo. He tu'nt out ter be a sma't man, en l'arnt de blacksmif trade; en Kunnel Pen'leton let 'im hire his time. En bimeby he bought his mammy en sot her free, en den he bought hisse'f, en tuk keer er Sis' Becky ez long ez dey bofe libbed."

My wife had listened to this story with greater interest than she had manifested in any subject for several days. I had watched her furtively from time to time during the recital, and had observed the play of her countenance. It had expressed in turn sympathy, indignation, pity, and at the end lively satisfaction.

"That is a very ingenious fairy tale, Julius," I said, "and we are much obliged to you."

"Why, John!" said my wife severely, "the story bears the stamp of truth, if ever a story did."

"Yes," I replied, "especially the humming-bird episode, and the mocking-bird digression, to say nothing of the doings of the hornet and the sparrow."

"Oh, well, I don't care," she rejoined, with delightful animation; "those are mere ornamental details and not at all essential. The story is true to nature, and might have happened half a hundred times, and no doubt did happen, in those horrid days before the war."

"By the way, Julius," I remarked, "your story doesn't establish what you started out to prove,—that a rabbit's foot brings good luck."

"Hit's plain 'nuff ter me, suh," replied Julius. "I bet young missis dere kin 'splain it herse'f."

"I rather suspect," replied my wife promptly, "that Sis' Becky had no rabbit's foot."

"You is hit de bull's-eye de fus' fire, ma'm," assented Julius. "Ef Sis' Becky had had a rabbit foot, she nebber would 'a' went th'oo all dis trouble."

I went into the house for some purpose, and left Julius talking to my wife. When I came back a moment later, he was gone.

My wife's condition took a turn for the better from this very day, and she was soon on the way to ultimate recovery. Several weeks later, after she had resumed her afternoon drives, which had been interrupted by her illness, Julius brought the rockaway round to the front door one day, and I assisted my wife into the carriage.

"John," she said, before I had taken my seat, "I wish you would look in my room, and bring me my handkerchief. You will find it in the pocket of my blue dress."

I went to execute the commission. When I pulled the handkerchief out of her pocket, something else came with it and fell on the floor. I picked up the object and looked at it. It was Julius's rabbit's foot.

Tobe's Tribulations[1]

About half a mile from our house on the North Carolina sand-hills there lay, at the foot of a vine-clad slope, and separated from my scuppernong vineyard by a rail fence, a marsh of some extent. It was drained at a somewhat later date, but at the time to which I now refer spread for half a mile in length and a quarter of a mile in breadth. Having been planted in rice many years before, it therefore contained no large trees, but was grown up chiefly in reeds and coarse grasses, with here and there a young sycamore or cypress. Though this marsh was not visible from our house, nor from any road that we used, it was nevertheless one of the most prominent features of our environment. We might sometimes forget its existence in the day-time, but it never failed to thrust itself upon our attention after night had fallen.

It may be that other localities in our neighborhood were infested with frogs; but if so, their vocal efforts were quite overborne by the volume of sound that issued nightly from this particular marsh. As soon as the red disk of the sun had set behind the pines the performance would begin, first perhaps with occasional shrill pipings, followed by a confused chattering; then, as the number of participants increased, growing into a steady drumming, punctuated every moment by the hoarse bellowing note of some monstrous bull-frog. If the day had perchance been rainy, the volume of noise would be greater. For a while after we went to live in the neighborhood, this ceaseless, strident din made night hideous, and we would gladly

---

1. Written by Chesnutt in 1898 for *The Conjure Woman*; rejected for the volume; published in the *Southern Workman*, 1900.

have dispensed with it. But as time wore on we grew accustomed to our nocturnal concert; we began to differentiate its notes and to distinguish a sort of rude harmony in these voices of the night; and after we had become thoroughly accustomed to it, I doubt whether we could have slept comfortably without their lullaby.[2]

But I had not been living long in the vicinity of this frog-pond before its possibilities as a source of food-supply suggested themselves to my somewhat practical mind. I was unable to learn that any of my white neighbors indulged in the delicate article of diet which frogs' legs might be made to supply; and strangely enough, among the Negroes, who would have found in the tender flesh of the batrachia[3] a toothsome and bountiful addition to the coarse food that formed the staple of their diet; its use for that purpose was entirely unknown.

One day I went frog-fishing and brought home a catch of half a dozen. Our colored cook did not know how to prepare them, and looked on the whole proceeding with ill-concealed disgust. So my wife, with the aid of a cook-book, dressed the hind legs quite successfully in the old-fashioned way, and they were served at supper. We enjoyed the meal very much, and I determined that thereafter we would have the same dish often.

Our supper had been somewhat later than usual, and it was dusk before we left the table and took our seats on the piazza. We had been there but a little while when old Julius, our colored coachman, came around the house and approaching the steps asked for some instructions with reference to the stable-work. As the matter required talking over, I asked him to sit down.

When we had finished our talk the old man did not go away immediately, and we all sat for a few moments without speaking. The night was warm but not sultry; there was a sort of gentle melancholy in the air, and the chorus from the distant frog-pond seemed pitched this night in something of a minor key.

"Dem frogs is makin' dey yuzh'al racket ternight," observed the old man, breaking the silence.

"Yes," I replied, "they are very much in evidence. By the way, Annie, perhaps Julius would like some of those frogs' legs. I see Nancy hasn't cleared the table yet."

"No ma'm," responded Julius quickly, "I's much obleedzd, but I doan eat no frog-laigs; no, *suh*, no *ma'm*, I doan eat no frog-laigs, not ef I knows w'at I's eatin'!"

"Why not, Julius?" I asked. "They are excellent eating."

2. With John's description of hearing the "drumming" and "chattering" of the frogs, Chesnutt recalls antebellum accounts by white residents of plantations of hearing goings-on from the slave quarters at night.
3. In the taxonomic system of biological classification, Batrachia is the order of the class Amphibia that comprises the frogs and toads.

"You listen right close, suh," he answered, "en you'll heah a per-tic'ler bull-frog down yander in dat ma'sh. Listen! Dere he goes now—callin', callin', callin'! sad en mo'nful, des lak somebody w'at's los' somewhar, en can't fin' de way back."

"I hear it distinctly," said my wife after a moment. "It sounds like the lament of a lost soul."

I had never heard the vocal expression of a lost soul, but I tried, without success, to imagine that I could distinguish one individual croak from another.

"Well, what is there about that frog, Julius," I inquired, "that makes it any different from the others?"

"Dat's po' Tobe," he responded solemnly, "callin' Aun' Peggy—po' ole Aun' Peggy w'at's dead en gone ter de good Marster, yeahs en yeahs ago."

"Tell us about Tobe, Julius," I asked. I could think of no more appropriate time for one of the old man's stories. His views of life were so entirely foreign to our own, that for a time after we got acquainted with him his conversations were a never-failing source of novelty and interest. He had seen life from what was to us a new point of view—from the bottom, as it were; and there clung to his mind, like barnacles to the submerged portion of a ship, all sorts of extravagant beliefs. The simplest phenomena of life were to him fraught with hidden meaning,—some prophesy of good, some presage of evil. The source of these notions I never traced, though they doubtless could be easily accounted for. Some perhaps were dim reflections of ancestral fetishism; more were the superstitions, fil-tered through the Negro intellect, of the Scotch settlers who had founded their homes on Cape Fear at a time when a kelpie[4] haunted every Highland glen, and witches, like bats, darkened the air as they flew by in their nocturnal wanderings. But from his own imagi-nation, I take it—for I never heard quite the same stories from any-one else—he gave to the raw material of folk-lore and superstition a fancifulness of touch that truly made of it, to borrow a homely phrase, a silk purse out of a sow's ear. And if perhaps, at times, his stories might turn out to have a purpose apart from any esthetic or *didactic* end, he probably reasoned, with a philosophy for which there is high warrant, that the laborer was worthy of his hire.

"'Bout fo'ty years ago," began Julius, "ole Mars Dugal McAdoo—*my* ole marster—useter own a man name' Tobe. Dis yer Tobe wuz a

4. Lowland Scottish mythological water-demon or spirit that is able to morph into different shapes, predominantly that of a horse. Kelpies are thought to haunt lakes and rivers and are believed to delight in drowning travelers. With the reference Chesnutt again stresses the cultural cross-pollination of Julius's tales, rejecting a racially bifurcated paradigm for the folk culture of the U.S. South.

slow kind er nigger, en w'iles he'd alluz git his tas' done, he'd hafter wuk harder 'n any yuther nigger on de place ter do it. One time he had a monst'us nice 'oman fer a wife, but she got bit by a rattlesnake one summer en died, en dat lef' Tobe kind er lonesome. En mo'd'n dat, Tobe's wife had be'n cook at de big house, en eve'y night she'd fetch sump'n down ter her cabin fer Tobe; en he foun' it mighty ha'd ter go back ter bacon and co'n-bread atter libbin' off'n de fat er de lan' all dese yeahs.

"Des 'bout a mont' er so atter Tobe's wife died, dey wuz a nigger run 'way fum ole Mars Marrabo McSwayne's—de nex' plantation— en in spite er all de w'ite folks could do, dis yer nigger got clean off ter a free state in de Norf, en bimeby he writ a sassy letter back ter Mars Marrabo, en sont 'im a bill fer de wuk he done fer 'im fer twenty yeahs er mo', at a dollah en a half a day—w'at he say he wuz gittin' at de Norf. One er de gals w'at wukked roun' de big house heared de w'ite folks gwine on 'bout it, en she say Mars Marrabo cusst en swo' des tarrable, en ole missis 'mos' wep' fer ter think how ongrateful dat nigger wuz, not on'y ter run 'way, but to write back sich wick'niss ter w'ite folks w'at had alluz treated 'im good, fed 'im en clothed 'im, en nussed 'im w'en he wuz sick, en nebber let 'im suffer fer nuffin all his life.

"But Tobe heared 'bout dis yer nigger, en he tuk a notion he'd lak ter run 'way en go ter de Norf en be free en git a dollah en a half a day too. But de mo' he studied 'bout it, de ha'der it 'peared ter be. In de fus' place, de Norf wuz a monst'us long ways off, en de dawgs mought track 'im, er de patteroles mought ketch 'im, er he mought sta've ter def ca'se he couldn' git nuffin ter eat on de way; en ef he wuz cotch' he wuz lakly ter be sol' so fur souf dat he'd nebber hab no chance ter git free er eber see his ole frien's nuther.

"But Tobe kep' on studyin' 'bout runnin 'way 'tel fin'lly he 'lowed he'd go en see ole Aun' Peggy, de cunjuh 'oman down by de Wim'l'ton Road, en ax her w'at wuz de bes' way fer him ter sta't. So he tuk a pa'r er pullets down ter Aun' Peggy one night en tol' her all 'bout his hank' in's en his longin's, en ax' her w'at he'd hafter do fer ter run 'way en git free.

"'W'at you wanter be free fer?' sez Aun' Peggy. 'Doan you git ernuff ter eat?'

"'Yas, I gits ernuff ter eat, but I'll hab better vittles wen I's free.'

"'Doan you git ernuff sleep?'

"'Yas, but I'll sleep mo' w'en I's free.'

"'Does you wuk too ha'd?'

"'No, I doan wuk too ha'd fer a slabe nigger, but ef I wuz free I wouldn' wuk a-tall 'less'n I felt lak it.'

"Aun' Peggy shuck her head. 'I dunno, nigger,' sez she, 'whuther you gwine ter fin' w'at you er huntin' fer er no. But w'at is it you wants me ter do fer you?'

"'I wants you ter tell me de bes' en easies' way fer ter git ter de Norf en be free.'

"'Well', sez Aun' Peggy, 'I's feared dey ain' no easy way. De bes' way fer you ter do is ter fix yo' eye on de Norf Stah en sta't. You kin put some tar on yo' feet ter th'ow de houn's off'n de scent, en ef you come ter a crick you mought wade 'long fer a mile er so. I sh'd say you bettah sta't on Sad'day night, fer den mos' lakly you won' be miss' 'tel Monday mawnin', en you kin git a good sta't on yo' jou'ney. En den maybe in a mont' er so you'll retch de Norf en you'll be free, en whar you kin eat all you want, ef you kin git it, en sleep ez long ez you mineter, ef you kin 'ford it, en whar you won't hafter wuk ef you'd ruther go to jail.'[5]

"'But w'at is I gwine ter eat dyo'in' er dis yer mont' I's trabblin'?' ax' Tobe. 'It makes me sick ef I doan git my reg'lar meals.'

"'Doan ax me', sez Aun' Peggy. 'I ain' nebber seed de nigger yit w'at can't fin' sump'n ter eat.'

"Tobe scratch' his head. 'En whar is I gwine to sleep dyo'in' er dat mont'? I'll hafter hab my reg'lar res'.'

"'Doan ax me,' sez Aun' Peggy. 'You kin sleep in de woods in de daytime, en do yo' trabblin' at night.'

"'But s'pose'n a snake bites me?'

"'I kin gib you a cha'm fer ter kyo snake-bite.'

"'But s'pose'n' de patteroles ketch me?'

"'Look a heah, nigger,' sez Aun' Peggy, 'I's ti'ed er yo' s'pose'n', en I's was'e all de time on you I's gwine fer two chick'ns. I's feared you wants ter git free too easy. I s'pose you des wants ter lay down at night, do yo' trabblin' in yo' sleep, en wake free in de mawn'in. You wants ter git a thousan' dollah nigger fer nuffin' en dat's mo'd'n any-body but de sma'test w'ite folks kin do. Go 'long back ter yo' wuk, man, en doan come back ter me 'less'n you kin fetch me sump'n mo'.'

"Now, Tobe knowed well ernuff dat ole Aun' Peggy'd des be'n talkin' ter heah herse'f talk, en so two er th'ee nights later he tuk a side er bacon en kyared it down ter her cabin.

"'Uh huh', sez Aun' Peggy, 'dat is sump'n lak it. I s'pose you still 'lows you-'d lak ter be free, so you kin eat w'at you mineter, en sleep all you wanter, en res' w'eneber you feels dat erway?'

"'Yas'm, I wants ter be free, en I wants you ter fix things so I kin be sho' ter git ter de Norf widout much trouble; fer I sho'ly does hate en 'spise trouble.'

"Aun' Peggy studied fer a w'ile, en den she tuk down a go'd off'n de she'f, en sez she:—

---

5. Aunt Peggy describes the incompleteness of "freedom" after legal emancipation.

"'I's got a goopher mixtry heah w'at'll tu'n you ter a b'ar.' You know dey use'ter be b'ars roun' heah in dem ole days.'

"Den she tuk down ernudder go'd. 'En,' she went on, 'ef I puts some er dis yuther mixtry wid it, you'll tu'n back ag'in in des a week er mont' er two mont's, 'cordin' ter how much I puts in. Now, ef I tu'ns you ter a b'ar fer, say a mont', en you is keerful en keeps 'way fum de hunters, you kin feed yo'se'f ez you goes 'long, en by de een' er de mont' you'll be ter de Norf; en w'en you tu'ns back you'll tu'n back ter a free nigger, whar you kin do w'at you wanter, en go whar you mineter, en sleep ez long ez you please.'

"So Tobe say all right, en Aun' Peggy mix' de goopher, en put it on Tobe en turn't 'im ter a big black b'ar.

"Tobe sta'ted out to'ds de Norf, en went fifteen er twenty miles wid-out stoppin'. Des befo' day in de mawnin' he come ter a 'tater patch, en bein' ez he wuz feelin' sorter hongry, he stop' fer a hour er so 'tel he got all de 'taters he could hol'. Den he sta'ted out ag'in, en bimeby he run 'cross a bee-tree en eat all de honey he could. 'Long to'ds ebenin' he come ter a holler tree, en bein' ez he felt kinder sleepy lak, he 'lowed he'd crawl in en take a nap. So he crawled in en went ter sleep.

"Meanw'ile, Monday mawn'in' w'en de niggers went out in de fiel' ter wuk, Tobe wuz missin'. All de niggers 'nied seein' 'im, en ole Mars Dugal sont up ter town en hi'ed some dawgs, en gun 'em de scent, en dey follered it ter ole Aun' Peggy's cabin. Aun' Peggy 'lowed yas, a nigger had be'n ter her cabin Sad'day night, en she had gun 'im a cha'm fer ter keep off de rheumatiz, en he had sta'ted off down to'ds de ribber, sayin' he wuz ti'ed wukkin' en wuz gwine fishin' fer a mont' er so. De w'ite folks hunted en hunted, but co'se dey did'n fin' Tobe.

"Bout a mont' atter Tobe had run 'way, en w'en Aun' Peggy had mos' fergot 'bout im, she wuz sett'n' in her cabin one night, wukkin' her roots, w'en somebody knock' at her do'.

"'Who dere?' sez she.

"'It's me, Tobe; open de do', Aun' Peggy.'

"Sho' 'nuff, w'en Aun' Peggy tuk down de do'-bar, who sh'd be stan'in' dere but Tobe.

"'Whar is you come fum, nigger?' ax' Aun' Peggy, 'I 'lowed you mus' be ter de Norf by dis time, en free, en libbin' off'n de fat er de lan'.'

"'You must 'a s'pected me ter trabbel monst'us fas' den,' sez Tobe, 'fer I des sta'ted fum heah yistiddy mawnin', en heah I is turnt back ter a nigger ag'in befo' I'd ha'dly got useter walkin' on all-fours. Dey's sump'n de matter wid dat goopher er yo'n, fer yo' cunj'in' ain' wuk right dis time. I crawled in a holler tree 'bout six o'clock en went ter sleep, en w'en I woke up in de mawnin' I wuz tu'nt back ag'in; en bein' ez I hadn' got no fu'ther 'n Rockfish Crick, I des 'lowed I'd come back en git dat goopher w'at I paid fer fix' right.'

"Aun' Peggy scratched her head en studied a minute, en den sez she:—

"'Uh huh! I sees des w'at de trouble is. I is tu'nt you ter a b'ar heah in de fall, en w'en you come ter a holler tree you crawls in en goes ter sleep fer de winter, des lak any yuther b'ar 'd do; en ef I had n' mix' dat yuther goopher in fer ter tu'n you back in a mont', you'd a slep' all th'oo de winter. I had des plum' fergot 'bout dat, so I reckon I'll hafter try sumpin' diff'ent. I 'spec' I better tu'n you ter a fox. En bein' ez a fox is a good runner, you oughter git ter de Norf in less time dan a b'ar,' so I'll fix dis yer goopher so you'll tu'n back ter a nigger en des th'ee weeks, en you'll be able ter enjoy yo' freedom a week sooner.'

"So Aun' Peggy tu'nt Tobe ter a fox, en he sta'ted down de road in great has'e, en made mo'd'n ten miles, w'en he 'mence' ter feel kinder hongry. So w'en he come ter a hen-house he tuk a hen en eat it, en lay down in de woods ter git his night's res'. In de mawnin', wen he woke up, he 'lowed he mought 'swell hab ernudder chick'n fer breakfus', so he tuk a fat pullet en eat dat.

"Now, Tobe had be'n monst's fon' er chick'n befo' he wuz tu'nt ter a fox, but he hadn' nebber had ez much ez he could eat befo'. En bein' ez dere wuz so many chick'ns in dis naberhood, en dey mought be ska'se whar he wuz gwine, he 'lowed he better stay 'roun' dere 'tel he got kinder fat, so he could stan' bein' hongry a day er so ef he sh'd fin' slim pickin's fu'ther 'long. So he dug hisse'f a nice hole under a tree in de woods, en des stayed dere en eat chick'n fer a couple er weeks er so. He wuz so comf'table, eatin' w'at he laked, en restin' w'en he wa'n't eatin', he des kinder los' track er de time, 'tel befo' he notice' it his th'ee weeks wuz mos' up.

"But bimeby de people w'at own dese yer chick'ns 'mence' ter miss 'em, en dey 'lowed dey wuz a fox som'ers roun'. So dey got out dey houn's en dey hawns en dey hosses, en sta'ted off fer a fox-hunt. En sho' nuff de houn's got de scent, en wuz on po' Tobe's track in a' hour er so.

"W'en Tobe heared 'em comin' he wuz mos' skeered ter def, en he 'mence' ter run ez ha'd ez he could, en bein' ez de houn's wuz on de norf side, he run to'ds de souf, en soon foun' hisse'f back in de woods right whar he wuz bawn en raise'. He jumped a crick en doubled en twisted, en done ev'ything he could fer ter th'ow de houn's off'n de scent but 't wa'n't no use, fer dey des kep' gittin' closeter, en closeter, en closeter.

"Ez soon ez Tobe got back to'ds home en 'skivered whar he wuz, he sta'ted fer ole Aun' Peggy's cabin fer te git her ter he'p 'im, en des ez he got ter her do', lo en behol'! he tu'nt back ter a nigger ag'in, fer de th'ee weeks wuz up des ter a minute. He knock' at de do', en hollered:—

"'Lemme in, Aun' Peggy, lemme in! De dawgs is atter me.'

"Aun' Peggy open' de do'.

"'Fer de Lawd sake! nigger, whar is you come fum dis time?' sez she. 'I 'lowed you wuz done got ter de Norf, en free long ago. W'at's de matter wid you now?'

"So Tobe up'n' tol' her 'bout how he had been stop' by dem chick'ns, en how ha'd it wuz ter git 'way fum 'em. En w'iles he wuz talkin' ter Aun' Peggy dey heared de dawgs comin' closeter, en closeter, en closeter.

"'Tu'n me ter sump'n e'se, Aun' Peggy,' sez Tobe, 'fer dat fox scent runs right up ter de do', en dey'll be 'bleedzd ter come in, en dey'll fin' me en kyar me back home, en lamb me,[6] en mos' lakly sell me 'way. Tu'n me ter sump'n, quick, I doan keer w'at, fer I doan want dem dawgs ner dem w'ite folks ter ketch me.'

"Aun' Peggy look' 'roun' de cabin, en sez she, takin' down a go'd fum de chimbly:—

"'I ain' got no goopher made up ter-day, Tobe, but dis yer bull-frog mixtry. I'll tu'n you ter a bull-frog, en I'll put in ernuff er dis yuther mixtry fer ter take de goopher off in a day er so, en meanw'iles you kin hop down yander ter dat ma'sh en stay, en w'en de dawgs is all gone en you tu'ns back, you kin come ter me en I'll tu'n you ter a sparrer er sump'n' w'at kin fly swif', en den maybe you'll be able ter git 'way en be free widout all dis yer foolishness you's be'n goin' th'oo.'

"By dis time de dawgs wuz scratchin' at de do' en howlin', en Aun' Peggy en Tobe could heah de hawns er de hunters blowin' close behin'. All dis yer racket made Aun' Peggy sorter narvous, en w'en she went ter po' dis yuther mixtry in fer ter lif' 'de bull-frog goopher off 'n Tobe in a day er so, her han' shuck so she spilt it ober de side er de yuther go'd en didn' notice dat it hadn' gone in. En Tobe wuz so busy lis'nin' en watchin' de do', dat he didn' notice nuther, en so w'en Aun' Peggy put de goopher on Tobe en tu'nt 'im inter a bull-frog, dey wa'n't none er dis yuther mixtry in it w'atsomeber.

"Tobe le'p' out'n a crack 'twix' de logs, en Aun' Peggy open' de do', en de dawgs run 'roun', en de w'ite folks come en inqui'ed, en w'en dey seed Aun' Peggy's roots en go'ds en snake-skins en yuther cunjuh-fixin's, en a big black cat wid yaller eyes, settin' on de h'a'th, dey 'lowed dey wuz wastin' dey time, so dey des cusst a little en run 'long back home widout de fox dey had come atter.

"De nex' day Aun' Peggy stayed roun' home all day, makin' a mixtry fer ter tu'n Tobe ter a sparrer, en 'spectin' 'im eve'y minute fer ter come in. But he nebber come. En bein' ez he didn' 'pear no mo', Aun'

---

6. Tobe fears that if he is caught he will be lamed, have his Achilles tendon severed so that he is not able to run or walk properly. This punishment for runaway slaves was pre-scribed by some eighteenth-century colonial laws. By using the dialect spelling, Chesnutt puns on the Bre'r Rabbit tales: Tobe fears being "lambed" or made into prey by the white hunters.

Peggy 'lowed he'd got ti'ed er dis yer animal bizness en w'en he had tu'nt back fum de bull-frog had runned 'way on his own 'sponsibility, lak she 'vised 'im at fus'. So Aun' Peggy went on 'bout her own bizness en didn' paid no mo' tention ter Tobe.

"Ez fer po' Tobe, he had hop' off down ter dat ma'sh en had jump' in de water, en had waited fer hisse'f ter tu'n back. But w'en he didn' tu'n back de fus' day, he 'lowed Aun' Peggy had put in too much er de mixtry, en bein' ez de ma'sh wuz full er minners en snails en crawfish en yuther things w'at bull-frogs laks ter eat, he 'lowed he mought 's well be comf'table en enjoy hisse'f 'tel his bull-frog time wuz up.

"But bimeby, w'en a mont' roll' by, en two mont's, en th'ee mont's, en a yeah, Tobe kinder 'lowed dey wuz sump'n wrong 'bout dat goopher, en so he 'mence' ter go up on de dry lan' en look fer Aun' Peggy. En one day w'en she came 'long by de ma'sh, he got in front er her, en croak' en croak'; but Aun' Peggy wuz studyin' 'bout sump'n e'se; en 'sides, she 'lowed Tobe wuz done gone 'way en got free long, long befo', so she didn' pay no 'tention ter de big bull-frog she met in de path, 'cep'n ter push him out 'n de road wid her stick.

"So Tobe went back ter his ma'sh, en dere he's be'n eber sence. It's be'n fifty yeahs er mo', en Tobe mus' be 'bout ten yeahs older 'n I is. But he ain' nebber got ti'ed er wantin' ter be tu'nt back ter hisse'f, en ter sump'n w'at could run erway ter de Norf. Co'se ef he had waited lak de res' un us he'd a be'n free long ago; but he didn' know dat, en he doan know it yet. En eve'y night, w'en de frogs sta'ts up, dem w'at knows 'bout Tobe kin reco'nize his voice en heah 'im callin', callin', callin' ole Aun' Peggy fer ter come en tu'n 'im back, des ez ef Aun' Peggy hadn' be'n restin' in Aberham's bosom[7] fer fo'ty yeahs er mo'. Oncet in a w'ile I notices dat Tobe doan say nuffin fer a night er so, en so I 'lows he's gittin' ole en po'ly, en trouble' wid hoa'seness er rheumatiz er sump'n er 'nuther, fum bein' in de water so long. I doan 'spec' he's gwine to be dere many mo' yeahs; but w'iles he is dere, it 'pears ter me he oughter be 'lowed ter lib out de res' er his days in peace.

"Dat's de reason w'y," the old man concluded, "I doan lak ter see nobody eat'n frogs' laigs out 'n dat ma'sh. Ouch!" he added suddenly, putting his hand to the pit of his stomach, "Ouch!"

"What's the matter, Uncle Julius?" my wife inquired with solicitude.

"Oh, nuffin, ma'm, nuffin wuf noticin'—des a little tech er mis'ry in my innards. I s'pose talkin' 'bout po' old Tobe, in dat col', wet ma'sh, wid nobody ter 'sociate wid but frogs en crawfish en watermoccasins en sich, en wid nuffin fittin' ter eat, is des sorter upsot me

---

7. In the parable of Dives and Lazarus (Luke 16:19–30), when both figures die and enter the abode of the dead, the disciple Lazarus is believed to occupy a place of honor with the patriarch Abraham, a place reserved only for the just.

mo' er less. If you is anyways int'rusted in a ole nigger's feelin's, I ruther 'spec' a drap er dem bitters out'n dat little flat jimmyjohn er yo'n git me shet er[8] dis mis'ry quicker'n anything e'se I knows."

Hot-Foot Hannibal[1]

"I hate you and despise you! I wish never to see you or speak to you again!"

"Very well; I will take care that henceforth you have no opportunity to do either."

These words—the first in the passionately vibrant tones of my sister-in-law, and the latter in the deeper and more restrained accents of an angry man—startled me from my nap. I had been dozing in my hammock on the front piazza, behind the honeysuckle vine. I had been faintly aware of a buzz of conversation in the parlor, but had not at all awakened to its import until these sentences fell, or, I might rather say, were hurled upon my ear. I presume the young people had either not seen me lying there,—the Venetian blinds opening from the parlor windows upon the piazza were partly closed on account of the heat,—or else in their excitement they had forgotten my proximity.

I felt somewhat concerned. The young man, I had remarked, was proud, firm, jealous of the point of honor, and, from my observation of him, quite likely to resent to the bitter end what he deemed a slight or an injustice. The girl, I knew, was quite as high-spirited as young Murchison. I feared she was not so just, and hoped she would prove more yielding. I knew that her affections were strong and enduring, but that her temperament was capricious, and her sunniest moods easily overcast by some small cloud of jealousy or pique. I had never imagined, however, that she was capable of such intensity as was revealed by these few words of hers. As I say, I felt concerned. I had learned to like Malcolm Murchison,[2] and had heartily consented to his marriage with my ward; for it was in that capacity that I had stood

---

8. "to get shut of": to get rid of; *bitters*: bitter medicine or liquor impregnated with substances such as wormwood; *jimmyjohn*: a liquor jug.
1. Written by Chesnutt in 1898 specifically for *The Conjure Woman*; published in the *Atlantic Monthly* in 1899 in advance of the release of the volume; included as the last story in the book.
2. This marriage story resurrects the Murchison family from the much darker story "The Dumb Witness," which had been rejected by the *Atlantic Monthly* the year before. Rather than giving Mabel's suitor the name "Roger Murchison," that of the young nephew of the family who had inherited his demented uncle's fortune at the end of the earlier story, Chesnutt calls him "Malcolm Murchison"—ominously giving him the name of the demented uncle himself.

for a year or two to my wife's younger sister, Mabel. The match thus rudely broken off had promised to be another link binding me to the kindly Southern people among whom I had not long before taken up my residence.

Young Murchison came out of the door, cleared the piazza in two strides without seeming aware of my presence, and went off down the lane at a furious pace. A few moments later Mabel began playing the piano loudly, with a touch that indicated anger and pride and independence and a dash of exultation, as though she were really glad that she had driven away forever the young man whom the day before she had loved with all the ardor of a first passion.

I hoped that time might heal the breach and bring the two young people together again. I told my wife what I had overheard. In return she gave me Mabel's version of the affair.

"I do not see how it can ever be settled," my wife said. "It is something more than a mere lovers' quarrel. It began, it is true, because she found fault with him for going to church with that hateful Branson girl. But before it ended there were things said that no woman of any spirit could stand. I am afraid it is all over between them."

I was sorry to hear this. In spite of the very firm attitude taken by my wife and her sister, I still hoped that the quarrel would be made up within a day or two. Nevertheless, when a week had passed with no word from young Murchison, and with no sign of relenting on Mabel's part, I began to think myself mistaken.

One pleasant afternoon, about ten days after the rupture, old Julius drove the rockaway up to the piazza, and my wife, Mabel, and I took our seats for a drive to a neighbor's vineyard, over on the Lumberton plank-road.

"Which way shall we go," I asked,—"the short road or the long one?"

"I guess we had better take the short road," answered my wife. "We will get there sooner."

"It's a mighty fine dribe roun' by de big road, Mis' Annie," observed Julius, "en it doan take much longer to git dere."

"No," said my wife, "I think we will go by the short road. There is a bay-tree in blossom near the mineral spring, and I wish to get some of the flowers."

"I 'spec's you 'd fin' some bay-trees 'long de big road, ma'm," suggested Julius.

"But I know about the flowers on the short road, and they are the ones I want."

We drove down the lane to the highway, and soon struck into the short road leading past the mineral spring. Our route lay partly through a swamp, and on each side the dark, umbrageous foliage, unbroken by any clearing, lent to the road solemnity, and to the air a refreshing coolness. About half a mile from the house, and about half-way to the mineral spring, we stopped at the tree of which my wife had spoken, and reaching up to the low-hanging boughs, I gathered a dozen of the fragrant white flowers. When I resumed my seat in the rockaway, Julius started the mare. She went on for a few rods, until we had reached the edge of a branch crossing the road, when she stopped short.

"Why did you stop, Julius?" I asked.

"I didn', suh," he replied. "'T wuz de mare stop'. G' 'long dere, Lucy! W'at you mean by dis foolis'ness?"

Julius jerked the reins and applied the whip lightly, but the mare did not stir.

"Perhaps you had better get down and lead her," I suggested. "If you get her started, you can cross on the log and keep your feet dry."

Julius alighted, took hold of the bridle, and vainly essayed to make the mare move. She planted her feet with even more evident obstinacy.

"I don't know what to make of this," I said. "I have never known her to balk before. Have you, Julius?"

"No, suh," replied the old man, "I neber has. It 's a cu'ous thing ter me, suh."

"What 's the best way to make her go?"

"I 'spec's, suh, dat ef I'd tu'n her 'roun', she'd go de udder way."

"But we want her to go this way."

"Well, suh, I 'low ef we des set heah fo' er fibe minutes, she'll sta't up by herse'f."

"All right," I rejoined; "it is cooler here than any place I have struck to-day. We'll let her stand for a while, and see what she does."

We had sat in silence for a few minutes, when Julius suddenly ejaculated, "Uh huh! I knows w'y dis mare doan go. It des flash' 'cross my recommemb'ance."

"Why is it, Julius?" I inquired.

"'Ca'se she sees Chloe."

"Where is Chloe?" I demanded.

"Chloe's done be'n dead dese fo'ty years er mo'," the old man returned. "Her ha'nt is settin' ober yander on de udder side er de branch, unner dat willer-tree, dis blessed minute."

"Why, Julius!" said my wife, "do you see the haunt?"

"No'm," he answered, shaking his head, "I doan see 'er, but de mare sees 'er."

"How do you know?" I inquired.

"Well, suh, dis yer is a gray hoss, en dis yer is a Friday; en a gray hoss kin alluz see a ha'nt w'at walks on Friday."

"Who was Chloe?" said Mabel.

"And why does Chloe's haunt walk?" asked my wife.

"It's all in de tale, ma'm," Julius replied, with a deep sigh. "It 's all in de tale."

"Tell us the tale," I said. "Perhaps, by the time you get through, the haunt will go away and the mare will cross."

I was willing to humor the old man's fancy. He had not told us a story for some time; and the dark and solemn swamp around us; the amber-colored stream flowing silently and sluggishly at our feet, like the waters of Lethe; the heavy, aromatic scent of the bays, faintly suggestive of funeral wreaths,—all made the place an ideal one for a ghost story.

"Chloe," Julius began in a subdued tone, "use' ter b'long ter ole Mars' Dugal' McAdoo,—my ole marster. She wuz a lackly gal en a smart gal, en ole mis' tuk her up ter de big house, en l'arnt her ter wait on de w'ite folks, 'tel bimeby she come ter be mis's own maid, en 'peared ter 'low she run de house herse'f, ter heah her talk erbout it. I wuz a young boy den, en use' ter wuk 'bout de stables, so I knowed eve'ythin' dat wuz gwine on 'roun' de plantation.

"Well, one time Mars' Dugal' wanted a house boy, en sont down ter de qua'ters fer ter hab Jeff en Hannibal come up ter de big house nex' mawnin'. Ole marster en ole mis' look' de two boys ober, en 'sco'sed wid deyse'ves fer a little w'ile, en den Mars' Dugal' sez, sezee:—

"'We lacks Hannibal de bes', en we gwine ter keep him. Heah, Hannibal, you'll wuk at de house fum now on. En ef you er a good nigger en min's yo' bizness, I'll gib you Chloe fer a wife nex' spring. You other nigger, you Jeff, you kin go back ter de qua'ters. We ain' gwine ter need you.'

"Now Chloe had be'n stan'in' dere behin' ole mis' dyoin' all er dis yer talk, en Chloe made up her min' fum de ve'y fus' minute she sot eyes on dem two dat she didn' lack dat nigger Hannibal, en wa'n't neber gwine keer fer 'im, en she wuz des ez sho' dat she lack' Jeff, en wuz gwine ter set sto' by 'im, whuther Mars' Dugal' tuk 'im in de big house er no; en so co'se Chloe wuz monst'us sorry w'en ole Mars' Dugal' tuk Hannibal en sont Jeff back. So she slip' roun' de house en waylaid Jeff on de way back ter de qua'ters, en tol' 'im not ter be down-hea'ted, fer she wuz gwine ter see ef she couldn' fin' some way er 'nuther ter git rid er dat nigger Hannibal, en git Jeff up ter de house in his place.

"De noo house boy kotch' on monst'us fas', en it wa'n't no time ha'dly befo' Mars' Dugal' en ole mis' bofe 'mence' ter 'low Hannibal wuz de bes' house boy dey eber had. He wuz peart en soopl', quick ez lightnin', en sha'p ez a razor. But Chloe didn' lack his ways. He wuz so sho' he wuz gwine ter git 'er in de spring, dat he didn' 'pear ter 'low he had ter do any co'tin', en w'en he 'd run 'cross Chloe 'bout de house, he'd swell roun' 'er in a biggity way en say:—

"'Come heah en kiss me, honey. You gwine ter be mine in de spring. You doan 'pear ter be ez fon' er me ez you oughter be.'

"Chloe didn' keer nuffin fer Hannibal, en hadn' keered nuffin fer 'im, en she sot des ez much sto' by Jeff ez she did de day she fus' laid eyes on 'im. En de mo' fermilyus dis yer Hannibal got, de mo' Chloe let her min' run on Jeff, en one ebenin' she went down ter de qua'ters en watch', 'tel she got a chance fer ter talk wid 'im by hisse'f. En she tol' Jeff fer ter go down en see ole Aun' Peggy, de cunjuh 'oman down by de Wim'l'ton Road, en ax her ter gib 'im sump'n ter he'p git Hannibal out'n de big house, so de w'ite folks 'u'd sen' fer Jeff ag'in. En bein' ez Jeff didn' hab nuffin ter gib Aun' Peggy, Chloe gun 'im a silber dollah en a silk han'kercher fer ter pay her wid, fer Aun' Peggy neber lack ter wuk fer nobody fer nuffin.

"So Jeff slip' off down ter Aun' Peggy's one night, en gun 'er de present he brung, en tol' 'er all 'bout 'im en Chloe en Hannibal, en ax' 'er ter he'p 'im out. Aun' Peggy tol' 'im she'd wuk 'er roots, en fer 'im ter come back de nex' night, en she'd tell 'im w'at she c'd do fer 'im.

"So de nex' night Jeff went back, en Aun' Peggy gun 'im a baby doll, wid a body made out'n a piece er co'n-stalk, en wid splinters fer a'ms en laigs, en a head made out'n elderberry peth, en two little red peppers fer feet.

"'Dis yer baby doll,' sez she, 'is Hannibal. Dis yer peth head is Hannibal's head, en dese yer pepper feet is Hannibal's feet. You take dis en hide it unner de house, on de sill unner de do', whar Hannibal'll hafter walk ober it eve'y day. En ez long ez Hannibal comes anywhar nigh dis baby doll, he'll be des lack it is,—light-headed en hot-footed; en ef dem two things doan git 'im inter trouble mighty soon, den I'm no cunjuh 'oman. But w'en you git Hannibal out'n de house, en git all th'oo wid dis baby doll, you mus' fetch it back ter me, fer it's monst'us powerful goopher, en is liable ter make mo' trouble ef you leabe it layin' roun'.'

"Well, Jeff tuk de baby doll, en slip' up ter de big house, en whistle' ter Chloe, en w'en she come out he tol' 'er w'at ole Aun' Peggy had said. En Chloe showed 'im how ter git unner de house, en w'en he had put de cunjuh doll on de sill, he went 'long back ter de qua'ters—en des waited.

"Nex' day, sho' 'nuff, de goopher 'mence' ter wuk. Hannibal sta'ted in de house soon in de mawnin' wid a armful er wood ter make a fire, en he hadn' mo' d'n got 'cross de do'-sill befo' his feet begun ter bu'n so dat he drap' de armful er wood on de flo' en woke ole mis' up a' hour sooner 'n yushal, en co'se ole mis' didn' lack dat, en spoke sha'p erbout it.

"W'en dinner-time come, en Hannibal wuz help'n' de cook kyar de dinner f'm de kitchen inter de big house, en wuz gittin' close ter de do' whar he had ter go in, his feet sta'ted ter bu'n en his head begun ter swim, en he let de big dish er chicken en dumplin's fall right down in de dirt, in de middle er de ya'd, en de w'ite folks had ter make dey dinner dat day off'n col' ham en sweet'n' 'taters.

"De nex' mawnin' he overslep' hisse'f, en got inter mo' trouble. Atter breakfus', Mars' Dugal' sont 'im ober ter Mars' Marrabo Utley's fer ter borry a monkey wrench. He oughter be'n back in ha'f a' hour, but he come pokin' home 'bout dinner-time wid a screw-driver stidder a monkey wrench. Mars' Dugal' sont ernudder nigger back wid de screw-driver, en Hannibal didn' git no dinner. 'Long in de atternoon, ole mis' sot Hannibal ter weedin' de flowers in de front gya'-den, en Hannibal dug up all de bulbs ole mis' had sont erway fer, en paid a lot er money fer, en tuk 'em down ter de hawg-pen by de ba'nya'd, en fed 'em ter de hawgs. W'en ole mis' come out in de cool er de ebenin', en seed w'at Hannibal had done, she wuz mos' crazy, en she wrote a note en sont Hannibal down ter de oberseah wid it.

"But w'at Hannibal got fum de oberseah didn' 'pear ter do no good. Eve'y now en den 'is feet 'd 'mence ter torment 'im, en 'is min' 'u'd git all mix' up, en his conduc' kep' gittin' wusser en wusser, 'tel fin'lly de w'ite folks couldn' stan' it no longer, en Mars' Dugal' tuk Hannibal back down ter de qua'ters.

"'Mr. Smif,' sez Mars' Dugal' ter de oberseah, 'dis yer nigger has done got so triflin' yer lately dat we can't keep 'im at de house no mo', en I's fotch' 'im ter you ter be straighten' up. You's had 'casion ter deal wid 'im once, so he knows w'at ter expec'. You des take 'im in han', en lemme know how he tu'ns out. En w'en de han's comes in fum de fiel' dis ebenin' you kin sen' dat yaller nigger Jeff up ter de house. I'll try 'im, en see ef he's any better 'n Hannibal.'

"So Jeff went up ter de big house, en pleas' Mars' Dugal' en ole mis' en de res' er de fambly so well dat dey all got ter lackin' 'im fus'rate; en dey'd 'a' fergot all 'bout Hannibal, ef it hadn' be'n fer de bad repo'ts w'at come up fum de qua'ters 'bout 'im fer a mont' er so. Fac' is, dat Chloe en Jeff wuz so int'rusted in one ernudder sence Jeff be'n up ter de house, dat dey fergot all 'bout takin' de baby doll back ter Aun' Peggy, en it kep' wukkin' fer a w'ile, en makin' Hannibal's feet bu'n mo' er less, 'tel all de folks on de plantation got ter callin' 'im Hot-Foot Hannibal. He kep' gittin' mo' en mo' triflin', 'tel he got de name er bein' de mos' no 'countes' nigger on de plantation, en Mars' Dugal' had ter th'eaten ter sell 'im in de spring, w'en bimeby de goopher quit wukkin', en Hannibal 'mence' ter pick up some en make folks set a little mo' sto' by 'im.

"Now, dis yer Hannibal was a monst'us sma't nigger, en w'en he got rid er dem so' feet, his min' kep' runnin' on 'is udder troubles. Heah th'ee er fo' weeks befo' he'd had a' easy job, waitin' on de w'ite folks, libbin' off'n de fat er de lan', en promus' de fines' gal on de plantation fer a wife in de spring, en now heah he wuz back in de co'n-fiel, wid de oberseah a-cussin' en a-r'arin' ef he didn' get a ha'd tas' done; wid nuffin but co'n bread en bacon en merlasses ter eat; en all de fiel'-han's makin' rema'ks, en pokin' fun at 'im 'ca'se he'd be'n sont back fum de big house ter de fiel'. En de mo' Hannibal studied 'bout it de mo' madder he got, 'tel he fin'lly swo' he wuz gwine ter git eben wid Jeff en Chloe, ef it wuz de las' ac'.

"So Hannibal slipped 'way fum de qua'ters one Sunday en hid in de co'n up close ter de big house, 'tel he see Chloe gwine down de road. He waylaid her, en sezee:—

"'Hoddy, Chloe?'

"'I ain' got no time fer ter fool wid fiel'-han's,' sez Chloe, tossin' her head; 'w'at you want wid me, Hot-Foot?'

"'I wants ter know how you en Jeff is gittin' 'long.'

"'I 'lows dat 's none er yo' bizness, nigger. I doan see w'at 'casion any common fiel'-han' has got ter mix in wid de 'fairs er folks w'at libs in de big house. But ef it'll do you any good ter know, I mought say dat me en Jeff is gittin' 'long mighty well, en we gwine ter git married in de spring, en you ain' gwine ter be 'vited ter de weddin' nuther.'

"'No, no!' sezee, 'I wouldn' 'spec' ter be 'vited ter de weddin',—a common, low-down fiel'-han' lack I is. But I's glad ter heah you en Jeff is gittin' 'long so well. I didn' knowed but w'at he had 'mence' ter be a little ti'ed.'

"'Ti'ed er me? Dat's rediklus!' sez Chloe. 'W'y, dat nigger lubs me so I b'liebe he'd go th'oo fire en water fer me. Dat nigger is des wrop' up in me.'

"'Uh huh,' sez Hannibal, 'den I reckon it mus' be some udder nigger w'at meets a 'oman down by de crick in de swamp eve'y Sunday ebenin', ter say nuffin 'bout two er th'ee times a week.'

"'Yas, hit is ernudder nigger, en you is a liah w'en you say it wuz Jeff.'

"'Mebbe I is a liah, en mebbe I ain' got good eyes. But 'less'n I *is* a liah, en 'less'n I *ain'* got good eyes, Jeff is gwine ter meet dat 'oman dis ebenin' 'long 'bout eight o'clock right down dere by de crick in de swamp 'bout half-way betwix' dis plantation en Mars' Marrabo Utley's.'

"Well, Chloe tol' Hannibal she didn' b'liebe a wo'd he said, en call' 'im a low-down nigger, who wuz tryin' ter slander Jeff 'ca'se he wuz mo' luckier 'n he wuz. But all de same, she couldn' keep her min' fum runnin' on w'at Hannibal had said. She 'membered she'd heared one er de niggers say dey wuz a gal ober at Mars' Marrabo Utley's planta- tion w'at Jeff use' ter go wid some befo' he got 'quainted wid Chloe. Den she 'mence' ter figger back, en sho' 'nuff, dey wuz two er th'ee times in de las' week w'en she'd be'n he'pin' de ladies wid dey dressin' en udder fixin's in de ebenin', en Jeff mought 'a' gone down ter de swamp widout her knowin' 'bout it at all. En den she 'mence' ter 'member little things w'at she hadn' tuk no notice of befo', en w'at 'u'd make it 'pear lack Jeff had sump'n on his min'.

"Chloe set a monst'us heap er sto' by Jeff, en would 'a' done mos' anythin' fer 'im, so long ez he stuck ter her. But Chloe wuz a mighty jealous 'oman, en w'iles she didn' b'liebe w'at Hannibal said, she seed how it *could* 'a' be'n so, en she 'termine' fer ter fin' out fer herse'f whuther it *wuz* so er no.

"Now, Chloe hadn' seed Jeff all day, fer Mars' Dugal' had sont Jeff ober ter his daughter's house, young Mis' Ma'g'ret's, w'at libbed 'bout fo' miles fum Mars' Dugal's, en Jeff wuzn' 'spected home 'tel ebenin'. But des atter supper wuz ober, en w'iles de ladies wuz settin' out on de piazzer, Chloe slip' off fum de house en run down de road,—dis yer same road we come; en w'en she got mos' ter de crick—dis yer same crick right befo' us—she kin' er kep' in de bushes at de side er de road, 'tel fin'lly she seed Jeff settin' on de bank on de udder side er de crick,—right unner dat ole willer-tree droopin' ober de water yander. En eve'y now en den he'd git up en look up de road to'ds Mars' Marrabo's on de udder side er de swamp.

"Fus' Chloe felt lack she 'd go right ober de crick en gib Jeff a piece er her min'. Den she 'lowed she better be sho' befo' she done anythin'. So she helt herse'f in de bes' she could, gittin' madder en madder eve'y minute, 'tel bimeby she seed a 'oman comin' down de road on de udder side fum to'ds Mars' Marrabo Utley's plantation. En w'en she seed Jeff jump up en run to'ds dat 'oman, en th'ow his a'ms roun' her neck, po' Chloe didn' stop ter see no mo', but des tu'nt roun' en run up ter de house, en rush' up on de piazzer, en up en tol' Mars' Dugal' en ole mis' all 'bout de baby doll, en all 'bout Jeff gittin' de goopher fum Aun' Peggy, en 'bout w'at de goopher had done ter Hannibal.

"Mars' Dugal' wuz monst'us mad. He didn' let on at fus' lack he b'liebed Chloe, but w'en she tuk en showed 'im whar ter fin' de baby doll, Mars' Dugal' tu'nt w'ite ez chalk.

"'W'at debil's wuk is dis?' sezee. 'No wonder de po' nigger's feet eetched. Sump'n got ter be done ter l'arn dat ole witch ter keep her han's off'n my niggers. En ez fer dis yer Jeff, I 'm gwine ter do des w'at I promus', so de darkies on dis plantation'll know I means w'at I sez.'

"Fer Mars' Dugal' had warned de han's befo' 'bout foolin' wid cunju'ation; fac', he had los' one er two niggers hisse'f fum dey bein' goophered, en he would 'a' had ole Aun' Peggy whip' long ago, on'y Aun' Peggy wuz a free 'oman, en he wuz 'feard she 'd cunjuh him. En w'iles Mars' Dugal' say he didn' b'liebe in cunj'in' en sich, he 'peared ter 'low it wuz bes' ter be on de safe side, en let Aun' Peggy alone.

"So Mars' Dugal' done des ez he say. Ef ole mis' had ple'd fer Jeff, he mought 'a' kep' 'im. But ole mis' hadn' got ober losin' dem bulbs yit, en she neber said a wo'd. Mars' Dugal' tuk Jeff ter town nex' day

en' sol' 'im ter a spekilater, who sta'ted down de ribber wid 'im nex'
mawnin' on a steamboat, fer ter take 'im ter Alabama.

"Now, w'en Chloe tol' ole Mars' Dugal' 'bout dis yer baby doll en dis
udder goopher, she hadn' ha'dly 'lowed Mars' Dugal' would sell Jeff
down Souf. Howsomeber, she wuz so mad wid Jeff dat she 'suaded
herse'f she didn' keer; en so she hilt her head up en went roun' lookin'
lack she wuz rale glad 'bout it. But one day she wuz walkin' down de
road, w'en who sh'd come 'long but dis yer Hannibal.

"W'en Hannibal seed 'er, he bus' out laffin' fittin' fer ter kill: 'Yah,
yah, yah! ho, ho, ho! ha, ha, ha! Oh, hol' me, honey, hol' me, er I 'll
laf myse'f ter def. I ain' nebber laf' so much sence I be'n bawn.'

"'W'at you laffin' at, Hot-Foot?'

"'Yah, yah, yah! Wat I laffin' at? W'y, I's laffin' at myse'f, tooby
sho',—laffin' ter think w'at a fine 'oman I made.'

"Chloe tu'nt pale, en her hea't come up in her mouf.

"'W'at you mean, nigger?' sez she, ketchin' holt er a bush by de road
fer ter stiddy herse'f. 'W 'at you mean by de kin' er 'oman you made?'

"'W'at do I mean? I means dat I got squared up wid you fer treatin'
me de way you done, en I got eben wid dat yaller nigger Jeff fer cuttin' me out. Now, he's gwine ter know w'at it is ter eat co'n bread en
merlasses once mo', en wuk fum daylight ter da'k, en ter hab a
oberseah dribin' 'im fum one day's een' ter de udder. I means dat I
sont wo'd ter Jeff dat Sunday dat you wuz gwine ter be ober ter Mars'
Marrabo's visitin' dat ebenin', en you want 'im ter meet you down by
de crick on de way home en go de rest er de road wid you. En den I
put on a frock en a sunbonnet, en fix' myse'f up ter look lack a
'oman; en w'en Jeff seed me comin', he run ter meet me, en you seed
'im,—fer I'd be'n watchin' in de bushes befo' en 'skivered you comin'
down de road. En now I reckon you en Jeff bofe knows w'at it means
ter mess wid a nigger lack me.'

"Po' Chloe hadn' heared mo' d'n half er de las' part er w'at Hannibal said, but she had heared 'nuff to l'arn dat dis nigger had fooled
her en Jeff, en dat po' Jeff hadn' done nuffin, en dat fer lovin' her too
much en goin' ter meet her she had cause' 'im ter be sol' erway whar
she'd neber, neber see 'im no mo'. De sun mought shine by day, de
moon by night, de flowers mought bloom, en de mawkin'-birds
mought sing, but po' Jeff wuz done los' ter her fereber en fereber.

"Hannibal hadn' mo' d'n finish' w'at he had ter say, w'en Chloe's
knees gun 'way unner her, en she fell down in de road, en lay dere
half a' hour er so befo' she come to. W'en she did, she crep' up ter de
house des ez pale ez a ghos'. En fer a mont' er so she crawled roun'
de house, en 'peared ter be so po'ly dat Mars' Dugal' sont fer a doctor; en de doctor kep' on axin' her questions 'tel he foun' she wuz des
pinin' erway fer Jeff.

"W'en he tol' Mars' Dugal', Mars' Dugal' lafft, en said he 'd fix dat. She could hab de noo house boy fer a husban'. But ole mis' say, no, Chloe ain' dat kin'er gal, en dat Mars' Dugal' sh'd buy Jeff back.

"So Mars' Dugal' writ a letter ter dis yer spekilater down ter Wim'l'ton, en tol' ef he ain' done sol' dat nigger Souf w'at he bought fum 'im, he'd lack ter buy 'im back ag'in. Chloe 'mence' ter pick up a little w'en ole mis' tol' her 'bout dis letter. Howsomeber, bimeby Mars' Dugal' got a' answer fum de spekilater, who said he wuz monst'us sorry, but Jeff had fell ove'boa'd er jumped off'n de steamboat on de way ter Wim'l'ton, en got drownded, en co'se he couldn' sell 'im back, much ez he 'd lack ter 'bleedge Mars' Dugal'.

"Well, atter Chloe heared dis, she wa'n't much mo' use ter nobody. She pu'tended ter do her wuk, en ole mis' put up wid her, en had de doctor gib her medicine, en let 'er go ter de circus, en all so'ts er things fer ter take her min' off'n her troubles. But dey didn' none un 'em do no good. Chloe got ter slippin' down here in de ebenin' des lack she 'uz comin' ter meet Jeff, en she 'd set dere unner dat willer-tree on de udder side, en wait fer 'im, night atter night. Bimeby she got so bad de w'ite folks sont her ober ter young Mis' Ma'g'ret's fer ter gib her a change; but she runned erway de fus' night, en w'en dey looked fer 'er nex' mawnin', dey foun' her co'pse layin' in de branch yander, right 'cross fum whar we're settin' now.

"Eber sence den," said Julius in conclusion, "Chloe's ha'nt comes eve'y ebenin' en sets down unner dat willer-tree en waits fer Jeff, er e'se walks up en down de road yander, lookin' en lookin', en waitin' en waitin', fer her sweethea't w'at ain' neber, neber come back ter her no mo'."

There was silence when the old man had finished, and I am sure I saw a tear in my wife's eye, and more than one in Mabel's.

"I think, Julius," said my wife, after a moment, "that you may turn the mare around and go by the long road."

The old man obeyed with alacrity, and I noticed no reluctance on the mare's part.

"You are not afraid of Chloe's haunt, are you?" I asked jocularly.

My mood was not responded to, and neither of the ladies smiled.

"Oh, no," said Annie, "but I've changed my mind. I prefer the other route."

When we had reached the main road and had proceeded along it for a short distance, we met a cart driven by a young negro, and on the cart were a trunk and a valise. We recognized the man as Malcolm Murchison's servant, and drew up a moment to speak to him.

"Who's going away, Marshall?" I inquired.

"Young Mistah Ma'colm gwine 'way on de boat ter Noo Yo'k dis ebenin', suh, en I'm takin' his things down ter de wharf, suh."

This was news to me, and I heard it with regret. My wife looked sorry, too, and I could see that Mabel was trying hard to hide her concern.

"He's comin' 'long behin', suh, en I 'spec's you'll meet 'im up de road a piece. He's gwine ter walk down ez fur ez Mistah Jim Williams's, en take de buggy fum dere ter town. He 'spec's ter be gone a long time, suh, en say prob'ly he ain' neber comin' back."

The man drove on. There were a few words exchanged in an undertone between my wife and Mabel, which I did not catch. Then Annie said: "Julius, you may stop the rockaway a moment. There are some trumpet-flowers by the road there that I want. Will you get them for me, John?"

I sprang into the underbrush, and soon returned with a great bunch of scarlet blossoms.

"Where is Mabel?" I asked, noting her absence.

"She has walked on ahead. We shall overtake her in a few minutes."

The carriage had gone only a short distance when my wife discovered that she had dropped her fan.

"I had it where we were stopping. Julius, will you go back and get it for me?"

Julius got down and went back for the fan. He was an unconscionably long time finding it. After we got started again we had gone only a little way, when we saw Mabel and young Murchison coming toward us. They were walking arm in arm, and their faces were aglow with the light of love.

I do not know whether or not Julius had a previous understanding with Malcolm Murchison by which he was to drive us round by the long road that day, nor do I know exactly what motive influenced the old man's exertions in the matter. He was fond of Mabel, but I was old enough, and knew Julius well enough, to be skeptical of his motives. It is certain that a most excellent understanding existed between him and Murchison after the reconciliation,[3] and that when the young people set up housekeeping over at the old Murchison place, Julius had an opportunity to enter their service. For some reason or other, however, he preferred to remain with us. The mare, I might add, was never known to balk again.

---

3. The term "reconciliation" was used in Chesnutt's era to denote the post-Reconstruction rapprochement between North and South, and more specifically between Northern and Southern whites. In fiction, reconciliation stories took the form of romances that married a Northerner to a Southerner, thereby effecting a new union between regions. Chesnutt takes up that popular plot in this story.

The Marked Tree[1]

I had been requested by my cousin, whose home was in Ohio, to find for him, somewhere in my own neighborhood in the pine belt of North Carolina, a suitable place for a winter residence. His wife was none too strong; his father, who lived with him, was in failing health; and he wished to save them from the raw lake winds which during the winter season take toll of those least fitted to resist their rigor. My relative belonged to the fortunate class of those who need take no thought today for tomorrow's needs. The dignity of labor is a beautiful modern theory, in which no doubt many of the sterner virtues find their root, but the dignity of ease was celebrated at least as long ago as the days of Horace, a gentleman and philosopher,[2] with some reputation as a poet.

Since my cousin was no lover of towns, and the term neighborhood is very elastic when applied to rural life, I immediately thought of an old, uncultivated—I was about to say plantation, but its boundaries had long since shrunk from those which in antebellum times would have justified so pretentious a designation. It still embraced, however, some fifteen or twenty acres of diversified surface—part sand-hill, part meadow; part overgrown with scrubby shortleaf pines and part with a scraggy underbrush. Though the soil had been more or less exhausted by the wasteful methods of slavery, neglected grapevines here and there, and gnarled and knotted fruit-trees, smothered by ruder growths about them, proved it to have been at one time in a high state of cultivation.

1. Presumably written by Chesnutt long after the publication of the former stories; published, in two parts, in *The Crisis* in 1924–25. This is the only one of Chesnutt's stories to have been published with illustrations. The illustrations are by Yolande Du Bois (1900–1960), daughter of *Crisis* editor and famed writer W. E. B. Du Bois, who produced illustrations for several issues of the magazine after her graduation from Fisk University in 1924. The group of illustrations she created for Chesnutt's story is one of the most extensive she produced for a single item in the magazine.
2. Horace (65 B.C.E.–8 B.C.E.), major lyric poet of the reign of Augustus, was the son of a Roman freedman (former slave).

I had often driven by the old Spencer place, as it was called, from the name of the family whose seat it had been. It lay about five miles from my vineyard and was reached by a drive down the Wilmington Road and across the Mineral Spring swamp. Having brought with me to North Carolina a certain quickness of decision and promptness of action which the climate and *laissez faire* customs of my adopted state had not yet overcome, upon receipt of my cousin's letter I ordered old Julius to get out the gray mare and the rockaway and drive me over to the old Spencer place.

When we reached it, Julius left his seat long enough to take down the bars which guarded the entrance and we then drove up a short lane to the cleared space, surrounded by ragged oaks and elms, where the old plantation house had once stood. It had been destroyed by fire many years before and there were few traces of it remaining—a crumbling brick pillar here and there, on which the sills of the house had rested, and the dilapidated, ivy-draped lower half of a chimney, of which the yawning, blackened fireplace bore mute witness of the vanished generations which had lived and loved—and perchance suffered and died, within the radius of its genial glow.

Not far from where the house had stood, there was a broad oak stump, in a good state of preservation, except for a hole in the center, due, doubtless, to a rotten heart, in what had been in other respects a sound and perfect tree. I had seated myself upon the top of the stump—the cut had been made with the axe, almost as smoothly as though with a saw—when old Julius, who was standing near me, exclaimed, with some signs of concern.

"Excuse me, suh, I know you come from de No'th, but did any of yo' folks, way back yonder, come from 'roun' hyuh?"

"No," I returned, "they were New England Yankees, with no Southern strain whatever. But why do you ask?" I added, observing that he had something on his mind, and having often found his fancies quaint and amusing, from the viewpoint of one not Southern born.

"Oh, nothin', suh, leas'ways nothin' much—only I seed you settin' on dat ol' stump, an' I wuz kind er scared fer a minute."

"I don't see anything dangerous about the stump," I replied. "It seems to be a very well preserved oak stump."

"Oh, no, suh," said Julius, "dat ain' no oak stump."

It bore every appearance of an oak stump. The grain of the wood was that of oak. The bark was oak bark, and the spreading base held the earth in the noble grip of the king of trees.

"It is an oak, Julius—it is the stump of what was once a fine oak tree."

"Yas, suh, I know it 'pears like oak wood, and it 'pears like oak bahk, an' it looked like a oak tree wen it wuz standin' dere, fifty feet high, fohty years ago. But it wa'n't—no, suh, it wa'n't."

"What kind of a tree was it, if not an oak?"

"It was a U-pass tree, suh; yes, sah, dat wuz de name of it—a U-pass tree."

"I have never heard of that variety," I replied.

"No, suh, it wuz a new kind er tree roun' hyuh. I nevah heard er any but dat one."

"Where did you get the name?" I asked.

"I got it from ol' Marse Aleck Spencer hisse'f, fohty years ago—fohty years ago, suh. I was lookin' at dat tree one day, aftuh I'd heared folks talkin' 'bout it, an' befo' it wuz cut down, an' ole Marse Aleck come erlong, an' sez I, 'Marse Aleck, dat is a monst'us fine oak tree.' An' ole Marse Aleck up an sez, sezee, 'No, Julius, dat ain' no oak-tree—dat is a U-pass tree.' An' I've 'membered the name evuh since, suh—de U-pass tree. Folks useter call it a' oak tree, but Marse Aleck oughter a knowd;—it 'us his tree, an' he had libbed close to it all his life."

It was evident that the gentleman referred to had used in a figurative sense the name which Julius had remembered so literally—the Upas tree, the fabled tree of death.[3] I was curious to know to what it owed this sinister appellation. It would be easy, I knew, as it afterwards proved, to start the old man on a train of reminiscence concerning the family and the tree. How much of it was true I cannot say; I suspected Julius at times of a large degree of poetic license—he took the crude legends and vague superstitions of the neighborhood and embodied them in stories as complete, in their way, as the Sagas of Iceland or the primitive tales of ancient Greece. I have saved a few of them. Had Julius lived in a happier age for men of his complexion, the world might have had a black Aesop or Grimm or Hoffman[4]—as it still may have, for who knows whether

---

3. The sap of the upas tree was used in Asia for poison arrows and darts. According to a spurious eighteenth-century British account that engaged the imaginations of many writers, the tree would destroy all human and animal life within a ten-mile radius of it.

4. E. T. A. Hoffman (1776–1822), German author of fantasy and horror stories, best known for the story upon which the ballet *The Nutcracker* is based. *Aesop*: author (620 B.C.E.–560 B.C.E.) who wrote fables in Greek featuring animal characters. According to tradition, he was enslaved and may also have been "black," of interior African descent. *Grimm*: Jacob (1785–1863) and Wilhelm (1786–1859) Grimm, German collectors of European folktales.

our civilization has yet more than cut its milk teeth,[5] or humanity has even really begun to walk erect?

Later in the day, in the cool of the evening, on the front piazza, left dark because of the mosquitoes, except for the light of the stars, which shone with a clear, soft radiance, Julius told my wife and me his story of the old Spencer oak. His low, mellow voice rambled on, to an accompaniment of night-time sounds—the deep diapason[6] from a distant frog-pond, the shrill chirp of the cicada, the occasional bark of a dog or cry of an owl, all softened by distance and merging into a melancholy minor which suited perfectly the teller and the tale.

"Marse Aleck Spencer uster be de riches' man in all dis neighborhood. He own' two thousan' acres er lan'—de ole place ovuh yonduh is all dat is lef'. Dere wus ovuh a hund'ed an' fifty slaves on de plantation. Marse Aleck was a magist'ate an a politician, an' eve'ybody liked him. He kep' open house all de time, an' had company eve'y day in de yeah. His hosses wuz de fastes' an' his fox-hounds de swiftes', his game-cocks de fierces', an' his servants de impidentes' in de county. His wife wuz de pretties' an' de proudes' lady, an' wo' de bes' clo's an' de mos' finguh-rings, an' rid in de fines' carriage. Fac', day alluz had de best er eve'ything, an' nobody didn' 'spute it wid 'em.

"Marse Aleck's child'en wuz de apples er his eye—dere wuz a big fambly—Miss Alice an' Miss Flora, an' young Marse Johnny, an' den some yeahs latuh, little Marse Henry an' little Marse Tom, an' den dere wuz ol' Mis' Kathu'n, Marse Aleck's wife, an' de chilen's mammy.

"When young Marse Johnny was bawn, and Aunt Dasdy, who had nussed all de child'en, put de little young marster in his pappy's arms, Marse Aleck wuz de happies' man in de worl'; for it wuz his fus' boy, an' he had alluz wanted a boy to keep up de fambly name an' de fambly rep'tation. An' eve'ybody on de plantation sheered his joy, fer when de marster smile, it's sunshine, an' when de marster frown, it's cloudy weather.

"When de missis was well enough, an' de baby was ol' enough, de christenin' come off; an' nothing would do fer Marse Aleck but to have it under de fambly tree—dat wuz de stump of it ovuh yonduh, suh, dat you was setting on dis mawnin'.

"'Dat tree,' said Marse Aleck, 'wuz planted when my great-gran'daddy wuz bawn. Under dat tree eve'y fus'-bawn son er dis fambly since den has be'n christen'. Dis fambly has growed an' flourish' wid dat tree, an' now dat my son is bawn, I wants ter hab him christen' under it, so dat he kin grow an' flourish 'long wid it. An' dis ole oak'—Marse Aleck useter 'low it wuz a oak, befo' he give it de new

<hr />

5. Deciduous or "baby" teeth.
6. Complete concord or harmony.

name—'dis ole oak is tall an' stout an' strong. It has weathe'd many a
sto'm. De win' cant blow it down, an' de lightnin' ain't nevuh struck
it, an' nothin' but a prunin' saw has ever teched it, ner ever shill, so
long as dere is a Spencer lef' ter pertec' it.

"'An' so my son John, my fus'-bawn, is gwineter grow up tall an'
strong, an' be a big man' an' a good man; an' his child'en and his
child'en's child'en an' dem dat follers shall be as many as de leaves er
dis tree, an' dey shill keep de name er Spencer at de head er de roll
as long as time shall las'.'"[7]

"De same day Marse Johnny wuz bawn, which wuz de fu'st er
May—anudder little boy, a little black boy, wuz bawn down in de
quahtahs. De mammy had worked 'roun' de big house de yeah befo',
but she had give er mist'iss some impidence one day, an' er mist'iss
had made Marse Aleck sen' her back ter de cotton-fiel'. An' when little
Marse Johnny wuz christen', Phillis,[8] dis yuther baby's mammy, wuz
standin' out on de edge, 'long wid de yuther fiel'-hands, fuh dey wuz
all 'vited up ter take part, an' ter eat some er de christenin' feas'.
Whils' de white folks wuz eatin' in de house, de cullud folks all had
plenty er good things pass 'roun' out in de yahd—all dey could eat an'
all they could drink, fuh dem wuz de fat yeahs er de Spencers—an' all
famblies, like all folks, has deir fat yeahs an' deir lean yeahs. De lean
yeahs er de Spencers wuz boun' ter come sooner er later.

"Little Marse Johnny growed an' flourish' just like the fambly tree
had done, an' in due time growed up to be a tall an' straight an' smart
young man. But as you sca'cely evuh sees a tree widout a knot, so
you nevuh sees a man widout his faults. Marse Johnny wuz so
pop'lar and went aroun' so much wid his frien's that he tuck ter
drinkin' mo' dan wuz good for him. Southe'n gent'emen all drunk
them days, suh—nobody had never dremp' er dis yer foolishness
'bout pro'bition dat be'n gwine roun' er late yeahs. But as a gin'ral
rule, dey drunk like gent'emen—er else dey could stan mo' liquor dan
folks kin dese days. An' young Marse Johnny had a mighty quick
temper, which mo'd'n once got 'im inter quarrels which it give 'im
mo' or less trouble to make up.

Marse Johnny wuz mighty fond er de ladies, too, an' wuz de pet
of 'em all. But he wuz jus' passin' de time wid 'em, 'tel he met Miss
Mamie Imboden—de daughter er de Widder Imboden, what own' a
plantation down on ole Rockfish. Ole Mis' Imboden didn' spen'
much time on huh place, but left it tuh a overseah, whils' she an'

---

7. Marse Aleck's speech recalls Greek tragedy as an act of hubris against the gods (self-
exaltation), which invites nemesis (retribution).
8. Chesnutt's name for the conjurer in this story, especially given its spelling, recalls that of
Phillis Wheatley (1753–1784), the famous African-born poet and founding figure of
African American literature.

Miss Mamie wuz livin' in de big towns, er de wat'rin-places, er way up yonduh in de No'th, whar you an' yo' lady come fum.

When de Widder Imboden come home one winter wid huh daughter, Marse Johnny fell dead in lub wid Miss Mamie. He couldn' ha'dly eat ner sleep fuh a week or so, an' he jus' natch'ly couldn' keep way fum Rockfish, an' jus' wo' out Marse Aleck's ridin' hosses comin' an' going', day, night an' Sunday. An' wharevuh she wuz visitin' he'd go visitin'; an' when she went tuh town he'd go tuh town. An' Marse Johnny got mo' religious dan he had evuh be'n befo' an' went tuh de Prisbyte'ian Chu'ch down tuh Rockfish reg'lar. His own chu'ch wuz 'Piscopal, but Miss Iboden wuz a Prisbyte'ian.

"But Marse Johnny wa'n't de only one. Anudder young gentleman, Marse Ben Dudley, who come fum a fine ole fambly, but wuz monst'us wild an' reckless, was payin' co't tuh Miss Mamie at de same time, an' it was nip an' tuck who should win out. Some said she favored one, and some said de yuther, an' some 'lowed she didn' knowed w'ich tuh choose.

"Young Marse Johnny kinder feared fuh a while dat she like de yuther young gentleman bes'. But one day Marse Ben's daddy, ole Marse Amos Dudley, went bankrup', an' his plantation and all his slaves wuz sol', an' he shot hisse'f in de head, and young Marse Ben wuz lef' po'. An' bein' too proud tuh work, an' havin' no relations ter live on, he tuck ter bettin' an' dicin' an' kyard-playin', an' went on jes' scan'lous. An' it wuz soon whispered 'roun' dat young Mistah Dudley wuz livin' on his winin's at kyards, an' dat he wa' n't partic'lar who he played wid, er whar er how he played. But I is ahead er my tale, fuh

all dis hyuh 'bout Marse Ben happen' after Marse Johnny had cut
Marse Ben out an' ma'ied Miss Mamie.

"Ol' Marse Aleck wuz monst'us glad when he heared Marse Johnny
wuz gwineter git ma'ied, for he wanted de fambly kep' up, an' he
'lowed Marse Johnny needed a wife fuh tuh he'p stiddy him. An'
Miss Mamie wuz one of dese hyuh sweet-nachu'd, kin'-hearted ladies
dat noboddy could he'p lovin'. An, mo'over, Miss Mamie's Mammy
wuz rich, an' would leave huh well off sume day.

"Fuh de lean yeahs er de Spencers wuz comin', an' Marse Aleck
'spicioned it. De cotton crop had be'n po' de yeah befo', de cawn had
ben wuss, glanders[9] had got in the hosses an most of 'em had had ter
be killed; an' old Marse Aleck wuz mo' sho't of money dan he'd be'n
fur a long, long time. An' when he tried tuh make it up by spekilatin',
he jus' kep' on losin' mo' an' mo' an' mo'.

"But young Marse Johnny had ter hab money for his weddin', an'
the house had to be fix' up fuh 'im an' his wife, an' dere had ter be a
rich weddin' present an' a fine infare,[1] an' all dem things cos' money.
An' sence he didn' wanter borry de money, Marse Aleck 'lowed he
s'posed he'd hafter sell one er his han's. An' ole Mis' Spencer say he
should sell Phillis's Isham.[2] Marse Aleck didn' wanter sell Isham, fur
he 'membered Isham wuz de boy dat wuz bawn on de same day
Marse Johnny wuz. But ole Mis' Spencer say she didn' like dat boy's
looks nohow, an' dat his mammy had be'n impident tuh huh one
time, an ef Marse Aleck gwine sell anybody he sh'd sell Isham.

"Prob'bly ef old Marse Aleck had knowed jus' what wuz gwineter
happen he mought not 'a' sol' Isham—he'd 'a' ruther gone inter debt,
er borried de money. But den nobody nevuh knows whats gwineter
happen; an' what good would it do 'em ef dey did? It'd only make 'em
mizzable befo' han', an' ef it wuz gwineter happen, how could dey
stop it? So Marse Aleck wuz bettuh off dan ef he had knowed.

"Now, dis hyuh Isham had fell in love, too, wid a nice gal on de
plantation, an' wuz jus' 'bout making up his min' tuh ax Marse Aleck
tuh let 'im marry her an' tuh give 'em a cabin tuh live in by deyse'ves,
when one day Marse Aleck tuck Isham ter town, an' sol' 'im to

---

9. A contagious disease in horses which can cause swelling beneath the jaw.
1. In Scottish tradition, an infare is a lavish reception held on entering a new house, particularly when a bride enters a new home.
2. The name of Phillis's son may be read as "is ham" or, in dialect, "I's ham." With this name
   Chesnutt calls back to the early story "Dave's Neckliss," in which the enslaved protagonist
   of Julius's tale believes he has been transformed into a ham. With the name, Chesnutt
   also more directly links this later protagonist to the biblical Ham, whose story in Genesis
   (9:20–27) was cited in the nineteenth-century United States as a godly sanction for racial
   slavery. In the biblical passage, often termed "the Curse of Canaan," the patriarch Noah
   condemns the descendants of his son Ham to be, in perpetuity, "servant of servants" to
   the descendants of his other sons. The biblical story resonates with this tale of Isham, the
   black son of the Spencer plantation, exchanged for the aggrandizement of Johnny, the
   white son.

another gent'eman, fuh tuh git de money fuh de expenses er his own son's weddin'.

"Isham's mammy wuz workin' in de cotton-fiel' way ovuh at de fah end er de plantation dat day, an' when she went home at night an' foun' dat Marse Aleck had sol' huh Isham, she run up to de big house an' wep' an' hollered an' went on terrible. But Marse Aleck tol huh it wuz all right, dat Isham had a good marster, an' wa'n't many miles erway, an' could come an' see his mammy whenevuh he wanter.

"When de young ma'ied folks came back f'm dey weddin' tower,[3] day had de infare, an' all de rich white folks wuz invited. An' dat same night, whils' de big house wuz all lit up, an' de fiddles wuz goin', an' dere wuz eatin' an' drinkin' an' dancin' an' sky-larkin' an' eve'body wuz jokin' de young couple an' wushin' 'em good luck, Phillis wuz settin' all alone in huh cabin, way at de fah end er de quarters, studyin' 'bout huh boy, who had be'n sol' to pay fer it all. All de other cullud folks wuz up 'round' de big house, some waitin' on de white folks, some he'pin in de kitchen, some takin' keer er de guest's hosses, an' de res' swa'min' 'round de yahd, gittin' in one anudder's way, an' waitin' 'tel de white folks got thoo, so dey could hab somethin' tuh eat too; fuh Marse Aleck had open' de big blade,[4] an' wanted eve'body to have a good time.

"'Bout time de fun wuz at de highes' in de big house, Phillis heared somebody knockin' at huh cabin do'. She didn' know who it could be, an' bein' as dere wa'nt' nobody e'se 'roun', she sot still an' didn' say nary word. Den she heared somebody groan, an' den dere wuz anudder knock, a feeble one dis time, an' den all wuz still.

"Phillis wait' a minute, an' den crack' de do', so she could look out, an' dere wuz somebody layin' all crumple' up on de do'step. An' den somethin' wahned huh what it wuz, an' she fetched a lighterd to'ch fum de ha'th. It wuz huh son Isham. He wuz wownded an' bleedin'; his feet wuz so' wid walkin'; he wuz weak from loss er blood.

"Phillis pick' Isham up an' laid 'im on huh bed an' run an' got some whiskey an' give 'im a drap, an' den she helt camphire tuh his nost'ils, meanwhile callin' his name an' gwine on like a wild 'oman. An' bimeby he open' his eyes an' look' up an' says—'I'se come home, mammy,'—an' den died. Dem wuz de only words he spoke, an' he nevuh drawed anudder bref.

"It come tuh light nex' day, when de slave-ketchers come aftuh Isham wid deir dawgs an' deir guns, dat he had got in a 'spute wid his marster, an' had achully *hit his marster*! An' realizin' what he had done, he had run erway; natch'ly to'ds his mammy an' de ole plantation. Dey had wounded 'im an' had mos' ketched him, but he had 'scaped ag'in an' had reach' home just in time tuh die in his mammy's ahms.

---

3. Wedding tour; honeymoon.
4. Made a show of the greatest extent of his possessions or capabilities.

"Phillis laid Isham out wid her own han's—dere wa'n't nobody dere tuh he'p her, an' she didn' want no he'p nohow. An' when it wuz all done, an' she had straighten' his lim's an' fol' his han's an' close his eyes, an' spread a sheet ovuh him, she shut de do' sof'ly, and stahted up ter de big house.

"When she drawed nigh, de visituhs wuz gittin' ready tuh go. De servants wuz bringin' de hosses an' buggies an' ca'iges roun', de white folks wuz laffin' an gwine on an' sayin' good-bye. An' whils' Phillis wuz standin' back behin' a bunch er rose-bushes in de yahd, listenin' an' waitin', ole Marse Aleck come out'n de house wid de young couple an' stood unduh de ole fambly tree. He had a glass er wine in his han', an' a lot er de yuthers follered:

"'Frien's,' says he, 'drink a toas' wid me tuh my son an' his lady, hyuh under dis ole tree. May it last anudder hunded yeahs, an' den anudder, an' may it fetch good luck tuh my son an' his wife, an' tuh deir child'en an' deir child'en's child'en.'

"De toas' wuz drunk, de gues's depahted; de slaves went back tuh de quahtuhs, an' Phillis went home tuh huh dead boy.

"But befo' she went, she *marked de Spencer tree*!

"Young Marse Johnny an' his wife got 'long mighty well fuh de fust six mont's er so, an 'den trouble commence' betwix' 'em. Dey wus at a pahty one night, an' young Marse Johnny seen young Marse Ben

Dudley talking in a cawnuh wid Miss Mamie. Marse Johnny wuz mighty jealous-natu'ed, an' didn' like dis at all. Endoyin' de same evenin' he overheard somebody say that Miss Mamie had th'owed Marse Ben ovuh beca'se he was po' an' married Marse Johnny beca'se he wuz rich. Marse Johnny didn' say nothin', but he kep' studyin' an studyin' 'bout dese things. An' it didn' do him no good to let his min' run on 'em.

"Marse Ben Dudley kep' on gwine from bad ter wuss, an' one day Marse Johnny foun' a letter from Marse Ben in his wife's bureau drawer.

"'You used ter love me' says Marse Ben in dis hyuh letter—'you know you did, and you love me yit—I know you does. I am in trouble. A few hun'ed dollahs'll he'p me out. Youer totin' mo' d'n dat 'roun' on yo' pretty little fingers. Git the money fuh me—it'll save my honor an' my life. I swear I'll pay it back right soon.'

"Den' all Marse Johnny's jealousy b'iled up at once, an' he seed eve'ything red. He went straight to Miss Mamie an' shuck de lettuh in her face an' 'cused her er gwine on wid Marse Ben. Co'se she denied it. Den he ax' huh what had become er huh di'mon' 'gagement ring dat he had give huh befo' dey wuz ma'ied.

"Miss Mamie look' at huh han' an' turn' white as chalk, fer de ring wa'n't dere.

"'I tuck it off las' night, when I went tuh bed, an' lef' it on de bureau, an' I fuhgot tuh put it on dis mawnin.'"

"But when she look' fer it on de bureau it wuz gone. Marse Johnny swo' she had give' it tuh Marse Ben, an' she denied it tuh de las'. He showed her de letter. She said she hadn' answered it, an' hadn't meant to answer it, but had meant to bu'n it up. One word led to another. Dere wuz a bitter quarrel, an' Marse Johnny swo' he'd never speak to his wife ag'in 'tel de di'mond ring wuz foun'. And he didn'.

"Ole Marse Aleck wuz 'way from home dat winter, to congress or de legislator, or somewhar, an' Marse Johnny wuz de boss er de plantation whils' he wuz gone. He wuz busy all day, on plantation, or in his office, er in town. He tuck moster his meals by hisself, an' when he et wid Miss Mamie he manage' so as nevuh to say nothin'. Ef she spoke, he purten' not to hear her, an' so she didn' try mo' d'n once er twice. Othe'wise, he alluz treated her like a lady—'bout a mile erway.

"Miss Mamie tuck it mighty ha'd. Fuh she was tenduh as well as proud. She jus' 'moped an' pined erway. One day in de springtime, when Marse Johnny wuz in town all day, she wuz tuck ill sudden, an' her baby wuz bawn, long befo' its time. De same day one er de little black child'en clum up in de ole Spencer tree an' fetch' down a jay-bird's nes', an' in de nes' dey foun' Miss Mamie's ring, whar de jay-bird had stole it an' hid it. When Marse Johnny come home dat night he found his wife an' his chile bofe dead, an' de ring on Miss Mamie's finger.

"Well, suh, you nevuh seed a man go on like Marse Johnny did; an' folks said dat ef he could 'a' foun' Marse Ben Dudley he sho' would a' shot 'im; but lucky fer Marse Ben he had gone away. Aftuh de fune'al, Marse Johnny shet hisse'f up in his room fer two er three days; an' as soon as Marse Aleck come home, Marse Johnny j'ind de ahmy an' went an' fit in de Mexican Wah an' wuz shot an' kill'.

"Ole Marse Aleck wuz so' distress' by dese yer troubles, an' grieve' migh'ly over de loss er his fus' bawn son. But he got ovuh it after a while. Dere wuz still Marse Henry an Marse Tom, bofe un' 'em good big boys, ter keep up de name, an' Miss Alice an' Miss Flora who wuz bofe ma'ied an' had child'en, ter see dat de blood didn' die out. An' in spite er dis hyuh thievin' jaybird, nobody 'lowed dat de ole tree had anything ter do wid Marse Johnny's troubles, fer 'co'se nobody but Phillis knowed dat it had evuh been mark'.

"But dis wuz only de beginnin'.

"Next year, in the spring, Miss Alice, Marse Aleck's oldes' daughter, wuz visitin' the fambly wid her nuss an' chile—she had ma'ied sev'al yeahs befo' Marse Johnny—an' one day de nuss wuz settin' out in de yahd, wid de chile, under de ole tree, when a big pizen spider let hisse'f down from a lim' when de nuss wa'n't lookin', an' stung the chile. The chile swoll up, an' dey sent fer de doctuh, but de doctuh

couldn' do nothin', an' the baby died in spasms dat same night, an' de mammy went inter a decline fum grief an' died er consumption insid' er six mont's.

"Of co'se de tree wuz watched close fer spiders aftah dis, but none er de white folks thought er blamin' de tree—a spider mought 'a' come from de ceiling' er from any other tree; it wuz jes' one er dem things dat couldn' be he'ped. But de servants commence' ter whisper 'mongs' deyse'ves dat de tree wuz conju'ed an' dere'd be still mo' trouble from it.

"It wa'n't long coming. One day young Marse Henry, de nex' boy ter Marse Johnny, went fishin' in de ribber, wid one er de naber boys, an' he clumb out too fah on a log, an' tip' de log up, an' fell in de ribber an' got drownded. Nobody could see how de ole tree wuz mix' up wid little Marse Henry's drowndin', 'tel one er de house servants 'membered he had seed de boys diggin' bait in de shade er de ole tree. An' whils' they didn' say nothin' ter de white folks, leas'ways not jes' den, dey kep' it in min' an' waited tuh see what e'se would happen. Dey didn' know den dat Phillis had mark' de tree, but dey mo' den half s'picioned it.

"Sho' 'nuff, one day de next' fall, Mis' Flora, Marse Aleck's secon' daughter, who wuz ma'ied an' had a husban', come home to visit her folks. An' one day whils' she wuz out walkin' wid her little boy, a sto'm come up, an' it stahted ter rain, an' dey didn' hab no umbreller, an' wuz runnin' ter de house, when jes' as dey got under de ole tree, de lightnin' struck it, broke a limb off'n de top, skun a little strip off'n de side all de way down, an' jump off an' hit Mis' Flora an' de boy, an' killt 'em bofe on de spot—dey didn't have time ter draw anudder bref.

"Still de white folks didn' see nuthin wrong wid de tree. But by dis time de cullud folks all knowed de tree had be'en conju'd. One un 'em said somethin' 'bout it one day ter old Marse Aleck, but he tol' 'em ter go 'long wid deir foolishness; dat it wuz de will er God; dat de lightnin' mought's well 'a' struck any yuther tree dey'd be'en under as dat one; an' dat dere wouldn' be no danger in de future, fer lightnin' nebber struck twice in de same place nohow.

"It wus 'bout a yeah after dat befo' anything mo' happen', an' de cullud folks 'lowed dat mo' likely dey had be'n mistaken an' dat maybe de tree hadn' be'n mark', er e'se de goopher wuz all wo' off, when one day little Marse Tom, de only boy dat wuz lef', wuz ridin' a new hoss Marse Aleck had give 'm, when a rabbit jump 'cross de road in front er him, an' skeered dis hyuh young hoss, an' de hoss run away an' thowed little Marse Tom up 'gins' de ole Spencer tree, an' bu'st his head in an' killt 'im.

"Marse Aleck wuz 'mos' heartbroken, fer Marse Tom wuz de only son he had lef'; dere wa'n't none er his child'en lef' now but Miss Alice, whose husban' had died, an' who had come wid her little gal ter lib wid her daddy and mammy.

"But dere wuz so much talk 'bout de ole tree 'tel it fin'lly got ter ole Miss Katherine's yeahs, an' she tol' Marse Aleck. He didn' pay no 'tention at fu'st, jes' 'lowed it 'uz all foolishness. But he kep' on hearin' so much of it, dat bimeby he wuz 'bleege' ter listen. An' he fin'lly 'lowed dat whether de tree was conju'd or not, it had never brought nuthin' but bad luck evuh sence Marse Johnny's weddin', an' he made up his min' ter git rid of it, in hopes er changin' de fambly luck.

"So one day he ordered a couple er han's ter come up ter de house wid axes an' cut down de ole tree. He tol' 'em jes' how ter chop it, one on one side an' one on de yuther, so's ter make it fall a partic'lar way. He stood off ter one side, wid his head bowed down, 'tel de two cuts had 'mos' met, an' den he tu'ned his eyes away, fer he didn' wanter see de ole tree fall—it had meant so much ter him fer so long. He heared de tree commence crackin', an' he heared de axemen holler, but he didn' know dey wuz hollerin' at him, an' he didn' look round'—he didn't wanter see de ole Spencer tree fall. But stidder fallin' as he had meant it ter, an' as by rights it couldn' he'p fallin', it jes' twisted squar' roun' sideways to'ds ole Marse Aleck an' ketched 'im befo' he could look up, an' crushed 'im ter de groun'.

"Well, dey buried Marse Aleck down in de fambly buryin'-groun'— you kin see it over at de ole place, not fur from de house; it's all growed up now wid weeds an' briars, an' most er de tombstones is fell down and covered wid green moul'. It wuz already pretty full, an' dere wa'n't much room lef'. After de fune'al, de ole tree wuz cut up inter firewood an' piled up out in de yard.

"Ole Miss' Kathun an' her daughter, Mis' Alice, an' Mis' Alice's little gal, went inter mo'nin' an' stayed home all winter.

"One col' night de house-boy toted in a big log fum de old Spencer tree, an' put it on de fire, an' when ole Miss' Kathun an' her daughter an' her gran' daughter went to bed, dey lef' de log smoulderin' on de ha'th. An' 'long 'bout midnight, when eve'ybody wuz soun' asleep, dis hyuh log fell out'n de fireplace an' rolled over on de flo' an' sot de house afire an' bu'nt it down ter de groun', wid eve'ybody in it.

"Dat, suh, wuz de end er de Spencer fambly. De house wuz nebber rebuil'. De war come erlong soon after, an' nobody had no money no mo' ter buil' houses. De lan', or what little wuz lef' after de mogages an' de debts wuz paid off, went ter dis hyuh young gentleman, Mistuh Brownlow, down to Lumberton, who wuz some kinder fo'ty-secon' cousin er nuther, an' I reckon he'd be only too glad ter sell it."

I wrote to young Mr. Brownlow, suggesting an appointment for an interview. He replied that he would call on me the following week, at an hour stated, if he did not hear from me beforehand that some other time would be more convenient.

I awaited him at the appointed hour. He came in the morning and stayed to luncheon. He was willing to sell the old place and we agreed upon a price at which it was to be offered to my cousin.

He was a shallow, amiable young fellow, unmarried, and employed as a clerk in a general store. I told him the story of the Spencer oak, as related by old Julius. He laughed lightly.

"I believe the niggers did have some sort of yarn about the family and the old tree," he said, "but of course it was all their silly superstition. They always would believe any kind of foolishness their crazy imaginations could cook up. Well, sir, let me know when you hear from your friend. I reckon I'll drive past the old place on my way home, and take a last took at it, for the sake of the family, for it was a fine old family, and it was a pity the name died out."

An hour later there was an agitated knock at my library door. When I opened it old Julius was standing there in a state of great excitement.

"What is the matter, Julius?"

"It's done gone an' happen', suh, it's done gone an' happen'!"

"What has done gone and happened?"

"De tree, suh, de U-pass tree—de ole Spencer tree."

"Well, what about it?"

"Young Mistuh Brownlow lef' here an' went ovuh tuh de old place, an' sot down en de ole stump, an' a rattlesnake come out'n de holler an' stung 'im, an' killt 'im, suh. He's layin' ovuh dere now, all black in de face and swellin' up fas'."

I closed my deal for the property through Mr. Brownlow's administrator. My cousin authorized me to have the land cleared off, preparatory to improving it later on. Among other things, I had the stump of the Spencer oak extracted. It was a difficult task even with the aid of explosives, but was finally accomplished without casualty, due perhaps to the care with which I inquired into the pedigree of the workmen, lest perchance among them there might be some stray offshoot of this illustrious but unfortunate family.

CONTEXTS

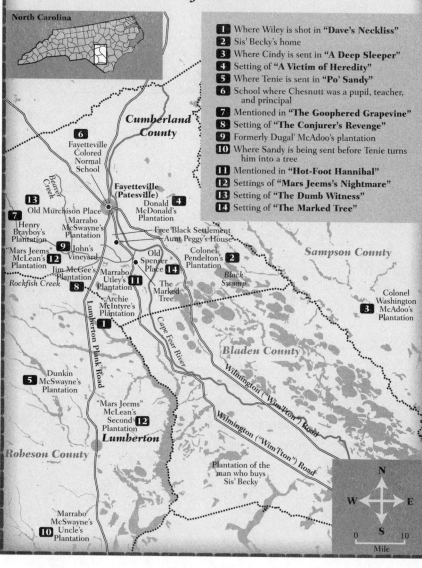

Map of the Terrain of Chesnutt's Conjure Tales

North Carolina

1 Where Wiley is shot in **"Dave's Neckliss"**
2 Sis' Becky's home
3 Where Cindy is sent in **"A Deep Sleeper"**
4 Setting of **"A Victim of Heredity"**
5 Where Tenie is sent in **"Po' Sandy"**
6 School where Chesnutt was a pupil, teacher, and principal
7 Mentioned in **"The Goophered Grapevine"**
8 Setting of **"The Conjurer's Revenge"**
9 Formerly Dugal' McAdoo's plantation
10 Where Sandy is being sent before Tenie turns him into a tree
11 Mentioned in **"Hot-Foot Hannibal"**
12 Settings of **"Mars Jeems's Nightmare"**
13 Setting of **"The Dumb Witness"**
14 Setting of **"The Marked Tree"**

Cumberland County

6 Fayetteville Colored Normal School

Beaver Creek

13 Old Murchison Place

Fayetteville (Patesville) 4

7 Henry Brayboy's Plantation

Marrabo McSwayne's Plantation

Donald McDonald's Plantation

Free Black Settlement
Aunt Peggy's House

Sampson County

"Mars Jeems" McLean's Plantation 12

9 John's Vineyard

Old Spenser Place

14

Colonel Pendelton's Plantation 2

Black Swamp

Jim McGee's Plantation

Rockfish Creek 8

Marrabo Utley's Plantation 11

The Marked Tree

3 Colonel Washington McAdoo's Plantation

Archie McIntyre's Plantation

1

Lumberton Plank Road

Cape Fear River

Bladen County

5 Dunkin McSwayne's Plantation

Wilmington ("Wim'l'ton") Road

"Mars Jeems" McLean's Second Plantation 12

Lumberton

Wilmington ("Wim'l'ton") Road

Robeson County

Plantation of the man who buys Sis' Becky

N
W   E
S

0   10
Mile

10 Marrabo McSwayne's Uncle's Plantation

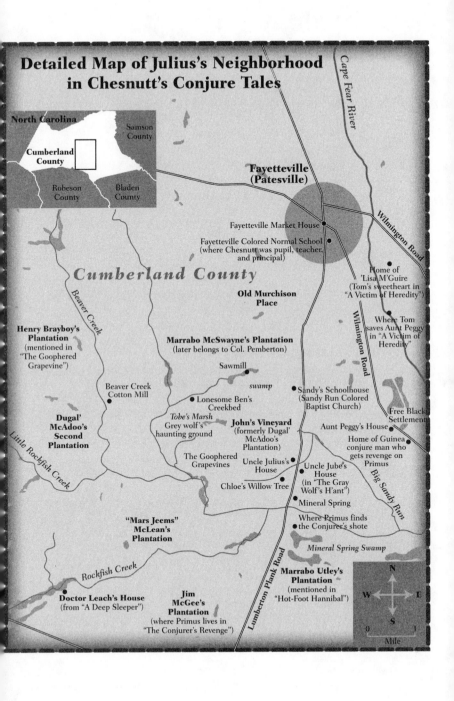

Detailed Map of Julius's Neighborhood in Chesnutt's Conjure Tales

North Carolina

Cumberland County

Samson County

Robeson County

Bladen County

Cape Fear River

Fayetteville (Patesville)

Fayetteville Market House

Fayetteville Colored Normal School (where Chesnutt was pupil, teacher, and principal)

Wilmington Road

Cumberland County

Beaver Creek

Henry Brayboy's Plantation (mentioned in "The Goophered Grapevine")

Old Murchison Place

Home of 'Lisa M'Guire (Tom's sweetheart in "A Victim of Heredity")

Where Tom saves Aunt Peggy in "A Victim of Heredity"

Wilmington Road

Marrabo McSwayne's Plantation (later belongs to Col. Pemberton)

Beaver Creek Cotton Mill

Sawmill

swamp

Lonesome Ben's Creekbed

Sandy's Schoolhouse (Sandy Run Colored Baptist Church)

Free Black Settlement

Tobe's Marsh Grey wolf's haunting ground

Dugal' McAdoo's Second Plantation

Little Rockfish Creek

John's Vineyard (formerly Dugal' McAdoo's Plantation)

Aunt Peggy's House

Home of Guinea conjure man who gets revenge on Primus

The Goophered Grapevines

Uncle Julius's House

Uncle Jube's House (in "The Gray Wolf's H'ant")

Chloe's Willow Tree

Mineral Spring

Big Sandy Run

Where Primus finds the Conjurer's shote

"Mars Jeems" McLean's Plantation

Mineral Spring Swamp

Rockfish Creek

Lumberton Plank Road

Marrabo Utley's Plantation (mentioned in "Hot-Foot Hannibal")

Doctor Leach's House (from "A Deep Sleeper")

Jim McGee's Plantation (where Primus lives in "The Conjurer's Revenge")

N

W   E

S

0   1

Mile

SARAH INGLE

The Terrain of Chesnutts Conjure Tales[†]

At the start of "The Goophered Grapevine," even before he introduces Uncle Julius, Chesnutt allows his readers to accompany John,
the narrator, and his wife, Annie, on a long, slow drive through the
countryside to the vineyard property that will soon become the narrative and geographical center of many of Julius's conjure tales. On the
way, the two Northerners become lost and stop to ask for directions:

> Once, at a crossroads, I was in doubt as to the turn to take, and
> we sat there waiting ten minutes—we had already caught some
> of the native infection of restfulness—for some human being to
> come along, who could direct us on our way. At length a little
> negro girl appeared, walking straight as an arrow, with a piggin
> full of water on her head. After a little patient investigation,
> necessary to overcome the child's shyness, we learned what we
> wished to know, and at the end of about five miles from the
> town reached our destination. (5)

The narrator, lost and stuck at a crossroads, ludicrously attempts to
deny his obvious status as an outsider by claiming to exhibit "the
native infection of restfulness," but the little girl, "walking straight
as an arrow," seems to know exactly where she is and where she is
going even if her answers to John's questions follow a more cir-
cuitous path that he attributes to "shyness." This encounter foreshadows the future interactions between John and Julius, which
often begin with John's condescension toward Julius's apparent
"embarrassment" and end with Julius telling a story that, in a cir-
cuitous but carefully crafted way, offers the Northern couple insight
into the local landscape, along with the people and the traumatic
history that inhabit it. This scene, which foregrounds the power of
local knowledge and the threat of disorientation, serves as an entry
point to the significance of real and imagined place in Chesnutt's
fictional landscape.[1]

[†] Published for the first time in this Norton Critical Edition.

1. Lorne Fienberg writes about the importance of the crossroads in this scene as a symbol of
   the liminality of Julius's and Chesnutt's positions. My concern is less with the symbolism
   of the crossroads than with the state of being lost and with the encounter and exchange
   that the narrator's disorientation precipitates. See Lorne Fienberg, "Charles W. Chesnutt
   and Uncle Julius: Black Storyteller at the Crossroads." *Studies in American Fiction* 15
   (Autumn 1987): 161–73.

Set in the vicinity of Fayetteville in Cumberland County, North Carolina, Chesnutt's conjure tales collectively constitute a geographical as well as literary community. Though born in Cleveland, Ohio, Chesnutt moved to Fayetteville with his family when he was eight and developed strong ties to the region. Like William Faulkner's fictional Yoknapatawpha County, the common setting of Chesnutt's conjure tales links the author's works together in ways that create a sense of continuity and familiarity. Unlike Faulkner, though, Chesnutt never drew a map of his conjure tales' setting, so the maps in this Norton Critical Edition are the first to represent the fictional landmarks described in Chesnutt's stories against the backdrop of the real geography of Cumberland County. By mapping the physical terrain of Chesnutt's conjure tales, we can gain insight into the ways in which geographical continuity, contested ownership, and disorientation shape the meanings of Chesnutt's conjure tales, both individually and collectively.

At the local level, Chesnutt maintains a striking degree of fidelity to the Fayetteville region's important landmarks and geographical features.[2] The stories mention by name three of the surrounding counties—Robeson, Bladen, and Sampson—and also identify local waterways such as Rockfish Creek and Beaver Creek. The Cape Fear River, a major feature of the region that flows just east of Fayetteville, is usually identified by Uncle Julius only as "de ribber," but the narrator specifically mentions "Cape Fear" in "Tobe's Tribulations" (111). Historical maps of Cumberland County also show the Lumberton Plank Road and two Wilmington Roads—one on each side of the Cape Fear River—extending south from Fayetteville. Although Chesnutt makes no mention of a second Wilmington Road—"Wim'l'ton" in Julius's dialect—he refers to the Lumberton and "Wim'l'ton" roads frequently, using them to connect the various plantations and settlements of his landscape, and also to connect the stories to one another. For example, every time Uncle Julius mentions Aunt Peggy in a story, he gives her more or less the same introduction: "Aun' Peggy, de free-nigger conjuh 'oman down by de Wim'l'ton Road." Although the exact wording of this introduction varies slightly each time, Julius invariably identifies Aunt Peggy by her name, her occupation, and her location. His consistency in doing so creates the sensation of listening to a refrain, suggesting that the tales are as intimately connected as the different verses of a

2. For an account of Chesnutt's use of actual Fayetteville landmarks and buildings in his first novel, *The House Behind the Cedars* (1900), see William L. Andrews, "Chesnutt's Patesville: The Presence and Influence of the Past in *The House Behind the Cedars.*" *College Language Association Journal* 15 (1972): 284–94.

single song. The repetition of familiar landmarks resonates with the repetition of characters to create a sense of community, but because the landmarks tend to remain relatively stable over time, they also connect the living with the dead, creating a sense of community across time as well as across space.

By bringing together scraps of information from different stories, many of Chesnutt's fictional landmarks can also be located with relative ease. John's vineyard, for example, is five miles from Patesville/ Fayetteville, according to "The Goophered Grapevine." "Po' Sandy" reveals that Sandy's schoolhouse lies on the northeast corner of John's property and fronts on the Lumberton plank-road. These descriptions alone are enough to locate John's property on a site that an 1884 map identifies as having "light sandy soil" suitable for growing grapes.[3] The same map shows the Beaver Creek Cotton Mill, whose construction is mentioned at the beginning of "Lonesome Ben," and another map from the 1860s locates the sawmill from "Po' Sandy" just north of John's property.[4] Most of Chesnutt's other fictional landmarks, including plantations, swamps, and haunted sites, are described with varying degrees of specificity in relation to their distance and direction from John's vineyard. Marrabo McSwayne's plantation, which figures prominently in many stories, including "Po' Sandy" and "Lonesome Ben," is also fairly easy to locate—just beyond the sawmill to the north of John's property. For other landmarks, though, Chesnutt often provides only vague descriptions such as "down on Wim'l'ton Road" and leaves the rest to his readers' imaginations. A few stories refer to Black Swamp and Mineral Spring Swamp, but current and historical maps of the area do not show swamps with those names. The maps in this book largely rely on contextual clues from the stories to locate those landmarks, but the Black Swamp's proximity to the Sampson County border reflects the fact that the river separating Cumberland and Sampson counties was labeled Black River on maps from as late as 1868, though most of it now goes by the name South River.[5] Although the locations of many of Chesnutt's fictional landmarks remain debatable, the two maps in this book represent a reasonable composite of the major fictional and non-fictional features of Chesnutt's literary landscape.

In addition to roads and streams, Chesnutt may even have drawn some of the names of his characters from real Fayetteville families

---

3. D.G. McDuffie, "McDuffie's map of Cumberland County, North Carolina" (1884). North Carolina Maps. U of North Carolina at Chapel Hill.
4. "Map of Fayetteville, North Carolina and surrounding area" (circa 1860–1865). North Carolina Collection. U of North Carolina at Chapel Hill.
5. D.G. McDuffie, "Map of Cumberland County representing the townships of said county" (circa 1868). North Carolina State Archives. U of North Carolina at Chapel Hill.

and places.[6] The many Scottish names that populate the conjure tales, including McAdoo, McSwayne, McLean, McGee, McDonald, and M'Guire, accurately reflect the origins of many settlers in the Cape Fear region. In a more specific parallel, the Fayetteville State Colored Normal School (now called Fayetteville State University), with which Chesnutt had strong ties as a pupil, a teacher, and a principal, moved to its current location on Murchison Road in 1908.[7] Although this move occurred several years after Chesnutt depicted members of the Murchison family in "The Dumb Witness" and "Hot-Foot Hannibal," he may have chosen the name for its local resonance. Likewise, the name of Marrabo Utley, whose plantation is mentioned in "Hot-Foot Hannibal," may have local roots. The Taylor-Utley House, listed today as one of Fayetteville's historic landmarks, was purchased by Joseph Utley in 1857.[8]

By far, though, Chesnutt's most ingenious use of local landmarks as a source of names occurs in "Po' Sandy." The story's frame narrative ends with the Sandy Run Colored Baptist Church experiencing a "split" over the issue of temperance, prompting Julius and his fellow "seceders" to relocate their meetings to a haunted schoolhouse built from the remains of a metamorphosed slave. Both the story's title character and the Sandy Run Colored Baptist Church get their names from a real waterway—Big Sandy Run, which rises on the map from Rockfish Creek and crosses the Lumberton Plank Road like a finger pointing directly to the site of John's property. In the name "Sandy Run," Chesnutt reflects the irony of his character's fate. Sandy tries to escape the devastating rootlessness and uncertainty of slavery by having his wife turn him into a tree, but when his

---

6. Although the maps and essays of this book focus on the conjure tales, Chesnutt incorporated local names and places from the Fayetteville area into many of his other stories and novels as well, and these references did not escape the notice of his contemporaries. Indeed, one anonymous "old inhabitant" of Fayetteville responded to Chesnutt's story "The Banquet" by wielding the authority of local knowledge to accuse Chesnutt of distorting the truth and of exaggerating the hardships endured by Fayetteville's African American population:

> The scene is not only laid in North Carolina by admission but in Fayetteville by description. Mary Myrover is a Fayetteville name. St. John's Episcopal church is a Fayetteville institution and is minutely described, except that it does not date from colonial times. There are several local touches, such as the profusion of flowers, the funeral customs, that remind an old inhabitant of Fayetteville. The old inhabitant desires to record a few facts.
>   * * * Mr. Chestnutt speaks of the colored people being denied access to the house of mourning and even to the galleries of the church during the funeral. One who has buried many dead in Fayetteville, including his own, may be permitted to testify to the fact that the sympathy of the colored people was always tendered and gratefully accepted and that there was not a single burial of the dead in which they did not occupy the galleries of the church and throng around the grave.

Anon., "Fiction and Fact." *The Wilmington Messenger* (Jan. 28, 1900): 7.
7. Jan S. Whitfield, "Fayetteville State University's History." Charles W. Chesnutt Library, Fayetteville State University. http://library.uncfsu.edu/archives/HistoryFSU.htm.
8. "Historic Sites." Fayetteville Area Convention & Visitors Bureau (2010). http://www .visitfayettevillenc.com/historicsites/index/list/page/3.

conjured disguise causes him to be milled and used as lumber, he finally achieves the stability he wanted at the cost of both his life and his humanity. Sandy hopes to put an end to his perpetual running back and forth from plantation to plantation at the whims of his master, but his attempt at escape leaves him in a state not only of permanent immobility but also of voicelessness, isolation, and fragmentation—a literal manifestation of the estrangement from his own humanity that he experienced as a slave. The full significance of Chesnutt's choice of names becomes apparent only when you realize that "Sandy Run" is not merely the name of a fictional church congregation that inhabits Sandy's schoolhouse but also a real feature of the landscape in Cumberland County, North Carolina. The real Big Sandy Run is both fixed in space and perpetually running, perpetually moving and changing with the flow of its waters. This combination of permanence and restlessness also characterizes Sandy's spirit, which, according to Uncle Julius, haunts the schoolhouse built from his lumber. Through his story, Chesnutt infuses the name "Sandy Run" with the power to reflect both the relentless commands of Sandy's master and the slave's ill-fated attempt to find a better life for himself and his wife. In doing so, Chesnutt mirrors Uncle Julius's technique of transforming features of the landscape by using the power of storytelling to alter their meaning. Julius's story transforms the abandoned schoolhouse on John's property from a handy source of cheap, recycled lumber into a haunted place worthy of awe and respect—at least in the eyes of Annie. By similar means, Chesnutt uses the power of his story to transform an ordinary stream in the middle of Cumberland County into a site of symbolic meaning and historical commemoration.

Chesnutt generally makes no attempt to conceal his use of real places in his conjure stories, but a striking exception to this rule occurs at the beginning of "The Goophered Grapevine" when the narrator describes his destination: "a quaint old town, which I shall call Patesville, because, for one reason, that is not its name" (3). Chesnutt's decision not only to change the name of Fayetteville but also to call attention to the name change in such an obvious fashion suggests that both the real and fictional names deserve careful scrutiny. The word "pate" in Patesville suggests an anatomical reading of the landscape in which Fayetteville/Patesville serves as the head, with its body unfolding to the south.[9] In this reading, John's vineyard and Uncle Julius's house seem to be at the geographical as well as narrative heart of the stories. Distant outposts such as

---

9. For another interpretation of the meaning of "Patesville" that associates the town with Golgotha, the place of Christ's crucifixion, see the Werner Sollors essay in this Norton Critical Edition, note 9; p. 295.

Colonel Washington McAdoo's plantation in Sampson County, where Cindy is sent in "A Deep Sleeper," are the appendages, and slaves are the blood that circulates among the various plantations throughout the region, going wherever their masters choose to send them. This anatomical reading of the landscape inverts the usual direction of transformation in the stories, in which human bodies are fused with the features of their physical environment—turned into trees and buildings in "Po' Sandy," into clay and muddy creek water in "Lonesome Ben," and into grapevines in "The Goophered Grapevine." Nevertheless, viewing the region as a living organism highlights the extent to which Chesnutt's conjure tales are interconnected across space and time, like the functioning networks of a body's organs. It should be no surprise that Chesnutt locates the head, and thus the mind, of this organism in Fayetteville, the site of the Fayetteville State Colored Normal School (called the Howard School until 1877) where Chesnutt received his own education and later became a teacher and then a principal. But though the mind behind Chesnutt's body of work may lie in "Patesville," his conjure tales focus on the geographical region of the body, where African Americans contend with the infection of slavery through the healing power of circulating stories.

However significant the fictional name "Patesville" may be, though, the narrator's ambiguous assertion that he calls the town Patesville "because, for one thing, that is not its name" suggests that the deliberate obfuscation of the name "Fayetteville" is at least as important as the suggestion of an embodied community. The most obvious explanation for such an omission is that Chesnutt does not want his readers to know where he has set his stories or wants them to believe that the stories are set in a purely fictional place. But this explanation falls short in the face of textual evidence that Chesnutt is more than willing to give his readers accurate names of major roads and waterways in the area as well as the names of the state, region, and three surrounding counties. So why should Chesnutt hold back the name of Fayetteville while revealing so many other place-names? I suspect the choice has something to do with the town's namesake—General Lafayette—and with the extent to which Julius's conjure tales are intricately concerned with the complex significance of enshrining a person in a place.

A man with no shortage of names, Marie Joseph Paul Yves Roche Gilbert du Motier, Marquis de Lafayette, was an officer in the French Royal Army in 1775 when he decided to join the American Revolution, eventually rising to the rank of Major General. In 1783, at the end of the war, the citizens of Campbellton, North Carolina, became the first of many American towns to change its name to Fayetteville to honor Lafayette's contributions to American independence. When Lafayette returned to the United States in 1825 for the fiftieth anniversary of the start of the Revolution, he visited Fayetteville, North Carolina, on a rainy day in March, was honored at several banquets and receptions, and offered the town a warm toast: "Fayetteville.—May it receive all the encouragements and attain all the prosperity which are anticipated by the fond and grateful wishes of its affectionate and respectful namesake."[1] Chesnutt well knew that the "prosperity" of Fayetteville came first at the expense of slaves and then at the expense of emancipated but economically and politically subjugated African Americans. As the narrator mentions in "The Goophered Grapevine," Patesville is "a county seat and a commercial emporium" and "one of the principal towns in North Carolina" largely because of its "considerable trade in cotton," the main cash crop of the plantation economy (3–4). The relatively facile and triumphant story of American independence evoked by Lafayette's name makes Fayetteville a profoundly ironic setting for Chesnutt's stories of slavery and of the "peculiar" institution's lingering consequences in the post-Reconstruction South. As usual, though, Chesnutt partially obscures his irony by making it visible only to those readers who possess enough local knowledge to recognize the thinly disguised setting of his stories. Chesnutt's decision to locate his stories in and around Fayetteville while veiling the irony of the town's name mirrors the strategy he employs when he mentions the four-faced clock tower of Patesville's market-house in "The Goophered Grapevine" but never calls attention to the historical irony embodied in that building, which used to hold slave markets and was built on the site of the old State House where North Carolina ratified the U.S. Constitution.[2] Chesnutt does give some hint of the region's connection to the American Revolution in "The Dumb Witness" when he describes the lineage of the Murchison family: "The first great man of the family, General Arthur Murchison, had won distinction in the war of independence, and during the Revolutionary period had been one of the most ardent of the Carolina patriots. . . . Elected a delegate to the Constitutional Convention at Philadelphia in 1787, it was largely due to his efforts that North Carolina adopted the Federal Constitution the following year" (63). Yet even this passage makes no direct reference to Murchison's fellow Revolutionary General, Lafayette, or to the location of the State House where the Constitution was adopted. Chesnutt's coyness about

---

1. Nicholas Graham, "This Month in North Carolina History: March 1825—Lafayette visits Fayetteville." UNC University Libraries. http://www.lib.unc.edu/ncc/ref/nchistory/mar2004/mar.html.
2. See "Market House, Fayetteville, North Carolina" and photograph, p. 165.

alluding to the historical ironies embedded in the town of Fayetteville mirrors the coyness of Uncle Julius's conjure tales.

In spite of the disparities between Lafayette's and Chesnutt's stories of American independence, Lafayette's enshrinement in Fayetteville also parallels Julius's attempts to enshrine the memory of
slavery in the swamps, creekbeds, marshes, trees, vineyards, sawmills,
abandoned buildings, and other landmarks of his rural community. A
historical map of Fayetteville from the period of Lafayette's visit visu-
ally enacts some of these similarities. This detailed map of the roads,
businesses, creeks, schools, churches, and homes of Fayetteville,
circa 1825, bears the following title on its right side: "This plate of
the town of Fayetteville North Carolina, so called in honor of that
distinguished patriot and philanthropist Gen'l La Fayette, is respectfully dedicated to him by the publisher." Just above the title is a
small oval portrait of Lafayette, and just below it is a drawing of the
Lafayette Hotel, which was hurriedly completed just in time for its
namesake's visit.[3] Despite Chesnutt's apparent misgivings about
invoking Lafayette in his conjure stories, this map resonates with
the thematic content of Chesnutt's work by suggesting the complex
network of meanings that are evoked by the act of verbally inscribing
a person in a place. The portrait of Lafayette that appears above the
map's title suggests the purely commemorative function of Fayetteville's name while the picture of the Lafayette Hotel represents the
artistic construction and even economic opportunism that can coex-
ist with the act of commemoration. Finally, the presence of the word
"patriot" in the title suggests the possibility that commemoration can
be a form of appropriation because it elides Lafayette's identity as a
Frenchman and appropriates him for what the map suggests is a
purely American narrative. Writing at a time when popular plantation
tales tended to depict contented slaves and benign masters and when
a wave of national amnesia about slavery and its role in the Civil War
was sweeping the country,[4] Chesnutt crafts his conjure tales in part
to commemorate the lives and folklore traditions of the those who
came before him—particularly of the Fayetteville storytellers whose
conjure tales first inspired his childhood imagination.[5] Julius, too,
functions as a commemorator every time one of his stories inscribes
the life of a slave into a particular landmark. At the same time, both

3. John McRae, "This plate of the town of Fayetteville North Carolina, so called in honor of
     that distinguished patriot and philanthropist Gen'l La Fayette is respectfully dedicated to
     him by the publisher" (circa 1825). North Carolina Collection. U of North Carolina
     Chapel Hill.
4. David W. Blight, *Race and Reunion: The Civil War in American Memory* (Cambridge,
     Mass.: Harvard UP, 2001).
5. Charles W. Chesnutt, "Superstitions & Folklore of the South" (1901). See pp. 199–205 in
     this Norton Critical Edition.

Chesnutt and Julius have their own economic and artistic goals beyond commemoration, and they are more than willing to appropriate what they need to meet them. By erasing Lafayette's name from the town of Fayetteville, Chesnutt inverts the usual tendency of maps to erase blacks from the visible landscape by assigning labels to white property owners while ignoring the black slaves and sharecroppers who frequently inhabit that property. Julius's conjure tales serve as gestures in opposition to the cartographical erasure of black life by re-inscribing the names of former slaves throughout the Fayetteville region.

It is no coincidence that when John hires Uncle Julius after hearing his tale in "The Goophered Grapevine," he employs him as a carriage driver. Just as John and Annie need Julius to explain the meaning of the regional word "goophered," they also need assistance in navigating the local landscape. In the opening paragraph of "Mars Jeems's Nightmare," the narrator gives his theory of Julius's relation to the land:

> We found old Julius very useful when we moved to our new residence. He had a thorough knowledge of the neighborhood, was familiar with the roads and the watercourses, knew the qualities of the various soils and what they would produce, and where the best hunting and fishing were to be had. He was a marvelous hand in the management of horses and dogs, with whose mental processes he manifested a greater familiarity than mere use would seem to account for, though it was doubtless due to the simplicity of a life that had kept him close to nature. Toward my tract of land and the things that were on it— the creeks, the swamps, the hills, the meadows, the stones, the trees—he maintained a peculiar personal attitude, what might be called predial rather than proprietary. He had been accustomed, until long after middle life, to look upon himself as the property of another. When this relation was no longer possible, owing to the war, and to his master's death and the dispersion of the family, he had been unable to break off entirely the mental habits of a lifetime, but had attached himself to the old plantation, of which he seemed to consider himself an appurtenance. We found him useful in many ways and entertaining in others, and my wife and I took quite a fancy to him. ("Mars Jeems's Nightmare" 90)

This passage appreciatively conveys the economic value of Julius's localized knowledge of the region, but it also reflects John's obtuseness regarding the contested status of his proprietary rights. Certainly, many of Julius's stories do depict characters who occupy a predial relation to the land as a consequence of their enslavement. The most prominent of these is Henry in "The Goophered Grapevine," who cyclically grows strong and feeble through his attachment to the grapevines until they finally send him to his grave. However, the complacency with which John uses the phrase "my tract of land" suggests that he remains unaware of his proprietary struggles with Julius and with the ghosts of the dead that recur throughout the stories.

The process of mapping the terrain of Chesnutt's conjure tales brings into sharp focus the struggles over contested ownership that permeate the narrative and the physical landscapes of Chesnutt's fictional North Carolina community. White landowners such as John, and before him Dugal' McAdoo, lay claim to most of the property in the region, but such legal property rights do not prevent Uncle Julius from using the power of his stories to lay his own claims of possession on the land and the resources it contains, both for himself and on behalf of the slaves who lived and died there as property. John seems largely aware of the ways in which Julius uses his stories to try to gain access to valuable resources such as the old schoolhouse in "Po' Sandy" and the honey-filled tree in "The Gray Wolf's H'ant," but he seems oblivious to the ways in which these stories also challenge his rights of ownership on a more fundamental level. Tobe's marsh, Sandy's schoolhouse, Lonesome Ben's creek bed, and the Gray Wolf's haunting ground are all, technically, on John's property, but Julius's stories provide John, his wife Annie, and the reader with new ways of naming each site as well as new ways of understanding their possession. While John may possess the deed to his tract of land, each individual site is also spiritually possessed by the ghost or metamorphosed presence of a former slave. This form of joint possession is inscribed visibly in this Norton Critical Edition's more detailed map, which juxtaposes the large-font labels of large-scale, formal property holdings such as "John's Vineyard" and "Marrabo McSwayne's Plantation" with the small-font labels of more localized, less formal forms of land possession such as "Chloe's willow tree" and "Sandy's schoolhouse." The possessive form of both the large and small labels suggests the dual ownership that Julius's stories inscribe on the landscape at the local level.

Land is not the only thing to which John lays claim. As narrator of the frame narrative in each conjure tale, John attempts to take possession of Uncle Julius's stories as well as of the physical territory on which many of them are situated. Just as John's property literally surrounds and contains each of the haunted landmarks within it, his frame narrative surrounds and contains Uncle Julius's dialect story within the pages of each conjure tale. Yet without Julius's story at its center, John's narrative would be as hollow, barren, and worthless as the neglected, pockmarked grounds of the old Murchison place in "The Dumb Witness" after Viney refuses to reveal the location of a hidden will to the master who cut out her tongue. The land surrounding the Murchison estate, described by John as "barren" and "rough and uneven, lying in little hillocks and hollows, as though it had been dug over at hazard, or explored by some vagrant drove of hogs" is the physical manifestation of the narrative devastation wrought by the denial of black storytelling (60). Viney, whose name evokes the predicament of the conjured slave Henry in "The Goophered Grapevine," finds herself in a relationship with the land that is the mirror image of Henry's. Rather than suffer and die like Henry in response to the violence done to the land, Viney projects her direct experience of violence onto the landscape as her silence provokes Malcolm Murchison to dig up and destroy his own property. This intimate connection between land and speech suggested by "The Dumb Witness" is equally evident in this Norton Critical Edition's detailed map of John's property, which is filled with landmarks—from Lonesome Ben's creek bed to Chloe's willow tree—that would not be landmarks without Julius's stories to give them meaning.

Although Chesnutt's conjure tales generally map onto the actual physical terrain of the Fayetteville region fairly accurately, there are occasionally times when the landscape described by the stories does not match the landscape depicted on the map—often in rather startling ways. These discrepancies shed light on the important distinctions between psychological and physical landscapes and on the ways in which both distance and direction can operate metaphorically. In "A Deep Sleeper," for example, Uncle Julius's conjure story pointedly privileges the psychological landscape over the physical one. In spite of her wish to remain with Skundus, Cindy is sent by her master to the plantation of Colonel Washington McAdoo, which Julius says is "down in Sampson County, 'bout a hundred mile erway" (45). Geographically, what Julius says is impossible because any spot a hundred miles away from Cindy's original home would be well beyond the borders of Sampson County, but such a literal understanding of Julius's words obscures their psychological resonance. However literal and accurate Julius's estimates of distance are at other times, in this story Julius seems to be engaging in a moment of free indirect discourse, merging his own narrative perspective with that of the young lovers whose separation he describes, and whose frustration and longing he evokes by exaggerating the distance between them. Julius's typical narrative style depends heavily on understatement and on a bluntness bordering on callousness, such as when he describes Cindy as "kinder down in de mouf" about being sent away from her home and family (47). Thus, for him, an emotional measurement of distance is a way of expressing empathy covertly, and of asking but not demanding empathy from his listeners. Moreover, an emotional rather than literal measurement of distance underscores the extent to which all of Julius's stories overlay the physical landscape with a psychological and figurative landscape. The psychological measurement of distance lends a surreal, dreamlike quality to the tale that complements the story's figurative depiction of sleep as a force powerful enough to distort time and space. Of course, the real power at work in the tale is not the power of sleep but the power of good storytelling, which both Julius and Skundus use for their own ends, thereby demonstrating that their power to manipulate others equals their skill at manipulating distance.

Mapping the title character's movements in "Tobe's Tribulations" reveals yet another insight into the relationship between the psychological and physical landscapes. Here, Chesnutt combines a distorted representation of distance and direction to suggest a critique of the forces undermining African Americans' freedom in the post-Reconstruction period. When Tobe decides to escape slavery, he asks Aunt Peggy to tell him the "easies' way fer ter git ter de Norf en be free" because he wants to eat and sleep as much as he chooses and never have to work "less'n I felt lak it." Despite her misgivings about Tobe's unrealistic expectations, Aunt Peggy temporarily turns him into a bear to help him on his journey. As Julius narrates, "Tobe sta'ted out to'ds de Norf, en went fifteen er twenty miles widdout stoppin'" before falling asleep, but after a month of hibernation as a bear, Tobe reverts to his human form and returns to Aunt Peggy, saying that "bein' ez I hadn' got no fu'ther 'n Rockfish Crick, I des 'lowed I'd come back en git dat goopher w'at I paid fer fix' right" (116). However, Julius's and Tobe's descriptions of the runaway's movements are inconsistent with one another; not only is Rockfish Creek significantly fewer than fifteen or twenty miles from both Marrabo McSwayne's plantation and Aunt Peggy's house, but it is also south, not north, of those landmarks. Thus, Tobe's comment to Aunt Peggy indicates that his first escape attempt fails not only because he falls asleep but also because he has been headed in the wrong direction from the start. Tobe's second escape attempt also ends in failure as Tobe succumbs to the black stereotypes of idleness and chicken-stealing and is forced to run south again to escape the hounds of a pursuing fox hunt. The story ends with Tobe, dehumanized by his permanent transformation into a frog, inhabiting a marsh on John's property and voicing his sadness and frustration in a "nocturnal concert" that John interprets alternately as a "strident din" and a soothing "lullaby" but which Annie interprets as "the lament of a lost soul" (111–13). The failure of Tobe's emancipation and the failure of John to recognize the sorrow or humanity of Tobe's voice suggest that the story can be read as a national allegory for the failures of post-Reconstruction America to protect and respect the rights and dignity of former slaves. Chesnutt highlights the allegorical resonance of his story with Julius's veiled, ironic allusion to the persisting limits on blacks' freedom: "Co'se ef [Tobe] had waited lak de res' un us he'd a be'n free long ago. But he didn' know dat, en he doan know it yet" (119). If Tobe still "doan know" that the slaves are free, Julius coyly suggests, that may be because the freedom of African Americans in the 1890s looks far too much like slavery.

While all of these clues support the reading of "Tobe's Tribulations" as an allegory for postbellum racial politics,[6] the discrepancy between the story's explicit and implicit geography—between the northward journey that Julius describes and the southward journey suggested by Tobe's comment about Rockfish Creek—adds an important dimension to that allegory. Tobe's progress toward freedom is not merely stalled by his month-long hibernation—an emphasis that might suggest the nation was simply weary of moving forward with the difficult pursuit of racial equality begun under Reconstruction. Instead, Tobe's geographical disorientation suggests a more profound social problem. Written in 1898, a time when Jim Crow laws, black disenfranchisement, and lynchings were increasingly widespread throughout the South, Chesnutt's story suggests that the nation, like Tobe, is fundamentally lost, headed in the wrong direction. In this respect, "Tobe's Tribulations" bears a remarkable similarity to Mark Twain's *Adventures of Huckleberry Finn,* in which Huck and Jim start out with a vague plan to convey Jim to freedom but end up drifting farther and farther south down the Mississippi River after passing Cairo in the fog. Like Twain, Chesnutt chooses not to call direct attention to the southern trajectory of his character's escape attempt or to the allegorical implications of that journey. Both writers rely instead on their readers' knowledge of regional geography to suggest the irony of their characters' voyages. This is a risky choice because it may shield the geographical irony from the attention of readers who are unfamiliar with the lay of the land, but it has the advantage of figuratively mirroring the discrepancy between the openly articulated goals of Reconstruction and silent consensus behind the Compromise of 1877 that signaled the ending of Reconstruction and the renewal of the nation's commitment to subjugating African Americans. Only by mapping the landscape of Chesnutt's conjure tales collectively rather than individually can readers gain a full sense of the irony and metaphorical power of their geography.

---

6. For more on "Tobe's Tribulations" as a postbellum political allegory, with a focus on Tobe's "voice" rather than on geography, see Eric J. Sundquist, "Charles Chesnutt's Cakewalk." *To Wake the Nations: Race in the Making of American Literature* (Cambridge, Mass: Harvard UP, 1993), pp. 313–23.

"Tobe's Tribulations" is not the only story in which Chesnutt depicts a slave who tries to reach freedom in the North and ends up south of where he started. In "Lonesome Ben," Ben tries to run north but becomes disoriented when clouds block out the North Star, and he ends up hiding in the woods between Dugal' McAdoo's plantation and Marrabo McSwayne's, a site just south of where he started. Ben's directional disorientation may reflect the changes that take place in his body as the clay he eats transforms him into a light-skinned, clay-colored "merlatter," rendering him unrecognizable to his white master and to his black wife and son, all of whom shun him (56). Like "Tobe's Tribulations," "Lonesome Ben" uses the image of a slave running south as an allegory to suggest a broad sense of social disorientation. Indeed, the "big bullfrog" that taunts Ben with the words "Turnt ter clay! Turnt ter clay!" (58) just before his complete absorption into the landscape underscores the important link between the two tales. However, "Lonesome Ben" associates its protagonist's geographical disorientation not with national politics but with the isolation, confusion, and self-alienation experienced by light-skinned African Americans living in a racially segregated society. In Chesnutt's conjure tales, property lines frequently mark the sites haunted by divided lovers and sundered relationships, highlighting the fact that such emotional separations were frequently the byproducts of cold-blooded property distributions. "Po' Sandy" and "Hot-Foot Hannibal" both feature haunted landmarks that are situated on a property line to represent both the artificial separation of the lovers and the liminal status of the possessing spirits, caught somewhere between life and death. The property line featured in "Lonesome Ben" shares all of the metaphorical meanings of the previous two, but this property line is also the color line, and its waters, turned "amber" by the dust of Ben's metamorphosed body, are as murky as the racial and social distinctions in Chesnutt's collection of northern color line stories.

Chesnutt's decision to locate his conjure tales in a fixed community generally aids readers in maintaining a sense of temporal and geographical orientation as they move from story to story. Even "Lonesome Ben," a story about a character whose directional disorientation thwarts his attempt at escape, provides plenty of orientation for its readers, who are told quite clearly that the site of Ben's transformation is the property line between two frequently mentioned landmarks—the plantations of Dugal' McAdoo and Marrabo McSwayne. However, the same expectations of geographical continuity that help keep readers grounded in "Lonesome Ben" can also lead unwary readers to disorientation and false recognition in "Hot-Foot Hannibal" in a way that mirrors the predicament of the story's tricked and divided lovers. The location of the haunted willow tree in "Hot-Foot

Hannibal" seems in many ways to resemble the site of Lonesome Ben's clay creek bed.[7] In both stories, the narrator describes a trip from his house to a small creek branch that crosses the road and is situated on or near a property line between Dugal' McAdoo's plantation and the land of one of his neighbors. The similarities appear even more striking when John mentions that Chloe's haunted tree lies on the other side of an "amber-colored stream" (123), recalling the amber tint that Lonesome Ben's dust gives to the waters near his creek bed. Finally, and perhaps most misleadingly, Julius frequently identifies the plantation that lies just beyond the swamp on the other side of the creek branch as the property of "Mars' Marrabo" and only occasionally clarifies that he is referring to Marrabo Utley, not Marrabo McSwayne. While Marrabo McSwayne is a recurring character in many of the conjure tales, Marrabo Utley is a cipher who appears only in "Hot-Foot Hannibal," and the story gives no indication of a relationship between the two characters to explain the extraordinary coincidence of their shared first name. Given that both Marrabos are contemporaries and neighbors of Dugal' McAdoo, though, their properties must lie in different directions, which means that Chloe's willow tree and Lonesome Ben's creek bed cannot be on the same spot.

The interpretive significance of this seemingly trivial geographical distinction is twofold. First, the "amber-colored stream" near Chloe's willow tree does indeed serve as a reminder of "Lonesome Ben," but because the stories are not set in the same place, the recurrence of amber-tinted water in a second spot suggests that Lonesome Ben's story of isolation, dissolution, and absorption into the landscape is not a unique case but a ubiquitous one. Second, the confusion and false sense of recognition that Chesnutt's tricky geography imposes on the reader mirrors the confusion that Hannibal creates between Chloe and Jeff when he tells Chloe that Jeff is cheating on her and then sets up an elaborate charade to prove his lie. Dressed in a "frock en a sun-bonnet" (128), Hannibal goes to the spot where he has convinced Chloe to spy on Jeff, and Jeff, mistaking his cross-dressed rival for Chloe, behaves in a way that seems to confirm her worst suspicions. Uncle Julius clearly intends his story to produce a sympathetic connection between Chloe and his listeners, and the story specifically targets Mabel, who has recently had an argument with her sweetheart and refused to reconcile it. After hearing the story, Mabel does indeed decide to forgive her sweetheart, suggesting that she identifies with Chloe's experience of hurt pride and lost love. Chesnutt's tricky geographical strategy for creating a sympathetic connection

7. See Candace Waid, "Chesnutt's Scenes from a Marriage," note 1, p. 322.

between his characters and his readers shows him to be an equally masterful storyteller.

The partly factual and partly fictional landscape that links Julius's conjure stories to one another also links them to the outside world through landmarks that sometimes embody as many layers of history and meaning as the tales themselves. The stories' blending of the factual with the fictional and the physical with the psychological can often make both distance and direction difficult to judge. The scene of John and Annie asking for directions that Chesnutt depicts at the beginning of his first conjure tale operates as an apt metaphor for the difficulties and rewards of mapping the conjure tales. From the perspective of an interloper, the landscape of Chesnutt's imagination can seem overwhelming and hopelessly complex. With the aid of some local knowledge, though, readers can reconstruct the landscape of Chesnutt's imagination in a way that highlights the tales' interconnectedness without undermining the productive potential of getting lost.

Market House, Fayetteville, North Carolina[†]

The Market House described by Chesnutt in the opening pages of "The Goophered Grapevine" is an actual structure, built in 1832, that still stands at the central intersection of the town of Fayetteville. The building embodies the ironies of the early history of the state of North Carolina: it was built to house a slave market below-stairs as well as the Town Hall above. It was also built on the site of the Convention Hall, which had been destroyed by fire in 1831, and within whose walls the North Carolina General Assembly had performed such laudable acts as ratifying the U.S. Constitution and chartering the first public university system in the United States. The clock and belfry of the Market House—which, as Chesnutt notes, tolled a daily schedule as well as the nightly curfew—both united the schedule of the community and enforced the policing of the enslaved people of the area.[1]

---

† Photograph copyright © Historic Preservation Foundation of North Carolina. Photographer: Tim Buchman.
1. See Catherine W. Bishir, *North Carolina Architecture* (Chapel Hill: U of North Carolina P, 1990), 172–73, and Federal Writers' Project, *North Carolina: A Guide to the Old North State* (Chapel Hill: U of North Carolina P, 1939), pp. 197, 199.

CHARLES W. CHESNUTT

From His Journal, Spring 1880[†]

Chesnutt wrote these journal entries at the age of twenty-one, while serving as a teacher at the North Carolina State Colored Normal School in Fayetteville (today, Fayetteville State University).

[*Why could not a colored man . . . write a far better book about the South?*]

Mar 16th, 1880. Judge Tourgee has sold the "Fool's Errand," I understand, for $20,000.[1] I suppose he had already received a large royalty on the sale of the first few editions. The work has gained an astonishing degree of popularity, and is to be translated into the French.

Now, Judge Tourgee's book is about the south,—the manners, customs, modes of thought, etc., which are prevalent in this section of the country. Judge Tourgee is a Northern man, who has lived at the South since the war, until recently. He knows a great deal about the politics, history, and laws of the South. He is a close observer of men and things, and has exercised this faculty of observation upon the character of the Southern people. Nearly all his stories are more or less about colored people, and this very feature is one source of their popularity. There is something romantic, to the Northern mind, about the southern negro, as commonplace and vulgar as he seems to us who come in contact with him every day. And there is a romantic side to the history of this people. Men are always more ready to extend their sympathy to those at a distance, than to the suffering ones in their midst. And the north, their eyes not blinded by the dirt and the hazy moral and social atmosphere which surrounds the average negro in the south, their interest not blunted by familiarity with the state of affairs in the south, or prejudiced by a love of "our institutions"—sees the south as it is; or is ever eager for something which will show it in a correct light. They see in the Colored people a race, but recently emancipated from a cruel bondage; struggling for education, for a higher social and moral life, against wealth, intelligence, and race prejudice, which are all united to keep them down. And they hear the cry of the oppressed and struggling ones, and extend a hand to help them; they lend a willing ear to all that is spoken or written concern-

---

[†] From *The Journals of Charles W. Chesnutt*, ed. Richard H. Brodhead (Durham: Duke UP, 1993), pp. 124–26 and pp. 139–40.

1. Albion W. Tourgée, author of *A Fools Errand* (1879), a best-selling fictional account of Reconstruction.

ing their character, habits, etc. And if Judge Tourgee, with his necessarily limited intercourse with colored people, and with his limited
stay in the South, can write such interesting descriptions, such vivid
pictures of Southern life and character as to make himself rich and
famous, why could not a colored man, who has lived among colored
people all his life; who is familiar with their habits, their ruling passions, their prejudices; their whole moral and social condition; their
public and private ambitions; their religious tendencies and habits;—
why could not a colored man who knew all this, and who, besides,
had possessed such opportunities for observation and conversation
with the better class of white men in the south as to understand their
modes of thinking; who was familiar with the political history of the
country, and especially with all the phases of the slavery question;—
why could not such a man, if he possessed the same ability, write a far
better book about the South than Judge Tourgee or Mrs. Stowe[2] has
written? Answer who can! But the man is yet to make his appearance;
and if I can't be the man I shall be the first to rejoice at his *début* and
give God speed! to his work.

I intend to record my impressions of men and things, and such
incidents or conversations which take place within my knowledge,
with a view to future use in literary work. I shall not record stale
negro minstrel jokes, or worn out newspaper squibs on the "man and
brother." I shall leave the realm of fiction, where most of this stuff is
manufactured, and come down to hard facts. There are many things
about the Colored people which are peculiar, to some extent, to
them, and which are interesting to any thoughtful observer, and
would be doubly interesting to people who know little about them.

[*I think I must write a book*]

May 29. I think I must write a book. I am almost afraid to undertake a
book so early and with so little experience in composition. But it has
been my cherished dream, and I feel an influence that I cannot resist
calling me to the task. Besides, I do not know but I am as well prepared as some other successful writers. A fair knowledge of the classics, a speaking acquaintance with the modern languages, an intimate
friendship with literature, etc.; seven years experience in the school
room, two years of married life, and a habit of studying character have
I think, left me not entirely unprepared to write even a book. Fifteen
years of life in the South, in one of the most eventful eras of its history; among a people whose life is rich in the elements of romance;
under conditions calculated to stir one's soul to the very depths;—
I think there is here a fund of experience, a supply of material, which a

2. Harriet Beecher Stowe, author of *Uncle Tom's Cabin* (1852).

skillful pers[on] could work up with tremendous effect. Besides, if I do write, I shall write for a purpose, a high, holy purpose, and this will inspire me to greater effort. The object of my writings would be not so much the elevation of the colored people as the elevation of the whites,—for I consider the unjust spirit of caste which is so insidious as to pervade a whole nation, and so powerful as to subject a whole race and all connected with it to scorn and social ostracism—I consider this a barrier to the moral progress of the American people; and I would be one of the first to head a determined, organized crusade against it. Not a fierce indiscriminate onslaught; not an appeal to force, for this is something that force can but slightly affect; but a moral revolution which must be brought about in a different manner. The Abolition[ist]s stirred up public opinion in behalf of the slave, by appealing in trumpet tones to those principles of justice and humanity which were only lying dormant in the northern heart. The iron hand of power set the slave free from personal bondage, and by admitting him to all the rights of citizenship—the ballot, education—is fast freeing him from the greater bondage of ignorance. But the subtle almost indefinable feeling of repulsion toward the negro, which is common to most Americans—and easily enough accounted for—, cannot be stormed and taken by assault; the garrison will not capitulate: so their position must be mined, and we will find ourselves in their midst before they think it.

This work is of a twofold character. The negro's part is to prepare himself for social recognition and equality; and it is the province of literature to open the way for him to get it—to accustom the public mind to the idea; and * * * while amusing them to * * * lead them on imperceptibly, unconsciously step by step to the desired state of feeling. If I can do anything to further this work, and can see any likelihood of obtaining success in it, I would gladly devote my life to the work.

WILLIAM WELLS BROWN

[Voudooism in Missouri][†]

Born into slavery in Lexington, Kentucky, William Wells Brown (1814–1884) was a major figure in American letters, writing what are considered to be the first novel (*Clotel, or The President's Daughter*, 1853) and the first play (*The Escape, or, A Leap for Freedom*, 1858) published by an African American author. After escaping from enslavement in St. Louis in 1834, Brown worked for the abolitionist movement in the northern United States and in England, eventually settling in Massachusetts after

† From *My Southern Home: or, The South and Its People* (Boston: A. G. Brown & Co., 1880), pp. 68–81.

the Civil War. His last book, *My Southern Home* (1880), recounts his youth in slavery in the environs of St. Louis, and includes one of the most extensive early accounts of conjure practices in southern culture.

Forty years ago, in the Southern States, superstition held an exalted place with all classes, but more especially with the blacks and uneducated, or poor, whites. This was shown more clearly in their belief in witchcraft in general, and the devil in particular. To both of these classes, the devil was a real being, sporting a club-foot, horns, tail, and a hump on his back.

The influence of the devil was far greater than that of the Lord. If one of these votaries had stolen a pig, and the fear of the Lord came over him, he would most likely ask the Lord to forgive him, but still cling to the pig. But if the fear of the devil came upon him, in all probability he would drop the pig and take to his heels.

In those days the city of St. Louis had a large number who had implicit faith in Voudooism. I once attended one of their midnight meetings. In the pale rays of the moon the dark outlines of a large assemblage was visible, gathered about a small fire, conversing in different tongues. They were negroes of all ages,—women, children, and men. Finally, the noise was hushed, and the assembled group assumed an attitude of respect. They made way for their queen, and a short, black, old negress came upon the scene, followed by two assistants, one of whom bore a cauldron, and the other, a box.

The cauldron was placed over the dying embers, the queen drew forth, from the folds of her gown, a magic wand, and the crowd formed a ring around her. Her first act was to throw some substance on the fire, the flames shot up with a lurid glare—now it writhed in serpent coils, now it darted upward in forked tongues, and then it gradually transformed itself into a veil of dusky vapors. At this stage, after a certain amount of gibberish and wild gesticulation from the queen, the box was opened, and frogs, lizards, snakes, dog liver, and beef hearts drawn forth and thrown into the cauldron. Then followed more gibberish and gesticulation, when the congregation joined hands, and began the wildest dance imaginable, keeping it up until the men and women sank to the ground from mere exhaustion.

In the ignorant days of slavery, there was a general belief that a horse-shoe hung over the door would insure good luck. I have seen negroes, otherwise comparatively intelligent, refuse to pick up a pin, needle, or other such object, dropped by a negro, because, as they alleged, if the person who dropped the articles had a spite against them, to touch anything they dropped would voudou them, and make them seriously ill.

Nearly every large plantation, with any considerable number of negroes, had at least one, who laid claim to be a fortune-teller, and who was regarded with more than common respect by his fellow-slaves.

Dinkie, a full-blooded African, large in frame, coarse featured, and claiming to be a descendant of a king in his native land, was the oracle on the "Poplar Farm." At the time of which I write, Dinkie was about fifty years of age, and had lost an eye, and was, to say the least, a very ugly-looking man.

No one in that section was considered so deeply immersed in voudooism, goopherism, and fortune-telling, as he. Although he had been many years in the Gaines family, no one could remember the time when Dinkie was called upon to perform manual labor. He was not sick, yet he never worked. No one interfered with him. If he felt like feeding the chickens, pigs, or cattle, he did so. Dinkie hunted, slept, was at the table at meal time, roamed through the woods, went to the city, and returned when he pleased, with no one to object, or to ask a question. Everybody treated him with respect. The whites, throughout the neighborhood, tipped their hats to the old one-eyed negro, while the policemen, or patrollers, permitted him to pass without a challenge. The negroes, everywhere, stood in mortal fear of "Uncle Dinkie." The blacks who saw him every day, were always thrown upon their good behavior, when in his presence. I once asked a negro why they appeared to be afraid of Dinkie. He looked at me, shrugged his shoulders, smiled, shook his head and said,—

"I ain't afraid of de debble, but I ain't ready to go to him jess yet." He then took a look around and behind, as if he feared some one would hear what he was saying, and then continued: "Dinkie's got de power, ser; he knows things seen and unseen, an' dat's what makes him his own massa."

It was literally true, this man was his own master. He wore a snake's skin around his neck, carried a petrified frog in one pocket, and a dried lizard in the other.

A slave speculator once came along and offered to purchase Dinkie. Dr. Gaines, no doubt, thought it a good opportunity to get the elephant off his hands, and accepted the money. A day later, the trader returned the old negro, with a threat of a suit at law for damages.

A new overseer was employed, by Dr. Gaines, to take charge of "Poplar Farm." His name was Grove Cook, and he was widely known as a man of ability in managing plantations, and in raising a large quantity of produce from a given number of hands. Cook was called a "hard overseer." The negroes dreaded his coming, and, for weeks before his arrival, the overseer's name was on every slave's tongue.

Cook came, he called the negroes up, men and women; counted them, looked them over as a purchaser would a drove of cattle that he intended to buy. As he was about to dismiss them he saw Dinkie come out of his cabin. The sharp eye of the overseer was at once on him.

"Who is that nigger?" inquired Cook.

"That is Dinkie," replied Dr. Gaines.

"What is his place?" continued the overseer.

"Oh, Dinkie is a gentleman at large!" was the response.

"Have you any objection to his working?"

"None, whatever."

"Well, sir," said Cook, "I'll put him to work to-morrow morning."

Dinkie was called up and counted in.

At the roll call, the following morning, all answered except the conjurer; he was not there.

The overseer inquired for Dinkie, and was informed that he was still asleep.

"I will bring him out of his bed in a hurry," said Cook, as he started towards the negro's cabin. Dinkie appeared at his door, just as the overseer was approaching.

"Follow me to the barn," said the impatient driver to the negro. "I make it a point always to whip a nigger, the first day that I take charge of a farm, so as to let the hands know who I am. And, now, Mr. Dinkie, they tell me that you have not had your back tanned for many years; and, that being the case, I shall give you a flogging that you will never forget. Follow me to the barn." Cook started for the barn, but turned and went into his house to get his whip.

At this juncture, Dinkie gave a knowing look to the other slaves, who were standing by, and said, "Ef he lays the weight ob his finger on me, you'll see de top of dat barn come off."

The reappearance of the overseer, with the large negro whip in one hand, and a club in the other, with the significant demand of "follow me," caused a deep feeling in the breast of every negro present.

Dr. Gaines, expecting a difficulty between his new driver and the conjurer, had arisen early, and was standing at his bedroom window looking on.

The news that Dinkie was to be whipped, spread far and near over the place, and had called forth men, women, and children. Even Uncle Ned, the old negro of ninety years, had crawled out of his straw, and was at his cabin door. As the barn doors closed behind the overseer and Dinkie, a death-like silence pervaded the entire group, who, instead of going to their labor, as ordered by the driver, were standing as if paralyzed, gazing intently at the barn, expecting every moment to see the roof lifted.

Not a word was spoken by anyone, except Uncle Ned, who smiled, shook his head, put on a knowing countenance, and said, "My word fer it, de oberseer ain't agwine to whip Dinkie."

Five minutes, ten minutes, fifteen minutes passed, and the usual sound of "Oh, pray, massa! Oh, pray, massa!" heard on the occasion of a slave being punished, had not yet proceeded from the barn.

Many of the older negroes gathered around Uncle Ned, for he and Dinkie occupied the same cabin, and the old, superannuated slave knew more about the affairs of the conjurer, than anyone else. Ned told of how, on the previous night, Dinkie had slept but little, had closely inspected the snake's skin around his neck, the petrified frog and dried lizard, in his pockets, and had rubbed himself all over with goopher; and when he had finished, he knelt, and exclaimed,—

"Now, good and lovely devil, for more than twenty years, I have served you faithfully. Before I got into your service, de white folks bought an' sold me an' my old wife an' chillen, an' whip me, and half starve me. Dey did treat me mighty bad, dat you knows. Den I use to pray to de Lord, but dat did no good, kase de white folks don't fear de Lord. But dey fears you, an' ever since I got into your service, I is able to do as I please. No white dares to lay his hand on me; and dis is all owing to de power dat you give me. Oh, good and lovely devil! please to continer dat power. A new oberseer is to come here to-morrow, an' he wants to get me in his hands. But, dear devil, I axe you to stand by me in dis my trial hour, an' I will neber desert you as long as I live. Continer dis power; make me strong in your cause; make me to be more faithful to you, an' let me still be able to conquer my enemies, an' I will give you all de glory, and will try to deserve a seat at your right hand."

With bated breath, everyone listened to Uncle Ned. All had the utmost confidence in Dinkie's "power." None believed that he would be punished, while a large number expected to see the roof of the barn burst off at any moment. At last the suspense was broken. The barn door flew open; the overseer and the conjurer came out together, walking side by side, and separated when half-way up the walk. As they parted, Cook went to the field, and Dinkie to his cabin.

The slaves all shook their heads significantly. The fact that the old negro had received no punishment, was evidence of his victory over the slave driver. But how the feat had been accomplished, was a mystery. No one dared to ask Dinkie, for he was always silent, except when he had something to communicate. Everyone was afraid to inquire of the overseer.

There was, however, one faint chance of getting an inkling of what had occurred in the barn, and that was through Uncle Ned. This fact made the old, superannuated slave the hero and centre of attraction, for several days. Many were the applications made to Ned for information, but the old man did not know, or wished to exaggerate the importance of what he had learned.

"I tell you," said Dolly, "Dinkie is a power."

"He's nobody's fool," responded Hannah.

"I would not make him mad wid me, fer dis whole world," ejaculated Jim.

Just then, Nancy, the cook, came in brim full of news. She had given Uncle Ned some "cracklin bread," which had pleased the old man so much that he had opened his bosom, and told her all that he got from Dinkie. This piece of information flew quickly from cabin to cabin, and brought the slaves hastily into the kitchen.

It was night. Nancy sat down, looked around, and told Billy to shut the door. This heightened the interest, so that the fall of a pin could have been heard. All eyes were upon Nancy, and she felt keenly the importance of her position. Her voice was generally loud, with a sharp ring, which could be heard for a long distance, especially in the stillness of the night. But now, Nancy spoke in a whisper, occasionally putting her finger to her mouth, indicating a desire for silence, even when the breathing of those present could be distinctly heard.

"When dey got in de barn, de oberseer said to Dinkie, 'Strip yourself; I don't want to tear your clothes with my whip. I'm going to tear your black skin.'

"Den, you see, Dinkie tole de oberseer to look in de east corner ob de barn. He looked, an' he saw hell, wid all de torments, an' de debble, wid his cloven foot, a-struttin' about dar, jes as ef he was cock ob de walk. An' Dinkie tole Cook, dat ef he lay his finger on him, he'd call de debble up to take him away."

"An' what did Cook say to dat?" asked Jim.

"Let me 'lone; I didn't tell you all," said Nancy. "Den you see de oberseer turn pale in de face, an' he say to Dinkie, 'Let me go dis time, an' I'll nebber trouble you any more.'"

This concluded Nancy's story, as related to her by old Ned, and religiously believed by all present. Whatever caused the overseer to change his mind in regard to the flogging of Dinkie, it was certain that he was most thoroughly satisfied to let the old negro off without the threatened punishment; and, although he remained at "Poplar Farm," as overseer, for five years, he never interfered with the conjurer again.

It is not strange that ignorant people should believe in characters of Dinkie's stamp; but it is really marvellous that well-educated men and women should give any countenance whatever, to such delusions as were practised by the oracle of "Poplar Farm."

The following illustration may be taken as a fair sample of the easy manner in which Dinkie carried on his trade.

Miss Martha Lemmy, being on a visit to Mrs. Gaines, took occasion during the day to call upon Dinkie. The conjurer knew the antecedents of his visitor, and was ready to give complete satisfaction in his particular line. When the young lady entered the old man's cabin, he met her, bade her be welcome, and tell what she had come for. She took a seat on one stool, and he on another. Taking the lady's right hand in his, Dinkie spit into its palm, rubbed it, looked at it, shut his one eye, opened it, and said: "I sees a young gentman, an' he's rich, an' owns plenty of land an' a heap o' niggers; an', lo! Miss Marfa, he loves you."

The lady drew a long breath of seeming satisfaction, and asked, "Are you sure that he loves me, Uncle Dinkie?"

"Oh! Miss Marfa, I knows it like a book."

"Have you ever seen the gentleman?" the lady inquired.

The conjurer began rubbing the palm of the snow-white hand, talked to himself in an undertone, smiled, then laughed out, and saying: "Why, Miss Marfa, as I lives it's Mr. Scott, an' he's thinkin' 'bout you now; yes, he's got his mind on you dis bressed minute. But how he's changed sense I seed him de lass time. Now he's got side whiskers an' a mustacher on his chin. But, let me see. Here is somethin' strange. De web looks a little smoky, an' when I gets to dat spot, I can't get along till a little silver is given to me."

Here the lady drew forth her purse and gave the old man a half dollar piece that made his one eye fairly twinkle.

He resumed: "Ah! now de fog is cleared away, an' I see dat Mr. Scott is settin in a rockin-cheer, wid boff feet on de table, an' smokin' a segar."

"Do you think Mr. Scott loves me?" inquired the lady.

"O! yes," responded Dinkie; "he jess sets his whole heart on you. Indeed, Miss Marfa, he's almos' dyin' 'bout you."

"He never told me that he loved me," remarked the lady.

"But den, you see, he's backward, he ain't got his eye-teef cut yet in love matters. But he'll git a little bolder ebbry time he sees you," replied the negro.

"Do you think he'll ever ask me to marry him?"

"O! yes, Miss Marfa, he's sure to do dat. As he sets dar in his rockin-cheer, he looks mighty solemcolly—looks like he wanted to ax you to haf him now."

"Do you think that Mr. Scott likes any other lady, Uncle Dinkie?" asked Miss Lemmy.

"Well, Miss Marfa, I'll jess consult de web an' see." And here the conjurer shut his one eye, opened it, shut it again, talked to himself in an undertone, opened his eye, looked into the lady's hand, and exclaimed: "Ah! Miss Marfa, I see a lady in de way, an' she's got riches; but de web is smoky, an' it needs a little silver to clear it up."

With tears in her eyes, and almost breathless, Miss Lemmy hastily took from her pocket her purse, and handed the old man another piece of money, saying: "Please go on."

Dinkie smiled, shook his head, got up and shut his cabin door, sat down, and again took the lady's hand in his.

"Yes, I see," said he, "I see it's a lady; but bless you soul, Miss Marfa, it's a likeness of you dat Mr. Scott is lookin' at; dat's all."

This morsel of news gave great relief, and Miss Lemmy dried her eyes with joy.

Dinkie then took down the old rusty horseshoe from over his cabin door, held it up, and said: "Dis horseshoe neffer lies." Here he took out of his pocket a bag made of the skin of the rattlesnake, and took from it some goopher, sprinkled it over the horseshoe, saying: "Dis is de stuff, Miss Marfa, dat's gwine to make you Mr. Scott's conqueror. Long as you keeps dis goopher 'bout you he can't get away from you; he'll ax you fer a kiss, de berry next time he meets you, an' he can't help hisself fum doin' it. No woman can get him fum you so long as you keep dis goopher 'bout you."

Here Dinkie lighted a tallow candle, looked at it, smiled, shook his head,—"You's gwine to marry Mr. Scott in 'bout one year, an' you's gwine to haf thirteen children—sebben boys an' six gals, an' you's gwine to haf a heap of riches."

* * *

JOEL CHANDLER HARRIS

The Sad Fate of Mr. Fox[†]

This is the last story in the first volume of Harris's extremely influential tales. Chesnutt echoes not only the frame narrative structure Harris employs but also many of his names: in addition to the "Uncle"-titled storyteller, we meet a fox named "Tobe" in the tale and hear of a "Mars Jeems" in the present.

"Now, den," said Uncle Remus, with unusual gravity, as soon as the little boy, by taking his seat, announced that he was ready for the evening's entertainment to begin; "now, den, dish yer tale w'at I'm agwine ter gin you is de las' row er stumps, sho. Dish yer's whar ole Brer Fox los' his breff, en he ain't fine it no mo' down ter dis day."

"Did he kill himself, Uncle Remus?" the little boy asked, with a curious air of concern.

"Hole on dar, honey!" the old man exclaimed, with a great affectation of alarm; "hole on dar! Wait! Gimme room! I don't wanter tell you no story, en ef you keep shovin' me forrerd, I mout git some er de facks mix up 'mong deyse'f. You gotter gimme room en you gotter gimme time."

The little boy had no other premature questions to ask, and, after a pause, Uncle Remus resumed:

"Well, den, one day Brer Rabbit go ter Brer Fox house, he did, en he put up mighty po' mouf. He say his ole 'oman sick, en his chilluns cole, en de fier done gone out. Brer Fox, he feel bad 'bout dis, en he tuck'n s'ply Brer Rabbit widder chunk er fier. Brer Rabbit see Brer Fox cookin' some nice beef, en his mouf gun ter water, but he take de fier, he did, en he put out to'rds home; but present'y yer he come back, en he say de fier done gone out. Brer Fox 'low dat he want er invite ter dinner, but he don't say nuthin', en bimeby Brer Rabbit he up'n say, sezee:

† From *Uncle Remus: His Songs and His Sayings—The Folk-Lore of the Old Plantation* (New York: D. Appleton and Company, 1881), pp. 143–48.

"'Brer Fox, whar you git so much nice beef?' sezee, en den Brer Fox he up'n 'spon', sezee:

"'You come ter my house ter-morrer ef yo' fokes ain't too sick, en I kin show you whar you kin git plenty beef mo' nicer dan dish yer,' sezee:

"Well, sho nuff, de nex' day fotch Brer Rabbit, en Brer Fox say, sezee:

"'Der's a man down yander by Miss Meadows's w'at got heap er fine cattle, en he gotter cow name Bookay,' sezee, 'en you des go en say *Bookay*, en she'll open her mouf, en you kin jump in en git des as much meat ez you kin tote,' sez Brer Fox, sezee.

"'Well, I'll go 'long,' sez Brer Rabbit, sezee, 'en you kin jump fus' en den I'll come follerin' atter,' sezee.

"Wid dat dey put out, en dey went promernadin' 'roun' 'mong de cattle, dey did, twel bimeby dey struck up wid de one dey wuz atter. Brer Fox, he up, he did, en holler *Bookay*, en de cow flung 'er mouf wide open. Sho nuff, in dey jump, en w'en dey got dar, Brer Fox, he say, sezee:

"'You kin cut mos' ennywheres, Brer Rabbit, but don't cut 'roun' de haslett,'[1] sezee.

"Den Brer Rabbit, he holler back, he did: 'I'm a gitten me out a roas'n-piece;' sezee.

"'Roas'n, er bakin', er fryin',' sez Brer Fox, sezee, 'don't git too nigh de haslett,' sezee.

"Dey cut en dey kyarved, en dey kyarved en dey cut, en w'iles dey wuz cuttin' en kyarvin', en slashin' 'way, Brer Rabbit, he tuck'n hacked inter de haslett, en wid dat down fell de cow dead.

"'Now, den,' sez Brer Fox, 'we er gone, sho,' sezee.

"'W'at we gwine do?' sez Brer Rabbit, sezee.

"'I'll git in de maul,' sez Brer Fox, 'en you'll jump in de gall,'[2] sezee.

"Nex' mawnin' yer cum de man w'at de cow b'long ter, an he ax who kill Bookay. Nobody don't say nuthin'. Den de man say he'll cut 'er open en see, en den he whirl in, en twan't no time 'fo' he had 'er intruls spread out. Brer Rabbit, he crope out'n de gall, en say, sezee:

"'Mister Man! Oh, Mister Man! I'll tell you who kill yo' cow. You look in de maul, en dar you'll fine 'im,' sezee.

"Wid dat de man tuck a stick en lam down on de maul so hard dat he kill Brer Fox stone-dead. W'en Brer Rabbit see Brer Fox wuz laid out fer good, he make like he mighty sorry, en he up'n ax de man fer Brer Fox head. Man say he ain't keerin', en den Brer Rabbit tuck'n brung it ter Brer Fox house. Dar he see ole Miss Fox, en he tell 'er dat he done fotch her some nice beef w'at 'er ole man sont 'er, but she ain't gotter look at it twel she go ter eat it.

"Brer Fox son wuz name Tobe, en Brer Rabbit tell Tobe fer ter keep still w'iles his mammy cook de nice beef w'at his daddy sont

---

1. When removed for roasting, the heart, liver, and other central vital organs of sheep, cows, hogs, etc.
2. Liver or gallbladder; *maul*: mouth.

'im. Tobe he wuz mighty hongry, en he look in de pot he did w'iles de cookin' wuz gwine on, en dar he see his daddy head, en wid dat he sot up a howl en tole his mammy. Miss Fox, she git mighty mad w'en she fine she cookin' her ole man head, en she call up de dogs, she did, en sickt em on Brer Rabbit; en ole Miss Fox en Tobe en de dogs, dey push Brer Rabbit so close dat he hatter take a holler tree. Miss Fox, she tell Tobe fer ter stay dar en mine Brer Rabbit, w'ile she goes en git de ax, en w'en she gone, Brer Rabbit, he tole Tobe ef he go ter de branch en git 'im a drink er water dat he'll gin 'im a dollar. Tobe, he put out, he did, en bring some water in his hat, but by de time he got back Brer Rabbit done out en gone. Ole Miss Fox, she cut and cut twel down come de tree, but no Brer Rabbit dar. Den she lay de blame on Tobe, en she say she gwineter lash 'im, en Tobe, he put out en run, de ole 'oman atter 'im. Bimeby, he come up wid Brer Rabbit, en sot down fer to tell 'im how 'twuz, en w'iles dey wuz a settin' dar, yer come ole Miss Fox a slippin' up en grab um bofe. Den she tell um w'at she gwine do. Brer Rabbit she gwineter kill, en Tobe she gwineter lam ef its de las' ack. Den Brer Rabbit sez, sezee:

"'Ef you please, ma'am, Miss Fox, lay me on de grindstone en groun' off my nose so I can't smell no mo' w'en I'm dead.'

"Miss Fox, she tuck dis ter be a good idee, en she fotch bofe un um ter de grindestone, en set um up on it so dat she could groun' off Brer Rabbit nose. Den Brer Rabbit, he up'n say, sezee:

"'Ef you please, ma'am, Miss Fox, Tobe he kin turn de' handle w'iles you goes atter some water fer ter wet de grinestone,' sezee.

"Co'se, soon'z Brer Rabbit see Miss Fox go atter de water, he jump down en put out, en dis time he git clean away."

"And was that the last of the Rabbit, too, Uncle Remus?" the little boy asked, with something like a sigh.

"Don't push me too close, honey," responded the old man; "don't shove me up in no cornder. I don't wanter tell you no stories. Some say dat Brer Rabbit's ole 'oman died fum eatin' some pizen-weed, en dat Brer Rabbit married ole Miss Fox, en some say not. Some tells one tale en some tells nudder; some say dat fum dat time forrer'd de Rabbits en de Foxes make frien's en stay so; some say dey kep on quollin'. Hit look like it mixt. Let dem tell you w'at knows. Dat w'at I years you gits it straight like I yeard it."

There was a long pause, which was finally broken by the old man:

"Hit's 'gin de rules fer you ter be noddin' yer, honey. Bimeby you'll drap off en I'll hatter tote you up ter de big 'ouse. I hear dat baby cryin', en bimeby Miss Sally'll fly up en be a holler'n atter you."

"Oh, I wasn't asleep," the little boy replied. "I was just thinking."

"Well, dat's diffunt," said the old man. "Ef you'll clime up on my back," he continued, speaking softly, "I speck I ain't too ole fer ter be yo' hoss fum yer ter de house. Many en many's de time dat I toted yo' Unk Jeems dat away, en Mars Jeems wuz heavier sot dan w'at you is."

OVID

The Transformation of Daphne into a Laurel[†]

William Wells Brown's conjure narratives and Joel Chandler Harris's tales were not the only precedents Chesnutt had in mind for his Julius tales. As early as "The Conjurer's Revenge" (1889), he has the narrator John refer to the transformative action of conjure as metamorphosis, referencing the classical stories of the Roman poet Ovid (43 B.C.E.–17? C.E.).

> Daphne, the daughter of the river god
> Peneus, was the first love of Apollo;[1]
> this happened not by chance, but by the cruel
> outrage of Cupid; Phoebus, in the triumph
> of his great victory against the Python,
> observed him bending back his bow and said,
>   "What are *you* doing with such manly arms,
> lascivious boy? That bow befits *our* brawn,
> wherewith we deal out wounds to savage beasts
> and other mortal foes, unerringly:
> just now with our innumerable arrows
> we managed to lay low the mighty Python,
> whose pestilential belly covered acres!
> Content yourself with kindling love affairs
> with your wee torch—and don't claim *our* glory!"
>   The son of Venus answered him with this:
> "Your arrow, Phoebus, may strike everything;
> mine will strike you: as animals to gods,
> your glory is so much the less than mine!"
>   He spoke, and soaring upward through the air
> on wings that thundered, in no time at all
> had landed on Parnassus' shaded height;
> and from his quiver drew two arrows out
> which operated at cross-purposes,
> for one engendered flight, the other, love;
> the latter has a polished tip of gold,

---

† From Charles Martin, trans., *Ovid: Metamorphoses*, with an introduction by Bernard Knox (New York: Norton, 2004), pp. 33–38. Copyright © 2004 by Charles Martin. Used by permission of W. W. Norton & Company, Inc.
1. Phoebus Apollo taunts Cupid for using the bow, a weapon of which he himself is master; Cupid, enraged, pierces Apollo with the dart that causes his unquenchable desire for the nymph Daphne.

the former has a tip of dull, blunt lead;
with this one, Cupid struck Peneus' daughter,
while the other pierced Apollo to his marrow.

One is in love now, and the other one
won't hear of it, for Daphne calls it joy
to roam within the forest's deep seclusion,
where she, in emulation of the chaste
goddess Phoebe, devotes herself to hunting;
one ribbon only bound her straying tresses.

Many men sought her, but she spurned her suitors,
loath to have anything to do with men,
and rambled through the wild and trackless groves
untroubled by a thought for love or marriage.

Often her father said, "You owe it to me,
child, to provide me with a son-in-law
and grandchildren!"
                                        "Let me remain a virgin,
father most dear," she said, "as once before
Diana's father, Jove, gave her that gift."

Although Peneus yielded to you, Daphne,
your beauty kept your wish from coming true,
your comeliness conflicting with your vow:
at first sight, Phoebus loves her and desires
to sleep with her; desire turns to hope,
and his own prophecy deceives the god.

Now just as in a field the harvest stubble
is all burned off, or as hedges are set ablaze
when, if by chance, some careless traveler
should brush one with his torch or toss away
the still-smoldering brand at break of day—
just so the smitten god went up in flames
until his heart was utterly afire,
and hope sustained his unrequited passion.

He gazes on her hair without adornment:
"What if it were done up a bit?" he asks,
and gazes on her eyes, as bright as stars,
and on that darling little mouth of hers,
though sight is not enough to satisfy;
he praises everything that he can see—
her fingers, hands, and arms, bare to her shoulders—
and what is hidden prizes even more.

She flees more swiftly than the lightest breeze,
nor will she halt when he calls out to her:
"Daughter of Peneus, I pray, hold still,
hold still! I'm not a foe in grim pursuit!
Thus lamb flees wolf, thus dove from eagle flies

on trembling wings, thus deer from lioness,
thus any creature flees its enemy,
but I am stalking you because of love!

"Wretch that I am: I'm fearful that you'll fall,
brambles will tear your flesh because of me!
The ground you're racing over's very rocky,
slow down, I beg you, restrain yourself in flight,
and I will follow at a lesser speed.

"Just ask yourself who finds you so attractive!
I'm not a caveman, not some shepherd boy,
no shaggy guardian of flocks and herds—
you've no idea, rash girl, you've no idea
whom you are fleeing, that is why you flee!

"Delphi, Claros, Tenedos are all mine,
I'm worshiped in the city of Patara!
Jove is my father, I alone reveal
what was, what is, and what will come to be!
The plucked strings answer my demand with song!

"Although my aim is sure, another's arrow
proved even more so, and my careless heart
was badly wounded—the art of medicine
is my invention, by the way, the source
of my worldwide fame as a practitioner
of healing through the natural strength of herbs.

"Alas, there is no herbal remedy
for the love that I must suffer, and the arts
that heal all others cannot heal their lord—"

He had much more to say to her, but Daphne
pursued her fearful course and left him speechless,
though no less lovely fleeing him; indeed,
disheveled by the wind that bared her limbs
and pressed the blown robes to her straining body
even as it whipped up her hair behind her,
the maiden was more beautiful in flight!

But the young god had no further interest
in wasting his fine words on her; admonished
by his own passion, he accelerates,
and runs as swiftly as a Gallic hound
chasing a rabbit through an open field;
the one seeks shelter and the other, prey—
he clings to her, is just about to spring,
with his long muzzle straining at her heels,
while she, not knowing whether she's been caught,
in one swift burst, eludes those snapping jaws,
no longer the anticipated feast;
so he in hope and she in terror race.

But her pursuer, driven by his passion,
outspeeds the girl, giving her no pause,
one step behind her, breathing down her neck;
her strength is gone; she blanches at the thought
of the effort of her swift flight overcome,
but at the sight of Peneus, she cries,
"Help me, dear father! If your waters hold
divinity, transform me and destroy
that beauty by which I have too well pleased!"

Her prayer was scarcely finished when she feels
a torpor take possession of her limbs—
her supple trunk is girdled with a thin
layer of fine bark over her smooth skin;
her hair turns into foliage, her arms
grow into branches, sluggish roots adhere
to feet that were so recently so swift,
her head becomes the summit of a tree;
all that remains of her is a warm glow.

Loving her still, the god puts his right hand
against the trunk, and even now can feel
her heart as it beats under the new bark;
he hugs her limbs as if they were still human,
and then he puts his lips against the wood,
which, even now, is adverse to his kiss.

"Although you cannot be my bride," he says,
"you will assuredly be my own tree,
O Laurel, and will always find yourself
girding my locks, my lyre, and my quiver too—
you will adorn great Roman generals
when every voice cries out in joyful triumph
along the route up to the Capitol;
you will protect the portals of Augustus,
guarding, on either side, his crown of oak;
and as I am—perpetually youthful,
my flowing locks unknown to the barber's shears—
so you will be an evergreen forever
bearing your brilliant foliage with glory!"

Phoebus concluded. Laurel shook her branches
and seemed to nod her summit in assent.

CHARLES W. CHESNUTT

Letters to Albion W. Tourgée and George Washington Cable (1889–1890)†

Both Tourgée (1838–1905) and Cable (1844–1925) had made names for themselves as authors of fiction set in the South, and as activists for civil and political rights for African Americans in the Southern states, following the end of Reconstruction in 1877. Tourgée, a native Ohioan, had fought for the Union Army and played an important role in the Reconstruction government of North Carolina, so he shared many geographic commonalities with Chesnutt; Cable, a native Louisianan, had fought for the Conferderacy and had become the most-read author in the United States in the 1880s for his wildly popular stories of antebellum Louisiana Creole life. After publishing his first Julius stories in the *Atlantic Monthly* in the late 1880s, Chesnutt sought out correspondence with both of the more prominent authors, who like him were interested in not only the aesthetics of fiction but also its potential to effect social change.

To Tourgée, Sept. 26, 1889:

My dear Sir:—

I do not know that I ever acknowledged receipt of your kindly letter in answer to the one in which I thanked you for a compliment paid. I found in your letter not only great pleasure but much encouragement.[1]

*   *   *

I take the liberty of sending you a copy of the October *Atlantic*, which contains one of my stories, which if you read it, I hope you may think the best of the series. I think I have about used up the old Negro who serves as mouthpiece, and I shall drop him in future stories,

---

† From *"To Be an Author": Letters of Charles W. Chesnutt, 1889–1905*, ed. Joseph R. McElrath, Jr., and Robert C. Leitz, III (Princeton: Princeton UP, 1997), pp. 44–46, 59–68. © 1997 Princeton University Press. Reprinted by permission. Footnotes have been edited.

1. While this is the earliest known letter to Tourgée, Chesnutt's correspondence with him was well advanced: on 8 December 1888, Tourgée wrote to him, "Few things have given me greater pleasure than your letters." The more recent compliment paid, to which Chesnutt refers here, was a reference to "Chestnut's [*sic*] curious realism" in "The South as a Field for Fiction," *Forum* 6 (December 1888), 404–13; and in an 8 December letter Tourgée apologized for its brevity: "I did not dare make the reference more explicit lest it should do you an injury. The fact of color is yet a curse the intensity of which few realize." * * *

as well as much of the dialect.[2] The punishment of tying the stolen meat around the thief's neck was a real incident of slavery—in fact I think it hardly possible to imagine anything cruel or detestable that did not have its counterpart in that institution. The setting of that incident is of course pure fiction. I tried in this story to get out of the realm of superstition into the region of feeling and passion—with what degree of success the story itself can testify.[3]

I presume you saw an article of mine in the *Independent* in June; that paper has accepted from me a Southern Story, dealing with a tragic incident, not of slavery exactly, but showing the fruits of slavery.[4] It is not in dialect, and while it has a moral, I tried to write as an artist and not as a preacher. I had a humorous dialect story in the June *Overland*, a rather out-of-the-way publication which it hardly pays to write for.[5]

I read with much interest your stirring weekly letters in the *Inter Ocean*.[6] I sincerely hope some of the Southern fire-eaters read them and profit by them. Recent events do not show, however, that the Southern whites have learned much; they certainly have not forgotten how to insult and oppress the Negro, and they still possess their old-time facility with the shot-gun and the cowhide. I see no remedy for the disease but for the colored people to learn to defend themselves.

I have had some thoughts of collecting in book form the stories I have published in the *Atlantic*, with some others I think as good, which have seen daylight elsewhere. If you have time to answer this letter, perhaps you would be kind enough to advise me from your own experience, whether such a book would be likely to pay for itself, or whether it would be of sufficient value as an advertisement to justify me in paying for it? I have been writing a good deal this Summer, among other things a novel which I shall try to inflict on the public sooner or later. With kindest regards, I am

Yours very respectfully,
Chas. W. Chesnutt.

2. The "mouthpiece" character in "Dave's Neckliss" is Uncle Julius McAdoo.
3. Chesnutt is here self-consciously describing himself as an African American artist in the terms employed by Tourgée in his 8 December letter: "I incline to think that the climacteric of American literature will be negroloid in character,—I do not mean in form—the dialect is a mere fleeting incident, but in style of thought, intensity of color, fervency of passion and grandeur of aspiration. Literature rather than politics, science or government, is the [medium] in which the American negro—not the African for there is really but little of the African left—will win his earliest perhaps his brightest laurels." * * *
4. The article was "What Is a White Man?" *Independent*, 30 May 1889, 5–6; the short story to be published was "The Sheriff's Children."
5. "The Conjurer's Revenge."
6. From 21 April 1888 through 5 January 1895 Tourgée wrote a weekly column, "A Bystander's Notes," for the Chicago *Inter Ocean*.

P.S.—

You said to me that you thought the fact of color would hurt me in literature—the knowledge of the fact rather. Perhaps it might with the public. It has not with the *Independent*—on the contrary I think it has helped me with that journal. I do not think it has hurt me with the *Atlantic*. The editors of both journals are aware of my connection with the colored race. The road to success in literature is not, I imagine, an easy one, and perhaps, if I have the patience and the industry to pursue it, the fact of color may in the course of time prove to be a distinction instead of a disadvantage.

Yours, etc.
C. W. Chesnutt.

To Cable, March 29, 1890:

My Dear Mr. Cable:—

*　　*　　*

I received a copy of your address to the Massachusetts Club.[7] It is a clear and able presentation of the Southern question in a new light—the hopeless struggle for pure government without free government.

I do not comprehend how a fair-minded opponent, however radically he might differ from you, could find anything harsh to say in reply to so fair and courteous an argument; if any one can lift the race question out of the mire of prejudice and partisanship into the clear light of reason and patriotism, I think you are the man. I don't agree with you, however, in the plea for one more chance for the Southern Democrats to deal fairly with their political opponents; it is true that something would be gained by a delay of Federal interference, and if the delay were long enough continued no Federal interference would be necessary to protect the Negroes in their rights. It is easy enough to temporize with the bull when you are on the other side of the fence, but when you are in the pasture with him, as the colored people of the South are, the case is different. I take it that every citizen is entitled to such protection as the government can extend to him in the enjoyment of his rights, and that he is entitled

---

7. Cable spoke before the Massachusetts Club in Boston on 22 February 1890. The text of his speech appeared in the *Boston Journal*, 24 February 1890, 1, as well as in pamphlet form, *The Southern Struggle for Pure Government. An Address . . . Delivered Before the Massachusetts Club, Boston, on Washington's Birthday, 1890* (1890).

to that protection *now*, and whenever his rights are invaded.[8] I sincerely hope the present Congress will pass a wise and practicable federal election law, and that the President will have brain enough and backbone enough to enforce it. The ever lengthening record of Southern wrongs and insults, both lawless and under the form of law, calls for whatever there is of patriotism, of justice, of fair play in the American people, to cry hands off and give the Negro a show, not five years hence or ten years hence, or a generation hence, but *now*, while he is alive, and can appreciate it; posthumous fame is a glorious thing, even if it is only posthumous; posthumous liberty is not, in the homely language of the rural Southerner, "w'u'th shucks."

*   *   *

To Cable, June 13, 1890:

Dear Mr. Cable:—

An absence of several days from the city has interfered with my answering your letter returning the MS. of "Rena Walden," which came duly to hand.[9] I thank you very much for sending me Mr. Gilder's letter which I do accept as a "faithful, wise word of friendly counsel."[1] Its faithfulness is obvious, its wisdom I cannot question, though I shall have to study both the letter and the story to avail myself of it, for

8. In his speech, Cable enumerated the restrictions imposed upon African Americans by Southern Democrats, but he avoided incendiary language and employed an optimistic, conciliatory tone. * * * He saw no immediate need for federal intervention in the Southern states, suggesting that they be given two years to begin eliminating Jim Crow laws. * * * Chesnutt, in responding to Cable with a more radical demand for immediate implementation of full civil rights for African Americans, articulates a theme running through his later correspondence with Booker T. Washington, and his tone with Washington is anticipated here.
9. When Chesnutt expresses strong emotion in his letters, it is typically provoked by outrages perpetrated against the African American community. His feelings concerning his own situation are normally restrained. The cri de coeur in the present letter is unique, even though Chesnutt toned down several passages in the original draft dated 5 June, as will be seen in the notes below focusing on his revisions. * * *
1. *Century* magazine editor Richard Watson Gilder wrote Cable on 28 May 1890 explaining his rejection of "Rena Walden": "This story of Chesnutts [sic] 'Rena Walden' I have read with great care. I'm extremely sorry not to find it feasible. Its subject is new, & the point of view. But somehow it seems to me amorphous—not so much in construction as in *Sentiment*. I could talk to you about it more clearly than I can write. There is either a lack of humor in the author or a brutality in the characters, & lack of mellowness, lack of spontaneous, imaginative life in the people, lack of outlook—I don't know what—that makes them—as here depicted—*uninteresting*. I think it is the writers [sic] fault, rather than the people's. The result seems to me a crude study; not a thoroughly human one. I wish I could see more of the author's work—some briefer study. The writing in the opening pages is excellent." In the left margin Gilder added: "The hero & heroine are such frauds both of them that they have no interest—*as here described*. The black boy is better, from a literary point of view & his father."

while there is something lacking, Mr. Gilder only very vaguely intimates what it may be. I do not think I am deficient in humor, though I dare say the sentiment of the story is a little bit "amorphous." It was written under the ever-present consciousness, so hard for me to get rid of, that a very large class of people consider the class the story treats of as "amorphous." I fear there is too much of this sentiment to make mulattoes good magazine characters,[2] and I notice that all of the good negroes (excepting your own creations) whose virtues have been given to the world through the columns of the *Century*, have been blacks, full-blooded, and their chief virtues have been their dog-like fidelity and devotion to their old masters. Such characters exist; not six months ago a negro in Raleigh, N.C., wrote to the Governor of the State offering to serve out the sentence in the penitentiary of seven years just imposed upon his old master for some crime. But I don't care to write about these people;[3] I do not think these virtues by any means the crown of manhood. I have read a number of English and French novels during the past few months dealing largely with colored characters, either in principal or subordinate parts. They figure as lawyers, as judges, as doctors, botanists, musicians, as people of wealth and station. They love and they marry without reference to their race, or with only such reference to it as to other personal disabilities, like poverty or ugliness for instance. These writers seem to find nothing extraordinary in a talented, well-bred colored man, nothing amorphous in a pretty, gentle-spirited colored girl.

But our American writers are different. Maurice Thompson's characters are generally an old, vulgar master, who, when not drunk or asleep, is amusing himself by beating an old negro. Thos. N. Page

2. In his draft Chesnutt here expatiated on the unlikelihood of any mulatto characters being attractive to American magazine editors and readers: "I suspect that my way of looking at these things is 'amorphous' not in the sense of being unnatural but unusual. There are a great many intelligent people who consider the [mulatto] class to which Rena and Wain belong as unnatural. I had a gentleman with whom I had just dined for whom I had been doing some difficult work, a man of high standing in his profession, of wide reading and as I had thought of great liberality, whom I had heard declare enthusiastically about the doctrine of human equality—which characterizes our institutions, I say this gentleman remarked to me in substance that he considered a mulatto an insult to nature, a kind of monster that he looked upon with infinite distaste, not to say disgust; that a black negro he looked upon with some respect, but any laws which permitted the intermarriage of the two races, or tended in any way to bring the two races nearer together, were pernicious and in the highest degree reprehensible."

3. In the draft, Chesnutt wrote more passionately, "But I can't write about those people, or rather I won't write about them." He then went on to make a self-disclosure appearing nowhere else in his correspondence: "I am a little surprised at Mr. Gilder's suggestion of a want of humor in the writer. Almost everything I have written has been humorous and I had thought that I had a rather keen sense of humor. But my position, my surroundings, are not such as to make me take a humorous view of life. They rather tend the other way. * * * The kind of stuff I could write, if I were not all the time oppressed by the fear that this line or this sentiment would offend somebody's prejudices, jar on somebody's American-trained sense of propriety, would I believe find a ready sale in England."

and H. S. Edwards and Joel C. Harris give us the sentimental and devoted negro who prefers kicks to half-pence.[4] Judge Tourgée's cultivated white negroes are always bewailing their fate, and cursing the drop of black blood that "taints"—I hate the word, it implies corruption—their otherwise pure blood.[5] An English writer would not hesitate to say that race prejudice was mean and narrow and provincial and unchristian—something to which a free-born Briton was entirely superior; he would make his colored characters think no less of themselves because of their color but infinitely less of those who despise them on account of it.

But I am wandering. Mr. Gilder finds that I either lack humor, or that my characters have "a brutality, a lack of mellowness, a lack of spontaneous imaginative life, lack of outlook." I fear, alas! that those are exactly the things that do characterize them, and just about the things that might be expected in them—the very qualities which government and society had for 300 years or so labored faithfully, zealously, and successfully to produce, the only qualities which would have rendered life at all endurable to them in the 19th century. But I suppose I shall have to drop the attempt at realism, and try to make my characters like other folks, for uninteresting people are not good subjects for fiction.[6]

I cannot find words to thank you for your expressions of kindness and confidence in my as yet almost untried powers. I have felt the same thing obscurely. Self-confidence is a good thing, but recognition is a better; and next to an accepted MS. there is nothing so encouraging as the recognition of those who have proved their right to criticise. I will endeavor to show that your judgment is not at fault and that it is based on something more than a sentimental sympathy with a would-be writer circumscribed in a manner so peculiar. Mr. Gilder shall see more of my work, and better. I shall write to please the editors, and the public, and who knows but that perhaps at some future day I may be best able to please others by pleasing myself?

*   *   *

4. James Maurice Thompson (1844–1901) served in the Confederate army and became a romancer famous for his fierce opposition to literary realism; his *A Tallahassee Girl* (1882), *His Second Campaign* (1883), and *At Love's Extremes* (1885) are sentimental works set in the South. Thomas Nelson Page (1853–1922) was a Virginia attorney whose "Marse Chan," published in *Century* in 1884, established his literary reputation as a writer adept at fictionalizing what he saw as the attractive life of the antebellum plantations. Joel Chandler Harris (1848–1908) was best known for his dialect stories narrated by his Uncle Remus in works such as *Uncle Remus: His Songs and His Sayings* (1881).
5. The pathos of the mulatto's situation receives heavy emphasis in Tourgée's *Toinette: A Tale of the South* (1874; published as *A Royal Gentleman* in 1881). * * *
6. Cable offered encouragement to Chesnutt on 31 May. "I feel you and this story stand in a very important relation to the interests of a whole great nation. If you will be patient and persevering, you can make of yourself a fictionist of a very high order. Your turning point is right before you. If you—with your vantage ground of a point of view new to the world and impossible to any other known writer—can acquire Gilder's clear discernment of all ungenuineness, you will become an apostle of a new emancipation to millions."

Original Cover of *The Conjure Woman*[†]

Despite Chesnutt's wish that Houghton Mifflin's presentation of his first book be as "dignified" as possible, the cover design sported an illustration of a stereotypical "Uncle" figure flanked by two drawings of white rabbits— a design that clearly seems to have been calculated to capitalize on the popularity of Joel Chandler Harris's renditions of the Brer Rabbit tales.

† Boston: Houghton Mifflin, 1899.

PAUL LAURENCE DUNBAR

The Deserted Plantation[†]

"The Deserted Plantation" is the first poem in Paul Laurence Dunbar's *Poems of Cabin and Field*, one of six illustrated editions of Dunbar's verse that appeared between 1899 and 1906. Published in the same year as Chesnutt's *Conjure Woman* volume, Dunbar's poem, with its accompanying photographs, touches upon many of the same registers as the Julius stories as it seeks to reconcile the landscape of the antebellum past with the post-emancipation present of the Southern states. At the time of publication of *The Conjure Woman*, reviewers often compared Chesnutt with Dunbar (1872–1906), whose poems written in dialect were especially popular with mainstream American readers at the end of the century.

The photographs that illustrate Dunbar's poem were taken by the members of the Hampton Institute Camera Club, who were faculty and staff members at the historically black college founded in Virginia after the Civil War. Ray Sapirstein's research informs us that the club operated during 1893–1926, and that while the membership was predominantly white, it did include seven African Americans, including two who were active during the production of the illustrated books.

† From *Poems of Cabin and Field*, illustrated with photographs by the Hampton Institute Camera Club (New York: Dodd, Mead & Company, 1899), pp. 11–29.

Oh, de grubbin'-hoe's a-rustin' in de co'nah,
　An' de plow 's a-tumblin' down in de fiel',
While de whippo'will's a-wailin' lak a mou'nah
　When his stubbo'n hea't is tryin' ha'd to yiel'.

In de furrers whah de co'n was allus wavin',
  Now de weeds is growin' green an' rank an' tall;
An' de swallers roun' de whole place is a-bravin'
  Lak dey thought deir folks had allus owned it all.

An' de big house stan's all quiet lak an' solemn,
    Not a blessed soul in pa'lor, po'ch, er lawn;
Not a guest, ner not a ca'iage lef' to haul 'em,
    Fu' de ones dat tu'ned de latch-string out air gone.

An' de banjo's voice is silent in de qua'ters,
  D' ain't a hymn ner co'n-song ringin' in de air;
But de murmur of a branch's passin' waters
  Is de only soun' dat breks de stillness dere.

Whah's de da'kies, dem dat used to be a-dancin'
  Ev'ry night befo' de ol' cabin do'?
Whah's de chillun, dem dat used to be a-prancin'
  Er a-rollin' in de san' er on de flo'?

Whah's ol' Uncle Mordecai an' Uncle Aaron?
    Whah's Aunt Doshy, Sam, an' Kit, an' all de res'?
Whah's ol' Tom de da'ky fiddlah, how's he farin'?
    Whah's de gals dat used to sing an' dance de bes'?

Gone! not one o' dem is lef' to tell de story;
    Dey have lef' de deah ol' place to fall away.
Couldn't one o' dem dat seed it in its glory
    Stay to watch it in de hour of decay?

Dey have lef' de ol' plantation to de swallers,
  But it hol's in me a lover till de las';
Fu' I fin' hyeah in de memory dat follers
  All dat loved me an' dat I loved in de pas'.

So I'll stay an' watch de deah ol' place an' tend it
    Ez I used to in de happy days gone by.
Twell de othah Mastah thinks it's time to end it,
    An' calls me to my qua'ters in de sky.

CHARLES W. CHESNUTT

Superstitions and Folk-lore of the South[†]

During a recent visit to North Carolina, after a long absence, I took occasion to inquire into the latter-day prevalence of the old-time belief in what was known as "conjuration" or "goopher," my childish recollection of which I have elsewhere embodied into a number of stories. The derivation of the word "goopher" I do not know, nor whether any other writer than myself has recognized its existence, though it is in frequent use in certain parts of the South. The origin of this curious superstition itself is perhaps more easily traceable. It probably grew, in the first place, out of African fetichism, which was brought over from the dark continent along with the dark people. Certain features, too, suggest a distant affinity with Voodooism, or snake worship, a cult which seems to have been indigenous to tropical America. These beliefs, which in the place of their origin had all the sanctions of religion and social custom, became, in the shadow of the white man's civilization, a pale reflection of their former selves. In time, too, they were mingled and confused with the witchcraft and ghost lore of the white man, and the tricks and delusions of the Indian conjurer. In the old plantation days they flourished vigorously, though discouraged by the "great house," and their potency was well established among the blacks and the poorer whites. Education, however, has thrown the ban of disrepute upon witchcraft and conjuration. The stern frown of the preacher, who looks upon superstition as the ally of the Evil One; the scornful sneer of the teacher, who sees in it a part of the livery of bondage, have driven this quaint combination of ancestral traditions to the remote chimney corners of old black aunties, from which it is difficult for the stranger to unearth them. Mr. Harris, in his Uncle Remus stories, has, with fine literary discrimination, collected and put into pleasing and enduring form, the plantation stories which dealt with animal lore, but so little attention has been paid to those dealing with so-called conjuration, that they seem in a fair way to disappear, without leaving a trace behind. The loss may not be very great, but these vanishing traditions might furnish valuable data for the sociologist, in the future study of racial development. In writing, a few years ago, the volume entitled "The Conjure Woman," I suspect that I was more influenced by the literary

[†] From *Modern Culture* 13 (1901): 231–35.

value of the material than by its sociological bearing, and therefore took, or thought I did, considerable liberty with my subject. Imagination, however, can only act upon data—one must have somewhere in his consciousness the ideas which he puts together to form a connected whole. Creative talent, of whatever grade, is, in the last analysis, only the power of rearrangement—there is nothing new under the sun. I was the more firmly impressed with this thought after I had interviewed half a dozen old women, and a genuine "conjure doctor;" for I discovered that the brilliant touches, due, I had thought, to my own imagination, were after all but dormant ideas, lodged in my childish mind by old Aunt This and old Uncle That, and awaiting only the spur of imagination to bring them again to the surface. For instance, in the story, "Hot-foot Hannibal," there figures a conjure doll with pepper feet. Those pepper feet I regarded as peculiarly my own, a purely original creation. I heard, only the other day, in North Carolina, of the consternation struck to the heart of a certain dark individual, upon finding upon his doorstep a rabbit's foot—a good omen in itself perhaps—to which a malign influence had been imparted by tying to one end of it, in the form of a cross, two small pods of red pepper!

Most of the delusions connected with this belief in conjuration grow out of mere lack of enlightenment. As primeval men saw a personality behind every natural phenomenon, and found a god or a devil in wind, rain, and hail, in lightning, and in storm, so the untaught man or woman who is assailed by an unusual ache or pain, some strenuous symptom of serious physical disorder, is prompt to accept the suggestion, which tradition approves, that some evil influence is behind his discomfort; and what more natural than to conclude that some rival in business or in love has set this force in motion?

Relics of ancestral barbarism are found among all peoples, but advanced civilization has at least shaken off the more obvious absurdities of superstition. We no longer attribute insanity to demoniac possession, nor suppose that a king's touch can cure scrofula. To many old people in the South, however, any unusual ache or pain is quite as likely to have been caused by some external evil influence as by natural causes. Tumors, sudden swellings due to inflammatory rheumatism or the bites of insects, are especially open to suspicion. Paralysis is proof positive of conjuration. If there is any doubt, the "conjure doctor" invariably removes it. The credulity of ignorance is his chief stock in trade—there is no question, when he is summoned, but that the patient has been tricked.

The means of conjuration are as simple as the indications. It is a condition of all witch stories that there must in some way be contact, either with the person, or with some object or image intended to represent the person to be affected; or, if not actual contact, at least close proximity. The charm is placed under the door-sill, or buried under the hearth, or hidden in the mattress of the person to be conjured. It may be a crude attempt to imitate the body of the victim, or it may consist merely of a bottle, or a gourd, or a little bag, containing a few rusty nails, crooked pins, or horsehairs. It may be a mysterious mixture thrown surreptitiously upon the person to be injured, or merely a line drawn across a road or path, which line it is fatal for a certain man or woman to cross. I heard of a case of a laboring man who went two miles out of his way, every morning and evening, while going to and from his work, to avoid such a line drawn for him by a certain powerful enemy.

Some of the more gruesome phases of the belief in conjuration suggest possible poisoning, a knowledge of which baleful art was once supposed to be wide-spread among the imported Negroes of the olden time. The blood or venom of snakes, spiders, and lizards is supposed to be employed for this purpose. The results of its administration are so peculiar, however, and so entirely improbable, that one is supposed to doubt even the initial use of poison, and figure it in as part of the same general delusion. For instance, a certain man "swelled up all over" and became "pieded," that is, pied or spotted. A white physician who was summoned thought that the man thus singularly afflicted was poisoned, but did not recognize the poison nor know the antidote. A conjure doctor, subsequently called in, was more prompt in his diagnosis. The man, he said, was poisoned with a lizard, which at that very moment was lodged somewhere in the patient's anatomy. The lizards and snakes in these stories, by the way, are not confined to the usual ducts and cavities of the human body, but seem to have freedom of movement throughout the whole structure. This lizard, according to the "doctor," would start from the man's shoulder, descend to his hand, return to the shoulder, and pass down the side of the body to the leg. When it reached the calf of the leg the lizard's head would appear right under the skin. After it had been perceptible for three days the lizard was to be cut out with a razor, or the man would die. Sure enough, the lizard manifested its presence in the appointed place at the appointed time; but the patient would not permit the surgery, and at the end of three days paid with death the penalty of his obstinacy. Old Aunt Harriet told me, with solemn earnestness, that she herself had taken a snake from her own arm, in sections, after a similar experience. Old Harriet may have been lying, but was, I imagine, merely self-deluded. Witches, prior to being burned, have often confessed their commerce with the Evil One. Why should Harriet hesitate to relate a simple personal experience which involved her in no blame whatever?

Old Uncle Jim, a shrewd, hard old sinner, and a palpable fraud, who did not, I imagine, believe in himself to any great extent, gave me some private points as to the manner in which these reptiles were thus transferred to the human system. If a snake or a lizard be killed, and a few drops of its blood be dried upon a plate or in a gourd, the person next eating or drinking from the contaminated vessel will soon become the unwilling landlord of a reptilian tenant. There are other avenues, too, by which the reptile may gain admittance; but when expelled by the conjure doctor's arts or medicines, it always leaves at the point where it entered. This belief may have originally derived its existence from the fact that certain tropical insects sometimes lay their eggs beneath the skins of animals, or even of men, from which it is difficult to expel them until the larvae are hatched. The *chico* or "jigger" of the West Indies and the Spanish Main is the most obvious example.

Old Aunt Harriet—last name uncertain, since she had borne those of her master, her mother, her putative father, and half a dozen husbands in succession, no one of which seemed to take undisputed precedence—related some very remarkable experiences. She at first manifested some reluctance to speak of conjuration, in the lore of which she was said to be well versed; but by listening patiently to her religious experiences—she was a dreamer of dreams and a seer of visions—I was able now and then to draw a little upon her reserves of superstition, if indeed her religion itself was much more than superstition.

"W'en I wuz a gal 'bout eighteen or nineteen," she confided, "de w'ite folks use' ter sen' me ter town ter fetch vegetables. One day I met a' ole conjuh man name' Jerry Macdonal', an' he said some rough, ugly things ter me. I says, says I, 'You mus' be a fool.' He did n' say nothin', but jes' looked at me wid 'is evil eye. W'en I come 'long back, date ole man wuz stan'in' in de road in front er his house, an' w'en he seed me he stoop' down an' tech' de groun', jes' lack he wuz pickin' up somethin', an' den went 'long back in 'is ya'd. De ve'y minute I step' on de spot he tech', I felt a sha'p pain shoot thoo my right foot, it tu'n't under me, an' I fell down in de road. I pick' myself up' an' by de time I got home, my foot wuz swoll' up twice its nachul size. I cried an' cried an' went on, fer I knowed I'd be'n trick' by dat ole man. Dat night in my sleep a voice spoke ter me an' says: 'Go an' git a plug er terbacker. Steep it in a skillet er wa'm water. Strip it lengthways, an' bin' it ter de bottom er yo' foot'. I never didn' use terbacker, an' I laid dere, an' says I ter myse'f, 'My Lawd, wa't is dat, wa't is dat!' Soon ez my foot got kind er easy, dat voice up an' speaks ag'in: 'Go an' git a plug er terbacker. Steep it in a skillet er wa'm water, an' bin' it ter de bottom er yo' foot.' I scramble' ter my feet, got de money out er my pocket, woke up de two little boys sleepin' on de flo', an' tol' 'em ter go ter de sto' an' git me a plug er terbacker. Dey didn' want ter go, said de sto' wuz shet, an' de sto' keeper gone ter bed. But

I chased 'em fo'th, an' dey found' de sto' keeper an' fetch' de terbacker—
dey sho' did. I soaked it in de skillet, an' stripped it 'long by degrees,
till I got ter de een', w'en I boun' it under my foot an' roun' my ankle.
Den I kneel' down an' prayed, an' next mawnin' de swelin' wuz all
gone! Dat voice wus de Spirit er de Lawd talkin' ter me, it sho' wuz!
De Lawd have mussy upon us, praise his Holy Name!"

Very obviously Harriet had sprained her ankle while looking at the
old man instead of watching the path, and the hot fomentation had
reduced the swelling. She is not the first person to hear spirit voices
in his or her own vagrant imaginings.

On another occasion, Aunt Harriet's finger swelled up "as big as a
corn-cob." She at first supposed the swelling to be due to a felon.
She went to old Uncle Julius Lutterloh, who told her that some one
had tricked her. "My Lawd!" she exclaimed, "how did they fix my finger?" He explained that it was done while in the act of shaking
hands. "Doctor" Julius opened the finger with a sharp knife and
showed Harriet two seeds at the bottom of the incision. He
instructed her to put a poultice of red onions on the wound over
night, and in the morning the seeds would come out. She was then
to put the two seeds in a skillet, on the right hand side of the fireplace, in a pint of water, and let them simmer nine mornings, and on
the ninth morning she was to let all the water simmer out, and when
the last drop should have gone, the one that put the seeds in her
hand was to go out of this world! Harriet, however, did not pursue
the treatment to the bitter end. The seeds, once extracted, she put
into a small phial, which she corked up tightly and put carefully
away in her bureau drawer. One morning she went to look at them,
and one of them was gone. Shortly afterwards the other disappeared. Aunt Harriet has a theory that she had been tricked by a
woman of whom her husband of that time was unduly fond, and
that the faithless husband had returned the seeds to their original
owner. A part of the scheme of conjuration is that the conjure doctor
can remove the spell and put it back upon the one who laid it. I was
unable to learn, however, of any instance where this extreme penalty
had been insisted upon.

It is seldom that any of these old Negroes will admit that he or she
possesses the power to conjure, though those who can remove spells
are very willing to make their accomplishment known, and to exercise it for a consideration. The only professional conjure doctor
whom I met was old Uncle Jim Davis, with whom I arranged a personal interview. He came to see me one evening, but almost immediately upon his arrival a minister called. The powers of light prevailed
over those of darkness, and Jim was dismissed until a later time,
with a commission to prepare for me a conjure "hand" or good luck
charm, of which, he informed some of the children about the house,

who were much interested in the proceedings, I was very much in need. I subsequently secured the charm, for which, considering its potency, the small sum of silver it cost me was no extravagant outlay. It is a very small bag of roots and herbs, and, if used according to directions, is guaranteed to insure me good luck and "keep me from losing my job." The directions require it to be wet with spirits nine mornings in succession, to be carried on the person, in a pocket on the right hand side, care being taken that it does not come in contact with any tobacco. When I add that I procured, from an equally trust-worthy source, a genuine graveyard rabbit's foot, I would seem to be reasonably well protected against casual misfortune. I shall not, how-ever, presume upon this immunity, and shall omit no reasonable pre-caution which the condition of my health or my affairs may render prudent.

An interesting conjure story which I heard, involves the fate of a lost voice. A certain woman's lover was enticed away by another woman, who sang very sweetly, and who, the jilted one suspected, had told lies about her. Having decided upon the method of punish-ment for this wickedness, the injured woman watched the other closely, in order to find a suitable opportunity for carrying out her purpose; but in vain, for the fortunate one, knowing of her enmity, would never speak to her or remain near her. One day the jilted woman plucked a red rose from her garden, and hid herself in the bushes near her rival's cabin. Very soon an old woman came by, who was accosted by the woman in hiding, and requested to hand the red rose to the woman of the house. The old woman, suspecting no evil, took the rose and approached the house, the other woman following her closely, but keeping herself always out of sight. When the old woman, having reached the door and called out the mistress of the house, delivered the rose as requested, the recipient thanked the giver in a loud voice, knowing the old woman to be somewhat deaf. At the moment she spoke, the woman in hiding reached up and caught her rival's voice, and clasping it tightly in her right hand, escaped, unseen, to her own cabin. At the same instant the afflicted woman missed her voice, and felt a sharp pain shoot through her left arm, just below the elbow. She at first suspected the old woman of having tricked her through the medium of the red rose, but was sub-sequently informed by a conjure doctor that her voice had been stolen, and that the old woman was innocent. For the pain he gave her a bottle of medicine, of which nine drops were to be applied three times a day, and rubbed in with the first two fingers of the right hand, care being taken not to let any other part of the hand touch the arm, as this would render the medicine useless. By the aid of a mirror, in which he called up her image, the conjure doctor ascer-tained who was the guilty person. He sought her out and charged

her with the crime which she promptly denied. Being pressed, however, she admitted her guilt. The doctor insisted upon immediate
restitution. She expressed her willingness, and at the same time her
inability to comply—she had taken the voice, but did not possess the
power to restore it. The conjure doctor was obdurate and at once
placed a spell upon her which is to remain until the lost voice is
restored. The case is still pending, I understand; I shall sometime
take steps to find out how it terminates.

How far a story like this is original, and how far a mere reflection of
familiar wonder stories, is purely a matter of speculation. When the
old mammies would tell the tales of Brer Rabbit and Brer Fox to the
master's children, these in turn would no doubt repeat the fairy tales
which they had read in books or heard from their parents' lips. The
magic mirror is as old as literature. The inability to restore the stolen
voice is foreshadowed in the Arabian Nights, when the "Open
Sesame"[1] is forgotten. The act of catching the voice has a simplicity
which stamps it as original, the only analogy of which I can at present
think being the story of later date, of the words which were frozen
silent during the extreme cold of an Arctic winter, and became
audible again the following summer when they had thawed out.

CHARLES W. CHESNUTT

The Free Colored People of North Carolina[†]

In our generalizations upon American history—and the American
people are prone to loose generalization, especially where the Negro
is concerned—it is ordinarily assumed that the entire colored race
was set free as the result of the Civil War. While this is true in a
broad, moral sense, there was, nevertheless, a very considerable tech-
nical exception in the case of several hundred thousand free people
of color, a great many of whom were residents of the Southern States.
Although the emancipation of their race brought to these a larger
measure of liberty than they had previously enjoyed, it did not confer
upon them personal freedom, which they possessed already. These
free colored people were variously distributed, being most numerous,
perhaps, in Maryland, where, in the year 1850, for example, in a state

---

1. The story of "Ali Baba and the Forty Thieves," in the epochal collection of Middle Eastern
   and South Asian folktales *One Thousand and One Nights*, involves a magical incantation
   that opens and closes the treasure cave of a gang of thieves. The greedy brother of Ali
   Baba, the hero of the tale, uses "Open Sesame" to get into the cave, but cannot remember
   it in order to get back out.
† From *The Southern Workman* 31.3 (Mar. 1902): 136–41.

with 87,189 slaves, there were 83,942 free colored people, the white population of the State being 515,918; and perhaps least numerous in Georgia, of all the slave states, where, to a slave population of 462,198, there were only 351 free people of color, or less than three-fourths of one per cent., as against the about fifty per cent. in Maryland. Next to Maryland came Virginia, with 58,042 free colored people, North Carolina with 30,463, Louisiana with 18,647, (of whom 10,939 were in the parish of New Orleans alone), and South Carolina with 9,914. For these statistics, I have of course referred to the census reports for the years mentioned. In the year 1850, according to the same authority, there were in the state of North Carolina 553,028 white people, 288,548 slaves, and 27,463 free colored people. In 1860, the white population of the state was 631,100, slaves 331,059, free colored people, 30,463.

These figures for 1850 and 1860 show that between nine and ten per cent. of the colored population, and about three per cent. of the total population in each of those years, were free colored people, the ratio of increase during the intervening period being inconsiderable. In the decade preceding 1850 the ratio of increase had been somewhat different. From 1840 to 1850 the white population of the state had increased 14.05 per cent., the slave population 17.38 per cent., the free colored population 20.81 per cent. In the long period from 1790 to 1860, during which the total percentage of increase for the whole population of the state was 700.16, that of the whites was 750.30 per cent., that of the free colored people 720.65 per cent., and that of the slave population but 450 per cent., the total increase in free population being 747.56 per cent.

It seems altogether probable that but for the radical change in the character of slavery, following the invention of the cotton-gin and the consequent great demand for laborers upon the far Southern plantations, which turned the border states into breeding-grounds for slaves, the forces of freedom might in time have overcome those of slavery, and the institution might have died a natural death, as it already had in the Northern States, and as it subsequently did in Brazil and Cuba. To these changed industrial conditions was due, in all probability, in the decade following 1850, the stationary ratio of free colored people to slaves against the larger increase from 1840 to 1850. The gradual growth of the slave power had discouraged the manumission of slaves, had resulted in legislation curtailing the rights and privileges of free people of color, and had driven many of these to seek homes in the North and West, in communities where, if not warmly welcomed as citizens, they were at least tolerated as freemen.

This free colored population was by no means evenly distributed throughout the state, but was mainly found along or near the eastern seaboard, in what is now known as the "black district" of North

Carolina. In Craven county, more than one-fifth of the colored population were free; in Halifax county, where the colored population was double that of the whites, one-fourth of the colored were free. In Hertford county, with 3,947 whites and 4,445 slaves, there were 1,112 free colored. In Pasquotank county, with a white and colored population almost evenly balanced, one-third of the colored people were free. In some counties, for instance in that of Jackson, a mountainous county in the west of the state, where the Negroes were but an insignificant element, the population stood 5,241 whites, 268 slaves, and three free colored persons.

The growth of this considerable element of free colored people had been due to several causes. In the eighteenth century, slavery in North Carolina had been of a somewhat mild character. There had been large estates along the seaboard and the water-courses, but the larger part of the population had been composed of small planters or farmers, whose slaves were few in number, too few indeed to be herded into slave quarters, but employed largely as domestic servants, and working side by side with their masters in field and forest, and sharing with them the same rude fare. The Scotch-Irish Presbyterian strain in the white people of North Carolina brought with it a fierce love of liberty, which was strongly manifested, for example, in the Mecklenburg declaration of independence, which preceded that at Philadelphia; and while this love of liberty was reconciled with slavery, the mere prejudice against race had not yet excluded all persons of Negro blood from its benign influence. Thus, in the earlier history of the state, the civil status of the inhabitants was largely regulated by condition rather than by color. To be a freeman meant to enjoy many of the fundamental rights of citizenship. Free men of color in North Carolina exercised the right of suffrage until 1835, when the constitution was amended to restrict this privilege to white men. It may be remarked, in passing, that prior to 1860, Jews could not vote in North Carolina. The right of marriage between whites and free persons of color was not restricted by law until the year 1830, though social prejudice had always discouraged it.

The mildness of slavery, which fostered kindly feelings between master and slave, often led to voluntary manumission. The superior morality which characterized the upper ranks of white women, so adequately protected by slavery, did not exist in anything like the same degree among the poorer classes, and occasional marriages, more or less legal, between free Negroes or slaves and poor white women, resulted in at least a small number of colored children, who followed the condition of their white mothers. I have personal knowledge of two free colored families of such origin, dating back to the eighteenth century, whose descendants in each case run into the hundreds. There was also a considerable Quaker element in the population, whose influence was cast against slavery, not in any fierce polemical spirit, but in such a way as to soften its rigors and promote gradual emancipation. Another source of free colored people in certain counties was the remnant of the Cherokee and Tuscarora Indians, who, mingling with the Negroes and poor whites, left more or less of their blood among the colored people of the state. By the law of *partitus sequitur ventrem*, which is a law of nature as well as of nations, the child of a free mother was always free, no matter what its color or the status of its father, and many free colored people were of female Indian ancestry.

One of these curiously mixed people left his mark upon the history of the state—a bloody mark, too, for the Indian in him did not passively endure the things to which the Negro strain rendered him subject. Henry Berry Lowrey[1] was what was known as a "Scuffletown mulatto"—Scuffletown[2] being a rambling community in Robeson county, N. C., inhabited mainly by people of this origin. His father, a prosperous farmer, was impressed, like other free Negroes, during the Civil War, for service upon the Confederate public works. He resisted and was shot to death with several sons who were assisting him. A younger son, Henry Berry Lowrey, swore an oath to avenge the injury, and a few years later carried it out with true Indian persistence and ferocity. During a career of murder and robbery extending over several years, in which he was aided by an organized band of desperadoes who rendezvoused in inaccessible swamps and terrorized the county, he killed every white man concerned in his father's death, and incidentally several others who interfered with his plans, making in all a total of some thirty killings. A body of romance grew up about this swarthy Robin Hood, who, armed to the teeth, would freely walk into the towns and about the railroad stations, knowing full well that there was a price upon his head, but relying for safety upon the sympathy of the blacks and the fears of the whites. His pretty yellow wife, "Rhody," was known as "the queen of Scuffletown." Northern reporters came down to write him up. An astute Boston detective who penetrated, under false colors, to his stronghold, is said to have been put to death with savage tortures. A state official was once conducted, by devious paths,

---

1. Henry Berry Lowrey, Lowrie, or Lowry (c. 1845–1872?), led a group of outlaws of Indian, white, and African American heritage in guerrilla warfare against the Confederate and Reconstruction governments of southeastern North Carolina, from 1864 until he disappeared in 1872. Lowrey's gang was rumored to have guided the army of Union general William Tecumseh Sherman through local swamps, enabling him to invade eastern North Carolina from the south; their propensity for stealing from local landowners and sharing the spoils with the desperately impoverished of the region garnered comparison, in *The New York Times* and elsewhere, to the legend of Robin Hood.
2. Present-day Pembroke. Robeson County borders Cumberland County, the site of the Julius tales, on the southwest.

under Lowrey's safeguard, to the outlaw's camp, in order that he might see for himself how difficult it would be to dislodge them. A dime novel was founded upon his exploits.[3] The state offered ten thousand, the Federal government, five thousand dollars for his capture, and a regiment of Federal troops was sent to subdue him, his career resembling very much that of the picturesque Italian bandit who has recently been captured after a long career of crime. Lowrey only succumbed in the end to a bullet from the hand of a treacherous comrade, and there is even yet a tradition that he escaped and made his way to a distant state. Some years ago these mixed Indians and Negroes were recognized by the North Carolina legislature as "Croatan Indians," being supposed to have descended from a tribe of that name and the whites of the lost first white colony of Virginia. They are allowed, among other special privileges conferred by this legislation, to have separate schools of their own, being placed, in certain other respects, upon a plane somewhat above that of the Negroes and a little below that of the whites.

I may add that North Carolina was a favorite refuge for runaway slaves and indentured servants from the richer colonies north and south of it. It may thus be plainly seen how a considerable body of free colored people sprang up within the borders of the state.

The status of these people, prior to the Civil War, was anomalous but tenable. Many of them, perhaps most of them, were as we have seen, persons of mixed blood, and received, with their dower of white blood, an intellectual and physical heritage of which social prejudice could not entirely rob them, and which helped them to prosperity in certain walks of life. The tie of kinship was sometimes recognized, and brought with it property, sympathy and opportunity which the black did not always enjoy. Many free colored men were skilled mechanics. The State House at Raleigh was built by colored workmen, under a foreman of the same race. I am acquainted with a family now living in the North, whose Negro grandfather was the leading tailor in Newbern, N. C. He owned a pew on the ground floor of the church which he attended, and was buried in the cemetery where white people were laid to rest. In the town where I went to live when a child, just after the Civil War, nearly all the mechanics were men of color. One of these, a saddler by trade, had himself been the owner, before the war, of a large plantation and several slaves. He had been constrained by force of circumstances to invest in Confederate bonds, but despite this loss, he still had left a considerable tract of land, a brick store, and a handsome town residence,

---

3. George Alfred Townsend, *The Swamp Outlaws, or, The North Carolina Bandits: being a complete history of the modern Rob Roys and Robin Hoods* (New York: Robert M. DeWitt, 1872).

and was able to send one of his sons, immediately after the war, to a Northern school, where he read law, and returning to his native state, was admitted to the bar and has ever since practiced his profession. This was an old free family, descended from a free West Indian female ancestor. For historical reasons, which applied to the whole race, slave and free, these families were, before the war, most clearly traceable through the female line.

The principal cabinet maker and undertaker in the town was an old white man whose workmen were colored. One of these practically inherited what was left of the business after the introduction of factory-made furniture from the North, and has been for many years the leading undertaker of the town. The tailors, shoemakers, wheelwrights and blacksmiths were men of color, as were the carpenters, bricklayers and plasterers.

It is often said, as an argument for slavery, by the still numerous apologists for that institution, that these skilled artisans have not passed on to the next generation the trades acquired by them under, if not in, slavery. This failure is generally ascribed to the shiftlessness of the race in freedom, and to the indisposition of the younger men to devote themselves to hard work. But the assumption is not always correct; there are still many competent colored mechanics in the South. In the town of which I have spoken, for instance, colored men are still the barbers, blacksmiths, masons and carpenters. And while there has been such a falling off, partly due to the unsettled conditions resulting from emancipation and inseparable from so sudden and radical a change, another reason for it exists in the altered industrial conditions which confront mechanics all over the country, due mainly to the growth of manufactures and the increased ease and cheapness of transportation. The shoes which were formerly made by hand are now manufactured in Massachusetts and sold, with a portrait of the maker stamped upon the sole, for less money than the most poorly paid mechanic could afford to make them for by hand. The buggies and wagons, to produce which kept a large factory, in the town where I lived, in constant operation, are now made in Cincinnati and other Northern cities, and delivered in North Carolina for a price prohibitive of manufacture by hand. Furniture is made at Grand Rapids, coffins in one place, and clothing in still another. The blacksmith buys his horseshoe ready made, in assorted sizes, and has merely to trim the hoof and fasten them on with machine-made nails. The shoemaker has degenerated into the cobbler; the tinner merely keeps a shop for the sale of tinware; the undertaker merely embalms the dead and conducts funerals, and tombstones are sold by catalogue with blanks for the insertion of names and dates before delivery. In some of the new industries which have sprung up in the South, such, for instance, as cotton-milling, Negroes are not employed.

Hence, in large part through the operation of social forces beyond any control on their part, they have lost their hereditary employments, and these have only in part been replaced by employment in tobacco factories and in iron mines and mills.

The general decline of the apprenticeship system which has affected black and white alike, is also in some degree responsible for the dearth of trained mechanics in the South. Even in Northern cities the finer grades of stone-cutting, bricklaying, carpentry and cabinet work, and practically all the mosaic and terra-cotta work and fine interior decorating, is done by workmen of foreign birth and training.

Many of the younger colored people who might have learned trades, have found worthy employment as teachers and preachers; but the servile occupations into which so many of the remainder have drifted by following the line of least resistance, are a poor substitute for the independent position of the skilled mechanic. The establishment, for the colored race, of such institutions as Hampton and Tuskegee, not only replaces the apprenticeship system, but fills a growing industrial want. A multiplication of such agencies will enable the "free colored people" of the next generation, who now embrace the whole race and will number some ten millions or more, to regain these lost arts, and through them, by industry and thrift, under intelligent leadership, to win that equality of citizenship of which they are now grasping, perhaps, somewhat more than the shadow but something less than the substance.

CHARLES W. CHESNUTT

Adaptation of "The Dumb Witness"†

In this adaptation of the unpublished story "The Dumb Witness," Chesnutt uses the story of Viney and Malcolm Murchison as background for his main plot, the romance of Ben Dudley and Graciella Treadwell. Viney's name remains unchanged, while Malcolm Murchison has become Malcolm Dudley, nephew of Ralph Dudley (old Roger Murchison) and mad uncle of Ben (young Roger Murchison). Ben is in love with Graciella, who will not marry him because he has no prospects for wealth, and instead courts the old, widowed and wealthy Colonel French of the title. In the first part of the excerpt, Ben shares the story of the hidden Dudley treasure with Graciella to try to convince her that he may someday become rich. In the second part of the excerpt, Ben witnesses the deaths of both Malcolm and Viney, as well

†   From *The Colonel's Dream* (Garden City, NY: Doubleday, Page, 1905), pp. 125–29, 272–75.

as the revelations that Viney can talk, and that the reputed fortune does not exist.

Other changes from the earlier story include the source of Viney's purported inability to speak (a stroke suffered when Malcolm Dudley had her whipped by an overseer), and the nature of the hidden treasure ($50,000 of Confederate gold).

*   *   *

Ben relapsed into gloom. * * * He could not give Graciella a house; he would not have a house until his uncle died. Graciella had never seemed so beautiful as to-day, as she sat, dressed in the cool white gown which Miss Laura's slender fingers had done up, and with her hair dressed after the daintiest and latest fashion chronicled in the *Ladies' Fireside Journal*. No wonder, he thought, that a jaded old man of the world like Colonel French should delight in her fresh young beauty!

But he would not give her up without a struggle. She had loved him; she must love him still; and she would yet be his, if he could keep her true to him or free from any promise to another, until her deeper feelings could resume their sway. It could not be possible, after all that had passed between them, that she meant to throw him over, nor was he a man that she could afford to treat in such a fashion. There was more in him than Graciella imagined; he was conscious of latent power of some kind, though he knew not what, and something would surely happen, sometime, somehow, to improve his fortunes. And there was always the hope, the possibility of finding the lost money.

He had brought his great-uncle Ralph's letter with him, as he had promised Graciella. When she read it, she would see the reasonableness of his hope, and might be willing to wait, at least a little while. Any delay would be a point gained. He shuddered to think that he might lose her, and then, the day after the irrevocable vows had been taken, the treasure might come to light, and all their life be spent in vain regrets. Graciella was skeptical about the lost money. Even Mrs. Treadwell, whose faith had been firm for years, had ceased to encourage his hope; while Miss Laura, who at one time had smiled at any mention of the matter, now looked grave if by any chance he let slip a word in reference to it. But he had in his pocket the outward and visible sign of his inward belief, and he would try its effect on Graciella. He would risk ridicule or anything else for her sake.

"Graciella," he said, "I have brought my uncle Malcolm's letter along, to convince you that uncle is not as crazy as he seems, and that there's some foundation for the hope that I may yet be able to give you all you want. I don't want to relinquish the hope, and I want you to share it with me."

He produced an envelope, once white, now yellow with time, on which was endorsed in ink once black but faded to a pale brown, and hardly legible, the name of "Malcolm Dudley, Esq., Mink Run," and in the lower left-hand corner, "By hand of Viney."

The sheet which Ben drew from this wrapper was worn at the folds, and required careful handling. Graciella, moved by curiosity, had come down from her throne to a seat beside Ben upon the porch. She had never had any faith in the mythical gold of old Ralph Dudley. The people of an earlier generation—her Aunt Laura perhaps—may once have believed in it, but they had long since ceased to do more than smile pityingly and shake their heads at the mention of old Malcolm's delusion. But there was in it the element of romance. Strange things had happened, and why might they not happen again? And if they should happen, why not to Ben, dear old, shiftless Ben! She moved a porch pillow close beside him, and, as they bent their heads over the paper her hair mingled with his, and soon her hand rested, unconsciously, upon his shoulder.

"It was a voice from the grave," said Ben, "for my great-uncle Ralph was dead when the letter reached Uncle Malcolm. I'll read it aloud—the writing is sometimes hard to make out, and I know it by heart:

> *My Dear Malcolm:* I have in my hands fifty thousand dollars of government money, in gold, which I am leaving here at the house for a few days. Since you are not at home, and I cannot wait, I have confided in our girl Viney, whom I can trust. She will tell you, when she gives you this, where I have put the money—I do not write it, lest the letter should fall into the wrong hands; there are many to whom it would be a great temptation. I shall return in a few days, and relieve you of the responsibility. Should anything happen to me, write to the Secretary of State at Richmond for instructions what to do with the money. In great haste,
>
> Your affectionate uncle,
>
> RALPH DUDLEY.

Graciella was momentarily impressed by the letter; of its reality there could be no doubt—it was there in black and white, or rather brown and yellow.

"It sounds like a letter in a novel," she said, thoughtfully. "There must have been something."

"There must *be* something, Graciella, for Uncle Ralph was killed the next day, and never came back for the money. But Uncle Malcolm, because he don't know where to look, can't find it; and old Aunt Viney, because she can't talk, can't tell him where it is."

"Why has she never shown him?" asked Graciella.

"There is some mystery," he said, "which she seems unable to explain without speech. And then, she is queer—as queer, in her own way, as uncle is in his. Now, if you'd only marry me, Graciella, and go out there to live, with your uncommonly fine mind, *you'd* find it—you couldn't help but find it. It would just come at your call, like my dog when I whistle to him."

Graciella was touched by the compliment, or by the serious feeling which underlay it. And that was very funny, about calling the money and having it come! She had often heard of people whistling for their money, but had never heard that it came—that was Ben's idea. There really was a good deal in Ben, and perhaps, after all——

But at that moment there was a sound of wheels, and whatever Graciella's thought may have been, it was not completed. As Colonel French lifted the latch of the garden gate and came up the walk toward them, any glamour of the past, any rosy hope of the future, vanished in the solid brilliancy of the present moment. Old Ralph was dead, old Malcolm nearly so; the money had never been found, would never come to light. There on the doorstep was a young man shabbily attired, without means or prospects. There at the gate was a fine horse, in a handsome trap, and coming up the walk an agreeable, well-dressed gentleman of wealth and position. No dead romance could, in the heart of a girl of seventeen, hold its own against so vital and brilliant a reality.

"Thank you, Ben," she said, adjusting a stray lock of hair which had escaped from her radiant crop, "I am not clever enough for that. It is a dream. Your great-uncle Ralph had ridden too long and too far in the sun, and imagined the treasure, which has driven your Uncle Malcolm crazy, and his housekeeper dumb, and has benumbed you so that you sit around waiting, waiting, when you ought to be working, working! No, Ben, I like you ever so much, but you will never take me to New York with your Uncle Ralph's money, nor will you ever earn enough to take me with your own. You must excuse me now, for here comes my cavalier. Don't hurry away; Aunt Laura will be out in a minute. You can stay and work on your model; I'll not be here to interrupt you. Good evening, Colonel French! Did you bring me a *Herald*? I want to look at the advertisements."

"Yes, my dear young lady, there is Wednesday's—it is only two days old. How are you, Mr. Dudley?"

"Tol'able, sir, thank you." Ben was a gentleman by instinct, though his heart was heavy and the colonel a favoured rival.

"By the way," said the colonel, "I wish to have an interview with your uncle, about the old mill site. He seems to have been a stock-holder in the company, and we should like his signature, if he is in condition to give it. If not, it may be necessary to appoint you his guardian, with power to act in his place."

"He's all right, sir, in the morning, if you come early enough," replied Ben, courteously. "You can tell what is best to do after you've seen him."

"Thank you," replied the colonel, "I'll have my man drive me out to-morrow about ten, say; if you'll be at home? You ought to be there, you know."

"Very well, sir, I'll be there all day, and shall expect you."

Graciella threw back one compassionate glance, as they drove away behind the colonel's high-stepping brown horse, and did not quite escape a pang at the sight of her young lover, still sitting on the steps in a dejected attitude; and for a moment longer his reproachful eyes haunted her. But Graciella prided herself on being, above all things, practical, and, having come out for a good time, resolutely put all unpleasant thoughts aside.

*   *   *

[One hundred forty-eight pages of the narrative have been omitted.]

At the same time that the colonel, dry-eyed and heavy-hearted, had returned to his empty house to nurse his grief, another series of events was drawing to a climax in the dilapidated house on Mink Run. Even while the preacher was saying the last words over little Phil's remains, old Malcolm Dudley's illness had taken a sudden and violent turn. He had been sinking for several days, but the decline had been gradual, and there had seemed no particular reason for alarm. But during the funeral exercises Ben had begun to feel uneasy—some obscure premonition warned him to hurry homeward.

As soon as the funeral was over he spoke to Dr. Price, who had been one of the pallbearers, and the doctor had promised to be at Mink Run in a little while. Ben rode home as rapidly as he could; as he went up the lane toward the house a Negro lad came forward to take charge of the tired horse, and Ben could see from the boy's expression that he had important information to communicate.

"Yo' uncle is monst'ous low, sir," said the boy. "You bettah go in an' see 'im quick, er you'll be too late. Dey ain' nobody wid 'im but ole Aun' Viney."

Ben hurried into the house and to his uncle's room, where Malcolm Dudley lay dying. Outside, the sun was setting, and his red rays, shining through the trees into the open window, lit the stage for the last scene of this belated drama. When Ben entered the room, the sweat of death had gathered on the old man's brow, but his eyes, clear with the light of reason, were fixed upon old Viney, who stood by the bedside. The two were evidently so absorbed in their own thoughts as to be oblivious to anything else, and neither of them paid the slightest attention to Ben, or to the scared Negro lad, who had followed him and stood outside the door. But marvellous to hear, Viney was talking, strangely, slowly, thickly, but passionately and distinctly.

"You had me whipped," she said. "Do you remember that? You had me whipped—whipped—whipped—by a poor white dog I had despised and spurned! You had said that you loved me, and you had promised to free me—and you had me whipped! But I have had my revenge!"

Her voice shook with passion, a passion at which Ben wondered. That his uncle and she had once been young he knew, and that their relations had once been closer than those of master and servant; but this outbreak of feeling from the wrinkled old mulattress seemed as strange and weird to Ben as though a stone image had waked to speech. Spellbound, he stood in the doorway, and listened to this ghost of a voice long dead.

"Your uncle came with the money and left it, and went away. Only he and I knew where it was. But I never told you! I could have spoken at any time for twenty-five years, but I never told you! I have waited—I have waited for this moment! I have gone into the woods and fields and talked to myself by the hour, that I might not forget how to talk—and I have waited my turn, and it is here and now!"

Ben hung breathlessly upon her words. He drew back beyond her range of vision, lest she might see him, and the spell be broken. Now, he thought, she would tell where the gold was hidden!

"He came," she said, "and left the gold—two heavy bags of it, and a letter for you. An hour later *he came back and took it all away*, except the letter! The money was here one hour, but in that hour you had me whipped, and for that you have spent twenty-five years in looking for nothing—something that was not here! I have had my revenge! For twenty-five years I have watched you look for—nothing; have seen you waste your time, your property, your life, your mind—for nothing! For ah, Mars' Ma'colm, you had me whipped—*by another man!*"

A shadow of reproach crept into the old man's eyes, over which the mists of death were already gathering.

"Yes, Viney," he whispered, "you have had your revenge! But I was sorry, Viney, for what I did, and you were not. And I forgive you, Viney; but you are unforgiving—even in the presence of death."

His voice failed, and his eyes closed for the last time. When she saw that he was dead, by a strange revulsion of feeling the wall of outraged pride and hatred and revenge, built upon one brutal and bitterly repented mistake, and labouriously maintained for half a lifetime in her woman's heart that even slavery could not crush, crumbled and fell and let pass over it in one great and final flood the pent-up passions of the past. Bursting into tears—strange tears from eyes that had long forgot to weep—old Viney threw herself down upon her knees by the bedside, and seizing old Malcolm's emaciated hand in both her own, covered it with kisses, fervent kisses, the ghosts of the passionate kisses of their distant youth.

With a feeling that his presence was something like sacrilege, Ben stole away and left her with her dead—the dead master and the dead past—and thanked God that he lived in another age, and had escaped this sin.

As he wandered through the old house, a veil seemed to fall from his eyes. How old everything was, how shrunken and decayed! The sheen of the hidden gold had gilded the dilapidated old house, the neglected plantation, his own barren life. Now that it was gone, things appeared in their true light. Fortunately he was young enough to retrieve much of what had been lost. When the old man was buried, he would settle the estate, sell the land, make some provision for Aunt Viney, and then, with what was left, go out into the world and try to make a place for himself and Graciella. For life intrudes its claims even into the presence of death.

When the doctor came, a little later, Ben went with him into the death chamber. Viney was still kneeling by her master's bedside, but strangely still and silent. The doctor laid his hand on hers and old Malcolm's, which had remained clasped together.

"They are both dead," he declared. "I knew their story; my father told it to me many years ago."

Ben related what he had overheard.

"I'm not surprised," said the doctor. "My father attended her when she had the stroke, and after. He always maintained that Viney could speak—if she had wished to speak."

CHARLES W. CHESNUTT

The Negro in Art: How Shall He Be Portrayed?[†]

We have asked the artists of the world these questions:

1. When the artist, black or white, portrays Negro characters is he under any obligations or limitations as to the sort of character he will portray?
2. Can any author be criticized for painting the worst or the best characters of a group?

[†] From *The Crisis* 33.1 (Nov. 1926): 28–29.

3. Can publishers be criticized for refusing to handle novels that portray Negroes of education and accomplishment, on the ground that these characters are no different from white folk and therefore not interesting?

4. What are Negroes to do when they are continually painted at their worst and judged by the public as they are painted?

5. Does the situation of the educated Negro in America with its pathos, humiliation and tragedy call for artistic treatment at least as sincere and sympathetic as "Porgy" received?

6. Is not the continual portrayal of the sordid, foolish and criminal among Negroes convincing the world that this and this alone is really and essentially Negroid, and preventing white artists from knowing any other types and preventing black artists from daring to paint them?

7. Is there not a real danger that young colored writers will be tempted to follow the popular trend in portraying Negro character in the underworld rather than seeking to paint the truth about themselves and their own social class?

Here are some answers. More will follow:

1. The realm of art is almost the only territory in which the mind is free, and of all the arts that of creative fiction is the freest. Painting, sculpture, music, poetry, the stage, are all more or less hampered by convention—even jazz has been tamed and harnessed, and there are rules for writing free verse. The man with the pen in the field of fiction is the only free lance, with the whole world to tilt at. Within the very wide limits of the present day conception of decency, he can write what he pleases. I see no possible reason why a colored writer should not have the same freedom. We want no color line in literature.

2. It depends on how and what he writes about them. A true picture of life would include the good, the bad and the indifferent. Most people, of whatever group, belong to the third class, and are therefore not interesting subjects of fiction. A writer who made all Negroes bad and all white people good, or *vice versa*, would not be a true artist, and could justly be criticised.

3. To the publisher, the one indispensable requisite for a novel is that it should sell, and to sell, it must be interesting. No publisher wants to bring out and no reader cares to read a dull book. To be interesting, a character in a novel must have personality. It is perhaps unfortunate that so few of the many Negro or Negroid characters in current novels are admirable types; but they are interesting, and it is the privilege and the opportunity of the colored writer to make characters of a different sort equally

interesting. Education and accomplishment do not of themselves necessarily make people interesting—we all know dull people who are highly cultured. The difficulty of finding a publisher for books by Negro authors has largely disappeared—publishers are seeking such books. Whether the demand for them shall prove to be more than a mere passing fad will depend upon the quality of the product.

4. Well, what can they do except to protest, and to paint a better type of Negro?

5. The Negro race and its mixtures are scattered over most of the earth's surface, and come in contact with men of other races in countless ways. All these contacts, with their resultant reactions, are potential themes of fiction, and the writer of genius ought to be able, with this wealth of material, to find or to create interesting types. If there are no super-Negroes, make some, as Mr. Cable did in his *Bras Coupé*.[1] Some of the men and women who have had the greatest influence on civilization have been purely creations of the imagination. It might not be a bad idea to create a few white men who not only think they are, but who really are entirely unprejudiced in their dealings with colored folk—it is the highest privilege of art to depict the ideal. There are plenty of Negro and Negroid types which a real artist could make interesting to the general reader without making all the men archangels, or scoundrels, or weaklings, or all the women unchaste. The writer, of whatever color, with the eye to see, the heart to feel and the pen to record the real romance, the worthy ambition, the broad humanity, which exist among colored people of every class, in spite of their handicaps, will find a hearing and reap his reward.

6. I do not think so. People who read books read the newspapers, and cannot possibly conceive that crime is peculiarly Negroid. In fact, in the matter of serious crime the Negro is a mere piker compared with the white man. In South Carolina, where the Negroes out number the whites, the penitentiary has more white than colored inmates. Of course the propagandist, of whatever integumentary pigment, will, of purpose or unconsciously, distort the facts. My most popular novel was distorted

---

1. In the late 1870s George Washington Cable wrote a story titled "Bras-Coupé"—the French name meaning, literally, "cut-arm"—about an African prince enslaved on a Louisiana Creole plantation who rises up against local slaveholders and, unsubdued under torture in retaliation, is ultimately beaten to death. Despite the popularity of his Creole fiction, Cable was unable to place the story in a northern magazine, and he ultimately refashioned it into an episode in his novel *The Grandissimes* (1880)—much as Chesnutt reworked the rejected story "The Dumb Witness" into an episode in *The Colonel's Dream*.

and mangled by a colored moving picture producer to make it appeal to Negro race prejudice.[2]

7. I think there is little danger of young colored writers writing too much about Negro characters in the underworld, so long as they do it well. Some successful authors have specialized in crook stories, and some crooks are mighty interesting people. The colored writer of fiction should study life in all its aspects. He should not worry about his social class. Indeed, it is doubtful whether the general reading public can be interested today in a long serious novel based upon the social struggles of colored people. Good work has been done along this line with the short story, but colored society is still too inchoate to have developed the fine shades and nuances of the more sophisticated society with which the ordinary novel of manner deals. Pride of caste is hardly convincing in a people where the same family, in the same generation, may produce a bishop and a butler, a lawyer and a lackey, not as an accident or a rarity but almost as a matter of course. On the other hand it can be argued that at the hand of a master these sharp contrasts could be made highly dramatic. But there is no formula for these things, and the discerning writer will make his own rules.

The prevailing weakness of Negro writings, from the viewpoint of art, is that they are too subjective. The colored writer, generally speaking, has not yet passed the point of thinking of himself first as a Negro, burdened with the responsibility of defending and uplifting his race. Such a frame of mind, however praiseworthy from a moral standpoint, is bad for art. Tell your story, and if it is on a vital subject, well told, with an outcome that commends itself to right-thinking people, it will, if interesting, be an effective brief for whatever cause it incidentally may postulate.

Why let Octavus Roy Cohen or Hugh Wiley[3] have a monopoly of the humorous side of Negro life? White artists caricatured the Negro on the stage until Ernest Hogan and Bert Williams[4] discovered that colored men could bring out the Negro's more amusing characteristics in a better and more interesting way.

---

2. Oscar Micheaux (1884–1951), regarded as the first African American feature film director, produced silent films of both Chesnutt's *The Conjure Woman* and *The House Behind the Cedars* in 1926; Chesnutt refers here to the latter. No prints of these films are known to exist today. Micheaux directed a second film based upon *The House Behind the Cedars* in 1932, with sound, titled *Veiled Aristocrats.* A trailer and fragments from two reels of this film are preserved in the Library of Congress.

3. Hugh Wiley (1884–1968) wrote popular stories for *Collier's* and is best remembered for creating the "famous Chinese sleuth" Mr. Wong; Octavus Roy Cohen (1891–1959), a white author from South Carolina, was famous for his comedic stories of backwoods southern African Americans published in *The Saturday Evening Post.*

4. Bert Williams (1874–1922), a vaudevillian, was one of the most popular American comedians of the first two decades of the twentieth century; Ernest Hogan (1865–1909), another veteran of vaudeville shows and populizer of ragtime songs, was the first African American entertainer to produce and star in a Broadway show.

Why does not some colored writer build a story around a Negro oil millionaire, and the difficulty he or she has in keeping any of his or her money? A Pullman porter who performs wonderful feats in the detection of crime has great possibilities. The Negro visionary who would change the world over night and bridge the gap between races in a decade would make an effective character in fiction. But the really epical race novel, in which love and hatred, high endeavor, success and failure, sheer comedy and stark tragedy are mingled, is yet to be written, and let us hope that a man of Negro blood may write it.

CHARLES W. CHESNUTT

Post-Bellum—Pre-Harlem[†]

My first book, *The Conjure Woman*, was published by the Houghton Mifflin Company in 1899. It was not, strictly speaking, a novel, though it has been so called, but a collection of short stories in Negro dialect, put in the mouth of an old Negro gardener, and related by him in each instance to the same audience, which consisted of the Northern lady and gentleman who employed him. They are naive and simple stories, dealing with alleged incidents of chattel slavery, as the old man had known it and as I had heard of it, and centering around the professional activities of old Aunt Peggy, the plantation conjure woman, and others of that ilk.

In every instance Julius had an axe to grind, for himself or his church, or some member of his family, or a white friend. The introductions to the stories, which were written in the best English I could command, developed the characters of Julius's employers and his own, and the wind-up of each story reveals the old man's ulterior purpose, which, as a general thing, is accomplished.

Most of the stories in *The Conjure Woman* had appeared in the *Atlantic Monthly* from time to time, the first story, "The Goophered Grapevine," in the issue of August, 1887, and one of them, "The Conjurer's Revenge," in the *Overland Monthly*. Two of them were first printed in the bound volume.[1]

---

† From *Charles W. Chesnutt: Essays and Speeches*, ed. Joseph R. McElrath, Jr., et al., (Stanford: Stanford UP, 1999), pp. 543–49. Originally published in *The Colophon*, February 1931. Notes have been edited.
1. Seeing previous periodical publication were four of the short stories. Three, rather than two, featuring Uncle Julius McAdoo appeared in print for the first time in the collection. Chesnutt also misremembered Aunt Peggy's more limited role; she is not present in all of the tales.

After the book had been accepted for publication, a friend of mine, the late Judge Madison W. Beacom, of Cleveland, a charter member of the Rowfant Club, suggested to the publishers a limited edition, which appeared in advance of the trade edition in an issue of one hundred and fifty numbered copies and was subscribed for almost entirely by members of the Rowfant Club and of the Cleveland bar. It was printed by the Riverside Press on large hand-made linen paper, bound in yellow buckram, with the name on the back in black letters on a white label, a very handsome and dignified volume.[2] The trade edition was bound in brown cloth and on the front was a picture of a white-haired old Negro, flanked on either side by a long-eared rabbit. The dust-jacket bore the same illustration.

The name of the story teller, "Uncle" Julius, and the locale of the stories, as well as the cover design, were suggestive of Mr. Harris's Uncle Remus, but the tales are entirely different. They are sometimes referred to as folk tales, but while they employ much of the universal machinery of wonder stories, especially the metamorphosis, with one exception, that of the first story, "The Goophered Grapevine," of which the norm was a folk tale, the stories are the fruit of my own imagination, in which respect they differ from the Uncle Remus stories which are avowedly folk tales.

Several subsequent editions of *The Conjure Woman* were brought out; just how many copies were sold altogether I have never informed myself, but not enough for the royalties to make me unduly rich, and in 1929, just thirty years after the first appearance of the book, a new edition was issued by Houghton Mifflin Company. It was printed from the original plates, with the very handsome title page of the limited edition, an attractive new cover in black and red, and a very flattering foreword by Colonel Joel Spingarn.

Most of my books are out of print, but I have been told that it is quite unusual for a volume of short stories which is not one of the accepted modern classics to remain on sale for so long a time.[3]

At the time when I first broke into print seriously, no American colored writer had ever secured critical recognition except Paul Laurence Dunbar, who had won his laurels as a poet. Phillis Wheatley, a Colonial poet, had gained recognition largely because she was a slave and born in Africa, but the short story, or the novel of life and manners, had not been attempted by any one of that group.

There had been many novels dealing with slavery and the Negro. Harriet Beecher Stowe, especially in *Uncle Tom's Cabin*, had covered

---

2. Chesnutt refers to the "Large-Paper Edition," which was the second 1899 printing of the first edition. Sheets for 160 copies were produced.
3. By "editions" Chesnutt means printings. The first edition plates were used for five printings in 1899–1900. Additional sheets (number unknown) were not produced until the sixth printing in 1928, rather than 1929.

practically the whole subject of slavery and race admixture. George W. Cable had dwelt upon the romantic and some of the tragic features of racial contacts in Louisiana, and Judge Albion W. Tourgée, in what was one of the best sellers of his day, *A Fool's Errand*, and in his *Bricks Without Straw*, had dealt with the problems of reconstruction.

Thomas Dixon was writing the Negro down industriously and with marked popular success. Thomas Nelson Page was disguising the harshness of slavery under the mask of sentiment.[4] The trend of public sentiment at the moment was distinctly away from the Negro. He had not developed any real political or business standing; socially he was outcast. His musical and stage successes were still for the most part unmade, and on the whole he was a small frog in a large pond, and there was a feeling of pessimism in regard to his future.

Publishers are human, and of course influenced by the opinions of their public. The firm of Houghton Mifflin, however, was unique in some respects. One of the active members of the firm was Francis J. Garrison, son of William Lloyd Garrison, from whom he had inherited his father's hatred of slavery and friendliness to the Negro. His partner, George H. Mifflin, was a liberal and generous gentleman trained in the best New England tradition. They were both friendly to my literary aspirations and became my personal friends.[5]

But the member of their staff who was of most assistance to me in publishing my first book was Walter Hines Page, later ambassador to England under President Wilson, and at that time editor of the *Atlantic Monthly*, as well as literary adviser for the publishing house, himself a liberalized Southerner, who derived from the same part of the South where the stories in *The Conjure Woman* are located, and where I passed my adolescent years. He was a graduate of Macon College, a fellow of Johns Hopkins University, had been attached to the staff of the *Forum* and the *New York Evening Post*, and was as broad-minded a Southerner as it was ever my good fortune to meet.

Three of the *Atlantic* editors wrote novels dealing with race problems—William Dean Howells in *An Imperative Duty*, Bliss Perry

4. Thomas Nelson Page wrote sentimental novels set in the antebellum and Reconstruction periods such as *Marse Chan* (1884), *In Ole Virginia* (1887), and the popular *Red Rock: A Chronicle of Reconstruction* (1898). Thomas Dixon (1864–1946) made his name with a virulently white-supremacist trilogy of "Reconstruction" or "Ku Klux Klan" novels published between 1902 and 1907 [*Editor*].
5. Francis Jackson Garrison (1848–1916) became particularly supportive of Chesnutt when he read the manuscript of *The Marrow of Tradition*; when that novel failed to realize Houghton Mifflin's sales expectations, Chesnutt's relationship with him ended. George H. Mifflin (1845–1921) became a partner of the firm succeeding Hurd & Houghton in 1872 and was president from 1908 to 1921. Their correspondence, too, was not maintained after the manuscript of *The Colonel's Dream*, published by Doubleday, Page & Co. in 1905, was declined by Garrison.

in *The Plated City*, and Mr. Page in *The Autobiography of Nicholas Worth*.[6]

The first of my conjure stories had been accepted for the *Atlantic* by Thomas Bailey Aldrich, the genial auburn-haired poet who at that time presided over the editorial desk.[7] My relations with him, for the short time they lasted, were most cordial and friendly.

Later on I submitted to Mr. Page several stories of post-war life among the colored people which the *Atlantic* published, and still later the manuscript of a novel. The novel was rejected, and was subsequently rewritten and published by Houghton Mifflin under the title of *The House Behind the Cedars*. Mr. Page, who had read the manuscript, softened its rejection by the suggestion that perhaps a collection of the conjure stories might be undertaken by the firm with a better prospect of success. I was in the hands of my friends, and submitted the collection. After some omissions and additions, all at the advice of Mr. Page, the book was accepted and announced as *The Conjure Woman*, in 1899, and I enjoyed all the delights of proof-reading and the other pleasant emotions attending the publication of a first book. Mr. Page, Mr. Garrison and Mr. Mifflin vied with each other in helping to make our joint venture a literary and financial success.

The book was favorably reviewed by literary critics. If I may be pardoned one quotation, William Dean Howells, always the friend of the aspiring author, in an article published in the *Atlantic Monthly* for May, 1900, wrote:

> The stories of *The Conjure Woman* have a wild, indigenous poetry, the creation of sincere and original imagination, which is imparted with a tender humorousness and a very artistic reticence. As far as his race is concerned, or his sixteenth part of a race, it does not greatly matter whether Mr. Chesnutt invented their motives, or found them, as he feigns, among his distant cousins of the Southern cabins. In either case the wonder of their beauty is the same, and whatever is primitive and sylvan or campestral in the reader's heart is touched by the spells thrown on the simple black lives in these enchanting tales. Character, the most precious thing in fiction, is faithfully portrayed.[8]

Imagine the thrill with which a new author would read such an encomium from such a source!

---

6. Perry succeeded Page as the *Atlantic Monthly* editor; *The Plated City* deals with the off-spring of inter-racial marriages. Page's *Autobiography of Nicholas Worth* (1909) indicts, among other regional shortcomings, racism in the South.
7. Aldrich (1836–1907) was editor of the *Atlantic Monthly* from 1881 to 1890.
8. Howells's review is reprinted in full in this Norton Critical Edition [*Editor*].

From the publisher's standpoint, the book proved a modest success. This was by no means a foregone conclusion, even assuming its literary merit and the publisher's imprint, for reasons which I shall try to make clear.

I have been referred to as the "first Negro novelist," meaning, of course, in the United States; Pushkin in Russia and the two Dumas in France had produced a large body of popular fiction.[9] At that time a literary work by an American of acknowledged color was a doubtful experiment, both for the writer and for the publisher, entirely apart from its intrinsic merit. Indeed, my race was never mentioned by the publishers in announcing or advertising the book. From my own viewpoint it was a personal matter. It never occurred to me to claim any merit because of it, and I have always resented the denial of anything on account of it. My colored friends, however, with a very natural and laudable zeal for the race, with which I found no fault, saw to it that the fact was not overlooked, and I have before me a copy of a letter written by one of them to the editor of the *Atlanta Constitution*, which had published a favorable review of the book, accompanied by my portrait, chiding him because the reviewer had not referred to my color.[1]

A woman critic of Jackson, Mississippi, questioning what she called the rumor as to my race, added, "Some people claim that Alexander Dumas, author of *The Count of Monte Cristo* and *The Three Musketeers*, was a colored man. This is obviously untrue, because no Negro could possibly have written these books"—a pontifical announcement which would seem to settle the question definitely, despite the historical evidence to the contrary.

While *The Conjure Woman* was in the press, the *Atlantic* published a short story of mine called "The Wife of His Youth" which attracted wide attention. James MacArthur, at that time connected with the *Critic*, later with *Harper's*, in talking one day with Mr. Page, learned of my race and requested leave to mention it as a matter of interest to the literary public. Mr. Page demurred at first on the ground that such an announcement might be harmful to the success of my forthcoming book, but finally consented, and Mr. MacArthur mentioned the fact in the *Critic*, referring to me as a "mulatto."[2]

---

9. In repeating this erroneous claim, Chesnutt ignores earlier authors of novels including William Wells Brown, Martin R. Delany, Julia C. Collins, and Frances Ellen Watkins Harper, as well as his turn-of-the-century contemporaries such as Pauline Hopkins and Sutton Griggs [*Editor*].
1. *The Conjure Woman* was reviewed by Lucian L. Knight in "The Literary World," *Atlanta Constitution*, 9 April 1899, Magazine Supplement, 9. A photograph of Chesnutt did not appear in this issue.
2. MacArthur (1866–1909) was co-editor of *The Bookman* (1894–1900). This revelation occurred not in *The Critic* but in "Chronicle and Comment," *Bookman* 7 (August 1898), 452. Chesnutt was described as a "coloured man of very light complexion."

As a matter of fact, substantially all of my writings, with the exception of *The Conjure Woman*, have dealt with the problems of people of mixed blood, which, while in the main the same as those of the true Negro, are in some instances and in some respects much more complex and difficult of treatment, in fiction as in life.

I have lived to see, after twenty years or more, a marked change in the attitude of publishers and the reading public in regard to the Negro in fiction. The development of Harlem, with its large colored population in all shades, from ivory to ebony, of all degrees of culture, from doctors of philosophy to the lowest grade of illiteracy; its various origins, North American, South American, West Indian and African; its morals ranging from the highest to the most debased; with the vivid life of its cabarets, dance halls, and theatres; with its ambitious business and professional men, its actors, singers, novelists and poets, its aspirations and demands for equality—without which any people would merit only contempt—presented a new field for literary exploration which of recent years has been cultivated assiduously.

One of the first of the New York writers to appreciate the possibilities of Harlem for literary purposes was Carl Van Vechten, whose novel *Nigger Heaven* was rather severely criticized by some of the colored intellectuals as a libel on the race, while others of them praised it highly.[3] I was prejudiced in its favor for reasons which those who have read the book will understand. I found it a vivid and interesting story which presented some new and better types of Negroes and treated them sympathetically.

The Negro novel, whether written by white or colored authors, has gone so much farther now in the respects in which it was criticized that *Nigger Heaven*, in comparison with some of these later productions, would be almost as mild as a Sunday School tract compared to *The Adventures of Fanny Hill*.[4] Several of these novels, by white and colored authors alike, reveal such an intimate and meticulous familiarity with the baser aspects of Negro life, North and South, that one is inclined to wonder how and from what social sub-sewers they gathered their information. With the exception of one or two of the earlier ones, the heroine of the novel is never chaste, though for the matter of that few post-Victorian heroines are, and most of the male characters are likewise weaklings or worse.

3. The white writer and photographer Van Vechten (1880–1964) published the controversially titled, sensational *roman à clef* about Harlem's artistic and intellectual scene in 1926 [*Editor*].
4. John Cleland's eighteenth-century novel about the life of a prostitute, *Memoirs of a Woman of Pleasure* (1748), is considered the first major work of prose pornography in English [*Editor*].

I have in mind a recent novel, brilliantly written by a gifted black author, in which, to my memory, there is not a single decent character, male or female.[5] These books are written primarily for white readers, as it is extremely doubtful whether a novel, however good, could succeed financially on its sales to colored readers alone. But it seems to me that a body of twelve million people, struggling upward slowly but surely from a lowly estate, must present all along the line of its advancement many situations full of dramatic interest, ranging from farce to tragedy, with many admirable types worthy of delineation.

Caste, a principal motive of fiction from Richardson down through the Victorian epoch, has pretty well vanished among white Americans. Between the whites and the Negroes it is acute, and is bound to develop an increasingly difficult complexity, while among the colored people themselves it is just beginning to appear.

Negro writers no longer have any difficulty in finding publishers. Their race is no longer a detriment but a good selling point, and publishers are seeking their books, sometimes, I am inclined to think, with less regard for quality than in the case of white writers. To date, colored writers have felt restricted for subjects to their own particular group, but there is every reason to hope that in the future, with proper encouragement, they will make an increasingly valuable contribution to literature, and perhaps produce chronicles of life comparable to those of Dostoievsky, Dumas, Dickens or Balzac.

---

5. Possibly Wallace Thurman's *The Blacker the Berry* (1929).

CRITICISM

Early Criticism

Critical Notices of *The Conjure Woman*†

From the *New York Times*, 15 Apr. 1899: 246:

Uncle Remus tells the black man's fairytales; Uncle Julius recites his creed, and it may be found in Mr. Charles W. Chesnutt's "The Conjure Woman." Certain persons, by "wukking de roots" and by means of "mixtries," can transform men into trees, birds, quadrupeds, or even into men of another race, sometimes controlling their movements by means of insect or animal messengers, and the spell may endure even after death of the conjuror. With the negro this is not a matter of faith; but of actual knowledge. The seven tales in Mr. Chesnutt's book are curious and interesting, and the shrewdness with which Uncle Julius relates each one at the moment when it will be most effective in his own interest suggests that the black man is no more above making his superstitions profitable than his white brother.

From the *Southern Workman* 28 (May 1899): 194–95:

In this little book we have one more addition to the already voluminous literature about the old plantation Negro, and at the same time an addition to the small, but constantly increasing library of English books by writers of African descent. Considered from both these points of view the volume is worthy of notice. As in the Uncle Remus books, the main story is a slight one, a mere thread upon which are hung the extraordinary conjure tales told by the old Negro, "Uncle Julius," who is the chief character of the book. There is in the manner in which the main story is told an irresistible reminder of Stockton,[1] not an imitation, but the same matter-of-fact attention to petty details in bringing out the effect, a resemblance so striking that it

---

† From *The Charles Chesnutt Digital Archive*, ed. Stephanie P. Browner (Berea College), www.chesnuttarchive.org.
1. Frank R. Stockton (1834–1902), a white American author of fables and fairy tales based upon folklore, best remembered for "The Lady, or the Tiger?" (1882).

would be possible to read page after page in the part where the distinctly Negro side of the work is not prominent, with the impression that it was Stockton's own writing.

In the character of Uncle Julius, we find the genial old Negro of "befo' de wah," engaged in the congenial task of initiating two guileless Northerners, his employers, into the ways and the folklore of the plantation darkey.[2] That he is not himself a firm believer in his own tales, seems pretty evident, although he affects entire faith, and expects his Northern friends to imitate it. In taking up the contemporary new line of the "conjuration" superstitions of the Negroes, Mr. Chesnutt has done well, although it seems to us as if at times he had embodied in his stories, not simply the conjuring powers ordinarily attributed by the Negroes to their local practitioners, but many of the magical tricks that belong rather to the witches and wizards of European and Asiatic folklore. It is our belief that Uncle Julius is not simply drawing on the stock of superstitions of his fellow slaves in the "quarters" but that from fairy tales of the young folks in the "great house" he has gathered many of the elements that go to make the book interesting and amusing. From our own study of the matter we have been led to think that the distinctly Negro belief in the power of the "conjure woman" did not include the trans-formation of her victims at will into trees, beasts, birds, etc., but was confined mainly to the power of working evil through sickness, or ordinary bad luck of one kind or another. We have known of cases in which an old woman was believed to have the power of self-transformation into some animal, but there has never come to our notice elsewhere any case in which a witch transformed her victim into another form. How far this enlargement of the "conjure woman's" powers is the use of literary license on Mr. Chesnutt's part, and how far it is his superior knowledge of Negro folklore, we would be very glad to know. For literary purposes, it is most effective, and the tales of Uncle Julius, with their gruesome African horrors enlarged through contact with the Aryan imagination, are entertaining reading enough, especially when we discover, as we soon do, that each one is told with a view to gaining some private end of the narrator.

We hope that Mr. Chesnutt has a literary future before him, and that we shall have many more of his works to notice. As his story, "The Wife of his Youth," published last summer in the *Atlantic Monthly*, has shown us, he has the power of entering into a hitherto unoccupied field, and brings before the reading public the little

---

2. Dismissive and now highly offensive term for an African American, used with irony here, but probably without irony by the reviewers for the *News and Observer* and the *Nation*, below.

understood life of the educated part of his own race. If he can, by sustained and serious work along this line, help us to a closer understanding of and sympathy with this struggling and often disappointed class, it seems to us that the work will be better worth doing than even this well executed series of stories about *The Conjure Woman*.

From the *News and Observer* [Raleigh], 30 Apr. 1899: 3:

The Conjure Woman by Charles W. Chestnutt * * * is the best book of short stories of the year. It has peculiar interest for North Carolina readers because the author shows a thorough acquaintance-ship with the superstitions and shrewdness of the negro character. The writer begins his first conjure story by stating that some years ago his wife was in poor health and his doctor advised a change from the temperature in the vicinity of the Great Lakes, and he came to North Carolina to visit a cousin who was in the turpentine business. The destination he writes, was "a quaint old town which I shall call Patesville, because for one reason, that is not its name. There was a red brick market-house in the public square with a tall tower which held a four-faced clock that struck the hours and from which there pealed out a curfew at nine o'clock." The further description of the place and surrounding country shows that Fayetteville was the town near which he bought a vineyard and settled. The seven conjure stories were told the new settler by an old-issue negro, "Uncle Julius," who was employed as coachman, and they bear every evidence of genuineness. They are admirably well told and each has a conclusion that gives "Uncle Julius" credit for smartness, as well as a vivid imagination. In the multitude of dialect [stories], Chas. Chestnutt's conjure stories deserve to rank with those of Joel Chandler Harris and Thomas Nelson Page.

We had scarcely finished reading this book, which charmingly tells of [the] harmless conjure faith of the old time darkey, when the *Newton Enterprise* gave an account of a trial in Lincoln[3] court, showing how faith in "conjuration" caused loss to a white man in North Carolina in the blazing light of this era's civilization. Here is the story of the trial:

> "Chris Detter was on trial on indictment for embezzlement and Martin Smith was the principal witness. Smith swore that Det-ter claimed to be a witch doctor and represented to him that his sister, an inmate of his house, was bewitched. After treating her some time, he said that the whole house and every crack in the

---

3. Newton, Lincolnton, and Burke County are located in the western part of the state.

house was full of witches and that the only way to get rid of them and cure the patient was to burn the house. Smith and his family had such implicit confidence in the witch doctor that the house was set on fire and burned down. During the burning the doctor stood by with a big stick to kill the witches as they came out. But after the fire he claimed that the witches had escaped up the chimney. Smith had a large hog and the doctor claimed that the witches had taken refuge in the hog, but that they could be driven out by hitting the hog between the eyes. Acting on the doctor's instructions Smith took a big stick of wood and hit the hog on the head, while the doctor held the hog's mouth open with a large butcher knife to enable the witches to escape. The first lick was not hard enough and the doctor called for a harder lick. The next blow killed the hog. Then the doctor said that a certain portion of the hog, if eaten by any member of the family, would cause instant death, but would have no deleterious effect on anybody else. He drew a mark close behind the shoulder blades and convinced Smith that if any of his family ate of the meat back of this line it would bring sure and immediate death. Smith therefore took the head and shoulders, and the doctor the hams and sides."

The *Charlotte Observer* adds some additional facts:

"Smith was living in Burke County all this time. The witches proving to be unusually tenacious in this case and refusing either to "banish" or be banished, Dr. Detter went into consultation with Smith again and informed him that he (Smith) would really have to leave, as the witches would not. The doctor recommended Lincolnshire as being peculiarly exempt from witches, and offered, at the sacrifice of his precious time and talents, to secure Smith a foothold in lovely Lincoln, where the hoo-doos[4] never trouble and the hoo-dooed might get a breathing spell and surcease from witches. He secured a home for Smith in this El Dorado for the small sum of $240, and Smith folded his tent like the soft-snap[5] that he was, and silently stole away to Lincoln. The most of the silent stealing, however, was done by Dr. Detter. Smith finally discovered that Dr. Detter had obtained this new home for him for $165, and had thus made $75 clear profit, although he told Smith that he paid exactly $240 for the place. Smith, as the *Enterprise* informs us, plucked up courage enough to consult a lawyer. They put the law on the learned Dr. Detter, and he was adjudged to be guilty of embezzlement. Judge Coble will doubtless give him a term in the pen."

4. Variant of "voudou."
5. Easy mark for a swindler.

The fact that such a thing could be possible among white people of North Carolina today almost staggers belief. It shows the crying need for education and proves that truth is stranger than fiction.

From the *Nation* 68 (1 Jun. 1899): 421:

The half-dozen tales of Aun' Peggy, the "cunjuh 'oman," told by an old plantation darky, are delightfully frank in their supernaturalism and lose in effectiveness only by the deep policy imputed to their relater. That the marvelous tale of the goophered grape-vine was concocted by Uncle Julius only to secure his own enjoyment of the vineyard, is a discovery which calls his own credulity in question. The thrill of the "Gray Wolf's Ha'nt" evaporates on finding the legend to be but the guardian of Uncle Julius's bee-tree. But in the current of the stories one has no thought of such a rude jar against the actual. The conjure woman "wuks" her roots, and Po' Sandy becomes a tree, Primus turns into a white mule, and Hot foot Hannibal, by the agency of a dollbaby with red-pepper feet, is brought low. Uncle Julius's scepticism cannot rob one of the belief that this was the real religion of the old plantation; the goopher "mixtry," not the overseer's lash, the dreaded power.

"Bruce Grit in Vanity Fair" in the *Colored American* [Washington] 25 Nov. 1899: 3:

I have just been bustin' my side a'laffin over Chesnutt's "Conjure Ooman," a copy of which has just been sent me by the publishers, Houghton, Mifflin and Co., Boston. They ain't na'er a book in the dialect language, that can 'proach it in originality, naturalness, and trueness to the life of the Negro of the day before yesterday. It has the flavor, which only a Negro writer could give to a collection of the folk lore of the race, and every page shows the master work of a consummate artist, who thoroughly understood his business when he evolved from his "think thing" "The Conjure Ooman." The white folks who write Negro dialect are not in it with the men of our race, who find this class of writing pleasurable, as well as profitable. Mr. Chesnutt can go on up to the haid of the class. He's a powerful smaht man, sholy.

WILLIAM DEAN HOWELLS

Mr. Charles W. Chesnutt's Stories[†]

The critical reader of the story called "The Wife of his Youth," which appeared in these pages two years ago, must have noticed uncommon traits in what was altogether a remarkable piece of work. The first was the novelty of the material; for the writer dealt not only with people who were not white, but with people who were not black enough to contrast grotesquely with white people,—who in fact were of that near approach to the ordinary American in race and color which leaves, at the last degree, every one but the connoisseur in doubt whether they are Anglo-Saxon or Anglo-African. Quite as striking as this novelty of the material was the author's thorough mastery of it, and his unerring knowledge of the life he had chosen in its peculiar racial characteristics. But above all, the story was notable for the passionless handling of a phase of our common life which is tense with potential tragedy; for the attitude, almost ironical, in which the artist observes the play of contesting emotions in the drama under his eyes; and for his apparently reluctant, apparently helpless consent to let the spectator know his real feeling in the matter. Any one accustomed to study methods in fiction, to distinguish between good and bad art, to feel the joy which the delicate skill possible only from a love of truth can give, must have known a high pleasure in the quiet self-restraint of the performance; and such a reader would probably have decided that the social situation in the piece was studied wholly from the outside, by an observer with special opportunities for knowing it, who was, as it were, surprised into final sympathy.

Now, however, it is known that the author of this story is of negro blood,—diluted, indeed, in such measure that if he did not admit this descent few would imagine it, but still quite of that middle world which lies next, though wholly outside, our own. Since his first story appeared he has contributed several others to these pages, and he now makes a showing palpable to criticism in a volume called *The Wife of his Youth, and Other Stories of the Color Line*; a volume of Southern sketches called *The Conjure Woman*; and a short life of Frederick Douglass, in the Beacon Series of biographies.[1] The last is a simple, solid, straight piece of work, not remarkable above many

† From the *Atlantic Monthly* 85.511 (May 1900): 699–701.
1. All three volumes by Chesnutt were published in 1899.

other biographical studies by people entirely white, and yet important as the work of a man not entirely white treating of a great man
of his inalienable race. But the volumes of fiction *are* remarkable
above many, above most short stories by people entirely white, and
would be worthy of unusual notice if they were not the work of a
man not entirely white.

It is not from their racial interest that we could first wish to speak
of them, though that must have a very great and very just claim upon
the critic. It is much more simply and directly, as works of art, that
they make their appeal, and we must allow the force of this quite
independently of the other interest. Yet it cannot always be allowed.
There are times in each of the stories of the first volume when the
simplicity lapses, and the effect is as of a weak and uninstructed
touch. There are other times when the attitude, severely impartial
and studiously aloof, accuses itself of a little pompousness. There
are still other times when the literature is a little too ornate for
beauty, and the diction is journalistic, reporteristic. But it is right to
add that these are the exceptional times, and that for far the greatest
part Mr. Chesnutt seems to know quite as well what he wants to do
in a given case as Maupassant, or Tourguénief, or Mr. James, or
Miss Jewett, or Miss Wilkins, in other given cases, and has done it
with an art of kindred quiet and force. He belongs, in other words, to
the good school, the only school, all aberrations from nature being
so much truancy and anarchy. He sees his people very clearly, very
justly, and he shows them as he sees them, leaving the reader to
divine the depth of his feeling for them. He touches all the stops,
and with equal delicacy in stories of real tragedy and comedy and
pathos, so that it would be hard to say which is the finest in such
admirably rendered effects as "The Web of Circumstance," "The
Bouquet," and "Uncle Wellington's Wives." In some others the comedy degenerates into satire, with a look in the reader's direction
which the author's friend must deplore.

As these stories are of our own time and country, and as there is not
a swashbuckler of the seventeenth century, or a sentimentalist of this,
or a princess of an imaginary kingdom, in any of them, they will possibly not reach half a million readers in six months, but in twelve
months possibly more readers will remember them than if they had
reached the half million. They are new and fresh and strong, as life
always is, and fable never is; and the stories of The Conjure Woman
have a wild, indigenous poetry, the creation of sincere and original
imagination, which is imparted with a tender humorousness and a
very artistic reticence. As far as his race is concerned, or his sixteenth
part of a race, it does not greatly matter whether Mr. Chesnutt
invented their motives, or found them, as he feigns, among his distant
cousins of the Southern cabins. In either case, the wonder of their

beauty is the same; and whatever is primitive and sylvan or campestral in the reader's heart is touched by the spells thrown on the simple black lives in these enchanting tales. Character, the most precious thing in fiction, is as faithfully portrayed against the poetic background as in the setting of the Stories of the Color Line.

Yet these stories, after all, are Mr. Chesnutt's most important work, whether we consider them merely as realistic fiction, apart from their author, or as studies of that middle world of which he is naturally and voluntarily a citizen. We had known the nethermost world of the grotesque and comical negro and the terrible and tragic negro through the white observer on the outside, and black character in its lyrical moods we had known from such an inside witness as Mr. Paul Dunbar;[2] but it had remained for Mr. Chesnutt to acquaint us with those regions where the paler shades dwell as hopelessly, with relation to ourselves, as the blackest negro. He has not shown the dwellers there as very different from ourselves. They have within their own circles the same social ambitions and prejudices; they intrigue and truckle and crawl, and are snobs, like ourselves, both of the snobs that snub and the snobs that are snubbed. We may choose to think them droll in their parody of pure white society, but perhaps it would be wiser to recognize that they are like us because they are of our blood by more than a half, or three quarters, or nine tenths. It is not, in such cases, their negro blood that characterizes them; but it is their negro blood that excludes them, and that will imaginably fortify them and exalt them. Bound in that sad solidarity from which there is no hope of entrance into polite white society for them, they may create a civilization of their own, which need not lack the highest quality. They need not be ashamed of the race from which they have sprung, and whose exile they share; for in many of the arts it has already shown, during a single generation of freedom, gifts which slavery apparently only obscured. With Mr. Booker Washington the first American orator of our time, fresh upon the time of Frederick Douglass; with Mr. Dunbar among the truest of our poets; with Mr. Tanner,[3] a black American, among the only three Americans from whom the French government ever bought a picture, Mr. Chesnutt may well be willing to own his color.

But that is his personal affair. Our own more universal interest in him arises from the more than promise he has given in a department of literature where Americans hold the foremost place. In this there is, happily, no color line; and if he has it in him to go forward on the way which he has traced for himself, to be true to life as he has known it, to deny himself the glories of the cheap success which

2. Paul Laurence Dunbar (1872–1906), nationally celebrated poet whose "The Deserted Plantation" is included in the Contexts section of this Norton Critical Edition.
3. Henry Ossawa Tanner (1859–1937), the first African American painter of international reputation.

awaits the charlatan in fiction, one of the places at the top is open to him. He has sounded a fresh note, boldly, not blatantly, and he has won the ear of the more intelligent public.

BENJAMIN BRAWLEY

[Fiction with a Firm Sense of Art]†

*   *   *

While in North Carolina Chesnutt studied to good purpose the tradi-tions and superstitions of the Negro people of the state, and in August, 1887, his short story, "The Goophered Grapevine," appeared in the *Atlantic Monthly*. This was the beginning of a series later brought together in a volume entitled *The Conjure Woman* (1899). "The Wife of his Youth" also appeared in the *Atlantic* (July, 1898) and gave the title to the second volume, *The Wife of his Youth, and Other Stories of the Color-Line* (1899). Three novels were published later, *The House behind the Cedars* (1900), *The Marrow of Tradition* (1901), and *The Colonel's Dream* (1905). All of these books except the last were issued by the Houghton Mifflin Company. Chesnutt also contributed a compact little work, *Frederick Douglass* (1899), to the Beacon Biographies of Eminent Americans, and at least three stories not in any collection appeared later, "Baxter's Procrustes" in the *Atlantic* (June, 1904), and "The Doll" and "Mr. Taylor's Funeral" in the *Crisis* (April, 1912, and April–May, 1915).

The *Conjure Woman* naturally evoked comparison with *Uncle Remus*, and the chief story-teller, Uncle Julius, stands up well by the side of Harris's famous character. With his shrewdness, his kindness, and his ability to look out for himself, he is, if anything, more clearly individualized than Uncle Remus. There are seven stories in the book. These are narrated by a man from Ohio who has gone to North Car-olina to engage in grape culture, but in one after another the story of Julius that is interpolated becomes the center of interest. The Conjure Woman is Aunt Peggy, who happens to be free and is quite expert in meddling with other people's affairs. In "The Goophered Grapevine," when the master of the plantation was missing too many scupper-nongs, she was engaged to call her arts into play, and "sa'ntered 'roun' 'mongs' de vimes, en tuk a leaf fum dis one, en a grape-hull fum dat one, en a grape-seed fum anudder one; en den a little twig fum here, en a little pinch er dirt fum dere,—en put it all in a big black bottle, en

† From *The Negro Genius: A New Appraisal of the Achievement of the American Negro in Literature and the Fine Arts* (New York: Dodd, Mead, 1937), pp. 145–51.

buried it under de root uv a red oak tree," and then remarked to one of the Negroes that anyone who ate the grapes would be dead within twelve months. Henry, one of her victims, found that as soon as the young grapes began to appear his hair "begun to quirl all up in little balls, des like dis yer reg'lar grapy ha'r, en by de time de grapes got ripe his head look des like a bunch er grapes." In telling his marvelous story so that a prospective owner would not feel inclined to purchase the vineyard, Julius remembered that he himself had been deriving a respectable revenue from the product of the neglected vines. So in "Po' Sandy," the sad story of a man who was turned into a tree and cut up as boards that went into a schoolhouse, it developed that Julius had in mind to use the old building for a church meeting. In "Hot-Foot Hannibal" he appears in a different light, helping to reconcile two young lovers higher in the world than himself. Chesnutt's dialect is not always above question, but, all told, *The Conjure Woman* showed that there had at last appeared among the Negro people a man who was able to write fiction with a firm sense of art.

*   *   *

HELEN M. CHESNUTT

Chesnutt and Walter Hines Page[†]

Chesnutt * * * went on to Boston to discuss his literary aspirations and plans with Walter Hines Page,[1] editor of *The Atlantic Monthly*, and with the members of the firm of Houghton, Mifflin and Company.

*   *   *

Chesnutt's spirit soared. Now, at last, perhaps, he could pass out of the world of dreams and preparation into the world of books and authorship.

[†]   From *Charles Waddell Chesnutt: Pioneer of the Color Line* (Chapel Hill: U of North Carolina P, 1952).

1. Page (1855–1918), a native North Carolinian close in age to Chesnutt, edited the *Atlantic Monthly* for five years at the close of the century. He went on to become a partner in the publishing house of Doubleday, Page & Co. from 1900 to 1913, and to serve as U.S. ambassador to the United Kingdom during World War I. He remained Chesnutt's principal supporter in the publishing industry, going on after collaborating with him on the shaping of *The Conjure Woman* volume to advise Chesnutt on revisions of what became his most popular novel, *The House Behind the Cedars*, and to publish Chesnutt's last published novel, *The Colonel's Dream*, under the Doubleday, Page imprint in 1905.

The visit to Boston was inspiring. Both Mifflin and Page were very much interested in his plans and encouraged him to keep on at his writing. Page suggested that Chesnutt send him any material he had on hand for criticism and comment. On his return he selected two stories and sent them to Page.

* * *

Walter H. Page to Chesnutt, October 2, 1897

It has given me great pleasure to read the two stories you sent after your return home, namely "The Dumb Witness" and "The Bouquet." I do not hesitate to say that I should keep one of them, most likely both, but for the reason that we have had such hard luck in making room for your other two stories which I value highly, I do not feel like keeping these when we may not be able to use them for so long a time. This field that you are working is a very profitable one I think, but we cannot give it undue attention, and I fear that the two stories that we now have are as many as we ought to commit ourselves to for the present. I shall watch with great interest, however, the continuance of your work if you will be good enough to permit me. When you get your long story done, I cannot help thinking that it will be a successful book if you write that as well as you write short stories, and I have thought, too, that a skillfully selected list of your short stories might make a book. Whenever you are in the humor to talk about these things, let me hear from you.

The two stories already in the hands of Houghton, Mifflin and Company were "The Wife of His Youth" and "The March of Progress."

* * *

Page to Chesnutt, October 20, 1897

I am very glad to have your letter of October 18th, and I like the frankness and spontaneity with which you write and the full explanation that you give of the stories you have on hand. Let us at once put the matter in practical shape and see what can be done. The best way to get at it, then, is for you to send us all the short stories, both published and unpublished, that you have, leaving out the longer ones (by the longer ones, I mean the story that contains 54,000 words and the other one that contains 29,000.) Send us all the rest, and let our readers take the whole collection up and see whether by selecting judiciously from them a selection can be made which seems likely to make a book of sufficient unity to put upon the market. If you will bundle up this whole lot and send them here by express, it will give us pleasure to take the matter immediately in hand, and I hope we shall be able to make a favorable report to you.

This seems to me the practical way to proceed, and we shall do our best to serve you.

Chesnutt to Houghton, Mifflin and Company, October 22, 1897

In accordance with letter of October 20th from your Mr. Page, I enclose the following stories, either typewritten or printed, with a view to a selection of them for a book:

A Matter of Principle	Uncle Peter's House
Lonesome Ben	The Fall of Adam
Jim's Romance	A Tight Boot
The Bouquet	Tom's Warm Welcome
Aunt Mimy's Son	The Goophered Grapevine
The Fabric of a Vision	Dave's Neckliss
The Dumb Witness	Po' Sandy
Mr. Taylor's Funeral	The Conjurer's Revenge
The Shadow of my Past	The Sheriff's Children
Uncle Wellington's Wives	A Deep Sleeper

October 22, 1897

MR. WALTER H. PAGE
BOSTON, MASSACHUSETTS
DEAR MR. PAGE:

I was duly in receipt of your favor of October 20, and I do not know of any better time than the present to act upon it. I have today forwarded to Messrs. Houghton, Mifflin and Company, by express, copies of twenty stories, including published and unpublished stories, from which I trust your readers will be able to select enough to make a book.

I think these stories will fall naturally into two or three groups, which will, of course, suggest themselves at once to the reader. This list is by no means complete without the two stories which you have on hand for the *Atlantic*, as I consider them, two of the best I have written, and I presume their publication in the *Atlantic* will help any book that might subsequently reproduce them. If I had to choose between having them printed in a book, and having them appear in the *Atlantic*, I should prefer the latter, but I presume you would use them in both.

Among the stories I send a few earlier stories and sketches; I do not know that they have much value, but the longest of them, "Uncle Peter's House," has some elements of strength, though it is not so well written as the later stories. It is quite likely, when a selection has been made, if such be the outcome of your examination, that I might want to retouch a few of the stories selected before they are put into type.

*   *   *

Thanking you for your promptness in answering my letter and for your personal interest in this matter, and trusting that a favorable report may be made, I remain,

Sincerely yours,
CHAS. W. CHESNUTT

1024 SOCIETY FOR SAVINGS BLDG.
CLEVELAND, OHIO
December 7, 1897

DEAR MR. PAGE:

I felt in a somewhat effusive mood the other day, and I sat down to write a long letter, in which I was going to tell you something about my literary plans, how long I had cherished them, the preparation I had made for them by study in our own language and other languages, by travel in our own country and in Europe; how I had in a measure restrained myself from writing until I should have something worth saying, and should be able to say it clearly and temperately, and until an opportune time should have come for saying it; how I had intended, for reasons which were obvious, and had in a measure paved the way financially, to make my literary debut on the other side of the Atlantic, and to follow it up immediately by devoting my whole time to the literary life, etc.

But it occurred to me that you were a busy man, and that anything I might say to you as an editor might be better said by what I should write for publication; that all my preparations and my hopes would be of no use to me, and of no interest to you, unless I followed them up with something like adequate performance; and that it would be in better taste to reserve personal confidences until I might have gained your friendship and your interest by having accomplished some worthy thing. So I concluded that I would write you a simple business letter, and say that I sincerely hope your house will see its way to publish that volume of stories for me. I feel confident that they have sufficient originality to secure a hearing, and that their chance of doing so will be very much enhanced if they are brought out by a concern of Houghton, Mifflin and Company's standing. It is not difficult to find a publisher of some kind, on some terms—but there are publishers and publishers.

I am prepared to follow up a volume of stories by a novel. I have completed the first draft of a long story which I mentioned to you when I saw you in Boston, and have started on the revision; in a month or two I hope to have it completed. It deals with no race problems, but mainly with a very noble order of human nature, more or less modified by circumstances. I have also the raw material, partly digested, of a story on the order of what you suggested might be written along the line of my shorter stories. When I get this other out of the way, I shall attack it seriously.

You may remember that you said to me that you hoped to get at least one of the two short stories you have for the *Atlantic*, in either the December or the January number. If that is not feasible for the January number, I am sure you will do the best you can for them.

I write to you thus fully—for I see I have written a long letter, in spite of my disclaimer—because I do not want you to forget me. I know you have a great many people on the ground, near at hand, and that distance puts me at a disadvantage with the relays of people waiting in the outer room to see you. I wish to secure your interest and your friendship in furtherance of my literary aims, and I do not think you will find it amiss that I write and tell you so, and tell you why.

Permit me to say in closing that I thought the book reviews in the December *Atlantic* exceedingly good, and that I remain,

Sincerely yours,
CHARLES W. CHESNUTT

HOUGHTON, MIFFLIN AND CO.
BOSTON
December 15, 1897

MR. CHAS. W. CHESNUTT
CLEVELAND, OHIO
DEAR SIR:

It has given me an unusual pleasure to receive your cordial letter—more pleasure than I shall now undertake to tell you when I am working against time to clear my desk of pressing tasks. But I write now to say simply this much—that your stories are undergoing a rather unusual experience here; because they are being read, I believe, by our whole staff of readers, and I hope to have in a very little while definite word to send you. The practical trouble presented is the miscellaneous quality of these stories. During the preliminary stages of our discussion about it there has seemed a better possibility of making two or three books (were there only enough stories of each group) than of making a single book of heterogeneous matter. But you shall hear our final judgment, which will be the most favorable one that can possibly be reached, without much greater delay.

I am delighted to hear that you have got a long novel so far ahead, for, as I think I told you, this seems to me a much more promising publishing opportunity, and a much more important step in your literary career than the book publication of any short stories whatever.

Again I wish to express my very cordial appreciation of your friendly letter, and it will give me and everybody here very great pleasure if it turns out that we can meet all your wishes, as I hope it may.

Very sincerely yours,
WALTER H. PAGE

* * *

March 15, 1898

MR. WALTER H. PAGE
BOSTON, MASSACHUSETTS
DEAR MR. PAGE:

I have written to you before about a long story I have been writing. I have finished it—at least, I am going to stop working on it for the time being—and take the liberty of sending it to you herewith. I have entitled it "A Business Career." I think it has some of the elements of a good story, and I should like to have your house consider it with that end in view. It would certainly strike a considerable class of people in large cities, if brought to their attention. I do not know whether in form or subject you would consider it suitable for the *Atlantic;* if so, I should be glad to see it there.

Any information as to my collection of stories that you have been considering or any intimation as to when you will probably be able to use the stories accepted for the *Atlantic* will be very much appreciated.

In the meantime, I remain

Cordially yours,
CHARLES W. CHESNUTT

HOUGHTON, MIFFLIN AND COMPANY
BOSTON
March 30, 1898

MR. CHAS. W. CHESNUTT
CLEVELAND, OHIO
DEAR MR. CHESNUTT:

The unpleasant task (for I assure you it is an unpleasant one) falls to my lot to write to you, saying that the firm is sorry that they do not see a way to make you an offer to publish either a book made up of your short stories or the longer story, "A Business Career," the manuscript of which you were kind enough to send at my suggestion a little while ago.

The novel, we have regretfully come to the conclusion, would be a doubtful venture on our list. It does not follow, of course, that it would not succeed on some other list, for it might very well do so;

but it has been impossible for us to reach the conclusion, after very careful deliberation and discussion, that it would be a wise venture for this firm to undertake—especially when the field is so absolutely over-crowded with novels as to compel a greater degree of conservatism on the part of publishers than was ever before warranted. A novel in these days must have some much more striking characteristic of plot or style to make its publication a good venture than was required a dozen years ago or less.

Concerning your short stories, the same general proposition holds, with an additional disadvantage from a publisher's point of view, that books made up of short stories become harder and harder to market; for the public seems thoroughly to have made up its mind that the business of the short story is completely done when it appears in a magazine.

This is a hard message to send you, because I have cherished the hope, ever since I read the first of your stories that came under my eye, not only that you would start a successful literary career with the first novel that you should put out, but that you would put out a novel which would fall properly within the scope of this house's publications. Now the first of these propositions—that "A Business Career" may be a success—is not at all denied by Messrs. Houghton, Mifflin and Company's conservative attitude towards it. You will doubtless be able to find a publisher, and my advice to you is decidedly to keep trying till you do find one.

There is yet a possibility of Messrs. Houghton, Mifflin and Company's doing something for you along this line—if you had enough "conjure" stories to make a book, even a small book. I cannot help feeling that that would succeed. All the readers who have read your stories agree on this—that "The Goophered Grapevine" and "Po' Sandy," and the one or two others that have the same original quality that these show, are stories that are sure to live—in fact, I know of nothing so good of their kind anywhere. For myself, I venture unhesitatingly the prediction of a notable and lasting success with them, but the trouble at present is there are only about three of these stories which have this quality unmixed with other qualities. If you could produce five or six more like these, I think I am safe in making you a double promise—first, of magazine publication, and then the collection, I think would make a successful book. This last opinion concerning the publication of them in a volume I make on my own responsibility, for the firm has not warranted me definitely to promise so much; but we are all so impressed with them that I think there would be no doubt about it.

You shall receive a proof of the two stories that the *Atlantic* has accepted from you now forthwith.

I need not tell you that I hoped quite as sincerely as you did that we should have a different answer to send you; and I need not say to you that this answer must not be interpreted in any sense as a discouragement.

I beg you to command me in any way that I can serve you.

Very truly yours,

WALTER H. PAGE

When Chesnutt finished reading this letter he was very much disappointed, but not at all discouraged. The *Atlantic Monthly* had already published three of his stories and had accepted two more for future publication; so he knew that he could really write. Very well, then, he would write some more conjure stories for that book that Page had practically guaranteed.

Chesnutt to Page, April 4, 1898

I have written you a business letter today, and sent it to you with some stories, under another cover. As this letter is of rather a personal nature, I enclose it separately.

A friend of yours, Mr. Keatings, of New York, with whom I have had more or less business for several years in connection with a railroad receivership out here, was in my office a few weeks ago. In the course of our conversation, the *Atlantic* was referred to, whereupon Mr. Keatings said that one of his best friends edited the magazine, and mentioned your name, also the fact that you were a North Carolinian by birth and breeding, and a member of the old Virginia family of the same name.

Of course, I ought to have known all this before, but when one lives far from literary centers, and is not in touch with literary people, there are lots of interesting things one doesn't learn. I had even read some of your papers on the South, and know of your editorial work in North Carolina, but when I met you in Boston I did not at the time connect you with them. I calmly assumed, as nine people out of ten would, off hand, that an editor of the *Atlantic* was, of course, a New Englander by birth and breeding. But when Keatings enlightened me on the subject, I immediately proceeded to correct my impressions by reference to a biographical dictionary. You may imagine my surprise, and it was an agreeable one, I assure you, to find that you were "bawn en raise'" within fifty or sixty miles of the town where I spent my own boyhood and early manhood, and where my own forebears have lived and died and laid their bones.

I hope you will find time to read my "conjah" stories, and that you may like them. They are made out of whole cloth, but are true, I think, to the general "doctrine" of conjuration, and do not stray very far beyond the borders of what an old Southern Negro *might* talk about.

I am going to work on the novel I have been speaking of; it is a North Carolina story. With your permission, I shall sometime soon write you a note briefly outlining the plot and general movement, and ask you whether there is anything in the subject that would make it unavailable for your house. I am not easily discouraged, and I am going to write some books, and I still cherish the hope that either with my conjure stories or something else, I may come up to your standard.

In the meantime, I remain,

Cordially yours,
CHAS. W. CHESNUTT

Toward the end of May, Chesnutt sent Page the collection of conjure stories and the following letter:

64 Brenton Street
CLEVELAND, OHIO
May 20, 1898

MR. WALTER H. PAGE
HOUGHTON, MIFFLIN AND COMPANY
BOSTON, MASSACHUSETTS
MY DEAR MR. PAGE:

I enclose you herewith the six "conjure" stories you suggested that I send with a view to magazine and book publication. They are entitled respectively: "A Victim of Heredity," "The Gray Wolf's Ha'nt," "Mars Jeems's Nightmare," "Sis' Becky's Pickaninny," "Tobe's Tribulations," and "Hot-foot Hannibal" or "The Long Road." In writing them, I have followed in general the lines of the conjure stories you have read already, and I imagine the tales in this batch are similar enough and yet unlike enough, to make a book.

In one of them, "Hot-foot Hannibal," the outside and inside stories are both strong, and I have given an alternative title, "The Long Road," so that there is room for editorial choice, one name being taken from the conjure story, and the other from the outside story.

In the case of "Mars Jeems's Nightmare" the transformation suggested is not an entirely novel one, but the treatment of it is, so far as I know. I have thought a good title for the story would be "De Noo Nigger," but I don't care to dignify a doubtful word quite so much; it is all right for Julius, but it might leave me under the suspicion of bad taste unless perchance the whole title's being in dialect should redeem it.

Speaking of dialect, it is almost a despairing task to write it. What to do with the troublesome *r*, and the obvious inconsistency of leaving it out where it would be in good English, and putting it in where correct speech would leave it out, how to express such words as "here" and "hear" and "year" and "other" and "another", "either" and "neither", and so on, is a "'stractin'" task. The fact is, of course, that there is no such thing as a Negro dialect; that what we call by that name is the attempt to express, with such a degree of phonetic correctness as to suggest the sound, English pronounced as an ignorant old southern Negro would be supposed to speak it, and at the same time to preserve a sufficient approximation to the correct spelling to make it easy reading. I do not imagine I have got my dialect, even now, any more uniform than other writers of the same sort of matter. If you find these stories available, I shall be glad to receive any suggestions in the matter of the dialect or anything else.

I hope you will like the stories and that you may find it possible to use them, or some of them, for the magazine, as well as for book publication, within the current year, if possible.

Of the three conjure stories heretofore written by me and published, one, "The Conjurer's Revenge," which appeared in the *Overland Monthly*, the mule transformation story, has a good deal of extraneous matter in it, and is a trifle coarse here and there. I shall rewrite it at once, as I think it was checked by your house as suitable for book publication.

Hoping that these stories may meet with favorable consideration, which I know you will be glad to find them worthy of, I remain,

Sincerely yours,
CHARLES W. CHESNUTT

EDITORIAL OFFICE OF
THE ATLANTIC MONTHLY
BOSTON
June 24, 1898

MR. CHARLES W. CHESNUTT
CLEVELAND, OHIO
DEAR MR. CHESNUTT:

"The Wife of His Youth" as you have by this time found out, appears in the July *Atlantic* and does its full share, too, to make this number interesting. The other story shall follow very soon. Very soon, too, you shall hear about the "conjure" stories.

Very truly yours,
WALTER H. PAGE

EDITORIAL OFFICE OF
THE ATLANTIC MONTHLY
BOSTON
June 28, 1898

MR. CHARLES W. CHESNUTT
CLEVELAND, OHIO
DEAR MR. CHESNUTT:

The enclosed letter will, I am sure, please you. I send it to you in confidence and with uncommon pleasure.

WALTER H. PAGE

The letter which Page sent Chesnutt was the following, which he had received from James Lane Allen:[2]

120 MADISON AVENUE
NEW YORK, 27 June

DEAR PAGE,

Who—in the name of the Lord!—is Charles W. Chesnutt? Half an hour ago, or an hour, I came in from the steaming streets and before beginning my day's work, picked up your ever faithful Atlantic. I read at once Bliss Carman's poem, which is mighty true, and then turned to the wife of my youth—I beg your pardon—to "The Wife of His Youth." I went through it without drawing breath—except to laugh out two or three times. It is the freshest, finest, most admirably held in and wrought out little story that has gladdened—and moistened—my eyes in many months.

If it is worth while, in your opinion, send the man my thanks, and my blessings on his pathway. And thank *you!*

Heartily,
JAMES LANE ALLEN

June 29, 1898

MR. WALTER H. PAGE
THE ATLANTIC MONTHLY
BOSTON
DEAR MR. PAGE:

I had written the other letter that I send you herewith, and it was lying on my desk, when I received your favor, enclosing Mr. Allen's letter. It is needless for me to say that I experienced genuine emotion at so spontaneous and full an expression of approval from one

---

2. Allen (1849–1925), a native Kentuckian writer known for his "local color" fiction, in which he often employed dialect.

who speaks with authority, as one of the scribes. If there is any quality that could be desired in such a story that Mr. Allen has not found
in it, I am unable to figure out what it is. His letter has given me
unfeigned delight, for I have read his books and know how to value
his opinion. If you will be good enough to let him know that his
praise and his good wishes are both a joy and an inspiration to me,
I shall be obliged to you. You don't say anything about my returning
Mr. Allen's letter. Of course, I should like to keep it, but if you think
it would not be right to let me do so, I will content myself with a
copy, which you will doubtless permit me to retain, in confidence, of
course. In the meantime, I will keep the original until I hear from
you again.

Cordially yours,
CHARLES W. CHESNUTT

EDITORIAL OFFICE OF
THE ATLANTIC MONTHLY
BOSTON
July 6, 1898

MR. CHARLES W. CHESNUTT
CLEVELAND, OHIO
MY DEAR MR. CHESNUTT:

Keep Mr. Allen's letter. Do not say anything about it for the present, because I really had no clear right to give it to you, but I do not
feel sufficiently guilty to ask you to return it. Keep it as long as you
like—permanently, in fact, and if by accident it ever comes out that I
took the liberty to give it away, I am sure Mr. Allen will forgive me;
but I should prefer at present that he would not know it.

I hope to see him before very long, and when I do I shall simply
repeat to him in conversation that you know of the compliment he
paid you and appreciate it very highly indeed.

Very truly yours, with Tar-heel[3] cordiality
WALTER H. PAGE

P. S. The other story comes out forthwith and the conjure stories
are in our readers' hands.

*   *   *

---

3. A nickname for North Carolinians, which gained in popularity after the Civil War.

Page to Chesnutt, September 6, 1898

I write this personal note to tell you that Messrs. H. M. and Company will publish the book of Conjure stories for you. They reached this decision unanimously today. A formal letter will follow in a day or two.

BOSTON, MASS.
September 9, 1898

MR. CHARLES W. CHESNUTT
CLEVELAND, OHIO
DEAR SIR:

It gives us pleasure to report that after thorough consideration we feel disposed to publish for you your collection of short stories which we have nick-named "conjure" stories, (for we think that a better title may possibly be found.)

Let us say first that it gives us unusual pleasure to add a book by you to our list; and then we ought frankly to say that this particular book we cannot help regarding with some doubt as to any great financial success. The workmanship is good—of some of the stories, indeed, we think it is exceedingly good; but whether the present interest in this side of the Negro character is sufficient to carry the book to the success we hope for can be determined only by experiment. We are willing to make the experiment, however, and hope for the best results. We have felt disposed to express this doubt, not as a discouragement, but simply to record our present feeling as regards the financial outlook, so that you may have documentary evidence, when the book shows unusual popularity, of the lack of foresight on the part of your publishers!

We wish to bring out this book early on our spring list, and to do this we ought to have the manuscript ready at your earliest convenience. We return the whole lot of stories to you, so that you may make the changes that we suggest and any others that occur to you. Please return them as soon as practicable.

We shall be glad to pay you the customary royalty on a book of this sort of ten per cent on the retail price of all copies sold. If this be satisfactory to you, a contract in regular form will be sent to you forthwith and the transaction formally concluded.

With thanks and best wishes for the success towards which we shall do our utmost, we are

Very truly yours,
HOUGHTON, MIFFLIN AND CO.
W. H. P.

September 19, 1898

MESSRS. HOUGHTON, MIFFLIN AND COMPANY
BOSTON, MASS.
GENTLEMEN:

I was duly in receipt of your favor of the 9th instant, notifying me of your decision to publish the book of conjure stories for me. Permit me to assure you that I appreciate the privilege of "coming out" under the auspices of your House, and that I thank you for the complimentary terms in which you announce your decision.

With regard to the financial success of the book, I am only solicitous that you may not lose by the experiment, and I am sure we should all be glad to see it turn out a pronounced success. I return the manuscript herewith. I have slightly enlarged the introduction to the first story, have revised the introduction to the others so as to avoid unnecessary repetition, and have arranged the stories in what I think good order. "The Goophered Grapevine" cannot well be anything but the first story, "Po' Sandy" is a good second, and "Hot-foot Hannibal" winds them up well and leaves a good taste in the mouth. Barring the first one, however, and perhaps the second, the order is not essential. I have left out the two stories, "Tobe's Tribulations" and a "Victim of Heredity." They are not, I will admit, as good as the others, and unless you think the book too small without them, I am content to leave them out. I have no idea, of course, of the form in which you think of bringing out the book, but should like to have it as dignified as the quantity of matter and the outlay you contemplate will permit.

The customary royalty of ten per cent on the retail price of all copies sold will be quite satisfactory to me, and I shall be very glad to close the transaction formally by signing a contract in regular form.

With sincere thanks for the interest and confidence you manifest in my work, which could not be better shown than by your decision in the case of the book, and with the sincere hope that the outcome may be satisfactory to us both, and that this may be but the beginning of a connection which I am proud to have made, I remain,

Yours very sincerely,
CHARLES W. CHESNUTT

Modern Criticism

ROBERT HEMENWAY

[Black Magic, Audience, and Belief]†

One fact often overlooked about *The Conjure Woman* is that Julius believes all his conjure stories are true. When Annie questions that belief in "The Goophered Grapevine," he responds "It's des es true as I'm a-settin' here, miss. Dey's a easy way ter prove it: I kin lead de way right ter Henry's grave ober yander in de plantation buryin'-ground." Julius's confidence in the verity of his materials makes it possible to consider all seven of Chesnutt's stories as literary representations of supernatural legends; Brunvand defines the genre as a prose narrative, regarded by its tellers as true, taking the form of a supposedly factual account of occurrences which seem to validate superstitions.[1] This is a definition for an oral rather than a written form, but the dialectics of belief which surround the folk legend process contribute greatly to an understanding of Chesnutt's fiction. Linda Dégh and Andrew Vázsonyi have provided an important analysis of the legend transmission process in two articles published in 1971 and 1973.[2] In the earlier essay they argued that in any given legend situation, the participants interacting in the legend process could be classified according to the level of their belief: (1) believers, (2) indifferents, (3) skeptics, (4) nonbelievers, and (5) opponents. Most recently they have suggested that these categories contribute to a "dispute" in each legend-telling situation during "which the legend teller discusses his belief with himself, but mostly with a real or an imaginary incredulous audience." As they put it, "the dispute, the exchange of opposing opinions, appears in almost all accurately recorded legend texts; it is not only to be read from the context of the telling situation."

† From "The Functions of Folklore in Charles Chesnutt's *The Conjure Woman* (*Folklore Institute Journal* 13.3 [1976]: 297–303). Reprinted by permission. Notes have been edited.
1. Jan Harold Brunvand, *Study of American Folklore* (New York: Norton, 1968), pp. 88–89.
2. Linda Dégh and Andrew Vázsonyi, "Legend and Belief," *Genre* 4 (1971): 281–304, and "The Dialectics of the Legend," *Folklore Preprint Series*, Indiana University Folklore Institute 1, no. 6 (Dec. 1973).

This "dispute" is characterized by both positive and negative belief, and may be accompanied by "nonbelief," which Dégh and Vázsonyi would consider "not an active part of the legend formation process," for it presents "socially accepted objective knowledge" to disprove the legend. The key to the distinction between negative and nonbelief is whether the "opponent derives his statement from *knowledge*," and draws evidence "conceived as objective and correct according to the ruling norms of society." It is the difference between saying "I do not believe this" and "I know that this is untrue."

These theories provide a model for understanding the effect of folklore in *The Conjure Woman*. The folkloric influence on the fiction is to enlist the reader in a transmission process whereby black conjure beliefs are granted a credence, just as a legend is validated and perpetuated by the dialectics of its dispute. Julius represents the legend teller who believes in what he is transmitting. John's wife, Annie, falls somewhere between indifference and nonbelief at the beginning of the book, but by the time we reach the last story, "Hot Foot Hannibal," she has come to believe. John consistently represents nonbelief and opposition, a person who "knows" Julius's tales are absurd because he is the arbiter of "the ruling norms" of his society which is rationalistic, antisuperstitious, and as we shall see shortly, racist.

The conflict in each story between John and Julius over the magic of conjure is the literary representation of the folkloristic process of legend transmission. Both Annie and the reader enter into what Dégh and Vázsonyi term the legend "conduit" whereby the folk legend is perpetuated through space and time. In so far as the reader identifies with Julius, he enters into a conspiracy with Annie against the disbelieving John. The literary effect is to encourage an ironic view of John's scientific rationalism, while the cultural effect is to make some readers a part of the process whereby "childish superstition" is granted the dignity of cultural belief.

The tension between John and Julius is the tension between two systems of thought which operate throughout *The Conjure Woman*: John's scientific rationalism, which depends on abstraction and object classification for validation, and Julius's secular faith in magic, which depends solely on subjective experience and the warrant of tradition. By aligning the first with the white man and the second with the black man, Chesnutt might seem to be playing into the hands of racist stereotypes which depict blacks as childishly superstitious, but actually he is only expressing the attitude common in black tradition that rootwork explains more than the white man's science. In a manner similar to legend transmission, belief in the supernatural may become a function of communal identity, the effect being to reverse social pressures against folk belief. One knows one is not supposed to be superstitious and yet if superstition is a distinguishing characteristic of a social group it can become a matter of self-assertive pride. Just as it might come from Julius, one of Whitten's informants reported:

> White folks don' put much stock in roots and the like no mo'. They thinks that science has solve jes' about every thin—but there's lots of times they'd be better off if they'd pay mo' attention to us what knows.[3]

Any situation in modern literature exposing science as an unreliable explanation for reality becomes inherently ironic. When John discovers the rabbit foot in his wife's dress he is satirized, his belief in medical science, a cultural norm of his society, proving an inadequate explanation for his wife's return to health. This sort of irony enables *The Conjure Woman* to address two audiences simultaneously, one John's, one Julius's. John's audience are rationalistic nonbelievers in the conjure phenomena; Julius's audience are participants in the folkloristic process whereby conjure is dignified by belief and transmitted from author to reader.

The irony in *The Conjure Woman* centers around the idea of conjure as a "childish superstition," and one of its better illustrations is John's introduction to "The Gray Wolf's Ha'nt." His narration begins as he and his wife sit on the piazza during a rainy, gloomy day. She finds the whole atmosphere dull, and asks him to read to her from his book to break the boredom.

> "I'll read to you with pleasure," I replied, and began at the point where I had found my bookmark:—
>
> "The difficulty of dealing with transformations so many-sided as those which all existences have undergone, or are undergoing, is such as to make a complete and deductive interpretation almost hopeless. So to grasp the total process of redistribution of matter and motion as to see simultaneously its several necessary results in their actual interdependence is scarcely possible. There is, however, a mode of rendering the process as a whole tolerably comprehensible. Though the genesis of the rearrangement of every evolving aggregate is in itself one, it presents to our intelligence"—
>
> "John," interrupted my wife, "I wish you would stop reading that nonsense and see who that is coming up the lane."
>
> I closed my book with a sigh. I had never been able to interest my wife in the study of philosophy, even when presented in the simplest and most lucid form.

The person coming up the lane is Julius, and his subsequent tale of the gray wolf contrasts nicely with the academic abstractions of

---

3. Norman E. Whitten Jr., "Contemporary Patterns of Malign Occultism among Negroes in North Carolina," *Journal of American Folklore* 75 (1962): 311.

John. A trickster-teller, Julius is not only trying to stop the field from being cleared, his narration also provides a lesson in the mental outlook necessary to deal with conjure as something other than the abstractions of a philosophical tract. John's passage is "nonsense" only because it is a pretentious discussion of the same "redistribution of matter and motion" that characterized the transformations of conjuration; his philosophy is so abstract that he can not even recognize it when Julius dramatizes it for him. The ironic effect of the passage is to fix the sensibilities of the two narrators in relation to a major Chesnutt theme: man's capacity for abstraction. John reads (and listens) but does not understand. Julius "believes," and since superstition is not an enemy in his system of thought, he does not require abstractions for proof.

Abstraction is important thematically because it was the process of abstraction which permitted slave owners to artificially objectify the human beings that stood before them: men and women became property, and as pieces of property did not demand the dignity of human status. Julius captured the essence of this process when he described the horse trader's "conscience": "A live hoss wuz better'n a dead nigger." John's propensity for abstract philosophical thought leads him to the same conception of black people as slave owners had of slaves. Julius is paternally considered "entertaining"; abstractly considered "useful." In either event John is pleased with the notion that Julius thinks of himself as an "appurtenance," though this perception is nothing more than a projection of John's own fantasy:

> He [Julius] had been accustomed, until long after middle life, to look upon himself as the property of another. When this relation was no longer possible, owing to the war, and to his master's death and the dispersion of the family, he had been unable to break off entirely the mental habits of a lifetime, but had attached himself to the old plantation, of which he seemed to consider himself an appurtenance. We found him useful in many ways and entertaining in others.

John's abstract, utilitarian conception of Julius is part and parcel of his conception of slavery as essentially a quaint institution characterized by a slave's unswerving loyalty to his paternalistic master. Chesnutt made it very clear how he felt about such paternalism, telling George Washington Cable, "I can't write about slaves who have a dog-like fidelity to their old master . . . or rather I won't write about them."[4] Any beginning field worker recognizes the utilitarian and paternalistic fallacies—that one will use the "folk" to further one's own career; that one patronizes their "ignorant" beliefs—yet a useful way to

4. See Contexts, note 3, p. 188 [Editor].

conceive of John arises from folkloristics. In some ways he is a culture-
bound folklore collector in much the same manner as the early white
collectors of black lore who were paternalistically racist.

*   *   *

What *The Conjure Woman* also does is to underline and refute the
common attitude of the culture towards black beliefs in magic, an
attitude that folklore collectors have done little to dispel. John's problem is that like Puckett and other ethnographers, he is culturally
blind to the significance of his data. Chesnutt ironically undercuts
John's narration, showing him not only to be an abstract-minded philosopher but also a racist and elitist. Julius, John tells us,

> was not entirely black, and this fact . . . suggested a slight strain
> of other than negro blood. There was a shrewdness in his eyes
> too, which was not altogether African, and which . . . was indica-
> tive of a corresponding shrewdness in character.

John must believe that conjure is a childish superstition racially
characteristic of blacks, and the reader who identifies with John proceeds with a paternalistic interpretation of the folklore of conjure.
For readers without a need to generalize from conjure belief towards
a theory of racial types, however, the use of conjure becomes another
example of the ingenuity of the folk in protecting and perpetuating
systems of belief. In terms of literary history, perhaps this method of
addressing two audiences simultaneously was the only way a black
writer could affirm the psychological resources of his people at a time
when white supremacy had just regained control of the South, and
the minstrel show was a major form of American entertainment.
Whatever the reason, it is clear that Chesnutt's utilization of literary
irony and folklore process enables him to address two different audiences in *The Conjure Woman*, yet his exposure of the inadequacies of
one part of that audience does not alienate because it appeals to cultural skepticism about supernatural happenings.

The concept of "audience" has been largely ignored by literary
criticism, partially because the nature of a literary audience is extraor-
dinarily difficult to establish.[5] No one can be completely certain how
Charles Chesnutt conceived of his audience for *The Conjure Woman*,
but Chesnutt was aware of the problems encountered by a black
writer addressing a predominantly white 19th century reading public. He once bitterly wrote Cable that he could present upper class
blacks in his fiction, "if I were not all the time oppressed by the fear

---

5. Two good discussions of the "audience" problem for a black author are Richard Baldwin,
   "The Art of the Conjure Woman," *American Literature* 43 (1971): 385–98, and William
   Couch Jr., "The Problem of Negro Character and Dramatic Incident," *Phylon* 11 (1950):
   127–133.

that this line or this sentiment would offend somebody's prejudices, jar on somebody's American trained sense of propriety."[6] Chesnutt knew that his books would be read by black readers ("My *Conjure Woman*, I think, has sold very well among them"[7]) but only late in his life did he openly acknowledge the demands his audience had made; he told the predominantly black crowd gathered in his honor as he received the NAACP's Spingarn Award in 1928: "I had to sell my books chiefly to white readers."[8]

Chesnutt's idea of his own audience is important, because it combines with the folkloristic process of legend dialectics to explain the irony of his presentation. The artist can never be as certain of his audience as a legend teller, for he is without the interchange of the telling situation, the shared assumptions, the gestures, emphases, inflections—indeed the whole context—which contributes to the performance. But irony enables an artist to make certain that at least some readers will see things his way, for the technique divides readers into two separate groups, their identity defined by their degree of vision: either one sees the irony or one does not. In *The Conjure Woman* you either see that John's abstractions are satirized, that his science does not fully explain the events of the tales, or one concludes that conjure is a quaint but childish superstition. The effect of Chesnutt's use of folklore is to dignify conjure as an agency of life in a death-dealing environment, a system of belief worthy of a slave's faith. The effect of his irony is *to permit one to be blind to this fact without apparent penalty*. As Robert Farnsworth has put it, Chesnutt's stories "were usually carefully gauged" to avoid "a direct, emotional confrontation."[9] The reason that the irony does not alienate much of the audience is because Chesnutt understood very well that both racial stereotyping and repudiation of superstition were cultural norms in the white, elitist society that would form the major segment of the *fin de siècle* reading public. Folklore provided a way for Chesnutt to write honestly without being "oppressed by the fear" that his presentation of black people would "jar on somebody's American trained sense of propriety." What you see is what you get, and if you can not see beyond John to Julius, you can still understand the tales at the literary level of Julius's trickster schemes. But if you do look beyond John to Julius, beyond rationality to magical belief, you will encounter a folkloristic level of significance to these tales; one's understanding of it depends largely on the reader's capacity to assimilate a positive attitude toward the magic beliefs of conjure.

6. See Contexts, note 3, p. 186 [*Editor*].
7. Helen Chesnutt, *Charles Waddell Chesnutt*, p. 120.
8. Quoted by Robert Farnsworth, "Introduction," to Chesnutt's *The Marrow of Tradition* (Ann Arbor: U of Michigan P, 1969), p. xvi.
9. Robert Farnsworth, "Testing the Color Line—Dunbar and Chesnutt," in *The Black American Writer*, ed. C. W. E. Bigsby (Deland, Fla.: Everett Edwards, 1969), p. 120.

WILLIAM L. ANDREWS

[A Critique of the Plantation Legend]†

As has been often pointed out, the plantation tradition offered anything but a realistic and critical view of the peculiar institution upon which the agricultural economy of the Old South rested. The postwar celebrators of the Old South dismissed leftover abolitionist sentiment against the old order by showing ex-slave retainers longing for the prewar era, when life was carefree and harmonious for both races. The classic statement about the good old days comes from Sam, the narrator of Thomas Nelson Page's "Marse Chan": "'Dem wuz good ole times, marster—de bes' Sam ever see! Dey wuz, in fac'! Niggers didn' hed nothin' 't all to do—jes' hed to 'ten' to de feedin' an' cleanin' de hosses, an' doin' what de marster tell 'em to do; an' when dey wuz sick, dey had things sont 'em out de house, an' de same doctor come to see 'em whar 'ten' to de white folks when dey wuz po'ly. Dyar warn' no trouble nor nothin'.'"[1] However, the point of view from which the aging ex-slaves of Page or [Joel Chandler] Harris take their memories is that of the privileged servant in the plantation "big house." By contrast, Julius "never indulged in any regrets for the Arcadian joyousness and irresponsibility which was a somewhat popular conception of slavery; his had not been the lot of the petted house-servant, but that of the toiling field hand."[2] By locating the point of view of his dialect stories in Julius, one of the large mass of ordinary field hands, Chesnutt was able to take a new look at the Old South's social and economic system, a look undistorted by the affection and nostalgia Uncle Remus and Page's uncles harbor for their erstwhile masters and former positions. The possibility lay open to examine the mundane, everyday life of the slave and his master replete with the stresses, complications, and threats which could, if handled sensitively, reveal a more reliable picture of individual black and white characters than was usually shown in the hackneyed romantic plots of plantation fiction.

The slave-master relationship in Chesnutt's dialect fiction differs significantly from the typical relationship of benevolent aristocrat and loyal retainer which dominated plantation fiction in Chesnutt's

† From *The Literary Career of Charles W. Chesnutt* (Baton Rouge: Louisiana State University Press, 1980), 55–60 and 67–69. Reprinted by permission. Notes have been edited.
1. Thomas Nelson Page, *In Ole Virginia* (Chapel Hill, N.C.: U of North Carolina P, 1969; orig. pub. 1887), 10.
2. See "Dave's Neckliss," p. 33 [*Editor*].

day. Accurate depiction of antebellum life in the sandhills region of North Carolina demanded a departure from the plantation norm. Unlike the Tidewater region of Virginia, which Page memorialized, and the middle Georgia farmland where Harris set his Uncle Remus tales, the part of North Carolina represented in the conjure tales possessed neither the rich soil that supported vast plantations in the deep South nor the old, established families that owned great holdings in land and slaves in Virginia and South Carolina. The land in southeastern North Carolina around "Patesville" was cultivated by small farmers who often worked in the fields beside the few slaves they owned. As one historian has noted, the North Carolina gentry "came, in most instances, from those middle class families who by thrift and energy were able to get ahead in life."[3]

The desire to "get ahead" is what distinguishes the Mars Dugals, Mars Marrabos, and the other slaveholders of Julius' tales from the stereotyped plantation gentlemen of Page, F. Hopkinson Smith, Harry Stillwell Edwards, and their ilk. While the aristocrats in Page's stories duel and dance, court and politic, and glory in the southern cause, the parsimonious Scots in Chesnutt's conjure tales cheat each other, indulge their gambling vices, hunt down their runaways, argue with their wives, curse their slaves, and worry over their bankbooks. These are the descendants of those hard-bitten small farmers, merchants, and ruffians who enliven the work of early southwestern humorists like Johnson Jones Hooper and Augustus Baldwin Longstreet. They are not derived from the diabolic man-stealers and overseers of abolitionist fiction; their salient characteristics are not outrageous cruelty and inhumanity but meanness and selfishness. Mars Dugal of "The Goophered Grapevine" receives his due when Julius says of him, "'it ha' ter be a mighty little hole he couldn' crawl thoo, en ha' ter be a monst'us cloudy night when a dollar git by him in de dahkness'." Another conjure tale, "A Victim of Heredity," describes how a planter cheats his own nephew out of his inheritance and cuts his slaves' rations by more than half in order to increase his own miser's horde. There is only one harsh overseer in Julius' tales, but practically all the white people he recollects exhibit a fundamental callousness which stems from their inability to see their slaves as anything other than property to be maintained and machinery to be worked. The slaveowners in "Hot-Foot Hannibal" and "Mars Jeems's Nightmare" attain a certain liberality toward their slaves, but it is engendered out of hard-headed business sense, not humanitarian concern. They learn that to work slaves too hard or to separate children from parents or spouse from spouse produces friction, leads to diminished vitality among the

---

3. Guion G. Johnson, *Ante-Bellum North Carolina* (Chapel Hill: U of North Carolina P, 1937), 59.

slaves, and reduces work output. Thus at times the slaves abused out of the master's ignorance and insensitivity receive eventual improved treatment in some of Julius' tales, notably in "Mars Jeems's Nightmare," where a master's change of heart toward his slaves occasions much "'juneseyin' en singin' en dancin''" in the quarters at the conclusion of the story. But Chesnutt does not romanticize unduly such "reformed" white people. Mars Jeems's humane treatment of his slaves improves their lot, but it also boosts his profit margin. He got "'a finer plantation, en slicker-lookin' niggers'" as a result of his kinder attitudes; he also "'uz makin' mo' cotton en co'n, dan any yuther gent'emen in de county'."

Just as the southwestern humorists countered the infant myth of the South with realistic reports of the majority of poorer southern whites cheating and scrambling for a place on the frontier, so Chesnutt offered his reader a picture of the representative slaveowner untinted by the rose-colored plantation myth. The whites of Julius' memory are only sketchily portrayed, but they do emanate from a more balanced view of the typical slaveholder than may be found in the picturesque, lovably eccentric aristocrats of the Page tradition. Through Julius' bland commentary, Chesnutt joined early local color depicters of the southern middle and lower classes—authors like Richard Malcolm Johnston, Mary Noailles Murfree, and Joel Chandler Harris—in their efforts to give an accurate impression of those regions of the South which did not resemble the world of most plantation fiction. Chesnutt did not focus on these aspects of the South with the thoroughness and breadth of a Johnston or a Murfree, but his efforts do represent an introduction to a seldom-discussed people in a region largely ignored by the plantation-dialect writers of his day.

If Chesnutt's conjure stories are significant because they helped to introduce the typical southern slaveholder to the post–Civil War American reading audience, they deserve even greater attention for their treatment of a type of slave unfamiliar to readers of southern local color. Within the confines of the local color tradition, Chesnutt depicted the situation of the average slave on an average plantation with greater care and sympathy than any of his white fiction-writing contemporaries. This does not mean that Chesnutt created rounded, complex black characters in his conjure stories. The brevity of his genre prevented this. Julius usually paints his slave protagonists in broad strokes; most are introduced by epithets and accompanied throughout their stories with a minimum of descriptive or analytic details. The hero of "Po' Sandy" is called simply a "'monst'us good nigger'" who does his work exceedingly well. The heroine of "Hot-Foot Hannibal" is termed "'a lackly gal en a smart gal.'" "'One nigger man is de same as ernudder,'" Julius quotes his master's wife in

"A Deep Sleeper," and the presumption is shared by all the slave-holders in *The Conjure Woman*, as it was, no doubt, by many of Chesnutt's late-nineteenth-century readers. To undermine this prejudice, Chesnutt constructed his conjure stories so as to bring his slave characters out of the shadows of their anonymity and separate slave status and into the light of a common humanity with the reader.

Chesnutt's strategy in promoting the idea of a common humanity between blacks and whites did not insist on the elevation of the slave protagonists of his conjure stories to the idealized plane of genteel white literature. Unlike his contemporaries in Afro-American fiction, Chesnutt did not try in Julius' tales to combat subhuman plantation fiction stereotypes with superhuman counter-stereotypes. One will find in Julius' memories no descendants of the magnificent heroic slaves who figure so strongly in the propagandistic fiction of William Wells Brown, Martin R. Delany, or Frances E. W. Harper.[4] Instead, the reader discovers an extensive survey of black characters, ranging from Dave, the saintly slave preacher in "Dave's Neckliss," to the malevolent, Iago-like conjure man in "The Gray Wolf's Ha'nt." Most of the slaves in Julius' stories, however, belong in the realistic middle ground of representative humanity, no better and no worse than they should be. Julius' fellow slaves are capable of great fidelity (Tenie in "Po' Sandy") and equal perfidy (Hannibal in "Hot-Foot Hannibal"), admirable self-sacrifice (Aunt Nancy in "Sis' Becky's Pickaninny") and petty vengefulness (the conjure man in "The Conjurer's Revenge"), patient dignity (Dan in "The Gray Wolf's Ha'nt") and pathetic pride (Chloe in "Hot-Foot Hannibal"). In most of the conjure stories, the slave protagonists demonstrate some primary character trait, predilection, or obsession which motivates them and which brings them into conflict either with white slaveholding institutions or with other black antagonists. In these conflicts, conjure practice can be used by slaves to express and preserve marriage ties ("Po' Sandy"), family solidarity ("Sis' Becky's Pickaninny"), love relationships ("Hot-Foot Hannibal"), and general group welfare ("Mars Jeems's Nightmare"). Other stories show conjuring in the service of less positive and humane purposes. In "The Goophered Grapevine," Aunt Peggy, the conjure woman, accepts a white man's money for bewitching an old slave who eventually dies as a result of the spell. The employment of conjuring for more spiteful reasons is the theme of "The Conjurer's Revenge" and "The Gray Wolf's Ha'nt," two tales concerned solely with internecine struggles between plantation slaves and free black conjure men.

4. I refer to the heroines of Brown's *Clotel; Or, The President's Daughter* (New York: Macmillan, 1970; orig. pub. 1853) and Harper's *Iola Leroy* (College Park, Md.: McGrath, 1969; orig. pub. 1892) and the hero of Delany's *Blake; or, The Huts of America* (Boston: Beacon, 1970; orig. pub. 1859).

The most impressive of Julius' stories from the standpoints of character development and thematic diversity are those in which conjure practice functions as the ally of slaves whose most deeply felt emotions and relationships, whose essential dignity and human identity are threatened by the inhuman slavery system. The least effective tales in *The Conjure Woman* put conjuring in the service of the depraved and selfish, leaving the reader feeling the perplexity and dissatisfaction which Annie, Julius' most perceptive listener, registers at the conclusion of "The Conjurer's Revenge": "'That story does not appeal to me, Uncle Julius, and is not up to your usual mark. It isn't pathetic, it has no moral that I can discover, and I can't see why you should tell it. In fact, it seems to me like nonsense.'" Actually of course, the story is not nonsensical in a practical sense. Julius' story of a slave transformed into a mule and then returned almost completely to his human shape helps to gain the old man's advantage in a horse trade at his employer's expense. However, in an aesthetic sense the story is a failure, for it lacks the twin appeals of Julius' best conjure tales—an emotionally moving, "pathetic" human situation and a "moral," a message relating to the character or situation of blacks in the South.

*   *   *

Time after time in Uncle Julius' stories the exigencies of the slave condition force a particular slave into a desperate situation which elicits from him or her some kind of action. At times the slave's action may constitute a direct challenge to the authority of the master, though not all of the conjure stories may be schematized into a narrative formula pitting conventional white societal power against supernatural black conjure power. Whatever their circumstances, Chesnutt's slave heroes and heroines need not perform superhuman acts of resistance or express their superiority through daring escapes to freedom to confirm their human worth. None of the main characters in any of Chesnutt's dialect stories ever permanently escapes his or her physical bondage, but the actions of a number of slaves attest to a freedom from the enslavement of the spirit. Within the restrictions of the slave condition, Becky, Tenie, Jeems, and Dave each illustrate a realistic standard of heroism. It is not the deathless loyalty of family servants and retainers celebrated by the plantation writers before Chesnutt. Nor is it the open militancy and ineffaceable defiance of slave insurrectionists and fugitives who were the special favorites of the abolitionist writers. Whether or not the slave's reaction to his predicament is successful is less important than the fact that the action itself confirms the slave's identity in his story as a serious figure who deserves the reader's respect and empathy. What is at stake ultimately in Chesnutt's dialect fiction is not the black man's triumph over the institution of slavery (something which Chesnutt could not depict and remain true to his version of the ordinary field hand's experience). Something more important to the black man's social progress in postwar America is at stake, namely, his triumph over the attitude toward Afro-Americans that the Old South and its apologists had perpetrated.

When Charles Chesnutt first began publishing his dialect fiction, the writers of the plantation tradition had largely won the sympathy of northern reading audiences for an ideal and a social system which an earlier generation of Yankees had fought to extirpate from American soil forever. More ironically, the aristocratic ideal of the Old South resurrected by Page and his followers was displayed as more than a relic to be venerated; the idea of the aristocrat as the black man's "natural leader," patron, and "best friend" was proposed as one solution to the racial unrest of Reconstruction and its aftermath.[5] Viewing the black man as happiest in slavery, Page and many of those who subscribed to his opinions often showed the ex-slave unfitted for life outside its confines. To these reactionaries, the erstwhile slave, though no longer his master's property, remained the white man's burden even after emancipation because he lacked the ability to deal independently and competently with the kinds of problems faced every day by whites. Stories like Joel Chandler Harris' "Free Joe and the Rest of the World"[6] played on the long-standing stereotype of the Negro as "wretched freeman" and implied that white authority provided much-needed discipline and identity for blacks before the war. But Chesnutt's picture of blacks in slavery, by concentrating on their tenacity of purpose, their depth of feeling, their resourcefulness, strength of character, and practicality, denied this insinuation that blacks were not qualified for the responsibilities of free people. By showing slavery not as a sheltered condition tailored to meet an inferior race's needs but as a difficult and fortuitous way of life in which great determination, courage, and fortitude were needed in order to survive, Chesnutt proved once again his fundamental thesis in his dialect fiction—that in the midst of slavery's worst depredations the black man and woman had confirmed their human dignity and heroic will. Chesnutt left little doubt to the sensitive reader of *The Conjure Woman* that having endured the crucible of slavery and having been tempered by it, the Afro-American could meet and overcome the problems of a free status.

5. Theodore Gross, "The Negro in the Literature of the Reconstruction," *Phylon*, XXII (1961), 5–14; Rayford W. Logan, *The Betrayal of the Negro* (New York: Macmillan, 1965), pp. 77–78, 173–74.
6. Joel Chandler Harris, "Free Joe and the Rest of the World," in *Free Joe and Other Georgian Sketches* (New York: Scribner's, 1887), pp. 1–20.

ROBERT B. STEPTO

[The Cycle of the First Four Stories]†

*　　*　　*

The first four stories complete a cycle unto themselves of which many readers are not aware since it is not reduplicated in the pages of *The Conjure Woman*.

*　　*　　*

Two of these stories present the first departure-and-return and revenge tales in the series, and * * * the other two offer Chesnutt's second efforts with these tale types. In other words, by the time "Dave's Neckliss" saw print, Chesnutt had not only struck upon his two strongest tale types but was already in the process of revising them. The two revenge tales—"The Conjurer's Revenge" and "Dave's Neckliss"—present an especially interesting study in this regard, partly because the revision of the former in the latter is so overt, and partly because Julius, as a result of this activity, becomes for the first and last time a character in one of his tales. The development of Julius as a character—indeed, as an intimate friend of the tale's protagonist—parallels that of John and Annie becoming increasingly reliable listeners. This brings into view a second point: the frames of these stories offer the most complete plotting of John and Annie's journey to listenership.

Julius's first four tales instruct John and Annie in various subjects, not the least of which being local geography. The tales take place on three different plantations, and John and Annie are further intro-duced to their new environs in "Po' Sandy" when they go out with Julius in the carriage. As a group, the tales generate a narrative rhythm of departure-and-return which circumscribes the Patesville region but always brings matters back to the McAdoo plantation where Julius was a slave and where his listeners, John and Annie, have rather innocently put down their roots. This rhythm appears first in "The Goophered Grapevine" and then is cunningly rephrased

† From "'The Simple But Intensely Human Inner Life of Slavery': Storytelling, Fiction and the Revision of History in Charles W. Chesnutt's 'Uncle Julius Stories,'" in *History and Tradition in Afro-American Culture*, ed. Günter H. Lenz (Frankfurt; New York: Campus Verlag, 1984), pp. 33–51. Reprinted by permission. Notes have been edited.

in "Po' Sandy." It is barely present in "Dave's Neckliss" and not at all apparent in "The Conjurer's Revenge." On the other hand, the fact that the tale in "Dave's Neckliss" is sited on the McAdoo plantation suggests that the four tales as a group present the rhythm on a grand scale. In other words, it seems clear that the pattern of departure from and return to the McAdoo plantation is both a macrorhythm in the tale group and a microrhythm in several individual tales.[1]

In "The Goophered Grapevine," the rhythm just described is best seen when the tale is reduced to its basic units:[2]

    A. Master visits Aunt Peggy, the conjurer; gains vineyard
       Master buys Henry; gains slave

I

    B. Henry visits Aunt Peggy
       Master sells and buys Henry (repeatedly); profits from
       vineyard *and* slave

    C. Master is duped by Yankee
       Master loses vineyard *and* Henry

II

    D. Master goes to War against Yankees
       Master returns to what's left of plantation

Once the tale is diagrammed in this way, we see rather clearly how the first two and second two units fuse into large blocks of narrative structure (I and II) and how closure in the second of these radically revises the conclusion of the first. The pattern of departure and return from the plantation which had been the lot of Henry in what were halcyon days for the master becomes that of the master in his demise. Aunt Peggy has worked her roots, the Yankee has fooled with those of the grapevines, and master Dugal McAdoo has been "uprooted" in more than one sense of the term. Of course, the great feature is that the tale squarely addresses the fact that its listeners are Yankees as well as inheritors of the Southern past. As figurations of Brer Rabbit and Brer Bear respectively, neither the know-it-all Yankee (as fresh from the North as are John and Annie) nor the greedy master are presented as models worth emulating. Julius rightly fears the destructive powers of white Northerners and Southerners alike—and his tale

1. Macrorhythms and microrhythms are usually discussed as narrative features within a single tale. I have taken the liberty of referring to their presence in a tale *group* chiefly because a sequence of "interlocking" tales (Hemenway's phrase, see n. 5) can be seen as a single evolving tale. My understanding of these narrative features is based primarily on the writings of Harold Scheub. See, for example, Scheub, *The Ntsomi* (New York: Oxford UP, 1975). I am also in debt to colleague Ronald Rassner who has freely shared his knowledge of oral literature scholarship.

2. My notion of a "basic unit" of narrative is loosely derived from Scheub's concept of a narrative "image block." See *The Ntsomi* and also "Oral Narrative Process and the Use of Models," *New Literary History* 6 (1975), 353–77.

says as much. In this regard, true to the traditions of the oral tale, instruction in "The Goophered Grapevine" is barely divisible from information: the answer to why the McAdoo land fell upon hard times in the past instructs John and Annie on how to behave in the future.[3]

"Po' Sandy" offers the sad tale of Sandy and Tenie, who had been slaves on the neighboring McSwayne plantation. In this tale, the pattern of departure-and-return makes three distinct appearances: first in the career of Sandy, secondly in that of Tenie, and finally in the tale's ingenious closing lines.

Sandy was, in Julius's words, "a monst'us good nigger" who "could do so many things erbout a plantation, en alluz 'ten' ter his wuk so well, dat w'en Mars Marrabo's chilluns growed up en married off, dey all un 'em wanted dey daddy fer ter gin 'em Sandy for a weddin' present." Marrabo McSwayne was apparently smart enough to real-ize that no one child could receive a gift as precious as Sandy with-out the others resenting it, and so he lent Sandy to all: ". . . he fix it by 'lowin' one er his chilluns ter take Sandy for a mont' er so, en den ernudder for a mont' er so, en so on dat erway tel dey had all had 'im de same lenk er time; en den dey would all take him roun' ag'in, 'cep'n' oncet in a w'ile w'en Mars Marrabo would len' 'im ter some er his yuther kinfolks 'roun' de country . . . tel bimeby it go to Sandy did n' hardly knowed whar he wuz gwine ter stay fum one week's een ter de yuther." Once, while Sandy was away on one of these many trips, McSwayne traded Sandy's wife for a "noo woman." When he returned, McSwayne apologized for breaking up "de fambly" and gave Sandy a dollar.

Clearly, Sandy is victimized by a vicious cycle of departure-and-return. But this is only the beginning of his tale. Further victimiza-tion awaits him chiefly because he, unlike Henry in the first tale, recognizes his oppression and attempts to do something about it. The cycle is arrested when Tenie, the "noo woman" in Sandy's life as well as that of the plantation, divulges that she is a conjure woman, and soon thereafter turns Sandy into a tree. All is well for a spell, but it is soon made obvious that the cycle has been only thwarted and not broken. Sandy's "disappearance" merely leads to Tenie being victim-ized by the same pattern from which he sought release. We expect the worse when she is forced to travel to a neighboring plantation and it does indeed occur: two men are sent out to cut down a tree for lumber and it is Po' Sandy who is felled. Tenie loses Sandy much as he lost his first wife while away on a mission occasioned by Marrabo's affection for his family. On the other hand, she suffers much

---

3. The roots of this tale in Afro-American folklore are discussed in Hemenway, "The Functions of Folklore," 287–90.

more than he, partly out of guilt (she thinks none of this might have happened if she had been near) but mostly because when she returns to the plantation and attempts to stop the milling of Sandy she is chained to a post and forced to watch her lover's dismemberment.

Irony piles upon irony when we realize that even the milling of Sandy is the result of Marrabo's largeness: the lumber is wanted for a new kitchen which will presumably please his wife and possibly create better conditions for the slaves who work there. Nor is it lost on us that even without knowing it the master has cut a "run-away" slave down to size, and, since Tenie goes mad and dies, destroyed the slave's accomplice in the process. Justice of a kind is eventually served when neither slave nor mistress will set foot in the new kitchen and Marrabo is forced to move the structure to the perimeter of the plantation and turn it into a schoolhouse. But none of this adds up to an eye for the eye lost: "Po' Sandy" is a tale about "monst'us" human waste.

Julius ends his tale in the following way:

> 'Hit wa'n't long atter dat befo' Mars Marrabo sol' a piece er his track er lan' ter Mars Dugal' McAdoo,—*my* ole marster,—en dat's how de ole school-'ouse happen to be on yo' place.

With this remark the tale fittingly concludes with yet another expression of the departure-and-return pattern. At the beginning of the tale, Julius, John, and Annie embarked upon a journey into the Patesville community, the past, and the "world" of storytelling. Here at its end, they are, in many senses of the term, "back home." In fashioning such a closure, Julius once again proves himself to be a teacher as well as a trickster.[4] The trickster role is clear enough: he is obviously getting ready to ask for the use of the old schoolhouse for his church. However, in the course of this maneuvering, meaningful lessons about John and Annie's new home are imparted. The lessons center around the fact that the old schoolhouse is now on *their* land. The legend of Sandy and Tenie is therefore now in some sense their story—as well as their responsibility. Whether or not they allow Julius to use the building, they have no business taking it—or what it symbolizes—apart.

While "Po' Sandy" does not fully revise "The Goophered Grapevine," it nonetheless retells many features of that tale. Most of the revisions show Chesnutt attempting to imbue his basic departure-and-return tale with greater "feeling and passion." Some of these suggest as well that he was equally concerned about creating a more

---

4. Of the many articles discussing Julius as a trickster figure, the following deserve special mention: David Britt, "Chesnutt's Conjure Tales: What You See Is What You Get," *CLA Journal* 15 (1972), 269–83; and Melvin Dixon, "The Teller as Folk Trickster in Chesnutt's *The Conjure Woman,*" *CLA Journal* 18 (1974), 186–97.

sophisticated narrative structure. The revision of Aunt Peggy as Tenie, for example, abets sentiment and structure alike. While Aunt Peggy resides at the edge of the plantation (*and* tale) and participates only in the sense that she sets certain things in motion, Tenie is a fully integrated major character; she, like others (notably Sandy), must live by the consequences of her conjuring gifts. The recasting of Henry as Sandy *and* Tenie achieves a similar result. The interaction between Sandy and Tenie introduces features which could not have been offered through Henry alone. From the standpoint of presenting greater "feeling and passion," the one "problem" with Henry is that he has no ties with family or friends; his individualism both creates him as a character and limits the opportunities within the tale for portraits of other kinds of human responses. Like Henry, Sandy and Tenie are assaulted as individuals, but they are oppressed as a couple as well. Insofar as their tale suggests some of the ways in which the slave family and even the slave community-at-large were affected by bondage, it is a more varied (though not necessarily better) study of human sentiment than Henry's.

In terms of narrative structure, the creation of Sandy and Tenie also had great effect. Much of what one would want to say here about the multiplication of departure-and-return patterns through the bifurcation of Henry into Sandy and Tenie has already been reviewed. To that should be added the point that the episodes in which Sandy and Tenie briefly live together are also structurally significant. When Sandy and Tenie debate which new form Sandy should assume, they consider three possibilities, the last being a tree. Once Sandy becomes a tree, he undergoes three tribulations, the last being his felling and milling. This tripartite patterning lends an additional "oral" quality to the tale while providing new and effective episodes. The patterning had not been used before but it would be employed again in many tales including the very next one, "The Conjurer's Revenge."

"The Conjurer's Revenge" is like the tales preceding it in several ways. To begin with, it turns on the disappearances and reappearances of a slave named Primus; in this regard, it reworks the departure-and-return motif used before. Moreover, like "Po' Sandy," it features a strong narrative rhythm involving tripartite actions and makes an effort (albeit not as remarkable) to introduce a female character affected by the male protagonist's plight. On the other hand, "The Conjurer's Revenge" is sufficiently different from the other tales to be considered a new tale in the series. Its episodes take place largely within the black world of the plantation community: more so than that of Henry, Tenie, or even Sandy, Primus's fate is in the hands of another black person. That this person is a conjurer is nothing new; however in Primus's tale the conjurer is a man. A third factor is that the tale introduces a revenge motif not used before. In this regard, it is the first of the revenge tales, the others including "The Dumb Witness," "Hot-Foot Hannibal," "The Gray Wolf's Ha'nt," "The Marked Tree," and the tale which succeeded it, "Dave's Neckliss."

The basic units of the tale may be described as follows:

A. Primus offends the Conjure Man (by killing his son in a fight)
    Conjure Man gets revenge (by turning Primus into a mule)

B. Master buys a mule (Primus) from a poor white
    (Primus is restored to the plantation in his new form)
    Conjure Man gets further revenge
    (Mule [1]eats tobacco, [2]gets drunk; slaves make "great 'miration")

C. Dan offends Primus (by courting Sally, Primus's wife)
    [3]Primus (as mule) gets revenge (by [i]throwing, [ii]kicking,
    [iii]scaring Dan)

D. Conjure Man gets religion, reforms, almost "re-forms"
    Primus into human shape before dying; Pete assists (Primus
    is "re-restored" to plantation in much of his old form; slaves
    make "great 'miration")

As a narrative structure, the tale is well ordered and full of effective rhythms. For example, the plantation episodes at the middle of the tale are ordered around three acts performed by Primus as a mule, each one more amazing and more elaborate than the one preceding it. The third act—Primus's harassment of Dan—completes the sequence of actions and neatly unifies the plantation episodes (units B and C) into a kind of tale within a tale. As a large action, it becomes unto itself a unit of the tale (unit C); as such, it harmonizes effectively with the tale's preceding parts both because it repeats the offense/revenge sequence which initiates the tale and because it offers its own tripartite form.

The two returns of Primus to the plantation constitute another key rhythm. In each case, Primus returns in a different form but of course *what* he is returning to is much the same thing. There is pitifully little difference between his working the fields as a mule and working them as a slave. Once we start thinking in these terms other analogies readily come to mind. There are, for example, certain sexual implications to Primus's return first as a mule and then as a man with a deformed, malfunctioning leg which cannot be completely ignored. In short, the returns of Primus appear to be a vehicle for one of Chesnutt's most serious themes: the great improbability of a slave's escape from slavery's "crippling" effects. In this regard, Primus is much like Henry and Sandy in the preceding tales except for the fact that he doesn't die as they do.

While "The Conjurer's Revenge" has this serious aspect, it is also a comic tale. The scenes in which Primus (as a mule) consumes his fill of tobacco and gets stumbling drunk on the master's wine are distinctly comic, as are those in which he harasses Dan to distraction for fooling with his wife. However, what is significant in these episodes is the way in which the serious and comic are fused and simultaneously expressed. When Primus *as a mule* gets hold of more tobacco and wine than he will ever see *as a man*, the "near-tragic" and "near-comic" qualities of his circumstance blend to create in mood, if not exactly in form, something close to what we would today call a blues.[5] In this regard, "The Conjurer's Revenge" is like all four of the first tales—they are all blues of a kind—but most like "The Goophered Grapevine." As a tale more about an individual than a family or community, and as a tale perhaps more comic than Chesnutt felt a revisionist plantation story should be, "The Conjurer's Revenge" was as likely to be reworked as was "The Goophered Grapevine." Greater "feeling and passion" entered the tale when it became "Dave's Neckliss."

This last statement should suggest that I am willing to argue that "Dave's Neckliss" doesn't just parallel or echo "The Conjurer's Revenge" but fully revises it. That is part of the argument I am about to make. The chart below will assist us here:

"THE CONJURER'S REVENGE"	"DAVE'S NECKLISS"
	A.[1] Dave offends Walker, the poor white overseer (w), by learning how to read and write Walker tells Master, Master pardons Dave Dave restored to plantation as Preacher to the slaves (Walker gets no revenge)
A. Primus offends the Conjure Man (b) by killing his son in a fight Conjure Man gets revenge by turning P. into a mule	A.[2] Dave offends Wiley, a new slave (b) by courting Dilsey, a woman Wiley likes Wiley gets revenge by framing D. as a thief
B. Master buys mule (P.) from poor white, P. restored to plantation as mule	B. Master turns D. over to poor white (Walker), D. restored to plantation as Outcast

5. I borrow the phrases "near-tragic" and "near-comic" from Ralph Ellison's famous definition of the blues in his essay, "Richard Wright's Blues." See Ellison, *Shadow and Act* (New York: Signet Books, 1966), p. 90.

Conjure Man gets further
  revenge
Mule [1]eats tobacco, [2]gets
  drunk; slaves make
  "great 'miration"

C. Dan offends Primus by
    courting Sally, Primus's
    wife
  [3]Primus (as mule) gets
    revenge by [1]throwing,
    [ii]kicking, and [iii]scaring
    Dan

D. Conjure Man gets religion,
    reforms, almost re-forms
    P. back to human shape
    (Pete, a slave, assists)
  Primus re-restored to
    plantation in much of
    his old form; slaves make
    "great 'miration"

Walker gets revenge
  (D. forced to wear iron
  "neckliss" to which the
  "stolen" ham has been
  attached); slaves scorn
  and ridicule Dave

C. Dilsey devastates Dave by
    not believing him
    innocent and by taking up
    with Wiley
  Dave (as outcast) begins
    to go mad, thinks he's
    a ham, tells Julius

D.[1] Wiley gets caught stealing,
    reforms, confesses to
    crimes and thereby
    attempts to re-form
    D. to prior status and
    human form
  Master announces Wiley's
    admission and thereby
    attempts to re-form Dave
    as well

D.[2] Dave is found by Julius in
    the smokehouse—a
    suicide (D. thus never
    re-restored to plantation
    in prior status and form)

  Master sells Wiley, fires
    Walker (gets revenge of a
    kind for the loss of D.
    while attempting to
    restore order to
    plantation)

w = white revenger
b = black revenger

I'm not altogether sure about how to chart the end of "Dave's Neck-liss." The events listed under items D[1] and D[2] could just as easily be distinguished as three full units of narrative, not two. However, I prefer the present charting chiefly because it brings out the tale's most remarkable structural innovation: the doubling of beginnings (A[1] and A[2]) and closures (D[1] and D[2]) and the virtual balancing of the two. Of course, this development was as necessary as it was novel. Much more so than "The Conjurer's Revenge," "Dave's Neckliss" begins and ends in both the black and white worlds of a plantation community and thus requires a structure which accommodates and possibly accentuates, the tale's multiple plottings.

Many other innovations appear in "Dave's Neckliss," and most of them can be most immediately seen as revisions of features in "The Conjurer's Revenge." The revision of the Conjure Man as two characters, the black Wiley and white Walker, is a case in point. As a comparison of the first two units in each tale should suggest, the idea for this development did not come from out of the blue: Wiley is a version of the Conjure Man and Walker a fuller configuration of the poor white who mysteriously comes into possession of Primus after the Conjure Man has "worked" his roots. While the collusion between black and white is not at all apparent in "The Conjurer's Revenge," it is brought to the fore in "Dave's Neckliss." Wiley gets his revenge not just by planting the stolen ham in Dave's cabin but by suggesting to Walker that Dave might be the thief. After Dave's fall from grace, Wiley and Walker both become (however briefly) the kings of their respective heaps. In all, they seem not only to be in league with each other but to be manifestations of the same evil force. This is further suggested by the fact that their names, though different, have a similar ring. The sounding of consonants prompts us to pair Wiley and Walker much as it encourages us to view Dave and Dilsey as a natural or perfect couple.

As versions of the Conjure Man and his poor white collaborator, Wiley and Walker stand out particularly because neither man is literally a conjurer in the sense forwarded by the preceding tales. In this regard, they are new characters of a sort. On the other hand, one must take into account the extent to which even this aspect of the tale may be seen as a logical development of previously used narrative features. While they may be more overt and sinister in their machinations, Wiley and Walker are not the first victimizers of slaves who aren't conjurers. Mars Dugal in "The Goophered Grapevine" isn't a conjurer but he clearly victimizes Henry and brings on his death. Mars Marrabo in "Po' Sandy" isn't a conjurer either, but when he sells Sandy's first wife he obviously occasions the depression and desperation which afflict Sandy and then consume Tenie as well. Dan in "The Conjurer's Revenge" is hardly in the same category as Dugal and Marrabo. However, he must be cited as well since his courting of Sally is evidently another trial Primus must endure. Certain lines of development can thus be clearly drawn: Wiley partakes of the Conjure Man but is also a more vindictive and lethal Dan; Walker is a recasting of the poor white which also incorporates the worst features of the masters in other tales. In short, it seems that Wiley and Walker are not so much new creations

as they are extensions and possible fulfillments of character proto-
types sketched before.

This suggests in turn that "Dave's Neckliss" as a whole is most
properly considered a tale which closes more narrative features than
it begins even though it is the first non-conjure tale in the Julius
series. What we see of Dave also supports this view. Dave seems new
because he appears to be both more heroic and more tragic than any
of the other major characters preceding him. He seems more heroic
because, as his hard-won literacy suggests, he is cast in the mold of
the "heroic slave" found in most slave narratives and abolitionist fictions. This is suggested further when Dave becomes the slaves'
preacher and the conventional link in pre-modern Afro-American letters between literacy and leadership is recognized and consummated.
As a tragic figure, Dave appears to outstrip the rest partly because he
is more conspicuously a victim of non-conjured oppression and
because his death may be considered self-inflicted. On the other
hand, the seeds for his portrait were clearly sown in the preceding
tales. As a revision of Primus, Dave is less a new character than a
revoicing of Sandy and Tenie. His desperation is no greater than
Sandy's; his depression no more profound than Tenie's. Tenie's death
upon the schoolhouse floor may not be as sensational as Dave's but it
is hardly less tragic or less self-inflicted. With Dave, as with Wiley and
Walker, we see features in "Dave's Neckliss" which both revise "The
Conjurer's Revenge" and possibly refine the entire tale cycle as it was
then constituted. What we also see is that despite the differences
between the departure-and-return and revenge tales as tale types, the
same tactics were being used to instill each kind of tale with greater
"feeling and passion." In short, the Julius tale as an assembly of a few
superb narrative ideas was indeed close to being used up.

This brings us to the revision of Pete as Julius, which stands out as
possibly the most interesting of the revisions since it develops tale
and frame alike. Julius is much more of an intimate of Dave than
Pete is of Primus; this in itself adds yet another layer, so to speak, of
"feeling and passion." But other, more complicated matters are afoot.
Once Julius enters the tale and thereby personalizes it more than any
other, the tale becomes somewhat autobiographical. This has two
great rhetorical effects. One is that the tale seemingly authenticates
itself. There is little or no need for Julius to defend his tale elsewhere
(in the epilogue, for example) since entry into the tale readily conveys
the idea that it is true because "he was there."[6] The other effect is
that we as readers are forced to consider if a change has come about

6. Andrews also makes this point in his discussion of "Dave's Neckliss." See William
Andrews, *The Literary Career of Charles W. Chesnutt*, p. 66.

in Julius's relations with his listeners, John and Annie. Is there a new
sensitivity on their part which makes the telling of a *personal* tale just
and appropriate? A lot of machinery is turning here and not all of it is
well-oiled. However, it seems clear that the personalization of Julius's
tale, specifically occasioned by the revision of Pete as Julius, is part of
a strategy for authenticating tale and frame alike. Julius's intimacy
with Dave is of a piece with his greater intimacy with his listeners—
or so we are encouraged to believe. How far we go in this belief
depends more on developments in the frames than in the tales, and it
is to them that we must now turn.

The prologue to "The Goophered Grapevine" is unusually long,
partly because it offers the various reasons for John and Annie's
removal from Ohio to the South. It is also long because it has the
double task of introducing Julius as a storyteller and presenting John
and Annie as listeners. John in particular requires special attention
since he, as the apparent custodian of the story's frame, must be
sketched as a listener who may eventually assume the responsibilities of storytelling. Much of this begins when John offers the
following description of Julius:

> He resumed his seat with somewhat of embarassment. While
> he had been standing, I had observed that he was a tall man,
> and, though slightly bowed by the weight of years, apparently
> quite vigorous. He was not entirely black, and this fact,
> together with the quality of his hair, which was about six inches
> long and very bushy, except on the top of his head, where he
> was quite bald, suggested a slight strain of other than negro
> blood. There was a shrewdness in his eyes, too, which was not
> altogether African, and which, as we afterwards learned from
> experience, was indicative of a corresponding shrewdness in his
> character. He went on eating the grapes, but did not seem to
> enjoy himself quite so well as he had apparently done before he
> became aware of our presence.

John and Annie have, in Faulkner's terms, "abrupted" upon the
scene. John has cordially greeted Julius by saying, "Don't let us disturb you . . . There is plenty of room for us all." These friendly words
from a white stranger understandably throw Julius into a quick
study, the visible traces of which John attempts to describe in the
passage above. As he proceeds, Julius is introduced not just as a
likely trickster figure but as a particular hybrid of that strain, the
Crafty Mulatto. That John sees Julius in these terms—even after
untold hours in his presence—indicates that the passage is as much
or more descriptive of him as Julius; most certainly, his resort to
clichés both complicates and qualifies the impression first advanced
by his solicitous, democratic air.

Julius is thus presented as a type—and John emerges as one as well. Together they assume the interlocking roles of the former slave and Helpful American, roles which became an integral part of American life when former slaves began to encounter abolitionists. John's inability to *see* Julius in other than stereotypic terms seemingly reenacts the average abolitionist's inability to *hear* a fugitive slave's tale. This is further suggested when he allows that Julius's first allusions to magic and conjure left him ". . . somewhat interested, while Annie was . . . much impressed . . ." As a rational *man* instinctually dubious of tales of the improbable, John doesn't fall into the role of the unreliable listener so much as he chooses it. Julius of course sees all of this and soon remarks, "'I wouldn' spec' fer you ter b'lieve me 'less you know all 'bout de fac's.'" With that, his conjure tale begins, it being no less factual (or fanciful) than any portion of John's opening narration.

The epilogue to "The Goophered Grapevine" is a much shorter affair but it still gets its business done. When Annie sincerely asks, "Is that story true?", a transition from tale to frame is effected while she is further characterized as a listener somewhat distinct from her husband. With Julius's reply to her question, we enter into the requisite conversation balancing that in the prologue which initiated the storytelling performance. Part of what Julius says is worth noting here:

> 'It's des ez true ez I'm a-settin' here, miss. Dey's a easy way ter prove it: I kin lead de way right ter Henry's grave ober yander in de plantation buryin'-groun.'

The fact that Julius can show Annie (and John) where Henry is buried proves nothing about the extraordinary episodes attributed to Henry's life, but of course that is the point. When seen whole, "The Goophered Grapevine" is about nothing so much as the inherent usefulness of certain facts to certain versions of reality. Julius's "proof" hardly substantiates his tale but it does announce the posture from which he will attempt to chip away at John's notions of what is empirical and what real. As the epilogue ends, John once again assumes control of the narration. Before he is done, we know that he's gone ahead with his purchase of the vineyard (contrary to Julius's advice) and that Julius is now in his employ. This censoring of the tale—rejecting its "moral" while patronizing its teller surely amounts to that—further confirms John's initial position *vis-à-vis* Julius's "fac's." The stage is now set for future storytelling performances in which it is always possible that John and Julius will burst beyond their initial, culturally ordained postures as listener and teller, the transformation of John into something other than a censor being a prerequisite for any change in Julius.

In all, the frame of "The Goophered Grapevine" performs many of the same narrative functions readily attributed to the General Prologue of Chaucer's *Canterbury Tales*. Instead of initiating a series of serialized portraits of Julius, John, and Annie, it presents them all at once, as a group. Moreover, a hierarchy within the group is firmly established, especially when the image of all three individuals democratically sharing a seat upon a log gives way to that of John, Annie, and Julius respectively becoming the master, mistress, and coachman of a plantation once run by slaveholders. There is, in short, as in Chaucer, an ordering of the group of tellers and listeners which partakes of history, caste, and custom as well as the present moment. Even more to the point, the frame announces that no matter how questioning we might be of John's abilities or intentions as a listener, it is his "feat of memory" upon which we are dependent for access to Julius's tales.[7] The ordering of the group in "The Goophered Grapevine" is therefore nascent rather than static: in order to perform these "feats" John must become something more than a censor—and he does so through hearing more of Julius's tales and weighing Annie's opinions of them against his own. The fact that much of this develops in the stories *not* collected in *The Conjure Woman* is one more reason for questioning those assessments of Chesnutt's achievement which solely discuss that volume. Something begins in "The Goophered Grapevine" that is not completed in *The Conjure Woman*.

The transition from "The Goophered Grapevine" to the second Julius story, "Po' Sandy," is deftly made once Julius assumes his new position as coachman and tells his next tale while he, John, and Annie have paused for a moment while out in the carriage. In this story, John and Annie are further developed as listeners but not quite to the point where they become story-collectors, let alone storytellers. In this instance, John's penchant for empiricism takes the form of a primitive literary criticism while Annie's interest in the "truth" prompts remarks of a historiographical cast. As is usually the case, what John has to say appears in the prologue portion of the frame:

> 'And who was poor Sandy?' asked my wife, who takes a deep interest in the stories of plantation life which she hears from the lips of the older colored people. Some of these stories are quaintly humorous; others wildly extravagant, revealing the Oriental cast of the negro's imagination; while others, poured freely into the sympathetic ear of a Northern-bred woman, disclose many a tragic incident of the darker side of slavery.

---

7. "Feat of memory" is Donald R. Howard's phrase; most of the points made in this comparison of Chesnutt and Chaucer come in response to Howard's discussion of "Memory and Form" in *The Canterbury Tales*. See Howard, *The Idea of the Canterbury Tales* (Berkeley: U of California P, 1976), pp. 134–209.

This assessment is hardly remarkable; John is still ordering and expressing his thoughts with clichés. On the other hand, the fact that the remarks are about the stories, not Julius, suggests that he is slowly becoming a listener. This is further suggested when he admits, in his way, that not all of the stories contribute to the myth of the Happy Slave—some expose the "darker side of slavery." Above all, John appears to be something of a listener when he distinguishes the tragic tales from the humorous and extravagant ones principally in terms of teller-audience relations and performance contexts. He is not yet fully articulate about this—"the sympathetic ear of a Northern-bred woman" is, for example, another time-worn phrase. But that is in keeping with where he is presently situated on the path to listenership: as an apprentice storylistener, he is beginning to hear the tales but cannot yet speak of them.

The epilogue to "Po' Sandy" is the first of many which Annie truly dominates. Right after Julius finishes his tale, she exclaims, "'What a system it was' . . . 'under which such things were possible!'" When John somewhat peevishly asks, "What things," Annie can only reply, "Poor Tenie!'" This exchange above all others confirms the point often made regarding Annie's heartfelt sympathy for the female victims of the slave system. On the other hand, from the point of view of narrative structure, it seems equally significant that Annie's remarks parallel John's in that she, too, is beginning to hear the tales but cannot fully express her responses. Perhaps this is why she grants every request Julius seems to make as the story concludes. It is often supposed that when she does this Julius has duped her and possibly taken advantage of that "feminine sensibility" John is always so quick to invoke if not always defend. But it is equally possible that her actions result from something other than her being deceived. Finding herself in a situation in which she is at a loss for words, Annie *acts* within the sustained event (in Braudel's terms, *longue durée*) of Julius's *performance* in ways which allow her to "say" much more than "Poor Tenie!" In short, while neither John nor Annie fully participate in the event of "Po' Sandy" linguistically, Annie approximates an articulate response to the tale she has heard when she combines actions with words.

In the frame of the third story, "The Conjurer's Revenge," three features stand out. The first is that the piazza of John and Annie's new southern home is introduced as a site for Julius's storytelling. In terms of the contextualization of story performances, this is where the story series has been heading all along. The movement from the log of the first story to the carriage of the second to the piazza of the third communicates that John and Annie are now fully in residence in the South and that a traditional context for storytelling has been constructed. Moreover, it suggests a didactic strategy expressed through the siting of storytelling which plays a major role in the education of John and Annie as listeners. More so than the log or carriage, the "reconstructed" piazza of a southern plantation Big House is a "charged field," full of reference to history and ritualized human behavior. Neither John and Annie nor Julius can successfully ignore these aspects of the past while attempting to live with each other in the present. The temporal relations between tale and frame in most of the stories allude to much of this. However, what the siting of storytelling on the piazza adds is the suggestion that the past and present (and correspondingly the tale and frame) constitute a single time frame that is far more synchronic than diachronic.

The most noteworthy feature of the prologue is the absence of commentary from John on Julius's storytelling; Chesnutt is beginning to "fiddle" with his story formula. What is there in its place is John's oblique admission that Julius's "plantation legends" are often to be preferred over the missionary reports and "rudimentary" novels with which he and Annie usually pass a Sunday afternoon. More could be done with this: comparisons between the spoken and written word in stories about storytelling are always rhetorically useful. However, more isn't done probably because any such development in the prologue would necessarily interfere with the more daring and significant innovation found in the epilogue.

Right after the end of Julius's tale, Annie remarks:

> 'That story does not appeal to me, Uncle Julius, and is not up to your usual mark. It isn't pathetic, it has no moral that I can discover, and I can't see why you should tell it. In fact, it seems to me like nonsense.'

Julius replies:

> 'I'm sorry, ma'm . . . ef you doan lack dat tale. I can't make out w'at you means by some er dem wo'ds you uses, but I'm tellin' nuffin but de truf. Co'se I didn' see de cunjuh man tu'n 'im back, fer I wuzn' dere; but I be'n hearin' de tale fer twenty-five yeahs, en I ain' got no 'casion fer ter 'spute it. Dey's so many things a body knows is lies, dat dey ain' no use gwine roun' findin' fault wid tales dat mought dez es well be so ez not. . . . dis is a quare worl', anyway yer kin fix it. . . .'

Many things are at work in this important exchange. To begin with, Chesnutt is clearly experimenting within the limits of his formula to discover what happens when the major comment on Julius's storytelling is shifted from the prologue to the epilogue, the most apparent development being that Annie becomes the principal unreliable listener. Once she assumes this role, it seems likely that John will perform the narrative chores she otherwise pursues in a story's closure. This is exactly what happens: it is he, not her who gives in to Julius's requests, he who gropes toward sensitive listenership by offering responsive actions when language fails him. While there are many ways to view this feature, I prefer to think that Chesnutt is (1) honestly experimenting with his formula, chiefly to test its limits; (2) successfully establishing a parity between John and Annie as developing listeners; and (3) creating a plausible context (within the frame) in which Julius can defend his storytelling in his own words and on his own terms.

This latter point figures greatly in any explanation as to why Chesnutt would tell Albion Tourgée that Julius was "used up" and that he could go no further with a written black dialect. The issue had less to do with how ingenious or accurate Chesnutt could be with diacritical representations of dialect than with what Julius, as a purveyor of black speech, could fully explain either through telling tales or conversing with listeners in the framing units of the story event. At the beginning of his response, he claims that he's been telling "nuffin but de truf"; this comes partly in response to the persistent issue of whether his seemingly more fanciful notion of reality is indeed less valid than that proffered by John's rationalism. In the rest of his remarks, he offers a defense of storytelling that is at least as old in English letters as *The Canterbury Tales*: he's been a *reliable listener* for many a year and has thereby earned the right as well as the ability to *tell* the tale *well*—"well" meaning in this instance truthfully. Nothing more can be said, especially by someone still very much rooted in a given expressive culture. It's one of those situations in which the storyteller has to say, as many have, "If you didn't understand the tale, I'll have to tell it again."

Julius and Annie's exchange anticipates some of the key developments found in the last story of the first phase, "Dave's Neckliss." Their debate voices that which Chesnutt was unquestionably pursuing regarding just how efficacious conjure tales in dialect were to his efforts to create honest fictions of antebellum plantation life. Once these doubts were confronted, not just within the borders of authorial reflection but also within those of a surprisingly self-reflexive fiction, it was likely that he would continue his experiments and attempt a Julius story in which conjure and superstition did not figure. In this way, innovations in the outer form of "The Conjurer's Revenge" led to a new kind of tale. However, they prompted new developments in the frame of "Dave's Neckliss" as well. Once Annie and John both had been portrayed as unreliable listeners, certain decisions had to be made regarding whether she or John or the two of them together would be transformed into the reliable performers Julius's tales deserved. In other words, the Julius story had developed to a point where Chesnutt had to decide whether John and Annie were to remain foils to Julius or whether they were to become collaborators in storytelling and possibly storytellers in their own right. The prologue of "Dave's Neckliss" clearly shows that Chesnutt decided to pursue the latter course of action.

The site for storytelling is once again the piazza. That Julius, John, and Annie are on increasingly familiar terms is suggested when Julius is invited to partake of Sunday dinner. Of course, certain proprieties are observed: Julius sits at the table and consumes the same food his employers enjoy but this occurs only after John and Annie have retired outdoors. When Julius joins them on the piazza, the stage is set for the next phase of the story formula—the conversation which inevitably prompts a tale. In this instance, it is John not Annie who assumes the role of the eager listener. When he asks, "'Who was Dave, and what about him?'" we immediately sense that he is a different man from the one who was so quick to effect impatience and disinterest in the past. This is further borne out when John launches into the most lengthy and extraordinary commentary on Julius's storytelling to be found in the early stories:

> The conditions were all favorable to storytelling. There was an autumnal languor in the air, and a dreamy haze softened the dark green of the distant pines and the deep blue of the Southern sky. The generous meal he had made had put the old man in a very good humor. He was not always so, for his curiously undeveloped nature was subject to moods which were almost childish in their variableness. It was only now and then that we were able to study, through the medium of his recollection, the simple but intensely human inner life of slavery. His way of looking at the past seemed very strange to us; his view of certain sides of life was essentially different from ours. He never indulged in any regrets for the Arcadian joyousness and irresponsibility which was a somewhat popular conception of slavery; his had not been the lot of the petted house-servant, but that of the toiling field-hand. While he mentioned with a warm appreciation the acts of kindness which those in authority had shown to him and his people, he would speak of a cruel deed, not with the indignation of one accustomed to quick feeling and spontaneous expression, but with a furtive disapproval which suggested to us a doubt in his own mind as to whether he had a right to think or to feel, and presented to us the curious psychological spectacle of a mind enslaved long after the shackles had been struck off from the limbs of its possessor. Whether the sacred name of liberty ever set his soul aglow with a generous fire; whether he had more than the most elementary ideas of love, friendship, patriotism, religion—things which are half,

and the better half, of life to us; whether he had even realized except in a vague, uncertain way, his own degradation, I do not know. I fear not; and if not, then centuries of repression had borne their legitimate fruit. But in the simple human feeling, and still more in the undertone of sadness, which pervaded his stories, I thought I could see a spark which, fanned by favoring breezes and fed by memories of the past, might become in his children's children a glowing flame of sensibility, live to every thrill of human happiness or human woe.

In this carefully developed passage, John is persuasively presented as a storylistener somewhere in the midst of becoming reliable. While there are echoes here and there of the clichés exclusively used before in describing Julius and his tales, they are balanced and occasionally cancelled by the many new insights and assessments John now expresses. Insofar as he both valorizes and devalorizes Julius, John speaks as much for Chesnutt as for himself. This is not to say that what appears to be John's insensitivity or opacity is Chesnutt's, but to suggest that what comes across as such is a surfacing figuration of Chesnutt's lingering distrust of the "stifling" culture he left behind when he moved North. Through John, as through Annie in the previous story, Chesnutt is coming to terms with what he has wrought as a northern black writer of southern black tales. What may be taken as John's ambivalence toward Julius expresses as well Chesnutt's mixed feelings about pursuing a literary career seemingly dependent on the further proliferation of Julius stories.

But let us not dwell overly much on what the passage fairly or unfairly suggests about the limitations of Julius or of the Julius story. John also remarks—and here he speaks for Chesnutt as well—on the ways in which Julius's portraits of slavery's "intensely human inner life" challenge the popular conceptions of antebellum times. One effect of this is that, in terms of the emerging story series, a defense of the tales in literary English as well as one in dialect had been attempted. The former from John is no better than the latter from Julius; the two statements are not in conflict, indeed, they are complementary. This union of rhetorical purpose, far more than any apparent eloquence on John's part, provides the most plausible indication that he is no longer an unreliable listener. If we accept the idea that he is in the process of being transformed, it is because he seems to have fully *heard* what Julius had to say in the previous story and is now, in true accord with the aesthetics of storytelling, *revoicing* what he learned. In short, John now seems to be at that point in his journey to listenership where he can, in Chaucer's words, "tell a tale after a man" or "reherse."[8]

8. See Howard, pp. 195–96.

JOHN EDGAR WIDEMAN

[Julius's Ex-Slave Narrative]†

"A Deep Sleeper" begins on a soporific, July afternoon in the rural south during Reconstruction. The first-person narrator, a transplanted northerner who owns the plantation upon which the action occurs, decides that the eating of a watermelon might break the monotony of the sultry July day so he commandeers the aid of Uncle Julius, a relic from the days of slavery inherited when the plantation was purchased. Julius complains of "rheumatiz" and instead of fetching the watermelon himself goes off to waken Tom and instruct him to bring a wheelbarrow to the piazza. When Julius returns to the whites sitting on the piazza he mentions that Tom is one of the "Seben Sleepers" and that the boy's grandfather had once slept a month. The curiosity of the whites is aroused and Julius complies with the women's clamor for a story. Julius' tale takes place during slavery days and concerns the deep sleeper Skundus, his courting of Cindy, their enforced separation, Skundus' "deep sleep" which caused him to disappear for a month and the eventual marriage of the slaves Cindy and Skundus. Julius' dialect narrative is the centerpiece of Chesnutt's story, taking up nearly five of its seven pages. When Tom finally arrives with the wheelbarrow, the group from the piazza stroll out to the watermelon patch and find the prize melon they intended to harvest is gone.

The title "A Deep Sleeper" is enigmatic, becoming more so after several readings of the text it commands. Does the title refer to a quality of the tale which follows? Is this story "a sleeper?" Are its form and message cunning, sly, crafty? Is the tale difficult to fathom or understand, is it obscure? Or do these meanings of the word "deep" describe Skundus, the sleeper whose tale Julius narrates? Or is it Uncle Julius himself who is deep-learned, understanding, wise? Who is sleeping? Skundus? His grandson Tom? All black people? All whites who continue to delude themselves about the depth, the humanity of the black folk over whom they wield lethal power? To whom is the title addressed? To a white audience which accepts the archetype of the sleepy, lethargic black and for whom Skundus and progeny would be humorous examples? Or instead of holding up the black clown (and watermelon thief) for derision, is the butt of the

† Currently collected in *The Slave's Narrative*, ed. Charles T. Davis and Henry Louis Gates, Jr. (New York: Oxford UP, 1985), pp. 62–69. Copyright © 1985 by John Edgar Wideman, used with pemission of The Wylie Agency.

story's joke the self-enforced gullibility of the master-class, the masters who must accept the pilfering of their property, the tall tales of their slaves, accept "deep sleeps" which last for a month? However the title is construed, the words "deep" and "sleep" alert a reader to look below the surface and to be on the watch for someone asleep. The action of the story becomes a gloss on the multiple significations of these words.

"A Deep Sleeper" is composed of a number of movements, internal and external, and these movements can be understood as the result of exercises of power. The exercise of power is being dramatized in the tale. The movement of the words of the story, their linear progress from the title to last word, is a comment on the exercise of power. The first-person narrator (who for convenience will be called "John" as he is in subsequent stories) is compromised by the structure of the story he is relating; what he wishes to say is conditioned by how he must say it. A large part of his story is delivered by Uncle Julius' voice. The convention of labeling or titling a story allows another voice, not necessarily the first-person narrator's, to have the first word, or words, to set the scene and qualify all that comes after. The action of a story, the events portrayed, can have meaning which arises independent of the significance alleged by the narrator; so in fact "A Deep Sleeper" is bracketed by a first "word" (the title) and a last "word" (the disappearance of the popular watermelon), signifiers not controlled by the voice of the plantation-owner/narrator. What seems on the surface to be John's story is rather a demonstration of authorial control over the voice of a first-person narrator. The reader has no way of knowing how John would react to having his story called "A Deep Sleeper." The reader can only guess at the depth of John's understanding of the function or meaning of the story Julius tells. The reader's questions about such matters must be referred to someone outside the story, to an implied author as he is manifested in the weave of voices and events which constitute the story.

That we should be prepared to hear other voices and add their testimony to John's is emphasized by Uncle Julius' "tale within a tale." When the dialect voice of Julius takes over, the first-person narrator, John, disappears and is forgotten; he and the world he described in the opening "literary" paragraphs of "A Deep Sleeper" return only when Julius has finished his narration, only when, to put the matter another way, Julius permits him to speak again. An action has been completed that is a statement about power and authority. The literate narrator's role as proprietor of the story and owner of the watermelon, as master of words and property, has been undermined. The reader is left at the conclusion of the story to sort out his or her own conclusions rather than accept the words of the single, stable guide who seemed to be on hand in the story's first paragraphs.

If the movement of the story, its linear progression from beginning to end, expresses the tension between apparent power and power not so apparent, then one might expect to find parallel movements within the story illustrative of hidden versus apparent power. Like buckets to catch rain from a leaky roof, blacks are moved around in the story according to the needs, wills, and whims of whites. Cindy's removal to Kunnel Wash'n'ton McAdoo's place a hundred miles away from Skundus, her intended husband, is an obvious case. That black people had no control over such removals is made clear by Julius; "Skundus didn' lack ter hab Cindy go, but he couldn' do nuthin." Cindy "didn' hab no mo' ter say 'bout comin' dan she did 'bout goin!" The balance of power seems clear. The master class is absolutely in control. Promises made to blacks are not binding. When Marse Dugal's wife reminds him that niggers have no rights a white man need respect, he breaks his word to Cindy and Skundus, salving his conscience with a few little white lies, to them and to himself. John, Julius' employer, seems to have the same command over Julius' movements as masters had over their slaves. After all, the story occurs on a Sunday afternoon and Julius is on his way home from the church he serves as a deacon, but John does not hesitate to mobilize the old man into his watermelon-fetching scheme.

These apparent exercises of power describe only the surface of black-white relationships. Below the surface, other kinds of power affect other kinds of movement. Though the slaves Cindy and Skundus appear to be pawns, they make adjustments, and these 'justments allow them to subvert the power of the master class over their lives. Skundus can "steal himself" by running away from the plantation to the swamp. Cindy can pretend her health is dependent on certain elusive roots which she must gather each day from the swamp, a dependency providing a daily excuse for being away from the Big House. Julius and his extended family work for the narrator and must follow his orders, yet Julius is a magician, a trickster, who enchants the whites lounging on the piazza, capturing them in his tale about other times and places so he controls their movements in the present. Julius contrives a fiction to entertain his listeners, to distract them from interfering with his plans. Marse Dugal' manufactures a fiction to smooth over Cindy's removal from Skundus. The parallel loses its symmetry when one recalls that at stake in one deception was a watermelon, while in the other are the lives, love and happiness of two human beings.

A series of confrontations between the powerful and powerless are enacted in the story and in each case an obvious kind of power is balanced by an unexpected force wielded by the supposed powerless. The pairs brought into opposition—Julius and the narrator, Skundus and Marse Dugal', Cindy and her Mistress on the McAdoo plantation—reflect a larger system of black-white power relationships in the South, the struggle to establish personal space and territorial rights. Because of its persistence over time, its pervasiveness in people's lives, this struggle has assumed the formal coherence, the stability and predictability of a ritual dance.

The elements of this dance provide a structural unity in "A Deep Sleeper" and are exhibited in the WPA narratives gathered in the 1930's. First the separation of black from white, a formal assumption paralleling the segregation of the sexes in many traditional African dances. The two groups regard each other over a broad, hard-packed dirt floor, a stage, arena, threshing ground where encounters will be choreographed. An individual dancer sallies out of each group of participants. The dancer's movements are strictly patterned. Facial expression, posture, tone of voice, all are predetermined by ancient canons of behavior. The object of the dance is complex. The whites, who have the advantage of establishing the outward forms of the dance, design the ritual to display their superiority, their dominance; the dance is a metaphor of their power. For the blacks who, like the whites, must perform for two audiences at once, the objective is to find room for maneuver within the rigid forms dictated by the whites, maneuver which allows space for private communication with the other black participants. This communication coded into the space disciplined by the whites becomes another version of the action in the exposed center of the floor. Like a good boxer, the white dancer crowds the black into a corner, cutting off the ring, systematically diminishing room for black display and maneuver, but of course such a strategy also defines the area in which the white must perform. Each pair that enacts the ritual embodies both individual norms of behavior and archetypal relationships. Though these confrontations occur within the framework sanctioned by white power, their inevitability can be turned to the advantage of blacks, can be incorporated into black routines. (Recall Muhammad Ali's "rope-a-dope" tactics vs. George Foreman.) An observer wishing to understand any movement of the dance must visualize it from the dual perspective of the two groups which are its audience.

The separation of black from white and the consequent rituals produce, among other things, two distinct types of speech which may be exemplified by the narrator, John's literary English, and Julius' dialect. These varieties of speech describe two different worlds; each speech form (speech community) represents a version of reality. At some levels the languages of blacks and whites are mutually intelligible, or at least *seem* to allow a variety of exchanges. Chesnutt explores the forms and uses of language where the *seams* of mutual intelligibility burst. What Chesnutt's characters are saying cannot be understood unless the reader has an awareness of the total version of reality which a particular utterance signifies. Dell Hymes' discussion of the socio-linguistic concept *key* is useful here. In speech acts, *key* provides the tone, manner, or spirit of the words spoken. Speech acts, often the same as regards setting, participants, form of message, etc., may differ in *key*, that is, may be serious or mocking, painstaking or perfunctory depending on a signal (verbal or otherwise, i.e., wink, gesture) which is part of the speech act. *How* something is said (the "how" being defined by the speech community of a speaker) is part of *what* is said. The more a way of speaking has become shared and meaningful within a group, the more likely that crucial cues will be efficient or small in scale. Chesnutt employs numerous subtle keys, often drawn from the repertoire of Afro-American oral tradition, to achieve density of meaning in "A Deep Sleeper."

Manipulation of key can call attention to playful or artistic dimensions of speech. Satire, irony, ridicule, as Sylvia Render points out in her introduction to *Chesnutt's Short Fiction*, are called into play by *signifying*, a traditional resource of black speech communities signalled by key. Signifying is verbal art. Claudia Mitchell-Kernan has succinctly described the dynamics of signifying: the apparent meaning of an utterance is cancelled by the introduction of a key which signals to those who recognize the key that the utterance should not be taken "straight." The speaker who is signifying depends upon a body of experience he shares with the audience to whom the signifying is addressed. The signifier expects his audience to process his utterance metaphorically, because their shared experience allows them to recognize the key and supplies the material for re-interpreting the utterance. In the street a skillful signifier can talk behind a victim's back while looking him in the face. Manipulation of key, employed as a rhetorical device in fiction, permits the writer to address several audiences simultaneously by appealing to pools of knowledge only segments of his readers share with him. In effect, the writer can profit from the diversity among his readers rather than be limited by it. Chesnutt took full advantage of this possibility by playing to multiple audiences, designing his "A Deep Sleeper" in layers, layers corresponding to the conflicting versions of reality perceived by blacks and whites.

> "Tom's gran'daddy wuz name' Skundus," he began. "He had a brudder name' Tushus en' ernudder name' Cottus en' ernudder name' Squinchus." The old man paused a moment and gave his leg another hitch.
> My sister-in-law was shaking with laughter. "What remarkable names!" she exclaimed. "Where in the world did they get them?"

Uncle Julius is speaking, *sho nuff*, like an old ignorant southern darky is supposed to speak in Negro dialect. And sho nuff he gets his laugh, the laughter Chesnutt could count on from the majority of his readers, the ones who enjoyed Joel Chandler Harris, Sidney Lanier and Irwin Russell, the ones who turned, as Mabel and Annie and John on the piazza, to Uncle Julius for an entertaining interlude. The laughter of such readers is encouraged, sanctioned by Mabel's. Julius' performance is that of a virtuoso dialect story-teller; he is rhyming "brudder" and "enudder" so they fall as syncopated beats in his narration. He is probably twisting his mouth in absurd ways to pronounce the strange names Skundus, Tushus, Squinchus. That his performance for the piazza is conscious and calculated is keyed by the "hitch" he gives his leg. One of the roles Julius is projecting for the whites is an old, feeble man whose ailments prevent him from fetching a watermelon. With sighs, grimaces, and explicit references, Julius sustains this role throughout the story. Given Julius' intentions and the successful working-out of his plan for appropriating the melon, his comments on his pain and the mannerisms by which he pantomimes its effects become a source of humor for those readers who appreciate the art of fooling master.

The source of the "remarkable names" turns out to be Marse Dugal' McAdoo, who named all the babies "wat wuz bawn on de plantation." The absolute power of the master licenced him to name his chattel. For some readers who share with Chesnutt a knowledge of Latin, the humor of the names is enriched because the slaves' names correspond to the Latin words for second, third, fourth and fifth. Recognizing the Latin key, certain readers have their classical learning rewarded, their vanity touched and their prejudice confirmed since Julius exhibits the Negro's darned comical funny habit of muddling words when he reaches above his proper sphere of ignorance. Within the small class that recognized the Latin key, a smaller grouping might respond with indignation towards the old Regime which allowed such abuses of power. Some of this group might even feel slightly ashamed that human beings were given numbers for names, numbers for the master's convenience, numbers which reverberate ironically since they are disguised in Latin, one of the classical languages and cultures which are the oft-exalted and extolled sources of Western Civilization. But some readers may be keyed to other kinds of power at work here. Julius calls the names "Hebrew" suggesting that their source, like the source of so many other mysterious indignities the master class imposes on its slaves, is the Bible, the Bible Julius admits he cannot read. Uncle Julius makes it clear that "Hit ain' my fault I ain't able ter read," so his confession of illiteracy is also an indictment of the ignorance enforced upon the slave by his master. In this light, the source of the remarkable names might as well be Hebrew as Greek since, for Julius, access to this kind of knowledge has been systematically withheld. Chesnutt rightfully, ironically dismisses the question of origin and points to another kind of meaning the names contain. When the Latin words are trans-lated into Blackspeech and given their unique pronunciation, an identity is created for the brothers apart from the dehumanizing numerical designations. Skundus is "Skundus," not *Secundus*. He is baptised by the slave community and becomes a distinct individual. His distinction, his individuality is defined and preserved in the tale Julius narrates. Marse Dugal's joke (like so many kinds of humor, a sadistic exercise of power) is turned back on him and the culture he represents. Originally named for the convenience of a white man, Secundus has been transformed by Blackspeech and oral tradition into Skundus, a legendary Deep Sleeper. The source of his name is as much of an enigma for Mabel as his behavior is an embarrassment and thorn in the side of Marse Dugal'. While Mabel laughs at the remarkable names, some readers are laughing at her. When Marse Dugal' threatens Skundus: "I'm gwine ter hang yer up by yer thumbs en take ev'y bit er yer black hide off'n yer," he is declaiming the lit-eral power of the master over his slaves. But Julius also states that "evey'body knowed Marse Dugal' bark uz wuss'n his bite," and this knowledge shared by the slave community is the key for interpreting Dugal's empty words, as well as the absurd actions he has no choice but to perform when Skundus returns from his deep sleep.

In his fiction, Chesnutt is cleaning up Negro dialect, tinkering not so much with its outward form, which he inherited and felt was hope-lessly artificial at best, but with its validity to carry a message apart from the demeaning one with which it was traditionally burdened. Chesnutt's illiterate speakers from Uncle Julius to Mammy Jane are distinctive not only because of the form (Negro dialect) of their speech, but because what they say is true. Oral history in Chesnutt is a vehicle for reconstructing the past so that the lies and misrepresen-tations of the master class become part of the written record. Negro dialect has come full circle. Rather than being an instrument of power in the hands of the enemy (Black speech framed in an inimical literary tradition), it is turned against the oppressor.

Can I get a Witness! Chesnutt's answer is yes. He allows Julius to speak for himself. The point of view of the slave can be understood apart from and in spite of the voice of the white plantation owner. The Works Progress Administration oral history project nearly half a century later is another kind of attempt to record the black man's version of slavery and reconstruction. What Julius and the former slaves have to say is of crucial importance if one wishes a rounded view of the "peculiar institution," and scholars have begun to incor-porate the slaves' view into the historiography of the period. But how the former slaves told their stories, the notions of style and form, the values embodied in the narratives have been neglected by scholars even though studying the narratives from this perspective perhaps could illuminate fundamental elements of Afro-American culture, the incredible inner sense of purpose and worth, the integrity and resiliency which enabled a people to survive their time on the cross.

WERNER SOLLORS

[Reason, Property, and Modern Metamorphoses]†

* * *

Whatever John's frame narratives represent, Julius' inside tales can be read as their counterplots. Several readers have looked at Julius' tales as demythologizing John's and have emphasized Julius' own economic motives in telling his tales. This is less apparent in "Sis' Becky's Pickaninny"—where Julius only lends Annie his rabbit's foot, perhaps for a fee—but in "Dave's Neckliss" he gets a ham, in "A Deep Sleep" probably a watermelon, in "Po' Sandy" the infamous lumber, and in the "The Goophered Grapevine" he attempts, but fails, to keep control over his grapes.

* * *

Is the trickster Julius merely a selfish manipulator, a juggler who acts upon ulterior motives? However seriously such readings of con-jure tales are offered as counter-texts to John's narrative, they, too, still follow John's lead. As Jules Chametzky argues, Julius' serving of his own interest is, after all, a motive John "benignly understands".[1] John believes in nothing more than economic self-interest; he notes Julius' shrewdness (which, as we saw, he ascribes to the non-African part of his ancestry) and concludes "The Goophered Grapevine" with the comment:

> I found, when I bought the vineyard, that Uncle Julius had occu-pied a cabin on the place for many years, and derived a respectable revenue from the product of the neglected grapevines. This, *doubtless*, accounted for his advice to me not to buy the vineyard, though whether it inspired the goopher story I am unable to state.

---

† From "The Goopher in Charles Chesnutt's Conjure Tales: Superstition, Ethnicity, and Modern Metamorphoses." *Litterature d' America* 6 (1985): 120–29. Reprinted by permission. Notes have been edited.
1. *Our Decentralized Literature: Cultural Mediation in Selected Jewish and Southern Writers* (Amherst: U of Massachusetts P, 1986), p. 39.

Even more forcefully, John views the tale of "The Gray Wolf's Ha'nt" as a story told by Julius in order to keep his honey supply.

> The gray wolf's haunt had *doubtless* proved useful in keeping off too inquisitive people, who might have interfered with his monopoly.

That Julius is not a child of nature and that slavery as well as freedom meant living in the economic world is clear. However, the very fact that John regards Julius as an economic schemer, and the probability that the word "doubtless" was used ironically in those passages, should prompt us to look for more than shrewd profit motives in Uncle Julius. For this reason it is good to focus on "Sis' Becky's Pickaninny" where that motive is not directly present.

Melvin Dixon reads the rabbit's foot as a phallic symbol that accounts for the wife's "satisfaction" in the manner of a seduction tale[2]—which loosely fits into the theme of self-interest, I suppose. Of course, it goes without saying that the rabbit is a fertility symbol and has specific sexual and procreative connotations in much folklore; Claudia de Lys, for example, explains in *A Treasury of American Superstitions*:

> The mystic potency of the foot has always been used symbolically in relation to sex, and the hindfoot of an animal as prolific as the hare or rabbit added to the potency of the amulet.[3]

It is also meaningful that Annie and John are childless, whereas it is as a mother that Becky suffers in the inside tale. Thus one can easily guess what a Freudian could make of the fact that John pulls Julius' foot out of his wife's pocket. Yet it is the whole explanation of Julius' character that is problematic here.

David Britt argued strongly against an exclusive focus on John's ulterior motive (and we might include the ulterior sexual motive):

> it is a mistake to view a few jugs of wine or a crock of honey [and, we might add, Annie's "pocket"] as the prime objectives of Julius' maneuverings . . . Julius' tales are not aimed at manipulating John in the way the surface narrative implies.[4]

The struggle is not between ideology and profit, but between differing and conflicting ideologies, expressed in different forms of narration.

In this broader sense the stories may be viewed as tales of seduction (though not necessarily sexual seduction) of verbal persuasion,

2. "The Teller as Folk Trickster in Chesnutt's *The Conjure Woman*," *College Language Association Journal* 18 (December 1974): 186–97.
3. (New York: Philosophical Library, 1948), pp. 117–18.
4. "Chesnutt's Conjure Tales: What You See Is What You Get," *College Language Association Journal* 15 (March 1972): 274.

of attempted manipulation in more than monetary aspects. Robert Bone sees this as the connection, not only between inside and outside tale, but between Julius, John, and Chesnutt. The role of the Black writer, "conveyed through the metaphor of conjuration", is to "bewitch the white folks" with the help of fiction, to open their eyes to truth and imagination. In "Sis' Becky's Pickaninny", for example, Mose's singing is parallel to John's and Julius' tales and to Chesnutt's story. The story is thus, as Bone puts it, a "tribute to sorrow songs". The rabbit, too, as evidenced by John's first question about the rabbit's foot, parallels the slave—as the Brer Rabbit tradition documents:

> If Brer Fox, like Colonel Pendleton and the white narrator, is a symbol of power without imagination, Brer Rabbit, like Sis' Becky and Uncle Julius, is a symbol of the imagination without power, which sometimes manages to turn the tables, but always enables its possessor to endure.[5]

According to Bone's reading, Becky's rabbit foot is imagination, and Julius' is the "charming" power of story-telling.

In order to sway the reader (Chesnutt's dream was to undermine the garrison of white resentment), Chesnutt darkens John's world of imaginative "reason" and lightens the occult of Julius' conjuring. In Chesnutt's stories, as Hemenway points out, conjure

> never finally represents evil, because conjure is placed in a context in which the omnipresent evil is slavery itself. The terror in Chesnutt's tales comes not from the transformations of nature, fears of night, the irrationality of supernatural force, but from what men do to each other in the name of race.[6]

The evil of slavery itself appears as a voodoo which transforms men into commodities—whose value fluctuates seasonally and according to the market—or into people who are "socially dead". Chesnutt's stories are full of illustrations not only of the owners' cruelty, avarice, and thoughtlessness, but also of the slaves' denial of stability ("Po' Sandy") and learning ("A Dumb Witness"). Some scenes give vivid testimony to the slaves' experience of radical alienation and reification; in "Lonesome Ben", for example, Julius describes Ben's estrangement from himself:

> Well, po' Ben didn' know what ter do. He had been lonesome ernuff befo', but now he didn' eben hab his own se'f ter 'so'ciate wid, fer he felt mo' lak a stranger 'n he did lak Ben.

---

5. Bone, *Down Home*, pp. 86, 88.
6. Robert Hemenway, "Gothic Sociology: Charles Chesnutt and the Gothic Mode," *Studies in the Literary Imagination* 7 (Spring 1974): 112.

In "Dave's Neckliss", the ham on Dave's neck is like a "cha'm" that gives him a reified identity:

> W'en de ham had be'n tuk off'n Dave, folks kinder stopped talkin' 'bout 'im so much. But de ham had be'n on his neck so long dat Dave had sorter got use' ter it. He look des lack he'd los' sump'n fer a day er so atter de ham wuz tuk off, en didn' 'pear ter know w'at ter do wid hisse'f . . .

The dehumanizing processes of slavery outdo the most horrifying charms, spells, and metamorphoses. The slaves' goopher in Julius' tales is often directed against this state of affairs; and it is no threatening power, but a tool for liberation, or at least for fending off the worst of slavery. Whenever it is thus politicized, the occult tends to be less demonic and satanic than under other conditions.

John shares his belief in "reason" with the horse trader who finally surrenders Becky thinking that "a lame hoss wuz better 'n a dead nigger", and with the owners of the *ancien régime* of slavery, yet he fails to feel implicated. John's and the former slave owners' perceptions reduce life to commodities; conversely, what they disparage as mere goophers, as fetishes, superstitions, amulets, or talismans, can transform the reified objects back to life. John's rationality, Hemenway says, "becomes a function of his racism for he is incapable of granting conjure the dignity of belief".[7] John's blindness extends to his own world and to objects he believes he controls. In a frequently invoked scene in "The Gray Wolf's Ha'nt" John reads the following passage to his bored wife:

> "The difficulty of dealing with transformations so many-sided as those which all existences have undergone, or are undergoing, is such as to make a complete and deductive interpretation almost hopeless. So to grasp the total process of redistribution of matter and motion as to see simultaneously its several necessary results in their actual interdependence is scarcely possible. There is, however, a mode of rendering the process as a whole tolerably comprehensible. Though the genesis of the rearrangement of every evolving aggregate is in itself one, it presents to our intelligence"—
>
> "John," interrupted my wife, "I wish you would stop reading that nonsense and see who that is coming up the lane."
>
> I closed my book with a sigh. I had never been able to interest my wife in the study of philosophy, even when presented in the simplest and most lucid form.

What John reads is, of course, a theory of metamorphoses, the existence of which he so vehemently denies in Julius' tales. Hemenway comments perceptively: "John reads, but does not understand, Julius

7. Hemenway, p. 116.

'knows' but does not require abstractions for 'proof'".[8] Julius' "goo-pher" is what John can only imagine in the abstract, never as part of himself. John fails to connect "who is coming up the lane" with what he reads and believes he owns as if it were his racial patrimony.

Chesnutt's stories thus may appeal to the fear that the Western spirit (of the classical and biblical tradition) has been lost to the dead letter of form. The Pharisaic John reads abstractions about metamorphoses—in order to build a static sense of stable selfhood and to feel superior to Julius as well as to his wife who empathizes with Julius' stories of victims of metamorphoses. Julius, not John, is the new Ovid: "The Goophered Gravepine" is reminiscent of Bacchus (*Metamorphoses* VI:125), and "Po' Sandy" of Daphne (I:452–567). Julius' tales are art à la Horace: John himself calls Julius "entertain-ing" and "useful". Ironically, then, the slaves are identified with the classical tradition, which John merely invokes as a possession, as shallow form. More importantly, the same opposition also applies to the biblical allusions in Chesnutt's stories. The slaves are the salt of the earth and abide in God's vine (*John* 15:1–5) whereas John wants to leave no grapes for the poor and for the stranger, as God had instructed Moses (*Numbers* 19:10). Chesnutt's "John" does not understand li'l "Mose". As Monika Plessner has argued, the territory between superstition and rationality is filled by Chesnutt with reminders of Christ's suffering as a hope for redemption and recon-ciliation: thus Chesnutt transformed Fayetteville into "Patesville"—literally Golgotha (*Matthew* 27:33); the "scuppernong" grapes seem to echo Capernaum where Jesus preached parables and performed miracles (*Matthew* 17:24; 8:5; 13:18, 24); and "The Goophered Grapevine" alludes to the parable of the householder's vineyard (*Matthew* 21:33–44).[9] Though John wonders what Christianity may mean for ex-slaves, they live the spirit of the Bible that the compla-cent John arrogantly claims as his racial property. John is a Pharisee, a scribe, but Julius has a truly Christian moral vision to which John fails to respond. No wonder that Chesnutt emphasizes the "good" goopher, conjuring against the evils of slavery, ownership, compla-cency, and lack of empathy. Chesnutt shows with his ironic method that a proprietary relationship to truth is a lie.

Interestingly—as Jahoda points out[1]—modern attitudes toward superstition are always characterized by the hope that superstitions are dying out and will give way to rational progress. In this sense, "superstition" is opposed to "modernity" in the same way "ethnicity" is commonly considered a thing of the past. More than that, the first

---

8. Hemenway, p. 170.
9. "Nachwort," in Charles W. Chesnutt, *Der verwunschene Weinberg und andere Sklaven-märchen aus Nordamerika*. trans. Monika Plessner, (Frankfurt: Insel, 1979), pp. 132–33.
1. Gustav Jahoda, *The Psychology of Superstition* (Harmondsworth, Penguin, 1969), pp. 138–47.

occurrence of the word "ethnicity" recorded in the *Oxford English Dictionary* is of 1772 and in the sense of "pagan superstition": "From the curling spume of the celebrated Egeans waves fabulous ethnicity feigned Venus their idolatress conceived". "Ethnicity" and "superstition" are based on divisions, boundaries between an in-group (sacralized in the process) and an out-group. Though he thinks that he represents universal common sense, John constructs, and fails to see his own construction of, social boundaries. He cannot recognize much of himself in Julius. Though John thinks of the goopher as a vestige of darker ages, in Julius' tales it functions as a modern assault on John's artificial separation between his white male selfhood and all forms of otherness. The conjure woman's (and Chesnutt's) goopher dissolves prematurely hardened boundaries around self, gender and race; if it can change any form into any other form, it can turn masters into slaves and children into birds; and it can surely melt hardened hearts. Even an "object", a thing, such as a rabbit's foot can rescue humans from being mere commodities and fixities. In Chesnutt's world, the goopher spells process against reification, human wholeness against ethnic and sexual division, and reconciles human beings with their mortality.[2] It is no coincidence that Chesnutt placed the goopher at the very center of his short stories which, I suppose, have rightly been called "charming".

HOUSTON A. BAKER, JR.

[The Sound of the Conjure Stories][†]

The first edition of *The Conjure Woman*, Chesnutt's 1899 collection of short stories, immediately reveals what might be called the graphics of minstrelsy. On the cover, a venerably comic black man who is bald and possessed of big ears, rough features, and a great deal of woolly white hair merges—not unintentionally—with two rather malevolent looking caricatures of rabbits. The Houghton, Mifflin and Company designers outdid themselves in suggesting the link between Chesnutt's content and that of the ever popular Joel Chandler Harris's "Uncle Remus" and the crafty Brer Rabbit of Afro-American

---

2. One only has to remember the meaning of "goofer dust," the "graveyard" rabbit, and the resurrection motif in some of the metamorphoses. This aspect makes the rabbit's foot part of the rituals that "socially dead" people could invoke in order to undergo symbolic rebirths. See Orlando Patterson, *Slavery and Social Death: A Comparative Study* (Cambridge and London; Harvard UP, 1982), pp. 214–39; and Klaus Heinrich, *Vernunft und Mythos* (Frankfurt: Fischer, 1983), pp. 7–9.

† From *Modernism and the Harlem Renaissance* (Chicago: U of Chicago P, 1987), pp. 41–47. Reprinted by permission.

folk ancestry. There is, to be sure, justification for regarding Chesnutt's work as an expressive instance of the traditional trickster rabbit tales of black folklore, since his main character Uncle Julius manages to acquire gains by strategies that are familiar to students of Brer Rabbit. The real force of *The Conjure Woman*, however, does not reside in a febrile replay of an old Harris tune. Rather, the collection's strength lies in the deep and intensive recoding of form that marks its stories. The work is best characterized as a drama of transformation.

In a letter from Chesnutt to Walter Hines Page in 1898 we find the following:

> Speaking of dialect, it is almost a despairing task to write it. . . . The fact is, of course, that there is no such thing as a Negro dialect; that what we call by that name is the attempt to express, with such a degree of phonetic correctness as to suggest *the sound*, English pronounced as an ignorant old southern Negro would be supposed to speak it.

In these reflections shared with one of the most influential literary editors and brokers of his era, Chesnutt shrewdly gives and takes in a single, long breath. He unequivocally states that the task of the spokesperson who would render black life adequately is to "suggest the *sound*." At the same time, he knows to whom he is speaking and promptly gives Page something for his fancy—"an ignorant old southern Negro." In a phrase, then, we have encoded the injunction from Chesnutt to *heed the sound* and a disclaimer to Page that says there is no need—really, boss—to fear the sound: it is still that of an ignorant old darky.

Nothing, of course, could be farther from the truth. Chesnutt had been aware for years that the plantation tradition in American letters and even more studied efforts by white authors to write about the Afro-American were inadequate and frequently idiotic. He had also been fully aware that what editors like Page passed off as "Negrolife in story" was radically opposed to the story he wanted to tell. Listen again as Chesnutt gives and takes in a single breath.

Having been dithyrambic about the March 1899 issue of *Atlantic* in a letter to Page, he then says, "The dialect story is one of the sort of Southern stories that make me feel it is *my duty* to write a different sort, and yet I did not lay it down without a tear of genuine emotion." As an Afro-American spokesperson, Chesnutt was acutely aware of "his duty" to preserve fidelity to the *sound* of African ancestors and the phonics of their descendants in the "country districts." Rather than producing a simpleminded set of trickster stories framed by the ponderous pretensions of a white Ohio Buckeye as narrator, therefore, he offered a world of sounds and sweet airs that resonates with the transformative power of *conjure*.

Conjure is the transatlantic religion of diasporic and Afro-American masses in the New World. Descended from *vodun*, an African religion in which the priestess holds supreme power, conjure's name in Haiti and the Caribbean is *voodoo*. The force that transmutes and transforms in Chesnutt's volume of stories is the *root work* and empowering mediations of *The Spirit* that mark the efforts of voodoo's Houngans or conjure's "two-headed doctors." In the stories of *The Conjure Woman*, we find a struggle in progress as the white, Ohio narrator who has moved to southern "country districts" strives to provide empirical explanations—a certain species of philosophical "nonsense"—as a reassuring mask for the myriad manifestations of Uncle Julius's "spirit work." The seemingly comic old "uncle," in turn, ceaselessly transmits sounds about a cruel order of bondage that has transformed African harmony, as idealized and serene as a Dan mask, into family separation, floggings, and commercial negotiations. But even as Julius relays his sound, he introduces, valorizes, and validates a *root* phonics that is vastly different from the sounds of the Ohio narrator. The *difference* is conjure. For conjure is a power of transformation that causes definitions of "form" as fixed and comprehensible "thing" to dissolve. Black men, considered by slavery as "things" or "chattel personal," are transformed through conjure into seasonal vegetation figures, or trees, or gray wolves. White men, in turn, are transmuted into surly and abused "noo niggers." A black child is changed into a hummingbird and a mockingbird. A black woman becomes a cat, and an elderly black man's clubfoot is a reminder of his transformation—under a conjurer's "revenge"—into a mule.

The fluidity of *The Conjure Woman*'s world, symbolized by such metamorphoses, is a function of the black narrator's mastery of form. The old man knows the sounds that are dear to the hearts of his white boss and his wife, and he presents them with conjuring efficaciousness. In effect, he presents a world in which "dialect" masks the drama of African spirituality challenging and changing the disastrous transformations of slavery. A continuation of this historic masking ritual is at work in the "present" universe of *The Conjure Woman* (the space/time in which Julius relates his stories to Ohioans). For throughout all of the volume's stories the *sound* of African ancestry operates at a low, signifying, and effective register *behind* the mask of a narrational dialect that, in Chesnutt's words, is "no . . . thing." Finally, what is sharply modified by the transformative soundings of the work are the dynamics of lordship and bondage as a whole. When the work concludes, Julius has obtained a job, use of a building on the Ohioan's property for black community organizational purposes, employment for his grandson, and (possibly) profits from a duplicitous horse trade. In a sense, one might say that Julius has secured—in the very heart of the country districts—an enclave in which a venerable Afro-American spirit can sound off.

During all of the black narrator's tellings, the white Ohioan believes the stories are merely expressive of a minstrel type. He views Julius as, at best, a useful entertainment, one who can do odd jobs *and* tell stories. He considers him, at worst, an agent of annoyance and craftiness—never as a potent force of African transformations that can not be comprehended or controlled by Western philosophy.

But what is meant here by Western philosophy? The Ohioan's reading at the beginning of "The Gray Wolf's Ha'nt" provides an indication of the kind of rational control the white man seeks in the face of formal transmutations. He reads the following passage to his wife "with pleasure":

> "The difficulty of dealing with transformations so many-sided as those which all existences have undergone, or are undergoing, is such as to make a complete and deductive interpretation almost hopeless. So to grasp the total process of redistribution of matter and motion as to see simultaneously its several necessary results in their actual independence is scarcely possible. There is, however, a mode of rendering the process as a whole tolerably comprehensible."

"John," says his wife, "I wish you would stop reading that *nonsense* and see who that is coming up the lane." Indeed, the process of "redistribution" suggested in the passage is philosophically incomprehensible in Western terms, especially if that very redistribution is being effected from behind the minstrel mask—with the sound of minstrelsy seeming to dominate—by an African sensibility. The transformations wrought in and by Julius's tales are *conjure changes* necessitated by a bizarre economics of slavery. Only spiritual transformations of the "slave" self as well as the "master" self ("Mars Jeems's Nightmare") in a universe governed by *root work* (a work that demands that adherents pay in full to the priestess Aunt Peggy) will enable the progress and survival of a genuinely Afro-American *sound*.

Julius's voice is in fact a function of conjure and a conjuring function. It allows Chesnutt—who, like Julius, is a North Carolinian who has heard "de tale fer twenty-five years . . . and ain't got no 'casion for ter 'spute it"—to *sound* a common tale of Afro-American transformative resourcefulness under the guise of an ole "uncle" speaking *nonsense*. The power of Julius and Chesnutt resides in the change they work on their audiences. They put, so to speak, their white hearers through changes. Listen to the Ohioan's wife at the conclusion of "The Conjurer's Revenge"—the tale that appears in advance of the one in which her husband attempts to read "transformation." At the story's close, she condemns Julius's narration as follows: "That story does not appeal to me, Uncle Julius, and is not up to your usual mark. . . . In fact, it seems to me like nonsense." When the next story opens—"Sis' Becky's Pickaninny"—the mistress has fallen morosely ill and neither "novels" read by John, nor "plantation songs" sung by "the hands" can effect a cure.

In comes Uncle Julius with his *conjure*, and when his tale of Sis' Becky is done—a tale whose moral the wife is able to supply, bringing her and the teller into expressive accord—she begins to improve. *Conjure* is also known, of course, as folk medicine. "My wife's condition," says the Ohioan, "took a turn for the better from this very day, and she was soon on the way to ultimate recovery." Can it come as a surprise that the wife's characterization of two opposed *phonics*— Western philosophical rationalism meant to comprehend and control fluidity, and African conjure meant to move the spirit through a fluid repertoire of "forms"—grants the nod to *conjure*? The designation *nonsense* falls with a heavy thump upon rationalism's polysyllables at the commencement of "The Gray Wolf's Ha'nt." And we know by this token that Julius (like his creator) has played a mojo hand with the deft brilliance of a master of form.

What moves through Chesnutt's collection is the sound of a southern black culture that knew it had to *re-form* a slave world created by the West's willful transformation of Africans into chattel. Conjure's spirit work moves behind—within, and through—the mask of minstrelsy to ensure survival, to operate changes, to acquire necessary resources for continuance, and to cure a sick world. At the first appearance of Chesnutt's "conjure" stories in the *Atlantic*, (and in his correspondence, the word "conjure" is always in quotes, protected as a *tricky* or transformative sign—masked), a white audience thought they were hearing merely entertaining syllables of a lovable darky. The turn-of-the-century writer's goal, however, was "a different story" for a different world, and he achieved this black southern eloquence in a discourse unequaled in his day.

ERIC J. SUNDQUIST

[Chesnutt's Revision of Uncle Remus]†

Mark Twain's well-known compliment to Joel Chandler Harris that the framework of narration in his Uncle Remus tales was more important than the content of the tales ("The stories are only alligator pears [avocados]," wrote Twain in 1881, "one eats them merely for the sake of the dressing") goes against the grain of modern readings, which tend to value the tales' mythic action—their black folkloric

---

† Reprinted by permission of the publisher from *To Wake the Nations: Race in the Making of American Literature* by Eric J. Sundquist (Cambridge, Mass.: The Belknap Press of Harvard University Press, 1993), pp. 324–31, 333–34. Copyright © 1993 by the President and Fellows of Harvard College. Notes have been edited.

kernels—but lament the stereotypical plantation mythology gener-
ated by old Uncle Remus's storytelling to the little white boy. For
his part, Harris repeatedly insisted that he was only the "editor and
compiler" of the tales, that they were not "cooked" but "given in the
simple but picturesque language of the negroes, just as the negroes
tell them."[1] Nevertheless, Harris's narrative frame is important not
just for its enforcement of plantation mythology but because there
are certain signs that, in his own sometimes confused and contradic-
tory way, he went behind Remus's mask more frequently than some
readers have suspected. Welding his own imagination to that of
Remus, Harris used him to critique a range of southern problems
and to comment on a time before slavery—an African time. The
imaginative framework in which the animal tales of African American
folklore are set, whether by the most rudimentary collector or by a
publishing author such as Harris or Chesnutt, cannot always be
firmly distinguished from the tale itself, for the fabrication of storytelling is the essence of both. It is this aspect of Uncle Remus's own
role and his tales that Chesnutt would take further, turning it back on
Harris, in his creation of Uncle Julius.

The manifold relations between Harris and Chesnutt can perhaps
best be measured by a look at Harris's original portrait of Uncle
Remus and the Chesnutt story that most directly responds to it. "A
Story of the War" established Remus's position within the southern
family that first owned him and then, following the Civil War,
employed him. As it appeared in *Uncle Remus: His Songs and Sayings* (1881), the story also fixed the "faithful darky" characterization
of Remus that Harris would have great difficulty throwing off. But
what happened to the story between its first publication in the
Atlanta Constitution in 1877, under the title "Uncle Remus as a
Rebel," and its inclusion in the first Remus volume is even more
noteworthy. The central action of the story is Remus's shooting of a
Yankee sharpshooter who is about to kill his master, "Mars Jeems."
In the newspaper version the Yankee, John Huntingdon, is killed; in
the volume version he is only wounded (and loses an arm), thus
allowing him to be nursed back to health, marry Jeems's sister, Miss
Sally, and move with her to Atlanta after the war, taking with them
Uncle Remus as an employee. In his reworking of the tale into a
classic example of the North-South reunion theme so prevalent by
the 1880s, Harris's most brilliant structural stroke was to make John
and Sally's son the "little boy" to whom Uncle Remus tells his wealth
of animal stories.

These features of the story are familiar to any reader of Harris,
and critics have often enough taken Remus's shooting of John to be

---

1. Julia Collier Harris, *The Life and Letters of Joel Chandler Harris* (London: Constable,
1919), pp. 169–70; Harris, *Nights with Uncle Remus*, pp. xli–xlii.

the best evidence of Harris's reactionary mythology. Yet not only were there such instances of slave allegiance in the war's history available to Harris, if he needed a model, but also Remus is shown to be markedly ambivalent: "It sorter made cole chills run up my back" to shoot a Union soldier, Remus tells John's visiting northern sister in his own narration of the incident, "but w'en I see dat man take aim, en Mars Jeems gwine home ter Ole Miss en Miss Sally, I des disremembered all 'bout freedom en lammed aloose." The fact that it is John, his new employer, who was shot by Remus and lost an arm, is withheld until the last lines of the story, where Remus has an opportunity to tell us that in return for taking John's arm, he has given his own arms, to work for John. The theme of reconciliation thus operates on several levels. Remus pays tribute to his northern savior after shooting him in order to save his own southern master, and his story, during which he speaks "from the standpoint of a Southerner," is directed at an additional northern audience (not just John's visiting sister but by implication Harris's wider circle of readers who eagerly purchased his volume after the explosive popular reaction to his serialized Remus tales). A fine example of sectional reunion in literature, "A Story of the War" portrays the white South, in the immediate aftermath of Reconstruction, as restored to a loving, benevolent relationship with "the Negro." Despite his own liberal philosophy and demonstrable despair about purported racial progress in the South, Harris's stories seldom broke free from the careful containment of the "Negro problem" represented by Remus's narration of his participation in the war. Moreover, at the moment we meet him, in Atlanta in the 1870s, Remus is fed up with the "sunshine niggers" of Reconstruction (who beg his tobacco, borrow his tools, and steal his food) and longs to move back to the plantation with Mars Jeems.[2] Divided between the animal tales and the Atlanta sketches, *Uncle Remus: His Songs and Sayings* temporally displaces the "legends of the old plantation" and their narrative setting with urban satire, thus creating a structural nostalgia that corresponds to Remus's conservative opinions. In *Nights with Uncle Remus*, Harris not only moves Remus irrevocably back to the plantation (along with John, Sally, and the little boy) but in fact appears to transport the entire structure and setting of his storytelling into a vague antebellum past.

    * * * Remus is still the beast of burden for the new generation of white men (by the last Remus volumes it is the "little boy's" little boy—a fussy, spoiled representative of the New South, in Harris's imagination—who is listening to Remus's fireside tales). As this

---

2. Joel Chandler Harris, *Uncle Remus: His Songs and Sayings*, rev. ed. (New York: Appleton, 1896), pp. 212, 204–5.

allusion to Mars Jeems as the boy's uncle (one of several through-out the Remus volumes) reminds us, however, Remus was Mars Jeems's protector *and his slave* even when Jeems was a boy. Remus is not the "little boy's" slave in *Uncle Remus: His Songs and Sayings*, but he is in *Nights with Uncle Remus;* the second volume, as I will note, literalizes Remus's figurative slavery in the first through the retrogressive act of Harris's imagination. Although he has a very small, offstage role in the volumes, then, Mars Jeems represents plantation slavery in a very specific way: he remains the one saved by Remus's shooting of the Yankee, and he is the little boy's most direct male link to the past of slaveholding, as Remus is his link to the past of slavery.

If "A Story of the War" and Mars Jeems's role in it may be taken as constitutive of central structural features of Harris's mythological world, what relationship to it may be discovered in Chesnutt's story "Mars Jeems's Nightmare," which appeared as one of the seven stories in *The Conjure Woman?* "Mars Jeems's Nightmare" stands out among the conjure tales for several reasons. To begin with, it is one of the few that involve the conjuring of a white person, and it therefore occupies a more charged, potentially subversive political ground. In addition, the self-interested purpose of Julius's recital is more transparently figurative in this instance and the layering of the antebellum and postbellum time frames more instructive. In form the tale resembles a widely distributed African American folktale in the Master-John cycle, a group of stories in which the slave John (or Jack) and Master (ole massa, marster, and so on) square off in some kind of contest of wits; and as a tale of physical metamorphosis, it belongs with those that move in the direction of magic realism and can be allied to similar strategies in African folklore. But the story is also an example of Chesnutt's signifying upon Harris, for although Chesnutt might have taken his name from many sources, this Mars Jeems seems undeniably to be a reimagining of Harris's symbolically evocative character.

In the same letter, cited earlier, in which Chesnutt complained to Walter Hines Page about the difficulty of writing effective dialect, he remarked that he did not find the story of metamorphosis in "Mars Jeems's Nightmare" entirely novel but felt that his treatment of it was. "I have thought a good title for the story would be 'De Noo Nig-ger,'" he continued, "but I don't care to dignify a doubtful word quite so much; it is all right for Julius [to use the phrase], but it might leave me under the suspicion of bad taste unless perchance the whole title's being in dialect should redeem it."[3] This added insight into the issue of dialect on Chesnutt's part is important; but

---

3. Letter of May 20, 1898, quoted in Helen Chesnutt, *Charles Waddell Chesnutt*, p. 94.

more striking here is the alternate title itself, which underlines the two-pronged action of the story. In "Mars Jeems's Nightmare" there are two "new niggers"—first, Mars Jeems himself, who by conjure is turned into a slave, brought to his own plantation, and made to undergo the cruelties of his overseer's regime; and second, Julius's grandson, a lazy, incompetent worker, representative of that postwar generation of "new niggers" about whom Uncle Remus often complains. John fires the grandson after a short trial period, but Annie rehires him after the moral of Julius's tale sinks in. Chesnutt's alternate title, "De Noo Nigger," thus addresses a contemporary sociological issue, yet it does so by forcing us to locate the roots of that issue in slavery and racism.

Although Julius may tell his tale in order to gain a more charitable attitude toward his grandson, his tale is powerful in its own right. Stopping at a spring to fill their water jugs, John, Annie, and Julius observe a man riding his horse with furious brutality. It turns out that he is the grandson of the subject of Julius's ensuing story of Mars Jeems McLean, who ran a harsh, hardworking plantation in the old days. Suppressing black folk culture ("dey wa'n't 'lowed ter sing, ner dance, ner play de banjo"), denying slaves any right to court and marry ("said he wuzn' raisin' niggers, but wuz raisin' cotton"), and giving his mean overseer, Nick Johnson, a free hand for cruelty, Mars Jeems is every inch the bad master. When one slave, Solomon, is whipped and his girlfriend sold because of their courting, he employs the conjure woman, Aunt Peggy, to "wuk her roots" and put a "goopher" on master so as to get his girlfriend back. Even though Aunt Peggy admits that she "has ter be kinder keerful 'bout cunj'in' w'ite folks," she agrees to conjure Mars Jeems. His experience of slavery under Nick Johnson is a nightmare lesson in the reversal of roles, but it is also an allegory of the phenomenon of the "noo nigger," as Mars Jeems is called throughout his period of magical transformation. Mars Jeems's incompetence as a laborer and his astonishment at the overseer's brutality reflect two things at once: his own acculturation as a white master and his figurative representation of the new generation of blacks locked into the ambiguities of the post-Reconstruction years, those who feel pride in living and working freely on the one hand, despair at the failure of civil rights and pitiful educational and labor opportunities on the other. Julius's characterization of the new Mars Jeems applies in both cases: he "couldn' 'pear ter git it th'oo his min' dat he wuz a slabe en had ter wuk en min' de w'ite folks." Of course, when the conjure is removed and Jeems recovers from his "monst'us bad dream . . . a reg'lar, nach'ul nightmare," he has undergone at least a limited moral renovation. He fires his overseer, initiates a more humane regime for his slaves, and prospers personally and financially.

"Mars Jeems's Nightmare" stops a good deal short of undermining plantation slavery. Jeems does not free his slaves but only models his new plantation on the extended "family" advocated by proslavery idealists such as George Fitzhugh. In this respect, however, Julius's depiction of the slaves as recognizing Jeems's right as "de marster" to do as he pleases while despising Nick as "nuffin' but a po' buckrah" offers only a beggar's choice between benevolent and cruel subjugation. Similarly, his assertion that "in dem days any 'spectable pusson would ruther be a nigger dan a po' w'ite man," while it purports to illuminate the complex psychology of class on the plantation, more directly points to the half-truth of the postbellum southern contention that racial violence was a manifestation of lower-class white backlash. It cannot be proved that Julius is speaking entirely ironically in his statements. But his specious signifying on the rights of the master is clearly calculated to reveal the racist genealogy of John's naive framing comment about Julius's personality. Julius, he observes, had been so long accustomed to think of himself a slave that in the postwar years "he had been unable to break off entirely the mental habits of a lifetime, but had attached himself to the old plantation, of which he seemed to consider himself an appurtenance." It is Chesnutt who is speaking ironically now. Julius, although he is no Remus, is indeed an appurtenance of the plantation myth, inscribed by the habits of white thought into the southern (and national) consciousness. As a commentator on black attitudes he here repeats a "darky" view whose implications are scarcely less unsettling for the post-Reconstruction years than for the antebellum, no matter how certain we are that Chesnutt intended Julius's remarks as a test of his audience's moral acuity. The story, that is to say, employs Julius both as a character and as a symbol, the two forces not always in perfect congruity.

Before looking in more detail at Chesnutt's reworking of Harris's points of view, I would like to turn briefly to a second informing feature of "Mars Jeems's Nightmare" that will serve to characterize that difference more sharply. Chesnutt's tale, as he recognized, is novel in its treatment but not in its general plot. Although the story may have a number of antecedents, it strongly resembles a common example of the Master-John stories generally entitled the "Philly-Me-York" tale. In the tale's typical outline, Master pretends to go away on a trip (to "Philly-Me-York" or "Phillynewyork," as the slaves confusedly, or creatively, understand it) but dons a ragged disguise and returns to his plantation, where he catches his trusted slave John, as he had suspected, throwing a big "frolic" for the slaves, dancing, drinking, butchering Master's hogs, wearing his clothes, and so on. When Master reveals himself, John is caught and punished, or runs away, or, alternatively, talks his way out of the trouble.

Some versions of the tale have John escaping to the next county, getting whipped, or begging forgiveness at the end. But Zora Neale Hurston's version in *Mules and Men* (1935), which essentially combines two Master-John tales, is far more intricate and complimentary to John. When Master threatens to hang John for "killing up all my hogs and havin' all these niggers in my house," John engages his friend Jack to hide in the hanging tree and strike matches while John prays for God to throw bolts of lightning if he is willing to grant John's prayer that Master and his family and plantation will be destroyed. The trick works, of course. Master is so frightened that he gives John "his freedom and a heap of land and stock" before running away himself: "and that's how come niggers got they freedom today."[4] Hurston's tale traces emancipation not to patient subservience but to cunning and aggression.

The Master-John stories are a strong influence on Chesnutt's tales generally (the form seldom appears in Harris's Remus tales), and they are one of the most powerful examples of African American folklore. Sometimes Master wins the contest, and sometimes John; but the strategies at work make it clear that from John's black perspective they constitute a methodology of rebellion and a means of attacking the master directly, in deeds or more often in words. More than occasionally the tale ends with Master's defeat, even his death, as in a combination animal-John trickster tale recorded by Hurston in which Master is tricked into drowning himself. For the most part, however, the tales maintain a taut balance of power (an "uneasy partnership" in a "harsh and lethal conflict," as Richard Dorson remarks), and John is able to gain only limited victories through his verbal cunning and exploitation of the masked roles of slave existence. In this respect they measure the price of power and subjugation in more human terms, displaying both the rewards and the hazards of the trickster role. The Master-John tales were written down far less often than the animal trickster tales, suggesting a self-censorship by black informants more stringent than usual. Because they do not disguise their meaning in the costumes of animal mythology and are typically narrated as though they were memories rather than fantasies, the Master-John tales are more overtly threatening but also more pragmatic and balanced in their dramatization of the struggle for control. They demonstrate effectively that the great majority of slaves did not internalize the rules or humiliating

---

4. Roger D. Abrahams, *Afro-American Folktales* (New York: Pantheon, 1985), pp. 291–92; Lawrence W. Levine, *Black Culture and Black Consciousness* (Oxford: Oxford UP, 1978), p. 129; Richard M. Dorson, *American Negro Folktales* (New York: Fawcett, 1968), pp. 151–52; Zora Neale Hurston, *Mules and Men: Negro Folktales and Voodoo Practices in the South* (New York: Harper and Row, 1970), pp. 112–14.

postures of slavery but engaged, at the level of imagination as well as that of action, in outright rebellions against the master's power.[5]

*   *   *

His lesson for John and Annie, and for his readers, was that the generation of New Negroes must be given opportunities to prosper and that the sense of the southern as well as the national family must become truly interracial. Whereas Harris sometimes tentatively held forth plantation slavery, in its most humane forms, as a plausible labor relation (his ideal was a yeoman agrarianism) and a potentially fine realization of paternal society, Chesnutt maintained no such illusion. As always, Julius, playing the "John" role in a Master-John confrontation with his boss, gets the best of his own master, John. Even though the carpetbagger John has not yet undergone the moral transformation that affects Mars Jeems, Julius's grandson gets a second chance, while Remus's grandson, by contrast, will go to jail.

The fact that the narrated story ends not with freedom but with a more humane slavery, then, is misleading. For Julius's tale does gain from John a more lenient attitude toward his grandson, part of the new generation born after slavery; and in the nearly mad laughter of Mars Jeems as he interrogates his overseer about his cruelty toward the "noo nigger" who was "puttin' on airs, des lack he wuz a w'ite man," it registers a double frenzy, signaling both Jeems's vengeful hatred of the overseer (the emotion Chesnutt could easily imagine in a slave but could not, apparently, afford to portray except through dislocation) and the mad laughter of his own self-recognition as a master. Julius is so forward with the moral of his tale in this case—white folks must make allowances for "po' ign'ant niggers w'at ain' had no chanst ter l'arn"—that the discrepancy between John's and Annie's separate recognitions of it hardly matters. As the other "noo nigger" in the story, Julius's grandson represents the generation, Chesnutt says, for whom allowances must be made, economic opportunities and education carefully provided.

5. Hurston, *Mules and Men*, pp. 65–68; Dorson, *American Negro Folktales*, p. 124; Levine, *Black Culture and Black Consciousness*, pp. 127–29; Dickson A. Bruce, Jr., "The 'John and Old Master' Stories and the World of Slavery: A Study in Folktales and History," *Phylon* 35 (December 1974): 418–29; John W. Roberts, *From Trickster to Badman: The Black Folk Hero in Slavery and Freedom* (Philadelphia: U of Pennsylvania P, 1989), pp. 44–64; Charles Joyner, *Down by the Riverside: A South Carolina Slave Community* (Urbana: U of Illinois P, 1984), pp. 183–89.

RICHARD H. BRODHEAD

[Chesnutt's Negotiation with the Dominant Literary Culture]†

Chesnutt's conjure tales are in one sense remarkable for their massive conventionality. Brilliantly inventive in their conceits and suave in the manner of their telling, in their fictional structures these early tales stick close to the most formulaic features of their genre: the white speaker's prologue; the handing over of the speaking function to an old black uncle; the black folktale told in heavy dialect. One difference of Chesnutt's practice is that without in any sense exploding the artifice of this kind of tale, Chesnutt lightly underlines the fact of its artificiality. Chesnutt stays so close to generic conventions that they inevitably become revealed, though without comment or overt parody, as conventions: when, in the dozen conjure stories Chesnutt eventually wrote, Uncle Julius always shows up at an opportune moment *yet again*, with *yet another* story to tell in which someone *yet again* seeks out "the cunjuh wom'n up tuh deh Lumberton road" who *yet again* (for a price) "wukd huh roots," we learn to recognize the set moves of a certain formal protocol. The air of slight stiltedness or lightly indicated artificiality that Chesnutt produces for this form is also conveyed through his stories' half-exposed pastoralism, their manufacture of a version of history charmingly, even delightfully, ahistorical—as in the conceit that a quite bucolic grape industry, not the nonbucolic tobacco or textile industries of 1880s history, represents a principal form of North Carolina's postwar economic development. (Chesnutt's stories let us in on the joke of regionalism's "realism" if we recognize such fancies as fancies; if we do not, they pass this genre's pastoral fictions on us with straight face.)

But if Chesnutt embraces the unrealities of this form, he also achieves an unusual precision of historical identification for the parties to the regionalist transaction. The John of the conjure stories is thus the thousandth incarnation of the well-spoken frame narrator who comes to a region from afar, a fictional brother—if not formulaic substitute—for the white traveller of Page's "Marse Chan," the Cumberland vacationer of Murfree's "Dancin' Party at Harrison's Cove," the city girls on retreat in Jewett's *Deephaven*, and so on. But Chesnutt's rendering of this wholly stock figure is, by the standards

† From *Cultures of Letters: Scenes of Reading and Writing in Nineteenth-Century America* (Chicago: U of Chicago P, 1993), pp. 196–205. Reprinted by permission. Notes have been edited.

of this genre, unusually rich in social markers. John begins "The Goophered Grapevine":

> Some years ago my wife was in poor health, and our family doctor, in whose skill and honesty I had implicit confidence, advised a change of climate. I shared, from an unprofessional standpoint, his opinion that the raw winds, the chill rains, and the violent changes of temperature that characterized the winters in the region of the Great Lakes tended to aggravate my wife's difficulty, and would undoubtedly shorten her life if she remained exposed to them. The doctor's advice was that we seek, not a temporary place of sojourn, but a permanent residence, in a warmer and more equable climate. I was engaged at the time in grape-culture in Northern Ohio, and as I liked the business and had given it much study, I decided to look for some locality suitable for carrying it on. I thought of sunny France, of sleepy Spain, of Southern California, but there were objections to them all. It occurred to me that I might find what I wanted in our own Southern States. It was a sufficient time after the war for conditions in the South to have become somewhat settled; and I was enough of a pioneer to start a new industry, if I could not find a place where grape-culture had been tried. I wrote to a cousin who had gone into the turpentine business in central North Carolina. He assured me, in response to my inquiries, that no better place could be found in the South than the State and neighborhood where he lived; the climate was perfect for health, and, in conjunction with the soil, ideal for grape-culture; labor was cheap, and land could be bought for a mere song.

Every time he opens his mouth, this man says where he comes from in the America of his time. He is Northern, of course. But his Latinate diction and measured speech rhythms also mark him as of the educated class; his wife's health marks him as of the class in which women are leisured and inclined to neurasthenia; his deference to doctors ties him to the social formation in which medicine has become a province of certified professionals and nonprofessionals have been made into amateurs; his thoughts of Spain, France, and California link him to the class that practices international and domestic tourism; his history in the grape business says that he is used to owning the means of production (in Ohio he must have known Mr. Welch and Mr. Smucker); his wish to found industries where land and labor are cheap shows him of the class that initiates economic development in underdeveloped zones. All of these traits identify John as of the upper middle class stabilized in the North in the 1850s and after—a class which, as Chesnutt shows, is defined not by one or two traits but by a whole range of dispositions conformed together. By marking him as it does, Chesnutt's tale expresses its sense of where the contemporary incursion on regional cultures is coming from. It makes clear that the outside world is impinging on the local not through mere individual visits or the march of a generalized "modernity" but through a concrete social process, through a certain social group's pursuit of its particular investment and recreational interests.

Uncle Julius, the black vernacular speaker of Chesnutt's tales, is as conventional a figure as John, and his conventionality too is emphasized, not disguised: witness his minimal departure in name from Harris's Uncle Remus. But without realizing Julius out of his formulaic origin, Chesnutt is careful to link him too to a real contemporary culture—in this case the unmodernized black folk culture to be found in country districts. Here again Chesnutt takes pains to render the whole form of a social "world." Julius's is a world with a different verbal form: his speech is regionally accented, not delocalized; his is the language of speaking, not (like John's) of speech imitating writing. (Julius's words are often unintelligible when read but intelligible enough when mentally voiced.) Julius's world has its own differently constructed medical system, based on "cha'ms" and conjure women, not rest cures and male professionals. It has its own organization of religion, a voodoo-derived religion of "ha'nts" and spirit management most unlike John's decorous but despiritualized Christianity. It has its own economy, conducted through face-to-face exchanges of goods and services, not abstract market relations. It has its own different sense of space: in Julius's world people belong somewhere and stay there instead of moving around; places and things are not abstractly interchangeable (as Spain and California are for John) but wholly distinct, distinguished by the lived histories associated with them— so the swamp that to John is just more land to develop is to Julius a place in particular to be honored as such, the place where Mahaly was buried; the place where the branch creek crosses the short road is the place where Chloe drowned herself; and so on. And Julius's world has its own different mechanism of cultural self-maintenance: the telling of stories. Storytelling as *The Conjure Woman* presents it marks a distinction between America's local and postlocal societies: Julius knows a thousand stories, John (apparently) none. In a culture like Julius's, Chesnutt brilliantly suggests, tale-telling is not mere pastime but the means by which a sense of the world is stored and transmitted. When Julius wants John to realize what something around him means, he always tells him the whole story: the meaning is, as it were, lodged in the tale, which must be orally recollected for the meaning to be made present again. (When John's wife Annie asks "'And why does Chloe's haunt walk?'" in "Hot-Foot Hannibal," Julius replies: "'It's all in de tale, ma'm, it's all in de tale.'")

In Jewett the relations between an outlander and the native of an herbal, magical, storytelling, place-specific world are friendly, indeed hospitable. But one of Chesnutt's distinctions among local colorists is that he understands the parties to the regionalist dialogue to be antagonists, not friends. Once he has set up his juxtaposition of these two cultural formations, Chesnutt unfolds a contest between them, a contest of domination and indigenous resistance played out on several planes.

Within Julius's tales, slavery is the scene of this contention. The former white masters and their black slaves are the contending parties here, and the slaves' art of "cunjuh" forms the heart of the struggle between them. Always the object of special interest to fictional historians of African-American folk culture (Chesnutt's history of conjure has George Washington Cable's *The Grandissimes* behind it and Zora Neale Hurston's *Mules and Men* ahead of it), conjure is understood in *The Conjure Woman* at once as a magical art for the management of life forces and a quite practical social institution, the means for blacks to carry forward courtships, pay back injuries, and so on. But Chesnutt also shows that when this African-derived system gets enclosed within the system of American slavery it takes on a further function, as a recourse for the oppressed. These is no such thing as total domination in Chesnutt. When one group is subjugated by another its own cultural institutions get carried into subjugation with it, and institutions that were once just facts of its life are remade into forms for possible resistance. So conjure, part of the religion of the slaves before slavery, survives into slavery as a power slaves can resort to against the domination of their masters. And in Julius's tales this power works: by magically making their master the object of his own harsh work discipline, the slaves of "Mars Jeems's Nightmare" school him out of his cult of infinite productivity; through conjure's metamorphic powers the mother and child in "Sis' Becky's Pickaninny" overcome the slaveholder's power to break family bonds. But conjure's resistance, if it is never impotent, is never omnipotent either; and Chesnutt's tales are at their most moving in charting the limits of such power.

"Po' Sandy" provides an example here. The slave Sandy's story is a parabolic revelation of what slavery means. Sandy is such a good worker that all his master's children want to have his services. Since this father is generous he divides up Sandy's time, sending him off each month to work for a different child. The point here, as always wholly unstated, is that in slavery the more capable one is, the more others desire to own his labor; and that to be a slave means to be at someone else's disposal, literally not to be able to be where one wishes to be. When he reaches the limit of his ability to tolerate such domination, gets "monst'us ti'ed er dish yer gwine roun' so much," Sandy asserts his hunger to regain control of his own location—"I wisht I wuz a tree, er a stump, er a rock, er sump'n w'at could stay on de plantation fer a w'ile"; and with these words conjure magically reveals itself as a way out. Sandy's wife turns out to be a semiretired conjure woman, and through her potent art she changes Sandy, rescues him from the hardships of the human order by turning him into a tree. But the master owns Sandy the tree as surely as he owned Sandy the man, and when he needs lumber on a day when Sandy's wife has been sent to work elsewhere, he has the tree felled and milled to his ends. (The milling of Sandy is one of American literature's great images of the violence of manufacture.) The slave's imaginative recourse itself turns out to be at the master's disposal; so that the same story that reveals the power of residual cultural forms like conjure also plots that power's final limit, its inability to change the fact of domination within which it acts.

In content the conjure stories have antebellum slavery as their historical referent. But at the level of their telling they gauge dominances and resistances in another social situation, the new economic order of the postbellum South. Julius's stories are told on the site of impending development. Julius has what John calls a "predial rather than a proprietary" attitude toward "my tract of land and the things that were on it."[1] Together with his other different cultural understandings, he has a different understanding of property, based not on the alienable ownership of buying and selling but on possession through personal contiguity and association, and aimed not toward maximized return on investment but the maintenance of traditional uses. In this, Julius is linked to the historical populations of blacks who stayed on their former plantations after slavery but strove to work them to their own interests and in their own ways, according to the precapitalist ethic of their distinctive group culture.[2] John represents the incursion, upon such postemancipation black folk economies, of another form of domination based in another alien economics. He has come South to acquire land and labor "cheap" because not exploited for maximized profit and to manage it for such profit, sending his product to a national market by a newly built rail link (R. J. Reynolds might be his real-life prototype); and he represents the threatened expropriation of the possible economic resources of postwar Southern blacks for a Northern-style capitalist mode of production.[3]

In *The Conjure Woman* Julius always appears at the point where this new order impinges on his more traditional interests. And in the

1. The *Oxford English Dictionary* (1933 ed.) defines "predial" as "arising from or consequent upon the occupation of farms or lands," "attached to farms or to the land."
2. For a suggestive historical account using South Carolina materials, see John Scott Strickland, "Traditional Culture and Moral Economy: Social and Economic Change in the South Carolina Low Country, 1865–1910," in *The Countryside in the Age of Capitalist Transformation*, pp. 141–78.
3. For a historical account of the New South development of North Carolina—in 1860 the poorest Southern state but in 1900 the industrial leader of the South—see Dwight B. Billings, Jr., *Planters and the Making of a "New South": Class, Politics, and Development in North Carolina, 1865–1900* (Chapel Hill: U of North Carolina P, 1979).

face of this new domination, he too is not without resources. The residual culture of blacks in slavery has endowed him with his own cultural possession—stories—that can be redeployed as a means to cultural self-defense. By telling stories of "slabery days" Julius exerts his own conjurelike power, and here again this power works. Through the action of storytelling Julius persuades his hearers to curtail their development plans and so protects his residual uses of their land. By telling "Po' Sandy," Julius talks John out of making the old schoolhouse over into a new kitchen, and so preserves it as a place for his church to meet. By telling "Mars Jeems's Nightmare," he talks a new master out of a new cult of efficiency and productivity, and gets his shiftless relative rehired. By telling "The Gray Wolf's Ha'nt," he persuades John to leave the swamp undeveloped for agribusiness purposes, and so protects his own "monopoly" in the honey tree located there. But if Julius and his mode of enchantment exert real power, that power too has clear limits. Every time he wins a concession from a new property order, Julius pays tribute to the fact that that order can't not be dealt with. Julius wins local advantages through storytelling while conceding that his situation as a whole is under someone else's control.

Chesnutt's fables describe the asymmetrical power struggles of antebellum blacks against antebellum slavery. They describe the similarly asymmetrical struggles of postwar blacks against New South economic history. But these fables also engage a third historical situation, in which their author is much more nearly involved. Within *The Conjure Woman*, John and Annie may represent a certain mode of economics but they function primarily as an audience (what they do in the book is listen to stories); and their life as an audience is defined with the same social precision as the rest of their attributes. John and Annie listen to Julius's tales but they are more used to reading: this couple is found reading in several stories before better entertainment comes along. Unlike Julius, Annie and John come from a world where stories are assumed to be written by other people and circulated in print, not collectively known and shared. Their reading, in turn, is set in a larger ethos that ranges such entertainment under the values of high culture, respectable privacy, and decorous self-control. Reading has these affiliations (for instance) in John's opening to "The Conjurer's Revenge":

> [Sunday] afternoons we spent at home, for the most part, occupying ourselves with the newspapers and magazines, and the contents of a fairly good library. We had a piano in the house, on which my wife played with skill and feeling. I possessed a passable baritone voice, and could accompany myself indifferently well when my wife was not by to assist me.

All of these traits link Julius's audience with a particularized historical audience of Chesnutt's time that shared John and Annie's other marks as well: their wealth; their leisure; their disposition toward vacation travel; their attraction to undeveloped places. These hearers figure the class of readers addressed in the high-cultural literary journals of the post–Civil War decades. They embody the suggestion that the same socially assertive contemporary class that manifests itself in the economic realm in capitalistic development reappears in the cultural sphere as the public with "cultured" tastes.

Through these identifications Chesnutt puts his own audience at issue in his work and makes his fables figure a negotiation with a dominant literary culture. The periodicals that produced "high" literary writing toward a leisure-class public in the later nineteenth century, we have many times noted, were the chief cultural vehicles for American regional fiction. Genteel hearers form the frame for Chesnutt's conjure tales because Chesnutt knows that readers like these in their entertainment habits and social interests frame the scene of reception for stories like his own. (By the time of the conjure stories Chesnutt knows the social composition of "readers to the North" much more precisely than he did in his 1880 journal entries.) Faced with an audience so composed, Chesnutt was by no means wholly disadvantaged. This public's hunger for the colorful ways of "different" local cultures made Chesnutt's knowledge of Southern black voices and folktales into a marketable asset. In this situation Chesnutt too was able to activate a black vernacular heritage as a force in aid of his interests. And Chesnutt's conjure at a third remove, like Julius's, produced real results. By retelling these stories, by resynthesizing black oral culture within the written forms of a high-cultural genre, Chesnutt was able to make something of himself. When "The Goophered Grapevine" and "Po' Sandy" were accepted in the *Atlantic*, this literary nobody was able to establish himself as an author in the cultural site that carried the greatest degree of prestige.[4]

But the bleak wisdom of the conjure stories is that conjure exercises power only within situations that set limits to its power—a moral Chesnutt clearly applies to himself. Julius masters John and Annie's attention through his stories, and his hearers give him economic advantage and an improved position as a reward for his work. But Julius is not only a winner in this exchange: his audience gets, if it also

---

4. Chesnutt's letters make clear that he cared about where he was published in just such terms: "I would prefer that your house bring out the book; the author having first been recognized by you (so far as any high class publication is concerned,)" he wrote Houghton, Mifflin in 1891; in 1897 he reiterated of his stories: "their chance . . . will be very much enhanced if they are brought out by a concern of Houghton, Mifflin and Company's standing. It is not difficult to find publishers of some kind, on some terms—but there are publishers and publishers" (Helen Chesnutt, *Charles W. Chesnutt*, pp. 69, 86).

gives, through the transaction of storytelling. These hearers are often bored. The way of life they have organized for themselves makes things both scrupulously refined and—as John confesses at the end of his inventory of reading materials and musical accomplishments—"a little dull." At times this boredom mounts to the pitch of crisis: in "Sis' Becky's Pickaninny," Annie has fallen into a *tedium vitae* suggestive of the sickness unto death. It is against the background of this deep experiential deprivation that Annie turns to Julius for entertainment— "a story would be a godsend today," says this wife almost terminally bored; and when he tells his stories she recovers "delightful animation." *This is her gain.* By entering into Julius's stories, this person devitalized by her own cultural refinements can imaginatively possess the more amusing, or pathetic, or tragic, in short the more fully *animated* life of blacks in slavery, and thereby reclaim a life force she has forfeited. In exchange for this gain Annie makes concessions to Julius, but he has purchased them at a price. *He has put his peoples' life at someone else's disposal. He has served one group's life up as the stuff of another group's entertainment.*

CANDACE J. WAID

Conjuring the Conjugal: Chesnutt's Scenes from a Marriage†

"If I do write, I shall write for a purpose, a high, holy purpose, and this will inspire me to greater effort. The object of my writings would be not so much the elevation of the colored people as the elevation of the whites. . . . [T]he subtle almost indefinable feeling of repulsion toward the negro, which is common to most Americans— and easily enough accounted for—, cannot be stormed and taken by assault; the garrison will not capitulate: so their position must be mined, and we will find ourselves in their midst before they think it."—Charles Chesnutt's journal entry, May 29, 1880

Although the cultural trope of marriages between Southern men and Northern women has traditionally been seen as restoring union and moral balance to a dangerously divided nation, few if any of the writers for the national magazines in the postbellum decades proposed solving the race problem in America through intermarriage. Charles Chesnutt's tales repeatedly follow the convention of parallel plots; life in the quarters, even the stories of life from the past, has an effect on the relationships among the plantation class. Tales in

---

† Published for the first time in this Norton Critical Edition.

The Conjure Woman try to restore order through marriages which rewrite the stories of the past, linking the fate of the lovers among the white elite to the struggles of the black poor, in particular the trials of slaves who have been divided from their beloveds. Enacting narratives of exile and return, of estrangement and familiarization, entering into the at once painful and wishful narratives of both the African-American folk tradition and the white local color tradition, Chesnutt's conjure tales return to rituals of marriage and reunion to rehearse the ways in which these Southern communities are painfully joined as well as woundingly divided.

Chesnutt introduces the popular trope of a North-South wedding at an important moment in the history of his composition of the conjure tales—in "Hot-Foot Hannibal," the story he wrote specifically to conclude his 1899 story collection, *The Conjure Woman*. But "Hot-Foot Hannibal" is devoted to resolving more than the regional conflict raised in Chesnutt's tales; in particular, it revisits the narrative of a more disturbing story of marriage, "The Dumb Witness," which Chesnutt would not publish in his lifetime.[1] In this suppressed story about the silencing of tongues, a proposed marriage between North and South is thwarted because of the discovery of a deeper intimacy, the problem of a pre-existing and more profound union between the Southern master and the "comely" slave who has had (and maintains) control of the plantation household.[2] It is this hidden union, between the white man and black woman, which prevents the hot-tempered Southerner's marriage to the widowed Martha Todd from Pennsylvania—whose name echoes that of the most famous Northern widow of all time, Mary Todd Lincoln. Here the forbidden yet commonly enacted sexual union between the races pre-empts the cooling influence on the Southern man promised through his marriage to the Northern white woman, a figure who rises to the level of a type in Chesnutt's plantation tales. Like the reform-minded Annie (the Northern narrator's wife) and her high-minded sister Mabel, who is the sought-after woman in "Hot-Foot Hannibal," the Northern widow in "The Dumb Witness" is the locus of moral scruples in the pre-War era. Already well-schooled in the behavior of men through her experience of her previous marriage, the widow cites Saint Paul in the letter she writes refusing to sacrifice her widowed peace to the mission of reforming the hot-tempered, cruel, and passionate Murchison man.

1. "Hot-Foot Hannibal" refers as well to the uncollected tale "Lonesome Ben," since Julius tells the story of Chloe's loss of her lover as the stalled mule and buggy stand beside the amber stream which, according to the then-unpublished story, has become yellowed by the broken fragments of Ben's remains.
2. The story of this union not only cannot be told, it must be covered over. Not only are there no suggestions of interracial passion in *The Conjure Woman*, the stock figure of African American fiction and narrative—the jealous plantation mistress—is also absent.

Selecting what was already a familiar theme, a romantic plot that would become a standard feature in films as well as novels, "Hot-Foot Hannibal" begins by presenting the prospect of a marriage between North and South as Mabel, John's sister-in-law from Ohio, is set to marry the Southern Malcolm Murchison. However, this potential marriage is called into question by the opening lines of the story as John's sister-in-law in "passionately vibrant tones" tells her beloved: "I hate you and despise you! I wish never to see you or speak to you again!" Playing the piano loudly after Malcolm Murchison's exit, Mabel displays to John's ears "a dash of exultation, as though she were really glad that she had driven away the young man whom the day before she had loved with all the ardor of a first passion." John, who has "heartily consented to [this young man's] marriage with his ward," has also seen the coming marriage as an event that will unite him to his new home: "The match thus rudely broken off had promised to be another link binding me to the kindly Southern people among whom I had not long before taken up my residence." While John hopes that "time might heal the breach and bring the two young people together again," Annie sees the division as irrevocable. Doubting that the dispute could "'ever be settled,'" Annie insists "'there were things said which no woman of spirit could stand.'"

Predictably, in the story within the story, Uncle Julius once again tells a tale of the past which seems designed to resolve the difficulties of the present. His story of ill-fated lovers who have been divided forever brings about the healing of "the breach" between the proud Southern man and his high-spirited and willful Northern fiancée. In Julius's story, Mars Dugal and his wife consider two different slaves for their new houseboy; and as they select Hannibal instead of Jeff, Mars Dugal promises Hannibal "'ef you er a good nigger en min's yo' bizness, I'll gib you Chloe fer a wife nex' spring.'" In contrast to his support of individual preferences where he allows his slaves to select their own mates in "A Deep Sleeper" (Skundus and Cindy) and in "Dave's Neckliss" (Dave and Dilsey), here Mars Dugal McAdoo proposes a wedding without observing the preferences of the woman in question; and the house servant Chloe, watching her master and mistress make their decision, has come to a different conclusion. Trusting the bonds forged by slavery and the master's power to give ("gib") what he claims belongs to him, Hannibal is so "sho' he wuz gwine ter git 'er in de spring, dat he didn' 'pear ter 'low he had ter do any co'tin'.'" As he tells Chloe to come and kiss him, he insists "'you gwine ter be mine in de spring. You doan 'pear ter be ez fon' er me ez you oughter be.'" In her efforts to avoid being given as a gift at her own wedding, Chloe sends Jeff to the conjure woman who constructs a "baby doll," which she marks as Hannibal out of fragments of the natural world. The doll hidden under the doorstep has, among other things, red pepper shoes which cause Hannibal to become hot-footed and clumsy as he tries to perform his duties. After getting Hannibal sent back to the fields, Chloe informs him that she and Jeff are "'gwine ter git married in de spring, en you ain' gwine ter be 'vited ter de weddin' nuther.'"

In the end, Hannibal manages to part Jeff and Chloe forever by making an effigy of his own. After telling Chloe that Jeff is seeing another woman, Hannibal dresses himself in women's clothes so that from a distance Chloe watches as Jeff seems to meet another woman. Although both Jeff and Chloe end up bereft and drowned, there is an interesting turn in this story as the roles of husband and wife, master and missus, are reversed. This same mistress who has argued against the meaning of sentimental attachments in "A Deep Sleeper," saying "[o]ne nigger man is de same as ernudder," pleads Chloe's case here. As Mars Dugal insists that Chloe can marry the new house boy, "'ole mis' say, no, Chloe ain' dat kin'er gal, en dat Mars Dugal' sh'd buy Jeff back.'" In "Hot-Foot Hannibal," Mabel is moved by this story in which lovers are parted by misunderstanding and death and she is reunited with her estranged lover who is set to leave on the same day, having announced that he "'prob'ly . . . ain' neber comin' back.'" Following the narrative formula of the tales, "Hot-Foot Hannibal" concludes with John being "skeptical about [Julius's] motives." "[A]fter the reconciliation," as John observes, "a most excellent understanding existed between him [Julius] and Murchison." Closing with a union effected between North and South as the newly married couple "set[s] up housekeeping at the old Murchison place," this union, in an echo of the exchange of enslaved people as gifts precipitated by weddings before the War, threatens to bring about a scene of separation as well, as the Murchisons offer Julius an "opportunity to enter their service." Yet in this post-War economy he is free to decline the offer, allowing *The Conjure Woman* to conclude with yet another confirmation of unity as John announces that Julius "preferred to remain with us."

"Hot-Foot Hannibal" intimates that the story of a broken engagement between a slave couple from the past has the power to mend a ruptured romance among the white elite in the present. In Chesnutt's most disturbing story about conjugal union, though, the only marriage that is proposed is never consummated. "The Dumb Witness" is the story of a thwarted marriage between North and South in the years before the war, and it also concerns a childless bachelor named Malcolm Murchison—unquestionably, the ancestor of the Malcolm Murchison who suffers the broken engagement at the opening of "Hot-Foot Hannibal." When the younger Malcolm Murchison and Mabel, his Northern bride, move into what is called the "old Murchison place"—the place that is described in "The Dumb Witness"—they take part in the rewriting of an old and troubling legacy. While the earlier events are not mentioned, the relationship between the two tales (each of which concerns the prospective and endangered marriage of a Malcolm Murchison) is so important that "Hot-Foot Hannibal" might be called a silent partner to "The Dumb Witness."

"The Dumb Witness" tells an unspeakable story about a woman who appears to have been robbed of the power of speech. Ostensibly a composite version of what the narrator John has seen at the Murchison plantation, the tale Julius tells him, and information gathered from other sources, "The Dumb Witness" is the only one of the conjure tales in which John not only narrates the frame, but also tells the interior story in his own voice. In a disconcerting variation of what Richard Brodhead calls Chesnutt's "plot of bilingualism,"[3] the narration of this story about a horrible and obstinate silence for the most part is not rendered in dialect. Recalling the opening of the first published story of *The Conjure Woman*, "The Goophered Grapevine" (1887), John enters this story by driving between the "decaying gateposts" that mark an old homestead; like the seemingly abandoned vineyard of Chesnutt's first conjure tale, the dilapidated Murchison place is haunted by the living. The scene seems Edenic, and "some fragments" of what might be imagined as a more elegant past "still remained": "the one massive hinge, hanging by a slender rust-eaten nail, had been wrought into a fantastic shape." As John and Julius drive "through the gateway," the setting is definitely post-paradise: "a green lizard scampered down from the top of one of the posts, where he had been sunning himself, and a rattlesnake lying in the path lazily uncoiled his motley brown length, and, sounding his rattle the meanwhile, wriggled slowly off into the rank grass of weeds." This is a scene of a fallen hierarchy where the "rank" that once signified prestige and privilege now marks a luxuriant scene of rot, rich with fetid growth. While the weeds flourish, the Murchison place appears to have been despoiled, pocked with "hillocks and hollows, as though it had been dug over at hazard, or explored by some vagrant drove of hogs. At one side, beyond this barren area, lay an enclosed kitchen garden, in which a few collards and okra-plants and tomato vines struggled desperately against neglect and drought and poverty of soil."

In this ravaged garden, John encounters a man and a woman. Entering a "lonely," "desolate," and "untenanted" place, the Northern narrator recalls, "[a]s we approached we became aware of two

---

3. Richard H. Brodhead, Introduction, *The Conjure Woman and Other Conjure Tales* (Durham: Duke UP, 1993), p. 2.

figures on the piazza. At one end of it, in a massive arm-chair of carved oak, a man was seated. . . . His thin white hair hung down upon his shoulders. His face was of a high-bred and strongly marked type, with something of the hawk-like contour usually associated with extreme acquisitiveness. His eyes were turned toward the opposite end of the piazza, where a woman was also seated." The woman, suggestively named Viney, is said to seem "but little younger than the man, and her face was enough like his, in a feminine way, to suggest that they might be related in some degree, unless this inference was negatived by the woman's complexion of darker blood." As he approaches the porch, John hears a conversation that seems to have gone on for generations between Malcolm Murchison and the aged woman, once his slave and still his housekeeper. Both the symmetry in their arrangement and the similarity in their features indicate the presence of a strong relationship between these figures, suggesting that like Adam and Eve, or Faulkner's Charles Bon and Judith Sutpen, they too might share the same father.

Like the destruction of the Spencer oak in "The Marked Tree" and the fatally damaged roots of the grapes in "The Goophered Grapevine," "The Dumb Witness" tells of a violent cutting at the root of a primal source—in this instance Viney's tongue. This maiming causes the demise of a whole plantation and seems to contribute to the diversion of fertility which has prevented inheritance by direct descent among the Murchisons for at least two generations. In the conversation overheard by John, the fallen master pleads with his former slave to reveal an important secret; and then reverting to an older form, he insists: "tell me immediately, you hussy, or you will have reason to regret it. You take liberties that cannot be permitted. I will not put up with it. . . . I shall have to have you whipped." While Murchison's threat places the origins of this conversation in a different era, Viney, as she begins to speak, makes sounds that suggest that the distance that she articulates is finally not calculable in years. To the Northern narrator, her words sound like "a foreign tongue": "But after a moment I knew that no language or dialect, at least none of European origin, could consist of such a discordant jargon, such a meaningless cacophony as that which fell from the woman's lips."

As Malcolm Murchison continues his exasperated pleading, he speaks of knowing "it was wrong" and insists "I've always regretted it—always since the first day I did it." Without saying what "it" is, Murchison implores the listening woman to behave like a Christian: to "do good to them who despitefully use you." Throughout "The Dumb Witness," this woman with "inscrutable eyes" asks to be read; and as the "slumbrous fire" repeatedly flashes in her eyes in response to Murchison's pleas, the story reminds us that these are the same eyes with which she had once looked at him from what is called her "bed of pain." As the Northern narrator watches the mystery being enacted before him, in what must be read as a painfully suggestive gesture (whether recalling a scene of manumission or matrimony), John observes the former master "offering to take [Viney's] hand"; he observes that "she drew her hand away."

The deeper narrative that Julius later tells John, a story of "jealousy, revenge, and disappointment," has its beginnings in the years before the War, before the man and woman "'bofe [became] 'stracted . . . out'n dey min'.'" Viney's position in the Murchison place is suggested by the fact that aside from the aged cook, she ("the young comely quadroon") is the only woman mentioned as part of the Murchison household. Described as "single" "for ten or fifteen years," Malcolm Murchison has been the master of a household where "the foot of a white woman had not touched the floor for fifteen years"; and, as if to make the point more clearly, the narrative insists: "ladies never set foot in the Murchison house." Like Faulkner's Sutpen's Hundred before the windows and doors are put in, Murchison's house has been a place of masculine pleasures and pursuits where men smoked, drank, gambled, and "bought and sold produce or slaves." Viney, who has assumed the intimate offices of a wife by looking after "his clothing and his table" is described as having been "in power" over this realm for many years. Although the terms of Viney's "power" are never articulated, the sense of her authority in the Murchison household is suggested by the duration of her domestic rule.

The undisputed place of Viney in the Murchison world and the related depth of her passion appear most clearly when she learns that her master plans to replace her with another woman. What is for Viney a deeply emotional story, is for her master merely an act of exchange, a rearrangement of a hierarchy. After Murchison proposes marriage to a wealthy Northern widow, "[h]e broke the news to his housekeeper by telling her to make the house ready for a mistress." Viney, who is described as having "some passionate strain of . . . mixed blood in her veins—a very human blood," pleads with him in what is called "a fit of hysterical violence." Warning her to be "quiet and obedient," Murchison listens to the scene which "he had anticipated" and then warns her, "I have heard what you have to say—this once—and it will be useless for you to repeat it, for I shall not listen again." In this scene, his major threat is that he may not send Viney away, but rather keep her on in the house under the rule of his new bride: "If you are reasonable, I will send you to the other plantation. If not I will leave you here, with your new mistress."

As the title intimates, much remains unsaid in "The Dumb Witness"; and, even if things are known to have been said, little is repeated. Viney speaks to the "new object of Murchison's devotion," and following her visit, this "new object" writes to Murchison to revoke her decision to marry: "I have had my wedded happiness spoiled once. A burnt child dreads the fire—I do not care to go twice through the same experience. I have learned some things about you that will render it impossible for me ever to marry you." While Saint Paul argues it is better to marry than to burn,[4] the Northern widow has already learned something about the fiery hell that may be enshrined within marriage. Without any straining toward biblical exegesis, Murchison knows what open secret his fiancée has been told: "He had been wondering where Mrs. Todd got the information— he could not doubt what it was—that had been said to her."

Part of what the Northern widow understands is embodied by the messenger herself; Viney at this time is described as "a tall, comely young quadroon" who has been "in power" of a world that has long been outside the purview of white women who call themselves ladies. As Viney addresses the "new object" of her master's affections, there is no doubt about who has been the old object of his attentions. Murchison's "conspicuous vice" is called "avarice" in the story; this vice may "have kept him from marrying" in that, presumably, keeping a female slave is a less expensive proposition than taking on a wife. The secret that keeps the wealthy Northern widow from marrying him, on the other hand, is classified as a common practice rather than a vice: "If he had any other failings, they were the heritage of the period, and he shared them with his contemporaries of the same caste." This well-known secret, of course, is the story of his intimate relationship with Viney.

In the most disturbing part of the story, Murchison, after learning that Viney has spoken with the widow, threatens his "housekeeper," "I will teach you . . . to tell tales about your master. I will put it out of your power to dip your tongue in where you are not concerned." Like Ovid's Philomela, whose brother-in-law Tereus rapes her and then cuts out her tongue to ensure her silence, Viney's tongue is hurt in "The Dumb Witness" to punish her for having told a similarly unspeakable story, for telling "tales about [her] master." In a starkly revealing scene, the narrative offers its most explicit declaration of the terms of the relationship between the man and the woman: "There was no one to say him nay. The law made her his. It was a lonely house and no angel of mercy stayed his hand." In this isolated place, the enraged Murchison can mark his slave in any way he chooses, because "the law made her his."

From the outset, Viney's story has been one of subjugation, but it is also a story of other less public yokings, a story of conjugal relations

4. 1 Corinthians 7:9: "But if they cannot contain, let them marry: for it is better to marry than to burn."

that have taken place uncensored by the objections of white ladies over the course of many years. The secret story is not one of racial separation. The story which is so apparent that it does not have to be spoken in words is the story of inter-racial intimacy, the story of a union between Viney and Malcolm Murchison which is so profound that it goes beyond the intimation of a merely physical bond. Indeed, this slave woman who becomes the silent witness of Chesnutt's tale would not even have had to speak to tell her story. Among the things that John notices immediately upon his arrival at the Murchison place is the marked physical resemblance between the elderly man and woman seated in the symmetrically placed chairs at opposite ends of the piazza. Although Chesnutt himself came from a family in which not only the male but several of the female progenitors of his mixed-race ancestry were white, the more common story of miscegenation in the plantation South vehemently and violently insisted on a color line which could be crossed sexually in only one direction. Unlike Chesnutt's mixed-race world of a freedman elite in which Irish servant girls could become mothers with a place in the Chesnutt family tree, Viney's racial status as a quadroon on the Murchison plantation tells a different story. If she is a quadroon, in the simplest formulation, she herself is both the daughter of a white man and the daughter of a woman whose father was a white man. Long before her enraged master, "in the weakness of passion," marks her tongue, Viney, "with her passionate strain of mixed blood," has already been marked by Murchison passion: the powerful stamp of her relationship to the family is revealed by the fact that she has a Murchison face. Whether she is Malcolm Murchison's sister or first cousin—the daughter of one or the other of the only two men of the previous generation who are mentioned, Murchison's father or uncle—cannot be known. It also cannot be known whether Viney embodies some double strand of incestuous mingling, whether Viney's white father and white maternal grandfather represent two generations of Murchison masters, or whether this is a story that conceals even denser possibilities. As William Faulkner would remind readers of a later generation in works like *Go Down, Moses*, the Murchison blood in Viney may have come in the course of two generations from the same willful patriarch.

Whatever secret history Viney might embody, her connection is close enough to be described by the Murchisons as being "of our blood." In a piece of documentary evidence, a letter that John reads into the record of his account of the story, Malcolm Murchison's dying uncle tells his nephew that the valuables and the papers concerning the family wealth are hidden, and that "your housekeeper Viney knows their hiding place. She is devoted to you and to the family—she ought to be, for she is of our blood—and only she knows the secret." In the end, Viney's devotion, like her sense of vengeance, is deep. After separating Murchison from the "new object of his devotion," she follows a course that insists on the primacy of her relation to Malcolm Murchison. She is bound to him by a contract of her own making that follows the traditional terms of "'til death do us part."

Having announced that he will not listen to Viney again and having maimed her tongue, Malcolm Murchison suffers a punishment tailored to his crime. Without his uncle's will, he falls into increasing financial distress and spends the rest of his life pleading with Viney to speak, attending to every sound which comes from her mouth. Viney, who can be violated by Murchison because "the law made her his," fuses an irresolvable union through her refusal to speak; she makes him hers by using her only recourse to the law, the withholding of the legal papers that would prove Malcolm Murchison's rights of ownership to his "ancestral seat" and all the rest of his uncle's property.

With its emphasis on legal rights and property law, "The Dumb Witness" offers a critique of slavery which is also intimately tied to a story of marriage. Horrible though it may seem, in their opposing chairs Malcolm Murchison and Viney are enacting scenes from a marriage. Their bonds have gone past the era of bondage, yet they remain tied through the power of both property relations and blood. By holding her tongue, Viney has gained the upper hand and Murchison, driven by his avarice, has become her slave. Even before the war is over, he cannot sell her, because she has a value beyond her mere physical worth; she has within her grasp the power he has lost, the power of possession. Reversing the power of man and woman, of master and slave, "The Dumb Witness" takes the abstract and seemingly unlimited power of the law which supports Murchison's acts of violence as a slave master and, by a turn of plot, privileges the power of letters. The mystery surrounding the physical location of the testaments to Murchison's birthright demonstrates that the power of the law itself can be contained, conjured, and withheld in the form of an object as ephemeral as the sheets of paper on which the words are written. By continuing to be the dumb witness, meting out a lifelong punishment in her refusal to speak, Viney gains power by suppressing her voice, but at the same time she also robs her adversary of his legacy by suppressing the written word, denying Malcolm Murchison access to the "sworn oaths," the "con" "jure" that would decree his rights to their family's fortune. As she holds the power of the law by withholding it, Viney uses the law to secure her position as the de facto wife in the Murchison household. The law which once would have made her an object to be sold—the law which even in the present of the frame narrative would forbid interracial marriage—has become the means through which she has forced Malcolm Murchison into a lifetime commitment. Their indivisible union is indeed a marriage, albeit a union forged in hell.

In "Hot-Foot Hannibal," when the man who bears the name of his childless ancestor, Malcolm Murchison, takes his Northern bride to live at "the old Murchison Place," he revises the tortured union of "The Dumb Witness" into the more familiar and comforting story of the marriage between North and South. In this revision, Annie and her strong-willed sister play primary roles in the story itself. Intensifying the pattern seen in the other tales collected in *The Conjure Woman*, Annie stands in for the ethical reader who consistently insists on the presence of a moral in Uncle Julius's tales. In striking contrast, in "The Dumb Witness," Annie is named as a listener—a witness—but she neither speaks nor performs her usual role of articulating the moral of the story. The only other story where Annie's role disappears in a similar fashion is in "The Marked Tree" (1924), the last conjure tale that Chesnutt wrote. It is no accident that, like "The Dumb Witness," "The Marked Tree" tells—without explicitly naming—a story of interracial sexual relations between white masters and the slave women who have worked in their houses. When Annie herself—the white woman who represents the elite reader of the literary magazine—becomes the "dumb" witness in these stories, she is conspicuous in her absence. On one level, Annie might be said to be left "dumb" by stories that depict such deeply rooted evil. On another, like the white ladies who did not set foot in the Murchison house for fifteen years, Annie may refuse to acknowledge having heard Viney's story.

Since Annie has served as moral respondent in *The Conjure Tales*, providing ethical interpretations of the human costs of slavery to her profit-driven husband, her absence in "The Dumb Witness" and "The Marked Tree" is revelatory. As her reform-minded, moralizing commentary disappears, Chesnutt shifts the ethical burden of interpretation to the reader. Will the reader acknowledge the story of sexual violation and betrayal of familial ties, a story that remains so powerfully present precisely because it remains unspoken? The absence of the need to give a moral is an act of intimacy in itself: it means that the speaker trusts his or her interlocutor to understand what has been said without the summarily distancing act of needing to inscribe a response.[5]

None of the deviations from the previous formulas of the tales, though, explain why "The Dumb Witness" was "tentatively accepted," but never appeared in the pages of the *Atlantic*. The most likely reason is that editor Walter Hines Page—or perhaps even Chesnutt himself—realized the explicitness of the open secret, a

5. Brodhead, 23, 17–19.

sexual secret compounded in the story by other sexual secrets, notably the rather stark allusions to incest. Indeed, when Chesnutt incorporated a significantly altered version of Viney's story into his 1905 novel, *The Colonel's Dream*, he redacted it into a less violent and non-incestuous incarnation. In the novel, the passionate slave master does not maim the tongue of his dark and "comely" mistress; instead, she suffers a stroke after he has her beaten by the overseer. Decades later, Viney finally speaks at her former master's deathbed: "You had me whipped—whipped—whipped—by a poor white dog whom I despised and spurned! You had said that you loved me, and you had promised to free me—and you had me whipped. But I have had my revenge! . . . For twenty-five years, I have watched you look for—nothing; have seen you waste your time, your property, your life, your mind—for nothing! For ah, Mars' Ma'colm you had me whipped—*by another man*!"[6]

As in the short story, the later version includes the detail of a letter which informs Malcolm that Viney knows a secret about a hidden treasure, but there is a crucial and telling difference in this document. In this letter the "comely quadroon" is owned as "our girl Viney," no longer identified as "of our blood." Removed is the suggestion of incest; also absent are the details of the reflected countenance and family resemblance that link Viney so intimately to her former owner in "The Dumb Witness." Instead, Chesnutt substitutes a melodramatically dripping conclusion that tells the story of a "woman's heart that even slavery could not crush." While her "woman's heart" has "maintained" a "wall of outraged pride and hatred and revenge," after his death the Viney of *The Colonel's Dream* releases the "flood [of] the pent-up passions of the past." Crying from "eyes that had long forgotten to weep," the woman who has been described as the "wrinkled . . . mulattresse" throws herself to her knees by her former lover's bedside and "seizing old Malcolm's emaciated hand in both her own, covered it with kisses, fervent kisses, the ghosts of the passionate kisses of their distant youth." In the story of bitter yet explicit love told in *The Colonel's Dream*, the connection to the families of the conjure stories has been erased and, while several of the characters' names remain the same, Malcolm Murchison has silently become Malcolm Dudley.

Chesnutt holds his tongue—except insofar as "Hot-Foot Hannibal" is a silent witness of the earlier scene of violence that repressed the publication of "The Dumb Witness." Beginning with rupture, "Hot-Foot Hannibal" ends with a reassuring wedding; but the name of Malcolm Murchison, repeating exactly the name of the earlier character, would have had a deeper meaning to Chesnutt and Page.

6. Charles W. Chesnutt, *The Colonel's Dream* (Boston: Gregg Press, [1905] 1968), pp. 127, 273–74.

The earlier, unpublished story remains under the surface of the happy ending, whispering its brutal tale of blood ties and bloodlust. In displacing the scene of reconciliation to a marriage of North and South, following the bellicose "civil" argument that was ostensibly about the presence of slaves in the house of the Union, "The Dumb Witness" leaves unspoken the "negatived" family romance of race.

As early as 1887 in the third published tale, "The Conjurer's Revenge," Chesnutt's Northern couple suffers from what might be described as a feminized demise of the contemporary written word: Annie "wearily and conscientiously plow[s] her way through a missionary report while [John] . . . follow[s] the impossible career of the blonde heroine of a rudimentary novel."[7] Their sense of desperation as readers continues as Annie speaks, welcoming a story by Uncle Julius as "a godsend" that saves her from having to listen to her husband who, at his wife's request, reads aloud from a work of philosophy. These stultifying words read into the record of the story attest to the potentially moribund language of equally gendered—albeit highbrow—masculine fodder. From "The Goophered Grapevine" forward, Annie is concerned with what she names as "true": a concern, measured by accuracy of feeling, that becomes her moral calculus as her character develops in the arc of the conjure tales. In "Sis' Becky's Pickaninny," Annie conceives of a higher standard of truth than that which is limited to the actual, insisting that this "story bears the stamp of truth, if ever a story did." Arguing that the "ornamental details . . . are not at all essential," Annie concludes: "the story is true to nature and might have happened half a hundred times, and no doubt did happen, in those horrid days before the war." In "The Conjurer's Revenge," Annie explicitly criticizes the ethical shortcomings of a tale that actually follows a requisite religious formula by focusing on the religious conversion of a conjure man who has formerly kept his goophers in "go'ds": "gourds" in its dialect form articulates "gods" in the plural. Here, Annie complains: "That story does not appeal to me, Uncle Julius, and is not up to your usual mark. It isn't pathetic, it has no moral that I can discover, and I can't see why you would tell it. In fact, it seems to me like nonsense."

In Chesnutt's writing of the conjure tales, Annie, positioned from the outset as the serious listener, becomes the character who acts to try to correct problems from the plantation past that Uncle Julius's tales reveal as having consequences in the present. By 1888 in "Po' Sandy" (the second conjure story Chesnutt wrote), Annie with some frequency

7. This reading, which follows the arc of Annie's development as a character, insists upon the importance of the sequence in which Chesnutt's conjure tales were written, the sequence that becomes visible through this Norton Critical Edition of these fictions. See Robert Stepto's earlier analysis of the conjure tales, which argues for the importance of the publication sequence in the development of character and of community.

begins to commit acts of wifely insubordination; in particular she real-
locates contested resources that have been linked metaphorically or literally to the sacrificial bodies of slaves. Indeed, as John accedes to
Annie's most public overruling of his commands, he actually admits his
reluctance to have the servants observe "a conflict of authority in the
household." In "A Victim of Heredity; or, Why the Darkey Loves
Chicken" (1898), John explains that there were "dusky neighbors . . .
who did not shake off readily the habits formed under the old system,"
while Annie (who in an earlier story has rehired a hand fired by her
husband) has assumed the authority for releasing "a chicken-thief"
from "the smokehouse," sending away the law itself by dismissing the
constable who has been summoned by her husband. The Annie of this
late story reveals that although she may be weary of philosophy, she is
nevertheless versed in contemporary intellectual debates about human
behavior: "I have been thinking more or less about the influence of
heredity and environment, and the degree of our responsibility for the
things we do, and while I have not been able to get everything reasoned
out, I think I can trust my intuitions." As Annie introduces the scientis-
tic word "environment," this female adjudicator of morals insists on
white landowners' "responsibility" for the damaging past that remains
present. Listening to Uncle Julius tell tales of "po'ignant niggers,"
Annie is able to intuit what is written for all to see: the poor ignorant
("po'ignant") former slaves are indeed "poignant." Poverty and ignorance are related: these are not mere "habits," they are an "environment" that can be reformed. Poignancy appeals to the emotions, and
Annie's response based on "intuition" privileges female knowledge as a
source of deeper truth than any that she can "reason out" at the emotional distance provided by philosophy, biological determinism, or any
other intellectual field that has been book-ended by erudition.

   Chesnutt's last conjure tale, published a quarter of a century after
his culminating collection, *The Conjure Woman*, is telling in its subject: the annihilation of a family as a result of the evil perpetrated and
set in motion by the womanly jealousy of a plantation mistress. This
final story recounts the undying revenge of a slave mother whose son
has been sold and sacrificed. While Chesnutt's "The Marked Tree"
begins in the same way that the very first conjure tale had begun—an
invalid wife needing a Southern climate—here John as he seeks property that suits the needs of his "brother-in-law" finds a fatal tree
deeply rooted in the crimes of slavery. By this 1924 tale, Annie is not
only absent, she is not mentioned. Indeed, prior to this story, the
maleficent white mistress, popularized in abolitionist fiction, had
appeared only once in Chesnutt's conjure tales. This malfeasance in
which Mis' Dugal has denied the possibility of love between slaves in
"A Deep Sleeper" to contend "one nigger man is de same as ennud-
der" has undergone a change in *The Conjure Woman's* concluding

tale. In "Hot-Foot Hannibal," the formerly brutal Mis' Dugal insists that no slave besides the beloved man will do for Chloe "cause Chloe ain' that kin'er gal." While "The Dumb Witness" was written relatively early, Annie has already been identified in the narratives as a seeker of truth. She is the listener who insists that there be a "moral" to Uncle Julius's tales. This Northern-born reformer has already acted to reallocate used lumber, to deacquisition a ham, and (quixotically) to propose the rather hopeless removal of a clay bank that is being fed upon by dirt eaters, "sallow" poor whites as well as hungering blacks. As John narrates the "strange story" "of jealousy, revenge, and disappointment" entitled "The Dumb Witness," Julius interjects a few comments while Annie and her sister Mabel, explicitly designated as present, do not speak a word. Deviating from Chesnutt's formula that by 1889 had already developed an explicit pattern linking female sympathy to activist reform, this female silence is a politically sophisticated, literally provocative strategy, calling out the reader to fill in what is missing, to assume the place of the sympathetic reader. While in John's words "my wife and her sister and Julius and I" listen to "this strange story" "of jealousy, revenge and disappointment," this "romantic setting" tells of something that can still be heard, not unlike "[t]he voices of the night [that] came faintly from distant woods." Just as Annie has disappeared entirely from "The Marked Tree," her silence in the "The Dumb Witness," underlined by Mabel's silence, loudly insists that the unacknowledged be acknowledged and that the unspeakable be not just spoken but owned by female readers who would distance themselves from what the other tales aver is a continuing history, in this instance a continuing history of sexual violation and the reviling of the rights of maternity.

GLENDA CARPIO

[Black Humor in the Conjure Stories][†]

Repeated throughout the *Conjure Woman* and related stories are scenes of masters *and* slaves laughing to themselves, with each other, and even sometimes at each other, in what Uncle Julius, the ex-slave narrator in the tales, frequently describes as "laffin' fit ter kill." The phrase succinctly encompasses the extremes of humor and violence in the stories. In "Dave's Neckliss," a slave must enact the curse of

---

† From *Laughing Fit to Kill: Black Humor in the Fictions of Slavery* (New York: Oxford UP, 2008), 36–37, 53–56, 60–63. Reprinted by permission of Oxford University Press. Notes have been edited.

Ham by tying a ham around his neck as punishment for a crime he did not commit. Dave looks absurd with his "necklace," and the slaves laugh "fit ter kill" when they see him not only because he looks silly but also because they are made to work harder when Dave is falsely convicted of stealing. But the necklace becomes a sign of death and destruction, as the spelling of the word in the vernacular suggests: neck-less. In "Mars Jeems' Nightmare," a master is temporarily transformed into a slave and subjected to the cruelty of his own overseer. When he is turned back into a master he laughs "fit to kill" as the overseer recounts the extensive violence he used to try to break a mysterious "noo nigger" who refused to submit to his cruelty. In "Hot Foot Hannibal" Chesnutt presents the reader with the hilarious spectacle of a slave who, having been "goophered" (bewitched) cannot control his hands and feet and therefore creates chaos in the house in which he is enslaved. Ultimately, however, the tale is one of revenge, as the goophered slave ends by laughing "fit ter kill" at those who conspired against him, while those who first victimized him end in tragedy and loss when the master sells one of them down the river.

In these and other tales, Chesnutt produces what Pirandello calls "the feeling of the opposite" at the heart of tragicomedy. Whereas mere comedy produces laughter from the "perception of the opposite" (via inversion, incongruity, and juxtaposition), tragicomedy produces laughter that is "troubled and obstructed" by the lingering eventuality of doom.[1] One is caught between a desire to laugh and the suspicion that, in doing so, one could be cruelly laughing at a tragedy that is about to unfold. One is caught, that is, between wanting and not wanting to laugh. Chesnutt's stories produce the "feeling of the opposite" at both the narrative and the metanarrative level. In "Dave's Neckliss," the slaves' mocking laughter is always troubled by the tragedy of Dave's predicament and by the fact that their fate too is tied to his punishment. In "Mars Jeems' Nightmare," the master's laughter at once recognizes the cruelty to which he is temporarily subjected and the fact that he subjects others to the same cruelty. But the reader experiences the feeling of the opposite not only through the characters but also through the tensions that Chesnutt creates between the ironic, comic, and tragicomic aspects of his tales. The *Conjure Woman* tales operate at two levels: that of the outer frame, which takes place in the postbellum South and involves John and his sickly wife, Annie, and that of Uncle Julius, whose tales are set in the antebellum years that constitute the stories' inner frame. The two levels of narration inform one another in intricate ways, sometimes interlacing and sometimes putting in tension a

---

1. Luigi Pirandello, *On Humor*, trans. Antonio Illiano and Daniel Testa (Chapel Hill: U of North Carolina P, 1974), p. 118.

number of dichotomies: North and South, literate and illiterate, textual and oral, antebellum and postbellum. The various contrasts and parallels through which the story operates achieve rich levels of irony; it is this aspect of Chesnutt's work overall that has received the most sustained critical attention.[2]

The different levels of irony that Chesnutt creates through the structure of his tales and the comic aspects on which he relies—many of which engage with the racist images and ideologies of American popular culture—are often in conflict with the laughter that the stories represent, a laughter that, at its most powerful, suggests the violence and pain of slavery. That is, while the levels of irony and comedy in the tales refer to the power dynamics that inform interpretations of slavery and black culture, the laughter itself suggests that which is arguably beyond representation: the torture of bodies and psyches that the enslaved either endured or by which they perished.

*   *   *

"A Victim of Heredity," one of Chesnutt's Uncle Julius tales, opens with a ridiculous image: John, a white northerner, is so besieged by guilt that he cannot find adequate punishment for a "midnight marauder" who had tried to steal one of his chickens. Chesnutt humorously allows his readers to track John's thoughts: he begins by wanting to give the thief five years in the penitentiary to give him "time to break the habit" and to "strike terror [in]to hearts of other thieves." The disproportion between crime and punishment (as well as the rhetoric with which it is expressed) is so outrageous that even John, who is often morally blind and deaf, can sense it, and he begins to reduce the punishment, first to two years, then to one year, then to six months, then to three months (all within the space of a few paragraphs). At each step, the individual circumstances of the thief interpose John's convictions, slowly breaking down the stereotype of the chicken thief and giving way to the individual behind it: a "very much frightened," "insignificant-looking fellow" with a "large family and a sickly wife."

Despite the fact that John can sense the living human being behind the stereotype, he holds on to the image of the chicken thief and asks Julius "why is it that his people can't let chickens alone." "Is it in the blood?" When Julius responds affirmatively, Annie indignantly retorts, "Why, Uncle Julius! . . . I am ashamed of you, to be slandering your race in that way." If Annie thus voices the response that readers might have to Julius's affirmation of the stereotype,

---

2. For an excellent example, see Eric Sundquist's "Charles Chesnutt's Cakewalk," in *To Wake the Nations*, especially pp. 323–92.

after she hears Julius's tale about an avaricious master, she lets the thief go unpunished, concluding, "If slaves did contract the habit of stealing chickens and other little things to eat, they were not without some excuse for their conduct; and we [she and John] ought not to be too severe with them because they haven't outgrown the habit in a few years." Rather than take in the full force of Julius's tale, Annie is also besieged by guilt and, ironically, makes John's own guilt-produced elaborate deliberations come to naught.

Under the pretense of answering the mystery about chicken-loving darkies, Julius exposes a master's exploitation of and dependence on his slaves. He tells the story of a master who, having cheated his nephew of his inheritance, buys slaves and then, seeking to cut costs, pays Aunt Peggy, the local conjure woman, to devise a potion that will reduce his slaves' appetite and hence the rations he must provide for them. At first the slaves do not seem affected by the cut rations, but when the master's avarice gets the better of him and he applies a second dose, they become so weak that they cannot work, and the master risks losing not only his crops but also the investment that he has made in the slaves themselves. Just as the master's avarice doubles in on itself and creates a boomerang effect, the absurdity of the story doubles when the slaves, dying from starvation, eat vast amounts of food (the master's best hogs and cattle) but do not improve until the master begins to feed them chicken, upon which they require all the chicken in the county to recuperate.

In the end, Julius manages to answer the question that begins the tale—he claims that the slaves in the area now owned by John have genetically retained a taste for chicken—while contrasting the minor theft to the serious crime that the master commits in trying to cheat his slaves of one of the most basic forms of recompense they could receive for their labor. Exploiting another contrast, that between the response that Julius's tale merits and Annie's, Chesnutt reveals the inertia underneath both John's seemingly thoughtful consideration of the thief and Annie's paternalism. As Eric Sundquist notes, the master's successive reduction of rations in order to realize more profit can be taken "to represent the post-Reconstruction treatment of black labor through the inequities of sharecropping and convict lease." But rather than realize the connection between the exploitation of slaves and the exploitation of ex-slave employees like Julius, Annie is content to let people steal her "portable property" and John would rather punish the "victims of heredity" than examine his own complicity in perpetuating slavery.[3]

The strategy of appropriating racist caricatures in order to redefine their purpose is familiar to Chesnutt's readers, for it is a strategy

3. Sundquist, p. 380.

that characterizes all of his tales of conjure and transformation. In "The Passing of Grandison," the strategy results in the explosion of a stereotype; in "A Victim of Heredity," it works as a screen for Julius's critique of exploitation. In the tales I examine hereafter, Chesnutt uses the strategy as part of a tragicomedy of slavery. In these tales, laughter is the sound of the tragic recognition of dispossession. Particularly in "Dave's Neckliss," laughter is uttered in the face of the cruelty of slavery, a cruelty that Chesnutt invokes not through sentimental or Gothic elements but through a comedy that highlights the slaves' lack of control over their own bodies.

Chesnutt sets such laughter in uneasy relationship not only to the comedy of the body, which he creates in part by appropriating aspects of minstrelsy, but also to the comic resolutions that he gives all, except the last, of these tales. Involving cases of wrongdoing facilitated by conjure, the tales end in light, comic fashion with the righting of wrongs and the punishment of guilty parties. Yet such resolutions are always ironic in light of the fact that the crimes of slavery, which Chesnutt so potently invokes through laughter, are never redressed. John and Annie miss such irony and listen to Julius's tales for amusement, entertainment, and at best edification, and consider his motives only at the simple level of material gain. Although theirs are negative examples of how to interpret Julius's tales, Chesnutt's critics replicated them for decades. But the reader who is attuned to Chesnutt's brilliant interposition of comedy, laughter, and tragedy can appreciate not only the irony that John and Annie miss but also the fact that Julius's tales, and by extension Chesnutt's work, could be so dismissively consumed.

*   *   *

Henri Bergson argues that we *"laugh every time a person gives us the impression of being a thing,"* especially in "coarser forms of the comic, in which the transformation of a person into a thing seems to be taking place before our eyes." Machines, unlike living creatures, are predictable; it is the interposition of the two opposites, the rigidity of the mechanical clashing with the suppleness of life, specifically when something *"mechanical [is] encrusted upon the living,"* that produces laughter. Although Bergson could not have predicted it (he was capable of asking, in all seriousness, "[What] is there comic about a rubicund nose? And why does one laugh at a negro?"), his insights illuminate the kind of comedy that Chesnutt put to the service of tragedy.[4]

4. Henri Bergson, *Laughter: An Essay on the Meaning of the Comic*, trans. Cloudesley Brereton and Fred Rothwell (London: Macmillan, 1921), pp. 58, 61, 37, 40.

*   *   *

In Chesnutt's masterpiece, "Dave's Neckliss," the role of laughter
* * * is more complex and the comedy of the body has darker over-
tones. There are two significant forms of laughter in the story, that of
the slaves who mock Dave, and Dave's own laughter when he goes
mad. The slaves' laughter is cruel. One woman "bus' out laffin' fit ter
kill herse'f" when she describes to Dilsey, Dave's "junesey" (sweetheart), who deserts him once he is marked by the ham, what Dave
looks like with his "neckliss." Other slaves continually make jokes
about the ham and pester Dave so much that he takes to the "bushes
w'eneber he seed anybody comin', en alluz kep' hiss'f shet up in his
cabin atter he come in fum wuk." Their laughter drives him into isolation, which, along with his punishment and Dilsey's desertion, ultimately make him lose his mind. He begins to talk and sing to himself,
to have visions of hams growing in trees, and finally, when it is clear
that his punishment will cost the master and the ham is removed
from him, to miss the ham. Secretly he substitutes the ham with a fat
pine tied to a string to make a new "neckliss," eventually comes to
believe that he has turned into a ham, and hangs himself over a fire in
the smokehouse. In the midst of it all, Dave laughs "fit ter kill."

If, as Sundquist notes, "minstrelsy and chattelism are joined in
the ham, sign of labor, of stereotyped behaviors of consumption,"
laughter and horror are equally joined.[5] As the slaves witness Dave
transform from upstanding community leader before his punishment to the outcast he becomes, they laugh in mockery and bitter-
ness, but that laughter becomes shameful as they realize the madness
to which the punishment drives Dave. Julius's description of the
transformation also suggests an inwardly experienced dark comedy.
At work and in his limited leisure, Dave is haunted by the ham:
"W'enber he went ter lay down, dat ham would be in de way. Ef he
turn ober in his sleep, dat ham would be tuggin' at his neck. It wuz
the las' thing he seed at night, and de fus' thing he seed in the
mawnin'." The inanimate object has a strange agency: *it haunts
without actually doing anything*. Of course, the ham, as one of "the
stereotypical foods of coon songs, which figuratively dehumanized
blacks by making them into pathetic buffoons who are addicted to
watermelon, hams, chickens, and the like," has been endowed with
the power to haunt.[6]

In literalizing not only the curse of Ham but also the haunting
power of stereotypes, Chesnutt brilliantly underscores both the burden of stereotype as experienced from within and its absurdity. The

5. Sundquist, p. 379.
6. Ibid.

ham not only haunts Dave in his private moments, but it threatens to usurp his identity. "W'eneber [Dave] met a stranger," Julius recounts, "de ham would be de fus' thing de stranger would see" and the only thing the stranger would notice; most people "would 'mence ter laf, en whareber Dave went he could see folks p'intin' at him," telling jokes about the ham. In "A Victim of Heredity" we see John briefly discover the human being behind the stereotype of the chicken thief; here we see how a similar symbol dehumanizes Dave even in front of those who should know better.

The story, especially Dave's self-inflicted lynching, dramatizes not only the life-destroying effects of racial stereotyping, but also how laughter facilitates the internalization of such effects by the victims of racism. The enslaved people who mock Dave see in him their own enslavement carried to a literal and thus absurd level. They laugh at a man who, tethered to a ham, walks the plantation where they labor, a place that is supported by more quotidian forms of dehumanization. In laughing they assert the distance between their own lot and Dave's, whose absurd punishment becomes the nadir of subjection against which other slaves measure theirs. Laughter thus operates as a defense mechanism, expressed in bitter recognition of a shared subjection to cruelty and as a way of asserting some distance from that cruelty.

If those who laugh at Dave laugh in self-defense, Dave's own laughter is that defense mechanism carried to the extreme. Describing Dave's descent into madness, Julius notes that with "dat ham eberlastin' en eternally draggin' roun' his neck" Dave took to "laffin' fit ter kill 'bout nuffin." Enslaved people, as most accounts of black humor claim, laughed in order not to go mad. Dave laughs *because* he has gone mad, but in so doing he makes laughter expressive not of the cruelty of slavery, but of madness. At the same time, as he escapes into that realm, he succumbs to the literalness of the joke foisted upon him, staging his own lynching in an act that is a revolt against his master, since he becomes worthless property, but also his own gruesome end.

J. L. Styan suggests that "the real climax of a dark comedy" is not "the place where the hero is pressed to a decision, the villain unmasked, the situation brought to a crux, but the place where the tensions are so unbearable that we crave for relief."[7] Surely the crux of this tale is the moment Julius finds Dave in the smokehouse, hanging over the fire. The moment contains no suspense. By this time, the villain has been found, or rather, the real thief has confessed, and the master is ready to make it up to Dave and the rest of the slaves by giving them

---

7. J. L. Styan, *The Dark Comedy: The Development of Modern Comic Tragedy* (London: Cambridge UP, 1968), p. 252.

extra cider. He offers Dave a public apology, regardless of the fact that Dave has gone missing, which ends with, "Now take ernudder drink er cider all roun', en den git at dat cotton." But the reader has been warned of Dave's descent into madness, and when we follow Julius retracing Dave's footsteps to the smokehouse, we do so with the foreboding that something terrible has happened.

By this time, too, the reader has been subjected to John's racist ruminations on the limits of black sentience in the outer frame of the tale. The contrast between John's callous observations and the tremendous tragedy of the story heighten at the moment of Dave's suicide, a moment that also underscores Julius's act of narration and echoes precisely at the moment when Julius finds Dave. When the tale opens, John is counting the number of slices of a Sunday ham that Julius is eating; with each slice the ex-slave consumes, John becomes more and more convinced of Julius's base nature. When, in the midst of his eating, Julius sheds a tear, however, John's interest is piqued. Later, he asks for an explanation, which results in the story of Dave's "neckliss." Before Julius can relate his tale, however, John delivers a dense paragraph expressing his suspicion that Julius, as representative ex-slave, is not sentient enough to understand the degradation he experienced:

> It was only now and then that we were able to study, through the medium of [Julius's] recollection, the simple but intensely human inner life of slavery. His way of looking at the past seemed very strange to us; his view of certain sides of life was essentially different from ours. He never indulged in any regrets for the Arcadian joyousness and irresponsibility which was a somewhat popular conception of slavery; his had not been the lot of the petted house-servant, but that of the toiling field-hand. While he mentioned with warm appreciation the acts of kindness which those in authority had shown to him and his people, he would speak of a cruel deed, not with the indigna-tion of one accustomed to quick feelings and spontaneous expression, but with the furtive disapproval which suggested to us a doubt in his own mind as to whether he had a right to think or feel, and presented to us a curious psychological spectacle of a mind enslaved long after the shackles had been struck off from the limbs of its possessor.

Dave's story would seem to prove John's point, as it represents the plight of one whose mind remains "enslaved long after the shackles [have] been struck off." Julius's own relishing of the ham would seem to prove the point as well, for the ham, as Sundquist argues, is "trans-formed over the course of Chesnutt's narrative into . . . the body and blood of Dave," which Julius eats in "a ritual of remembrance in which comedy cloaks [Julius's] identification with a legacy of suffering."[8] Like Brown, however, Chesnutt fulfills the expectations of readers such as John only to create searing ironies. John doubts if Julius "even realized, except in a vague, uncertain way, his own degradation." But he finds evidence "in the simple human feeling, and still more in the undertone of sadness, which pervaded his stories," of a "spark which, fanned by favoring breezes and fed by the memories of the past, might become in his children's children a glowing flame of sensibility, alive to every thrill of human happiness or human woe." Ironically, it is John who seems not to be "alive to every thrill of human happiness or human woe." While he thinks Julius is incapable of "speak[ing] of a cruel deed" with freedom of thought and feeling due to his continued mental enslavement, Julius in fact delivers a story of "human woe" with a complexity beyond John's comprehension.

No sensitive reading of "Dave's Neckliss" fails to comment on this irony. Yet the laughter in the story escapes notice. To ignore it, however, is to miss the intensity of Chesnutt's tragicomedy. In at least one contemporary instance, Dave's death becomes merely an act of sacrifice that Chesnutt symbolically carries out in the service of saving the master's soul. In a puzzling introduction to the 2001 Riverside edition of Chesnutt's major works, Sally Ann H. Ferguson reads "Dave's Neckliss" as one instance, among many, in which Chesnutt "exploits the Christian promise to save devils at the expense of angels and creates dark-skinned, Jesus-like innocents who lead, or at least try to lead, reprobate whites to truth and goodness." In her reading "Mars Dugal comes to regret that he wrongly accused and punished Dave" only after Dave becomes an "unheralded" symbol "of mortal suffering whose rewards await [him] after death."[9]

Ferguson misses not only the biting sarcasm with which Chesnutt mocks the master's "regret," but also the complexity with which Chesnutt makes Dave into a sacrificial symbol. The slaves' laughter not only has a role to play in Dave's grief, but is a major factor in his descent into madness. He bears the intensity of the slaves' abjection in ritual sacrifice but *not* for the master's profit. When Julius eats the Sunday ham, he eats the body and blood of Dave in the ritual remembrance of an ancestor who was made to carry the burden of the tribe, arguably to ensure its psychic survival. Dave's own laughter at the moment when he finds himself alone, bearing his burden, seems to mock the Christian paradigm of sacrifice to which Ferguson alludes. Dave dies looking for a "cure" or, in Julius's bitter pun,

---

8. Sundquist, p. 382.
9. S. A. H. Ferguson, Introduction, *Charles W. Chesnutt: Selected Writings* (Boston: Houghton Mifflin, 2001), pp. 7–8.

a "kyo," but a cure for what? For the madness of racism that has produced the suffering he bears? It is a desperate and ultimately tragic attempt, expressive neither of saintliness nor heroism. It is absurd and yet full of pathos. And it is to this peculiar mix that Dave's laughter, ostensibly a laughter about "nuffin'," gives a sound "fit to kill."

Charles W. Chesnutt
A Chronology

1858	Charles Waddell Chesnutt born June 20 in Cleveland, Ohio, to Ann Maria Sampson Chesnutt and Andrew Jackson Chesnutt. His parents are free people of color from Fayetteville, N.C., who had emigrated to Cleveland in 1856. They name their first son for his paternal grandfather, Waddell Cade, a white landowner in Fayetteville.
1861–65	Chesnutt's father serves in the Union Army as a teamster.
1866–70	The family returns to Fayetteville, N.C., where Chesnutt's father opens a store and serves as county justice of the peace in the Republican Reconstruction government. Chesnutt attends the Howard School, a Freedman's Bureau school built on land purchased by his father and six other prominent local African American men.
1870–72	Father's store fails; Democrats oust the Republican ticket from office; the family moves out of town to the countryside; and Chesnutt becomes a teacher at the Howard School.
1873–76	Chesnutt helps to support his family by becoming assistant principal of the Peabody School in Charlotte, N.C. He continues his study of languages and literature, and begins keeping his journal.
1877–79	Chesnutt returns to Fayetteville as assistant principal of the State Colored Normal School, established when the University of North Carolina system funds the Howard School as an institute for the training of teachers, making it the first state-funded institution of higher education for African Americans in the United States. Chesnutt marries Susan Perry, a teacher at the Howard School, and starts a family. He begins to explore a career as a stenographer.
1882	Becomes principal of the Normal School; as stenographer, records a speech by Frederick Douglass for a Raleigh, N.C., newspaper; visits New York City. Reads

	Albion Tourgée's novel *A Fool's Errand* and begins to contemplate a career in writing fiction.
1883–85	Resigns as principal of the Normal School; moves briefly to New York and then to Cleveland, where he settles his family and goes to work as a legal stenographer. First short story published in December 1885 in the *Cleveland News and Herald*.
1886–87	Publishes multiple stories and sketches through the McClure syndicate, in the magazine *Family Fiction*, and in the humor magazine *Puck*. Passes the Ohio bar exam, and continues to work as a legal stenographer and court reporter. Breaks into the national literary scene with "The Goophered Grapevine" in the *Atlantic Monthly* in August 1887. Chesnutt is the first African American writer to be featured in the pages of that august magazine.
1888–89	"Po' Sandy" published in the *Atlantic Monthly* in May 1888, followed by "The Conjurer's Revenge" (*Overland Monthly*) and "Dave's Neckliss" (*Atlantic Monthly*). Chesnutt also publishes stories and essays in the New York *Independent* and writes "Rena Walden," the story upon which the novel *The House Behind the Cedars* will be based.
1891	Houghton Mifflin (publisher of the *Atlantic Monthly*) rejects Chesnutt's first proposal for a volume of short stories.
1893	"A Deep Sleeper" published in the short-lived Boston periodical *Two Tales*.
1896	Chesnutt tours England and France.
1897	Houghton Mifflin rejects Chesnutt's novel *Mandy Oxendine*, but Walter Hines Page, a North Carolina native and the new editor of the *Atlantic Monthly*, accepts two new stories for publication. Page requests manuscripts of all of Chesnutt's stories; Chesnutt sends him copies of twenty stories and goes to Boston to meet with Page.
1898	Houghton Mifflin rejects Chesnutt's novel *A Business Career*, but Page suggests publishing a volume of stories like "The Goophered Grapevine" and "Po' Sandy." In response, Chesnutt sends him six new stories featuring Julius as narrator, written in as many weeks.
1899	Houghton Mifflin publishes Chesnutt's first book, *The Conjure Woman*, a collection of seven stories. Its success leads the press to publish a second volume, *The Wife of His Youth and Other Stories of the Color Line*, before the year is out. Chesnutt also writes a biography

of Frederick Douglass for the *Beacon Biographies of Eminent Americans* series. He closes his stenography practice and devotes himself entirely to writing.

1900   "Lonesome Ben" and "Tobe's Tribulations," two Julius stories not included by Houghton Mifflin in The *Conjure Woman* volume, are published in the *Southern Workman*. Chesnutt publishes a controversial three-part essay on racial intermixture, "The Future American," in *The Boston Evening Transcript*. Houghton Mifflin rejects a novel titled *The Rainbow Chasers*, but publishes Chesnutt's first novel, *The House Behind the Cedars*, a story about two people of color who pass for white in the post-bellum South.

1901   Houghton Mifflin publishes *The Marrow of Tradition*, Chesnutt's fictional account of the Wilmington, N.C. riot of 1898. The riot occurred when a group of white supremacists, led by Alfred Moore Waddell, overthrew the municipal government and established martial law, encouraging terrorist violence against the African American population; as many as 100 African American citizens may have been killed. Chesnutt hopes that *The Marrow of Tradition* will function as an *Uncle Tom's Cabin* for his era, awakening readers to the atrocities of the Jim Crow regime consolidating in the Southern states. Sales and critical reception of the novel are disappointing, though, and Chesnutt feels pressed to reopen his legal stenography practice in Cleveland.

1903   Chesnutt contributes an essay to *The Negro Problem: A Series of Articles by Representative American Negroes of Today*, alongside Booker T. Washington and W. E. B. Du Bois.

1904–5 Chesnutt publishes his last story in the *Atlantic Monthly* ("Baxter's Procrustes"); Houghton Mifflin rejects *The Colonel's Dream*, but Walter Hines Page, now at the firm Doubleday Page, publishes it. This novel, the last published in Chesnutt's lifetime, incorporates a version of "The Dumb Witness," a Julius story that had tentatively been accepted for publication in the *Atlantic Monthly* in the 1890s but had never seen print.

1906–17 While continuing with his stenography business in Cleveland, Chesnutt remains active as an occasional lecturer on issues of racial prejudice and civil rights, and works with groups including Booker T. Washington's Committee of Twelve, Du Bois's Niagara Movement, and the National Association for the Advancement of Colored

People, founded in 1910. He publishes one story, "The Doll," in the magazine of the NAACP, *The Crisis*, in 1912.

1921　　Houghton Mifflin rejects Chesnutt's novel *Paul Marchand, F.M.C.* ("free man of color"). The *Chicago Defender*, a prominent African American newspaper, serializes *The House Behind the Cedars*, bringing it to a new generation of readers at the start of the Great Migration of African Americans from the Jim Crow states to northern urban centers.

1924　　The director Oscar Micheaux creates a film version of *The House Behind the Cedars*. Chesnutt's last Julius tale, "The Marked Tree," is published in *The Crisis*.

1927–28　　Houghton Mifflin brings out a new edition of *The Conjure Woman*. Chesnutt is awarded the Spingarn Medal of the NAACP. He completes the manuscript of his final novel, *The Quarry*, which is not published until 1999.

1931　　Chesnutt publishes the essay "Post-Bellum—Pre-Harlem" in *The Colophon*, in which he considers his position in the emerging modern African American literary tradition exemplified by the Harlem Renaissance.

1932　　Micheaux creates a second film version of *The House Behind the Cedars*, titled *Veiled Aristocrats*. Chesnutt dies on November 15.

Selected Bibliography

• Indicates works included or excerpted in this Norton Critical Edition.

WORKS OF CHARLES W. CHESNUTT

The Conjure Woman. Boston: Houghton, Mifflin & Co., 1899.
Frederick Douglass (Beacon Biographies of Eminent Americans). Boston: Small, Maynard & Co., 1899.
The Wife of His Youth and Other Stories of the Color Line. Boston: Houghton, Mifflin & Co., 1899.
The House Behind the Cedars. Boston: Houghton, Mifflin & Co., 1900.
The Marrow of Tradition. Boston: Houghton, Mifflin & Co., 1901.
The Colonel's Dream. New York: Doubleday, Page & Co., 1905.
Mandy Oxendine: A Novel [1897]. Ed. Charles Hackenberry. Urbana: U of Illinois P, 1997.
Paul Marchand, F.M.C. [1921]. Jackson: UP of Mississippi, 1998.
The Quarry [1928]. Ed. Dean McWilliams. Princeton: Princeton UP, 1999.
A Business Career [1898]. Ed. Matthew Wilson and Marjan A. van Schaik. Jackson: UP of Mississippi, 2005.

COLLECTIONS

Andrews, William L., ed. *The Portable Charles W. Chesnutt.* New York: Penguin Books, 2008.
Brodhead, Richard H., ed. *The Conjure Woman, and Other Conjure Tales.* Durham, N.C.: Duke UP, 1993.
Brodhead, Richard H., ed. *The Journals of Charles W. Chesnutt.* Durham, N.C.: Duke UP, 1993.
Crisler, Jesse S., Robert C. Leitz, III, and Joseph R. McElrath, Jr., eds. *An Exemplary Citizen: Letters of Charles W. Chesnutt, 1906–1932.* Stanford: Stanford UP, 2002.
McElrath, Joseph R., Jr., and Robert C. Leitz, III, eds. *"To Be an Author": Letters of Charles W. Chesnutt, 1889–1905.* Princeton: Princeton UP, 1997.
McElrath, Joseph R., Jr., Robert C. Leitz, III, and Jesse S. Crisler, eds. *Charles W. Chesnutt: Essays and Speeches.* Stanford: Stanford UP, 1999.
Render, Sylvia Lyons, ed. *The Short Fiction of Charles W. Chesnutt.* Washington, D.C.: Howard UP, 1974.
Sollors, Werner, ed. *Charles W. Chesnutt: Stories, Novels, and Essays (Library of America).* New York: Literary Classics of the United States, 2002.

BIBLIOGRAPHIES

Browner, Stephanie P., ed. *The Charles Chesnutt Digital Archive.* Berea, KY: Hutchins Library, 2001– (online resource).
Ellison, Curtis W., and E. W. Metcalf, Jr. *Charles W. Chesnutt: A Reference Guide.* Boston: G.K. Hall & Co., 1977.

Martin, Olivia J., ed. *The Charles Waddell Chesnutt Papers in the Library of the Western Reserve Historical Society (1889–1932)*. Ohio: Ohio Historical Society, 1972.

BIOGRAPHIES

- Andrews, William L. *The Literary Career of Charles W. Chesnutt*. Baton Rouge: Louisiana State UP, 1980.
- Chesnutt, Helen M. *Charles Waddell Chesnutt, Pioneer of the Color Line*. Chapel Hill: U of North Carolina P, 1952.
- Keller, Frances Richardson. *An American Crusade: The Life of Charles Waddell Chesnutt*. Provo: Brigham Young UP, 1978.

CRITICAL WORKS

- Babb, Valerie. "Subversion and Repatriation in *The Conjure Woman*." *Southern Quarterly* 25 (Winter 1987): 66–75.
- Baker, Houston A., Jr. *Modernism and the Harlem Renaissance*. Chicago: U of Chicago P, 1987.
- Baldwin, Richard E. "The Art of *The Conjure Woman*." *American Literature* 43 (Nov. 1971): 385–98.
- Brodhead, Richard H. *Cultures of Letters: Scenes of Reading and Writing in Nineteenth-Century America*. Chicago: U of Chicago P, 1993.
- Carpio, Glenda. *Laughing Fit to Kill: Black Humor in the Fictions of Slavery*. Oxford: Oxford UP, 2008.
- Gleason, William A. "Chesnutt's Piazza Tales: Architecture, Race, and Memory in the Conjure Stories." *American Quarterly* 51 (March 1999): 33–77.
- Goldner, Ellen J. "(Re)staging Colonial Encounters: Chesnutt's Critique of Imperialism in *The Conjure Woman*." *Studies in American Fiction* 26 (Spring 2000): 39–64.
- Hemenway, Robert. "The Functions of Folklore in Charles Chesnutt's *The Conjure Woman*." *Journal of the Folklore Institute* 13 (1976): 283–309.
- ———. "Gothic Sociology: Charles Chesnutt and the Gothic Mode." *Studies in the Literary Imagination* 7 (1974): 101–19.
- Hewitt, Elizabeth. "Charles Chesnutt's Capitalist Conjurings." *English Literary History* 76 (Winter 2009): 931–62.
- Howells, William Dean. "Mr. Charles W. Chesnutt's Stories." *Atlantic Monthly* 85 (May 1900): 699–701.
- Sollors, Werner. "The Goopher in Charles Chesnutt's Conjure Tales: Superstition, Ethnicity, and Modern Metamorphoses." *Litterature d'America* 6 (Spring 1985): 107–30.
- Stepto, Robert B. "'The Simple But Intensely Human Inner Life of Slavery': Storytelling, Fiction, and the Revision of History in Charles W. Chesnutt's 'Uncle Julius Stories,'" in *History and Tradition in Afro-American Culture*, ed. Gunter H. Lenz (Frankfurt: Campus Verlag, 1984), 29–55.
- Sundquist, Eric J. *To Wake the Nations: Race in the Making of American Literature*. Cambridge, Mass.: Harvard UP, 1993.
- Wideman, John Edgar. "Charles Chesnutt and the WPA Narratives: The Oral and Literate Roots of Afro-American Litearture," in *The Slave's Narrative*, ed. Charles T. Davis and Henry Louis Gates, Jr. (Oxford: Oxford UP, 1985), 59–77.